T0381552

GLOBAL WARMING
AND CLIMATE CHANGE

CLIMATE TEMPERATURE EARTH SEA LEVEL CHANGE IMGPACT IMGPACT EFFECTS CARBON OCREAN RISE DEFORESTATION AVERAGE POLLUTION GREENHOUSE ATMOSPHERE OZONE GASES EMISSIONS INCREASE

**CAUSES,
SYMPTOMS,
COPING STRATEGIES.**

ENWERE DIKE,
NGOZI DIKE

GLOBAL WARMING AND CLIMATE CHANGE
CAUSES, SYMPTOMS, COPING STRATEGIES

iUniverse books may be ordered through booksellers or by contacting:

iUniverse
1663 Liberty Drive
Bloomington, IN 47403
www.iuniverse.com
1-800-Authors (1-800-288-4677)

ISBN: 978-1-5320-3146-5 (sc)
ISBN: 978-1-5320-3147-2 (e)

Print information available on the last page.

iUniverse rev. date: 03/27/2018

DEDICATION

To the memory of our late parents, Richard Igboanusi Dike, Josephine Nwaikpeyi Dike, Sir (Chief) Michael Nwokem Amuzie (KSM) and Lady Lolo Ezigbonne Dorathy Nnola Amuzie (LSM), who started us off in the right direction and to our children Nwanneka, Ugonna, Obinna and Onyemaechi.

ACKNOWLEDGEMENTS

We acknowledge the support of the following academic colleagues who encouraged us in one way or another: Professors Ifeyori Ihimodu, Uka Ezenwe, Uche Nwogwugwu, Peter Nkeoye, late David Ogbonna, Nwachukwu Okeke, Augustine Ezealor, Sonnie Oniye; Drs. Victor Dike and Joshua Atta. We would like to register our gratitude to Dr. Lawrence Anukam who gave his time and effort to assess and review the manuscript and wrote the foreword. No less appreciated are the secretarial services of Mrs. Nkechinyere Emenwodo who provided the various draft copies of the manuscript.

Sincere appreciation is also extended to our children and their families: Nwanneka, her husband Mr. Uchenna Nwoguh and their children Chidubem and Adaeze; Ugonna, her husband Dr. Ikechukwu Durugbor and their children Tobenna and Chikamso; Obinna and Onyemaechi for their continuous love, support and encouragement.

PREFACE

Global warming and climate change is an important environmental degradation problem that is having sweeping effects on every continent and throughout planet Earth's environment. Academic writings in scientific journals, the popular and 'elite' press, policy speeches at international fora, etc, all stress that current global warming and climate change originates in increased emissions of greenhouse gases (GHGs). Greenhouse gases mainly caused by natural forces such as volcanic eruptions were previously roughly constant in Earth's atmosphere until the beginning of the Industrial Revolution of the 1700s and 1800s, when anthropogenic activities began to add significant amounts to Earth's atmosphere. By the beginning of the 2000s, 400 billion tons of carbon dioxide were estimated to have been emitted into Earth's atmosphere, mainly through fossil-fuel combustion and various land-use change processes, namely, deforestation, fire burning, livestock production, etc.

Fossil-fuel combustion not only releases carbon dioxide, it also releases various other GHGs such as nitrous oxide, methane, etc into Earth's atmosphere. As regards deforestation, trees are 50% carbon in content; when they are felled and burnt the carbon they store through photosynthesis gets released back to the atmosphere and thereby increasing carbon dioxide levels and contributing to the greenhouse effect.

For obvious reasons, popular thinking on global warming and climate change impacts tend to concentrate mainly on land/forests and atmosphere. But these are spheres of Earth's environment most easily perceptible to the human senses. Its effects on the aquatic ecosystems are far less known in spite of the fact that most of the warming caused by carbon dioxide atmospheric concentrations is found to be going into the oceans where a lot of ecosystem changes are occurring with disastrous consequences for human welfare. This book seeks to identify the various symptoms of global warming and climate change in all Earth's natural systems, ecosystems and socioeconomic systems/ human societies.

Though put together from a bi-disciplined perspective (the authors are an economist and biologist) it is not intended to be a magic wand to provide all the answers to the numerous and often elusive problems of global warming and climate change. Nonetheless, this book shows that global warming and climate change as a negative externality would require for its mitigation a multi-country (collective) approach in the form of international climate change agreements. It sets to sensitize readers to the symptoms of climate change on Earths natural and socioeconomic systems ás well as constraints on evolving effective international institutions to check atmospheric GHG emissions.

Natural scientists, meteorologists and geographers have authored most of the climate change literature, whose technical nature makes it largely inaccessible to readers not trained in the natural sciences. It is hoped that the content of this book would be helpful in providing the non-professional readers to appreciate the causes, effects, and solutions to the global warming and climate change problem. By explaining global warming and climate change to a wider reading public in a non-technical language, this book would have contributed to the discourse in climate change.

Professor Enwere Dike
Dr. Ngozi Dike

FOREWORD

Climate Change is real. It is a global problem and must be addressed at all levels. The world is currently facing one of its most serious environmental challenges in global warming and Climate Change. Humanity is at a crossroad. The Intergovernmental Panel on Climate Change had earlier provided scientific evidence that the earth is actually getting warmer as a result of mainly anthropogenic activities leading to the emission into the atmosphere of some gases referred to as Greenhouse Gases, which include carbon dioxide, methane, etc.

It took, unfortunately, many years before the wide acceptance of the phenomenon of Climate Change. The negotiation and adoption of the United Nations Framework Convention on Climate Change (UNFCC), which was opened for signature by Member States of the United Nations during the Earth Summit in Rio-de-Janeiro in 1992, was a watershed and marked a turning point in the global acceptance that humanity is actually approaching a tipping point and if no collective action is taken to address the growing problem it may be too late to correct it.

A lot has happed since the Earth Summit. Many countries have signed and ratified the UNFCC. Through the activities and programmes of the Conference of Parties (COP) of the Convention Secretariat, the issues about Climate Change have gained prominence and recognition. For example, the Kyoto Protocol on Clean Development Mechanisms arising from the Convention has provided a veritable instrument for emission reduction/control through carbon trading.

In addition, the Paris Agreement adopted by Member States at the 21st Session of the COP of the UNFCC in Paris, France in December, 2015 was a landmark agreement bringing together even those countries who did not believe in Climate Change before or were very slow to act, to collectively agree to chart a new course to control Climate Change and global warming. At the Conference, through the concept of Internal Nationally Determined Contributions (INDCs), member countries voluntarily stated their targets and strategies to reduce carbon emissions at country levels.

The publication of this book is timely. It is coming at the heels of the Paris Agreement and at a time when many climate action initiatives are beginning to evolve, and at a time when the reality of climate change is staring us in the face.

The authors Professor Enwere Dike and Dr. (Mrs.) Ngozi Dike, have done a great job. They have succeeded in expounding in detail and clarity a subject that touches on the survival of humanity. The work covers the causes, symptoms and coping strategies of this global challenge, drawing on various sources of data and information. It explains the key elements of adaptation and mitigation as applied to climate change. It also explains some national, regional and global efforts to address the problems of climate change. The authors have successfully welded together various perspectives and diverse disciplines to provide useful insights into the phenomenon of Climate Change and its impacts on various ecosystems.

By this publication, Prof. Enwere Dike and Dr. (Mrs.) Ngozi Dike have provided a rich discourse and better understanding of the Climate Change and global warming.

Lawrence Chidi Anukam, PhD,
Director General/CEO,
National Environmental Standards and
Regulations Enforcement Agency (NESREA)

CONTENTS

LIST OF TABLES

LIST OF FIGURES

INTRODUCTION

A. Background to the Study

Global warming and climate change constitutes the dominant environmental degradation threat confronting human society currently. Academic writings in the scientific literature, policy speeches at national and international fora, media publicity, etc. – all stress this fact: global warming and climate change is no longer just a hypothesis, but an established fact, whose symptoms are clearly visible in every continent and in all spheres of planet Earth's environment.

Global warming and climate change describes the phenomenon whereby solar radiation that has reflected off Earth's surface remains trapped at atmospheric levels, due to build-up of carbon dioxide (CO_2) and other greenhouse gases (GHGs), rather than being emitted back into space, which results in a warming of the global atmosphere. However, climate change is a long-standing phenomenon as the mix of the various gases constituting Earth's atmosphere have changed over long periods of time, so average temperatures have fluctuated. Two important issues are considered important in the current concern over global warming. First, it is occurring at an unprecedented pace; specifically, in the last 100 years – i.e. since the first decades of the 20th century – Earth's average surface temperatures have increased by about 0.8°C (33.44°F), with some 60% of this increase occurring over the 1970s. Second, it is caused by human activities; specifically, the combustion of fossil fuels (coal, petroleum, natural gas, etc.) to drive industrial development, transportation, and domestic activities, as well as land-use change activities (e.g. deforestation, livestock production, fire burning, etc.) emit enormous volumes of earth-heating GHGs into the atmosphere.

A number of climate-change related environmental disasters[1] in recent decades point to climate change as the dominant global environmental threat currently facing humanity: In the United States, Hurricane Sandy in New York in 2012, tornado in Oklahoma in 2013, and flooding in Texas in 2016 (April); in Asia and Pacific, Japan's 'megaquake and killer tsunami' of March, 2011 that spread across the entire Pacific and East Asia regions, typhoon Haiyan in the Philippines in 2013, and the tropical cyclone that devasted the South Pacific Island of Vanuatu in March 2015; in Europe, heatwaves in 2003 that claimed 1000s of lives, and flooding of the proportion of biblical deluge in parts of Central and Eastern Europe in 2013 and 2014; and in sub-Saharan Africa, increased incidence of drought beginning in the 1970s in the West African Sahel, the Horn of Africa (Ethiopia, Somalia, and Northern Kenya) and Southern Africa (e.g. Zimbabwe) resulting in crop failures and famine.

Available records show that climate-change induced environmental degradation events such as flooding, hurricanes, typhoons, droughts, etc. have tended to escalate over time, increasing 12-fold between 1950 and 2005, most of these occurring in the Asia-Pacific regions (see Thomas et al. 2014). At the same time recorded financial losses from such events have escalated: $48 billion in 1950-1959; $151.7 - $247 billion during 1970-1979; and $729 billion in 1999 (Hoffman, 2007; Mills, 2008). Estimates by the World Health Organization (WHO) put the growth rate of global losses from hurricane damages at 6% annually between 1995 and 2015.

The symptoms of climate change in Earth's natural systems, terrestrial and aquatic (marine) ecosystems, and socioeconomic systems are now clearly visible and carefully documented in scientific studies. Mountain ice caps and glaciers are almost everywhere shrinking, a problem which undermines their capacity to supply ecosystem services. For instance, Mount Kenya, some 5200 meters in altitude with alpine vegetation and wildlife, is threatened by human-induced climate change, which undermines its ecosystem functions in the form of water supply and wildlife (Adams, 2009, plate 1.2, p. 18). Permafrost in the polar (northern) tundra is thawing; organic matter long frozen in Arctic Ice since before human societies began to evolve is now melting, allowing it to decay and emit earth-heating GHGs. The Arctic ice-cap is shrinking each year[2], releasing large volumes of water into the oceans – a source of flooding and sea level rise (SLR) that threatens the very existence of several small island states and cities located on low-lying coastlines and river deltas. Inland lakes are shrinking due to a speeding up of the hydrologic (water) cycle – the most famous example is Lake Chad perched on the edge of the West African Sahel (Connah 1981; Mortimore 1989; UNEP, 2007; Onuoha 2008).

Growing seasons for plants are getting much longer in the middle and high latitudes; significant shifts in ecological cycles and animal behaviour are occurring – e.g. heat-loving insects, birds and even plants are being found in progressively high latitudes (formerly found inhospitable for such animal and plant species); timing of plant flowering, insect emergence and egg-laying in birds are occurring much earlier (Menzel et al., 2005); certain animal species are under extreme pressure from climate change and deforestation in many regions of the world, due to destruction of their natural habitats. Systematic changes are observed in rainfall patterns and ocean currents (Bryden et al., 2005); as well, there is systematic rise in the mean sea level, a result of thermal expansion of sea water and partial melting of vast sheets of polar glaciers

The authoritative Intergovernmental Panel on Climate Change (IPCC)[3] and other scientific sources[4] predict that within the present 21st century (the 2000s) the following climate change effects are likely to unfold:

- The drier sub-tropical regions – e.g. the West African Savanna and Sahel zones – will warm more than the wetter tropics such as the Congo basin rainforest.
- Northern and Southern Africa will become much hotter (as much as $4^0C = 39.2^0F$ or higher) and drier (precipitation falling by as much as by 15% or higher).
- Agricultural output (wheat in the northern hemisphere and maize or corn in the southern hemisphere) is likely to decline.
- Vector-borne diseases – e.g. malaria, dengue fever – may spread, becoming much more virulent.
- Sea level rise (SLR) will accelerate – increasing by as much as ½ meter-in the next 50 years posing serious challenges for the low-lying Nile Delta, the Ganges-Brahmaputra river systems, parts of West Africa, etc.
- Global precipitation will increase caused by more rapid evaporation from the oceans; but as with the rise in temperatures itself, there is likely to occur significant variation across latitudes, with the upper latitudes receiving more rainfall (e.g. Russia) and snow-fall, while some areas in and around the tropics experience diminishing rainfall: the Mediterranean, Mexico, Central America, North-East Brazil, Western Australia, etc. (Noble and Watson, 2006, p. 225).
- There will occur changes in migratory patterns of both humans and many animal species and even plants – as these find their supporting ecosystems degraded and themselves stressed by rising temperatures, changes in precipitation and other greenhouse effects. With the loss of so many species, many ecosystems will suffer "a devastating loss of biodiversity" (ibid., p. 226).
- Throughout the 21st century (the 2000s), climate change impacts will slow down economic growth, make poverty reduction much more difficult, further erode food security, and prolong existing and create new poverty traps, the latter particularly in urban areas and hot spots of hunger (IPCC AR5 2014); but also, Noble et al. 2005; Rosenzweig and Iglesia, 2006; Reuveny, 2007; Rose, 2009).

The major cause of global warming and climate change is human-induced GHG emissions into Earth's atmosphere. Huge atmospheric concentrations of GHGs beyond the assimilation capacity of Earth's atmosphere as a 'waste sink' have transformed the chemical composition of the atmosphere leading to global warming and climate change. The process of enhanced atmospheric GHG emissions began, in concrete terms, with the European Industrial Revolution starting in the mid-1700s and 1800s, which inaugurated socalled 'modern economic growth' (Kuznets, 1966), whose life-blood, as it were, is fossil-fuel energy (coal, petroleum, natural gas). Combustion of fossil fuels to drive industrial growth, transportation and myriad domestic activities, agricultural modernization linked to heavy use of nitrogen-based chemical fertilizers, land-use change (specifically, deforestation, livestock production, forestfires, etc.) – all these have constituted the key sources of Earth-heating GHGs.

B. Research Problems

The environmental economics literature (e.g. Field and Field, 2009) describes global warming and climate change as a global negative externality, a global 'public bad' created by the production and consumption activities of diverse economic agents (individuals, firms, governments) whose costs (burden) are borne by the world community rather than by the diverse economic agents who caused the damages in the first instance.

The following research questions seem, therefore, in order.

- What are the specific human activities causing this negative externality (global warming and climate change)?
- What are the symptoms of this negative externality in the various spheres of Earth's environment: atmosphere (air); lithosphere (soil); hydrosphere (water in all its various reservoirs – eg ocean, snow and ice; etc.); and biosphere (Earth's living sphere containing space for humans, animals, plants, microbial organisms, etc).
- What are the specific forms in which the environmental and health costs/damages arising from global warming and climate change manifest themselves?
- How have human societies and/or the world community attempted to cope with the global warming and climate change challenge? Or, what types of strategies, policies and institutions have human societies evolved to attempt to mitigate or, otherwise, adapt to, the environmental degradation posed by global warming and climate change?

C. Objectives and Justification

This study seeks to pursue four broad objectives. The first is to explain how global warming and climate change constitute a global environmental problem – that is, why and how the costs/damages arising from global warming and climate change are shared by the entire world community. The second is to identify, in concrete terms, and explain the specific human (anthropogenic) activities which emit the GHGs known to cause global warming and climate change. The third is to highlight the specific symptoms of global warming and climate change in the various spheres of Earth's environment: air, land, water, and living space. The fourth is to highlight the strategies, policies and institutions that have been evolved to attempt to cope with the global warming and climate change challenge.

CI. Justification for the Study

What particularly constitutes the motivation or justification for this study? First, we seek to provide the non-professional readers, namely, those individuals who do not possess the technical expertise and training to explore the otherwise highly specialized climate science literature with the relevant information and understanding of the causes and effects/symptoms of global warming and climate change.

It is important to note that the bulk of the studies on global warming and climate change has been produced by natural scientists[5] (physicists, biologists and ecologists, meteorologists, geographers, geologists, agricultural scientists) and climate economists, who, typically, employ terminologies and concepts unfamiliar to the general reader. While drawing on these specialist sources, we attempt to explain their concepts in more popular language. By this approach we hope to make the climate change narrative available and accessible to a wider audience. Popular thinking on global warming and climate change impacts tend to focus on land-use change (agriculture, deforestation) rainfall changes, etc. But these are the more easily perceptible elements of the Earth's environment. Its effects in the oceans, the ozone layer and ecosystems, etc are far less understood – again, because these elements of Earth's environment are not immediately perceptible to the ordinary, non-specialist observer.

Scientific studies have established that most of the warming caused by anthropogenic GHG emissions is absorbed by the oceans where a lot of ecosystem changes are occurring with disastrous consequences for human welfare. Rapidly rising carbon dioxide concentration are driving ocean systems towards conditions not observed for millions of years, with an associated risk of fundamental and irreversible ecological transformation: death, extinction and habitat loss – the ecological crisis problem. The latter began to register in the public consciousness, albeit in Europe and North America, only since the beginning of the 1980s.

In the academic sphere, the study of environmental externalities was for a long time neglected, or, at best, inadequately treated; in particular, neoclassical equilibrium economics, not enamoured, typically, of any notion of economic disequilibrium, failed to recognize environmental degradation as a case of a market failure: i.e. an outcome deriving from the self-interested behaviour of individuals in the context of unregulated economic activities, in which the collective interests of society fails to be properly taken into account. More technically, greenhouse gas emissions represent a negative externality; but they are a side-effect of economically valuable activities (e.g. applying chemical fertilizers to produce maize or corn) or burning coal to produce energy, etc.

Environmental externalities began to attract academic and policy interest only in recent decades – as from the 1980s – prompted by concerns over the effects of industrial pollution in the developed world, especially Western Europe and North America, the environmental conditions in the countries of Eastern Europe and the former Soviet Union caused by the failures of central planning, and, not the least, the environmental degradation caused by rapid urbanization and agricultural intensification in the developing world in the wake of the structural adjustment policies (SAPs) of the 1980s and 1990s focusing on production for export markets. At the international level, the problem of climate change arising from consumption of ozone-destroying chlorofluorocarbons (CFCs) has played no less a role in awakening interest in the economics of the environment.

However, inspite of the global awakening to the importance of the environment, sub-Saharan African populations, their governments and political leaders and academic institutions seem insulated from this global current. Few sub-Saharan African universities, for example, have serious programmes on environmental economics. Although sub-Saharan African governments have created separate Ministries of Environment, the latter often came off under-funded and ill-equipped, treated as one of the 'soft' ministries. But government policies in sub-Saharan Africa as a whole seem too overwhelmed by the problems of economic development to give the required attention to the issues connected with climate change challenge.

Although this particular study is not focused specifically on global warming and climate change as it affects Africa, several of the issues dealt with here touch on sub-Saharan Africa – e.g. drought and desertification in the African Sahel, climate change and its effects on the drying up of Lake Chad, etc. By explaining these specific African issues this study would have contributed to awakening the interests of the populations of sub-Saharan Africa and their governments to the global warming and climate change challenge.

D. Analytical Framework and Key Argument

The analytical framework to explain the phenomenon of global warming and climate change is premised on the economic theory of externality. The externality concept proposes that in a free-market economy (one in which production of goods and services as well as use of economic resources are not subject to government regulation other than normal competitive policy, but in which property rights exist and are upheld so that normal economic exchanges can proceed) rational individuals, typically, are motivated to pursue activities that maximize their own self interest and the costs and benefits arising from their activities for other parties not directly involved in their activities will not be reflected in the market prices of the goods / services they offer.

The present study proposes to argue that anthropogenic global warming and climate change is a market failure problem and represents a negative externality. But anthropogenic global warming and climate is a consequence of GHG emissions from diverse human activities, including fossil fuel combustion to drive industrial production, transportation and myriad domestic activities; land-use change (deforestation, livestock production, etc) – these are a result of rational activities of self-interested individuals, firms, and governments, whose cost functions do not reflect the value of the damages imposed on the global community by these activities. Briefly, global warming and climate change, a result of excessive exploitation of Earth's atmosphere as a waste 'sink', is the greatest example of a global negative externality the world community has ever confronted.

Why the over-exploitation and degradation of Earth's atmosphere as a waste 'sink'? The economic explanation is that Earth's atmosphere represents a common-pool resource *par excellence*, so that it is impossible to exclude any individual or firm or government from exploiting its services as a waste 'sink'. As a result, economic agents are free to make use of Earth's atmosphere at no charge (free). As a common-pool resource Earth's atmosphere raises problems similar to 'global public goods':[6] their 'carrying capacity' ultimately becomes destroyed through over-exploitation – the tragedy of the commons theory propounded by ecologist Garret Hardin (Hardin, 1968). Earth-atmosphere's 'carrying capacity' in the present context is the maximum amount of GHGs or gaseous pollutants the atmosphere as a natural waste 'sink' can effectively assimilate without its chemical composition changing to a vastly different state. As it has turned, that maximum amount of GHGs seems to have been exceeded; consequently, large unassimilated GHGs are left in Earth's atmosphere resulting in a fundamental change in its chemical composition – the source of current global warming and climate change facing the world community.

Strategies to reduce atmospheric GHG concentrations have involved mitigation and adaptation policies applied at national and international levels. Several policy initiatives aiming to steer the world away from "a course leading to tragedy" (United States Secretary of State John Kerry; quoted in Shiller, 2015), have foundered on a fundamental 'free rider problem' (no economic agent is willing to contribute towards the cost of supplying a good/service when he/she/it hopes that some other agent(s) will bear the cost instead). But reducing GHG emissions is an example of a global positive externality, whose benefits come as 'pubic goods' available and accessible to the global community at zero cost. This 'public goods' character of efforts to reduce GHG emissions does, indeed, undermine efforts at convincing countries and other individual economic agents (e.g. private firm) to volunteer to reduce GHG emission via taxes and legislation (See Shiller, 2015; also, Wagner and Weitzman, 2015).

E. Method and Data Sources

As has been stated, this study seeks to explain the causes of global warming and climate change, its symptoms, and the strategies for mitigating its effects. The main approach to the study is an extensive reliance on existing literature for an in-depth description and analysis of the nature of climate change, its causes, its symptoms in Earth's natural systems (e.g. deserts, oceans, etc.), ecosystems (e.g. inland freshwater lakes) and socioeconomic systems (e.g. agricultural production). These literatures, as already stated, are generated, largely, by natural scientists.

Scientists employ different approaches to attempt to discover the symptoms or effects of climate change on Earth's natural systems and ecosystems: use of instrumental records; palaeoclimatic analogues; and coupled general circulation models (CGCMs). In *instrumental records,* the natural variability of climate is used to predict rainfall patterns during sequences of extremes of dry and wet seasons. A limitation of this approach is the short periods of existing records; for example, it was only as from 1958 that Charles Keeling began recording, in any systematic way, carbon dioxide levels on Mauna Loa Observatory in Hawaii. Over such limited time spans, however, long-term changes in vegetation, sea surface temperatures, ocean currents, etc., which would be expected to have taken place are not adequately accounted for. This limitation notwithstanding, records for the past 30-40 years in many regions of the world, major river basins (especially in Africa), suggest changes directly related to global warming triggered by increase in GHGs (Evans: http://www.fao.org).

Palaeoclimatic analogues fall into the same category as instrumental records: estimating past climates is an extremely unreliable exercise. This approach deals with data gleaned from climates of earlier geological eras, which are based largely on the study of sediments that were laid down millions of years ago and of fossils (the remains or traces of any organisms) that lived in the geological past; in most fossils the organisms have been transformed into stones or fuels (coal, petroleum, natural gas, etc.).

Coupled general circulation models (CGCMs) are built by climate scientists and climatologists for exploring potential future impacts of enhanced GHGs; they are used to generate characteristics of future climate under anthropogenic forcing – i.e. under present and future emissions of GHGs as well as in climate impact assessment (e.g. Fischer et al., 2005; Reilly et al., 2001). They provide internally coherent climate change scenarios, being able to solve all globally climate-relevant physical equations. The United Nations IPCC **Assessment Reports** and most scientific views on climate conditions derive their predictions from CGCMs. Wright and Nebel (2004, p. 521) report that fourteen centres around the world (as at the beginning of the 2005) are engaged in running models coupling the atmosphere, oceans and land. Nevertheless, however, it has been found that CGCM projections present significant uncertainties, due in part to problems of imperfect knowledge of key climate dynamics such as water vapour-cloud feedbacks.

F. Structure of the Study

The rest of the study is structured into sixteen substantive chapters, as follows:

Chapter 1 surveys the theoretical and conceptual issues for explaining the problem of climate change as a global environmental degradation problem and, therefore, a negative externality that imposes costs on the global community. Global warming and climate change represents a global negative externality because its effects all nations and symptoms transcend national boundaries – and its cost must be borne by the international community as whole and not by the individuals or countries who inflicted the damage.

Chapter 2 examines the composition of Earth's environment and how the various spheres interact and interface. Specifically, understanding global warming and climate change would require explaining how the various spheres of Earth's environment are linked one to the other and how changes in the atmosphere-hydrosphere-lithosphere (or atmosphere – ocean – land systems) act as an enormous weather engine fuelled by solar radiation and strongly affected by Earth's rotation.

Chapter 3 examines human-activity sources of the GHGs that cause global warming and climate change. Specifically, it provides empirical insights into the human-activity sources of greenhouse gas emissions – socalled anthropogenic footprint in global warming. The final section of the chapter surveys the current controversies in 'climate sensitivity' – in particular, the hiatus between the predictions of climate science models and the actual behaviour of Earth's climate over the decades.

Chapter 4 examines the country and regional origins of global GHG emissions and, by extension, sources of human- induced climate change. Countries' GHG emissions tend to be correlated with their level of industrial and economic development. Expectedly, over all, the industrially developed countries, constituted largely by the OECD countries, account for over 80% of industrial carbon dioxide emissions over the long-term horizons.

Chapter 5 deals with the ozone layer and ozone layer depletion as a symptom of climate change, including the environmental consequences of ozone depletion. Ozone layer plays a vital positive role in determining the quality of life on Earth, absorbing, as it does, biologically harmful ultraviolet (UV) radiation from the Sun. Ozone depletion is largely linked to human activity: the atmospheric concentrations of chlorine and bromine through large emissions of anthropogenic nitrogen oxides produced from aircrafts and, more importantly, chlorofluorocarbons (CFCs). Five categories of environmental and health damages are known to be associated with ozone depletion: human health; plants; marine ecosystems; biogeochemical cycles; and materials.

Chapter 6 studies the symptoms of climate change in the hydrologic cycle (also called the water cycle) referring to the rate at which water evaporates and falls again as rain or snow, the circulation of water between Earth's atmosphere, lithosphere (land) and hydrosphere. Climate change has had the effect of speeding up the hydrologic cycle, which makes regions (e.g. the tropics) more sodden or yet wetter and humid, and arid regions (e.g. deserts) even drier; it brings longer droughts between more intensive periods of rain. Indeed, the hydrologic cycle is very much sensitive to global warming and climate change; much of the effect of climate change tends to be felt through its effects on precipitation (rain and snow). The circulation of water between Earth's atmosphere, land and oceans is enhanced through the warming up of local atmospheric temperatures, with great implications for the frequency, intensity and duration of hydrologic events, namely, precipitation, floods, droughts, etc.

Chapter 7 deals with climate change and the problem of retreating polar glaciers, melting ice caps and mountain snow caps. Glaciers provide the most sensitive indicators of global warming and climate change, constituting one of the most visually compelling symptoms of recent global warming. Globally, glaciers are showing signs of continuous melting and retreat, which are known to follow increases of atmospheric GHG concentrations. On the other hand, the melting of polar ice caps is predicted to release methane gas trapped in the frozen ice peats of the tundra, which could accelerate the pace of global warming. Other predicted impacts of glacier melting include sea level rise (SLR), alterations in ocean currents and thermohaline circulation.

Chapter 8 treats the symptoms of climate change in the oceans. Oceans constitute the largest single reservoir of water on Earth, for which single reason developments within the ocean systems have profound implications for global warming and climate change. Oceans occupy some 70% of Earth's surface, and absorb 80% of the temperature due to global warming – thus suggesting that but for the oceans global temperatures would be a lot warmer than they are presently. The thermohalin circulation (THC) pattern dominates ocean currents; because of its innate heat capacity and its role as a conveyor of heat, the ocean has a strategic role in climate and climate change. There is postulated slow down or even shutdown of the THC, as the effect of global warming: specifically, global warming resulting in thawing of Arctic ice sheets and retreat of glaciers could add enormous quantities of fresh water to the North Atlantic Ocean region, resulting in salinity changes that could shut down the THC, potentially triggering localized cooling in the North Atlantic and leading to cooling, or less warming in that region, especially in the British Isles and Nordic countries (Denmark, Norway, Sweden); other environmental consequences could include increases in flooding and storms, collapse of plankton stocks, etc.

Chapter 9 examines the symptoms of climate change in sea level rise (SLR). Sea level rise is a longer-term change in the volume or mass of the ocean leading to the long-term changes in world-wide sea level. Two primary sources of SLR are: thermal expansion (as ocean water warms, it expands); and contribution of land-based ice due to increased melting of polar glaciers and ice sheets. For many atoll island states – e.g. Maldives, Seychelles, etc. – known to be highly sensitive to SLR, the latter is a threat to their very existence. Similarly, low-lying deltas – e.g. the densely populated Nile delta, Ganges and Brahmaputra deltas, etc – are also threatened by SLR. Many of the world's largest cities, including many of the developing countries's most important, are built on coastlines threatened by SLR.

Chapter 10 treats drought and its climate change causes. Drought and desertification are two closely related environmental problems, whose climate change causes did not become a major international issue until the 1972-1974 Sahel drought. The fundamental causes of drought trace to changes in certain elements of climate that combine to support precipitation; most importantly, generally, rainfall is related to the amount and dew point (determined by air temperature) of water vapour carried by regional atmosphere, coupled with the upward forcing of the air mass containing that water vapour. So, drought occurs if these combined factors fail to support precipitation volumes sufficient to reach Earth's surface. Some common consequences of drought include: significant decline in crop yield; production and carrying capacity for livestock; shrinking of surface water reservoirs (e.g. lakes); dust bowles and dust storms; etc.

Chapter 11 focuses on symptoms of climate change in deserts and desertification. Also known as arid zones, deserts describe landscapes or regions of low precipitation: less than 150 millimeters (mm) per year. Most deserts tend to be located beneath areas or regions of high pressure into which rain-bearing, moisture- ladden, winds find difficult to penetrate, which results in those areas experiencing low, scattered rainfall patterns that are, besides, highly variable both seasonally and annually. Because (lack of) water emerges as the most important factor in desert ecosystems, changes in regional and global precipitation regimes tend to exert significant desertification outcomes. On the other hand, desertification refers to the spread of desert conditions for whatever reasons. In general, desertification is a product of two complementary processes: climate factors (climate change, drought) and unsustainable land-management practices in dry land or desert ecosystems – such as overgrazing and expansion of crop land due to demographic changes; fuelwood extraction; extraction of surface water beyond the recharge capacity of the hydrologic cycle; etc. (as in the Lake Chad basin experience). Both climate and desertification interface at a variety of scales through a complex of feedback loops: climate influences desertification through its impact on desert (dry land) soils and vegetation; in turn, desertification impacts on climate change indirectly during biomass combustion, a common practice in the tropics and semi-tropics, which generates a large volume of atmospheric aerosols and tract gas emissions.

Chapter 12 examines the effects of climate change in ecosystems. Ecosystems describe the processes by which plant and animal populations, including microbial organisms, interact with each other and the physical environment (air, water, and land) to reproduce and perpetuate the entire grouping. Thus, an inland freshwater lake, or a tropical rainforest, or a savanna grassland, or a wetland, or a mangrove swamp, etc. each with its plant (flora) and animal (fauna) species in a physical space, constitutes an ecosystem. The notion of ecosystems permits us to capture the fact of the complex interdependence between and among the living and non-living spheres of Earth's environment. Although humans can adjust to practically any climate change, this is hardly true of other living organisms – both animals and plants. If other living organisms in an ecosystem are adapted to their climate (i.e. temperature, precipitation, etc), a change in the latter represents a major threat to the structure and function(s) of that ecosystem. Certain ecosystems, especially tropical rainforests, harbour rich species diversity; their disturbance by climate change is a major cause of biodiversity loss. Climate change is a key factor shaping the capacity of ecosystems to supply their goods and services. Ecosystems face occasional disturbances in their equilibrium, but are, nonetheless, capable of recovering from such disturbances, provided their self- reproductive potentials are not destroyed. However, the frequency and severity of ecosystem disturbances determine the way they affect ecosystem functions. Long and reoccurring drought in the West African Sahel, for instance, has seriously undermined the natural capacity of the hydrologic cycle to replenish Lake Chad.

Chapter 13 examines the symptoms of climate change in socioeconomic systems, the extent socioeconomic systems are exposed to climate change, and their sensitivity and adaptive capacity to climate change. A socioeconomic system may be conceived as any structured or patterned or stable relationship between any number of human agents (as producers and consumers) possessing any degree of common interests (social, economic, political), values or goals, and who inhabit a specific geopolitical space, or who occupy a geographical entity defined by the boundaries of a state. As defined, the various countries of the world may be considered socioeconomic systems. On the world-scale, countries (as socioeconomic systems) may be classified into two categories: developed (industrialized), and developing (non-industrialized). These two categories of socioeconomic systems display different degrees of exposure, sensitivity and adaptive capacity to climate change. Developing countries, generally, have peculiar geographical characteristics - specifically, location nearer or within the tropics – which expose them more to the effects of climate change than developed countries. For example, agriculture is the economic sector most vulnerable to climate change. But rising temperatures are most likely to inflict the most change and, hence, causing the most damaging effect on land and agriculture. The effects of climate change on socioeconomic systems involve complex interactions between and among population growth rates, economic growth rates, technological change, geographical factors, etc. On the global level, agriculture will be affected adversely by climate change. However, even though technological change will likely offset the losses in agriculture due to climate change, the fact of the widening technological capability deficits in the developinhg world generally in contast to rapid technological change in the developed world will result in a further widening of the development gap between the developing and developed worlds as climate change proceeds a pace.

Chapter 14 deals with strategies to cope with climate change. Although those strategies differ across countries, they can be categorized into two broad types based on their role or the objective(s) they are meant to achieve. Thus, we have mitigation strategies, which aim to stabilize the atmospheric GHG concentrations, and adaptation, which seek to equip human societies with capabilities to function more effectively as Earth's temperatures continue to warm up with rise in GHG concentrations. Mitigation strategies thus include: innovations in fossil fuel technologies; developing biofuels as alternative to fossil fuels; developing 'new' technologies in non-carbon energy; improving energy efficiency; and land-use changes. Given that climate change is a global negative externality, a global 'bad', what is important for mitigation strategies to be effective is that all countries of the world and all income groups participate simultaneously, while acknowledging the principle of differentiated capacities and responsibilities between the industrial countries and developing countries respectively. Adaptation strategies are, essentially, means to manage the risk associated with climate change, which can be approached in three ways: by decreasing or minimizing the probability of incidence of climate-related events (e.g. constructing irrigation facilities to cope with drought); to mitigate the expected damage from climate-related events when they do occur; and by providing facilities to enhance communities' or individuals' ability to cope with climate-related change (e.g. by taking insurance policies against such events).

Chapter 15 highlights the economic and regulatory instruments evolved by the international community to cope with climate change challenge. By the end of the 1990s developments in the global environment, especially with regard to climate change, resurrected interest in taxation of fossil fuel consumption and/or removing subsidies on fuel prices, on the one side, and putting up legislation on legal rules and regulations guiding the activities of economic events (e.g. specifying minimum environmental standards on air quality, or imposing complete ban on the use of certain input, (e.g. CFCs), etc., on the other.

Chapter 16 highlights the international institutions and protocols so far set up to address the various problems relating to global warming and climate change, and the difficulties and incentives inherent in their formulation and execution. The setting up of international institutions on climate change has been motivated by the appreciation by the global community of the very nature of this environmental problem: it is an environmental global 'bad' inflicted by economic agents in one country but whose effects spill over into other countries.

Chapter 17 summarizes the study and draws conclusions. Climate change is a global negative externality and involves complex interactions between demographic, climatic, environmental, economic, health, political, institutional, social and technological processes. Climate change has impacted on Earth's environment as well as shaped prospects for food, water and health security.

End Notes

[1] Defined as those causing at least 100 deaths or affecting the survival needs of at least 1000 people, or prompting a declaration of a state of emergency or a call for international assistance (see Thomas et al. 2013, 2014; also, Vachani and Usman 2015).

[2] See The Economist (2012, 16th June). One positive outcome though, is that the Arctic Ocean (and, in particular, the 'North-West Passage') is expected to become navigable.

[3] The IPCC produces *Assessment Reports* which serve as the standard update on the global climate system.

[4] Scientific studies on climate change are now frequently published in major scientific journals – e.g. Science (by the American Association for the Advancement of Science), Climate Change, Nature, Journal of Climate, Quarterly Research, Quarterly of the Royal Meteorological Society, Gophysical Resarch Letters, The Integovernmental Panel on Climate Change (IPCC) Assessment Reports, Journal of Geophysical Research, etc.

[5] See end note no. 4 for relevant sources.

[6] Paul Samuelson (Samuelson 1954) is credited with pioneering the concept of 'public goods' in modern economics; he defined pubic goods as "collective consumption goods" – i.e. goods which everyone enjoys in

common, in the sense that each individual's consumption of such goods does not substract from any other individual's consumption of these goods – the non-rivalness principle. In addition, a public good has a second property: non-excludability meaning that it is impossible to barr or exclude others from consuming public goods. Some goods may be rivalrous but non-excludable, and are called common-pool resources – e.g. open sea fisheries. Common-pool resources raise similar problems to public goods – the tragedy of the commons problem.

CHAPTER 1

CONCEPTUAL AND ANALYTICAL FRAMEWORK

1.1 Introduction

This chapter surveys the conceptual and analytical categories for explaining global warming and climate change as an environmental degradation problem and, hence, constituting a global negative externality. The costs of a negative externality come in the form of a global public bad – quite the opposite of a global public good – so that its costs or burden must be borne by the world community and not by the economic agents who inflicted the environmental damages, in the first instance. But, first, let us explain the concept of global warming and climate change and how and when the concept itself evolved.

1.2 Evolution of the Global Warming and Climate Change Concept

Scientists had theorized on global warming and climate change till the 1800s (19th century), but not until the 1980s – about a century later – did the idea itself evolve into "one of the biggest arguments of our time" (The Economist, 9th September 2006, pp. 3-4). The first scientist to observe the connection between human activities and rising global temperatures was the Swedish physicist Svente Arrhenius (1859-1927), who developed a theory to explain the ice ages,[1] and in 1896 became the first scientist to attempt to calculate how changes in the level of atmospheric carbon dioxide (CO_2) could change global surface temperature through the greenhouse effect (Arrhenius, 1896, 1908). Arrhenius, however, did not use the term 'carbon dioxide' but, rather, 'carbonic acid'. He pioneered the theory that the CO_2 emissions from burning fossil fuels[2] and other combustible processes were large enough to result to global warming, including in his calculations the feedback from the changes in water vapour as well as latitudinal effects, while discounting the effects of clouds (which have cooling effects), convections of heat upwards in the atmosphere, and other forces that could affect temperature. Arrhenius seems to have been influenced by the cold climate in his native Scandinavia, when he believed that global warming would have a positive outcome by making colder regions warm. Arrhenius's ideas continued to circulate until the 1960s, even as most scientists dismissed as implausible his global warming propositions, believing, instead, that the oceans and other natural 'sinks' (e.g. forests) would absorb carbon dioxide faster than human activities would emit the gas. Later developments were to take the opposite direction: human activities (industrial, agricultural, transporation, domestic, etc.) create more carbon dioxide emissions (the major greenhouse gas) than natural 'sinks' can actually assimilate.

Earlier in 1824 the French scientist Jean-Baptiste Joseph Fourier pioneered propositions on the greenhouse effect, which was later discussed in 1860 by John Tyndall (Tyndall, 1861, 1863). The greenhouse effect was investigated quantitatively by Arrhenius in 1896 (Weart, 2008) and was developed in the 1930s through the 1960s by Guy Stewart Callendar (1867-1964), an English steam engineer (Callendar, 1938, 1939, 1940, 1941, 1949, 1958, 1961). Fourier's proposition of the possibility that Earth's atmosphere might act as an insulator of some kind became widely recognized as the first proposal of what came to be known as the greenhouse effect, although Fourier himself never called it that (see Fleming, 1999; Weart, 2008; Osman, 2011).

The global warming concept probably originated in modern scientific literature in the 1970s following a 1975 paper by oceanographer Wallace Smith Broecker (Broecker, 1975; Johnson, 2010). Thereupon, the phrase global warming began to feature in the scientific literature, and in 1976 the Soviet physicist Mikhail Budyko's statement that "a global warming had started" was widely reported (Weart, 2014; but see Budyko, 1969, 1971, 1972, 1975, 1977).[3] Prior to Broecker, while scientists admitted that human factors could affect Earth's temperatures and weather patterns, they were not quite certain the direction of those effects were taking: cooling or warming, and by how much? (see Conway, 2008).

The United States National Academy of Sciences adopted the terms 'global warming' and 'climate change' in 1979 in a paper called *The Charney Report*, which posited: "if carbon dioxide continues to increase (we find) no reason to doubt that climate change will result, and no reason to believe that these changes will be negligible". *The Charney Report* emphasized the distinction between rising Earth's surface temperature which it referred to as 'global warming' and changes originating in increased atmospheric carbon dioxide concentrations as 'climate change' (Conway, op. cit.; National Academy of Sciences, 1979). The term climate change came, henceforth, to be understood to refer to change in some property of atmospheric variables or phenomena: e.g. increased mean global temperatures, changes in the frequency/intensity of floods or droughts, urban heat islands, or volcanic-induced cooling; etc.

1.2.1 International Scientific Consensus

Scientific research continued to accumulate rapidly in the 1970s through the 1980s. The World Climate Conference in Geneva, Switzerland in 1978 had called attention to the problem of GHGs and human-induced climate change. In 1988 the Intergovernmental Panel on Climate Change (IPCC) was established by the World Meterological Organization (WMO) and the United Nations Environment Programme (UNEP) with three working groups: scientific evidence on climate change; environmental and socioeconomic impacts; and response strategies. IPCC's Assessment Reports were released for the first time in 1991, and came to represent "… authoritative statements of the contemporary views of the international scientific community" (Houghton, 1997, p. 159). IPCC's Scientific Evidence Working Group set out to fashion out a global consensus on the complex science of global warming and climate change. Scientific evidence began to confirm that atmospheric GHG concentrations are human-induced, and to establish that this is responsible for over 50% of the enhanced greenhouse effect, both historically and future (Jäger and O' Riordan, 1996).

1.2.2 Global Awareness of Global Warming and Climate Change

By the end of the 1970s,[4] the environmental impact of economic development referring, in its broadcast sense, to the expansion of industrial capacities and associated socioeconomic and technological changes, were beginning to register themselves. Specifically, the scale of human impact on Earth's environment and its resources were beginning to register in the public consciousness in the industrialized North and, to a less extent, the non-industrialised South. Perhaps, the most important indicator of the global awareness of the dangers posed by climate change came in the rise of the Green Parties in West European politics. By the 1970s concerns for the ecological stability of planet Earth and the quality of life in western societies had begun to sharpen perceptibly (Adams, 2009, especially chapter 7.). The German Greens, *Die Grünen* emerged the most articulate of the political lobby platforms espousing 'green development', evolving into a political party in the 1980s with representatives in the West German Parliament, the *Bundestag*. In the 2013 federal elections, *Die Grünen* came fourth with 8.4% of the votes and 63 out of 630 seats in the *Bundestag*. European Greens have since achieved significant successes in elections to the European Parliament (McLean and McMillan, 2005, pp. 231-2); currently European Green parties have 51 members of the 751 members of the European Parliament (2014 – 2019).

In the developing world, generally, public consciousness has been far more concerned with issues relating to economic development, poverty reduction, etc. than with environmental issues as such. Nevertheless, in the developing world, generally, the extension of the environmental pressure-group politics familiar with the western industrial societies starting in the 1970s, had evolved in the campaign against loss of species and natural habitats caused by deforestation. There was, for instance, the 'Save the Rainforest Organization' (STARO) – a charity organization founded by Jessica Hartfield and Dieter Bratschi. The emotional plea was to leave the vast expanse of flora and fauna in South America, especially the Amazon Rainforests considered by environmental scientists "the lung of the world" for its capacity to absorb up to 2.4 billion metric tons of carbon each year, apart from harbouring exotic flora and fauna now threatened by deforestation and mining exploration. Closely related to this problem is that as scientific understanding of environmental services began to improve in the 1990s onwards, new financial opportunities for the developing countries began to emerge: for instance, the importance of tropical rainforests in the protection of the ozone layer became appreciated in the developing world, which is probably behind the demand by the latter for monetary compensation from the rich industrial nations for their (developing countries') rainforests,[5] apart from current REDD+ (reducing deforestation and degradation and the role of conservation and sustainable forest management) mechanisms aimed at creating financial value for the massive stock of carbon stored in forests, to which we return in chapter 16.

At the international policy level, the academic debate on human-induced climate change became, in the 1970s onwards, fused with debates on sustainable development (Adams, op. cit.). A global consensus was now evolving to the effect namely, that the problems of economic development and environment are organically linked and should be treated as an "integrated whole" (Adams, op. cit., especially pp. 313-20). It is relevant to note, however, that the idea of sustainable economic development was introduced into the arena of international political economy following the publication of the World Commission on Environment and Development (WCEP), otherwise known as the Brundtland Report (1987), after the Norwegian Prime Minister Gro Harlem Brundtland, who chaired the Commission. The issue of environmental degradation was by the 1980s beginning to be treated as a global threat, a global environmental crisis, that could jeopardize economic development for future generations. Hence, the concept of sustainable development became conceived as "development that meets the needs of the present without compromising the ability of future generation to meet their own needs" (Brundtland Report, op. cit.). Rather than predicting greater environmental degradation in a world of continuously depleting natural resources, the Brundtland Report foresees "the probability of a new era of economic growth, based on policies that sustain and expand the environmental resource base."

The development literature of the 1980s had taken this as its point of reference. This literature expatiated on the idea that economic development requires a strong policy of protecting Earth's environmental resources as a component of natural wealth (Pezzy, 1989; Pearce et al., 1989). More recent literature goes further and separates out natural capital for special treatment, arguing that most forms of economic growth make demands on the environment, both by using (sometimes nonrenewable) natural resources and by generating wastes and pollution, which jeopardizes growth for future generations (Aronsson and Lofgreen, 2010). The notion of sustainable development attempts, therefore, to reconcile this apparent contradiction by insisting that economic policy choices should have utmost concern and consideration for their possible environmental outcomes.

To conclude this section, it should be stated that there are disputes, especially more pronounced in the popular press than in the scientific community, on global warming and climate change, which centre on the following: (i) causes of increased global average surface temperature, especially since the 1950s; (ii) whether this warming trend is imprecedented or within normal climate variations; (iii) whether human activities are partially responsible for rising temperatures or are artifact of poor measurements; and (v) others include disputes on estimates of climate sensitivity, predictions of additional warming, and what the outcomes of global warming will be (see, for instance, Bykoff and Bykoff, 2004; Oreskes and Conway, (no date). However these disputes should not detain us here.

1.3 Global Warming and Climate Change as Global Negative Externality

A negative externality (external diseconomy), generally, refers to the effect of a private agent's activity whose adverse consequences or outcomes for welfare or opportunity costs are not fully accounted for in the price or market system[6]. Global warming and climate change presents a perfect illustration of a negative externality, being the result, largely, of greenhouse gas emissions arising from the production and/or consumption activities of diverse economic agents, including firms, governments, and individuals or households, whose adverse outcomes for welfare (environmental and health costs) are not fully captured in the price system. For example: ozone layer depletion and associated environmental and health damages (e.g. skin cancer, cataract, a clouding of the eye lenses, inhibition of plant growth and photosynthesis, etc. caused by ultraviolet (UVB) radiation), created by greenhouse gas emissions by private agents who burn fossil fuels to drive economic activities, cause reductions in the welfare of people who may in no way be directly linked to the greenhouse gas emissions, in the first instance. Because third parties (individuals, firms, governments, etc. affected by the damages inflicted by ultraviolet radiation in our example) receive no compensation (do not charge) for these damages, these are costs of production (or consumption) not fully captured by the price or market system. We return to ozone layer depletion in chapter 5.

Externalities are important in determining the optimal use of economic resources; in a free-enterprise system, economic agents, typically, only attempt to maximize their own private benefits and so social costs and benefits – that is, costs and benefits in the context of society as a whole – will hardly be reflected in the prices of marketed goods and services. Take for example, a hypothetical case of a petroleum refinery producing and selling petroleum products cheaply, but, nevertheless, emitting gaseous fumes into the atmosphere as well as spilling wastes into nearby farmland, rivers and streams, to the detriment of other economic agents who may not be consumers of the refinery's cheap petroleum products. Our refinery's production costs will not capture the costs of the medical bills incurred by people whose health has been damaged by our refinery's air pollution, or even the costs of the lost production arising from the spillages on the nearby farmlands, rivers and streams. Yet the full cost (cost to society) of our refinery's production activity includes not only those that the refinery itself put down in its ledgers, but also the additional health bills and value of lost output incurred by economic agents affected by the pollution.

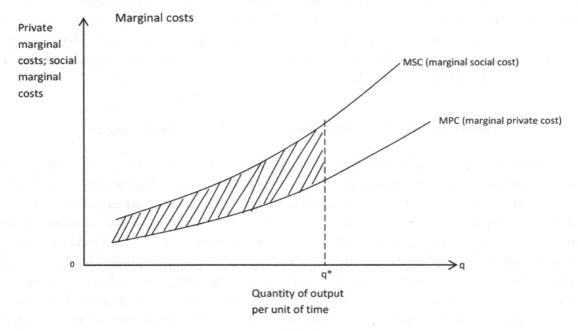

Figure 1.1 Divergence of private costs from social costs

Consider figure 1.1, which illustrates the marginal (additional) costs of producing our refinery's products as composed of two parts: MPC, the marginal private costs (MPC), as recorded in the refinery's ledger; and MSC, which is the sum of the refinery's MPC and the unrecorded costs to society of the refinery's production activities. Notice that at every point on the refinery's output curve, say q*, the MPC lies below the MSC; that is, private costs diverge clearly from social costs.

The policy literature admits though, that, in practice, there is difficulty in establishing the actual shape of the MSC curve; but it is not easy to isolate, unambiguously, the environmental externalities of an activity and quantify their impacts in relation to the actual private activity itself.

World Bank (1992) offers some insight on this, on which this study draws. To look for or assess environmental externalities there is need to establish a production decision boundary and time horizon. Establishing the production decision boundary enables us to determine the boundaries or limits of economic analysis – that is, what activities to include and what to exclude in the analysis. By assessing the boundaries or limits of economic activity, it becomes clear what benefits accrue to the production decision maker and what costs enter its production ledger. On the other hand, establishing a time horizon will enable us to establish, for example, how long the fumes or chemical emissions and wastes from our refinery might last and, possibly, the duration the impacts on health and environment of the gaseous fumes and spillages. Current debates on strategies to mitigate climate change often ask questions on how long the various GHGs emitted into Earth's atmosphere stay in the atmosphere before they dissipate or disappear (socalled average residence time of GHGs), which also determines their global warming potential (GMP), to which we return in chapters 2 and 3.

1.4 Interaction Between Economy and Environment

A more significant reason for the existence of externalities is that every human (economic) activity – be it production or consumption – starts and ends with interaction with Earth's environment. The latter refers to the natural world in which humans, animals, plants and microbial organisms live and reproduce themselves. Thus understood, Earth's environment includes: the nature of living space (sea or land, soil or water); the chemical constituents and physical properties of the living space; the climate; and the complexes of other organism's present – e.g. microbes. It is this physical world or natural environment occupied by living organisms (humans, animals, plants, microbes) that is being impacted on by human activity. We return to a more detailed treatment of Earth's environment in chapter 2.

To initiate an activity economic agents (individuals, firms, governments) necessarily draw inputs from Earth's environment – such as water, energy, soil, food, air, etc., which they transform into some output(s) partly for consumption, and partly for production of intermediate and final goods. The production and consumption processes generate materials that are returned to the environment as wastes – e.g., in the forms of gaseous fumes, polluted air or water, industrial and urban refuse composed of non-degradable plastic bags, metal cans, etc. and degradable material (e.g. oil sludges, kitchen and domestic refuse, etc.). 'Wastes' in this context refer to products of production and/or consumption that are not required for further production and/or consumptionm and are, therefore, excreted or expunged from these processes.

Figure 1.2 illustrates the economy-environment interactions analysed above. The direction of the arrows shows flows to initiating agents in the top half of the figure, the bottom half shows the waste disposal flows from initiating agents into the environment which then recycles these flows back to producers and consumers, which is shown by the dotted arrows from the environment as a waste 'sink'.

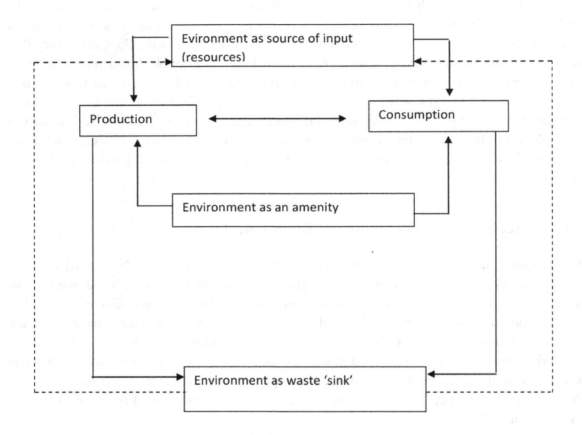

Figure 1.2 The Econonmy and Environment in Continous Interaction

The left-hand arrow originating in the box labeled 'environment as an amenity' to the production box represents the use of the environment as source of production inputs – e.g. crude refining to produce petroleum products (kerosene, aviation fuel, etc.). The arrow originating in this same box to the consumption box represents the use of environmental resources – e.g. lake resorts, beaches, etc. – as recreational activity. Briefly, the 'environment as an amenity' box indicates that Earth's environment contains resources that facilitate both production and consumption. As noted above, negative externalities are the outcome of human activities (production and consumption) which create 'wastes' in converting resources from Earth's environment into production and/or consumption inputs. Negative externalities arise, however, precisely because Earth's environment as a waste 'sink' is limited in its capacity to assimilate or absorb all the wastes created by human activities, which results in environmental degradation (destruction of the natural quality of Earth's environment) under certain circumstances. Much more importantly, negative externalities arise because the environmental resources like air, open seas, rivers, land, etc. cannot easily be owned privately (there is no private property rights over them, so that firms (producers) and consumers (individuals/households) cannot be excluded from exploiting them in ways which create negative externalities – i.e. create spillovers or affect third parties. If it were possible to create private property rights over Earth's atmosphere, for example, it would, perhaps, be possible to compel economic agents (users) to display sufficient regard for the environmental outcomes of their activeites – in terms of engaging in activeities that deplete their regenerative potentials.

1.5 Earth's Natural Environment as Global Commons

Why do private economic agents fail to consider the externality effects of their activities? Or, why do economic agents fail to consider the social cost or welfare cost implications of their production and consumption choices?

The answer is that simple: Earth's natural environment, including the atmosphere, is a common-pool resource, a global public good[7] **par excellence**, so that it is impossible to exclude any individual or firm or country from exploiting Earth's atmosphere as a waste 'sink'. As noted earlier, common-pool resources raise problems like those raised by global public goods: they ultimately get degraded through overexploitation, there is no 'exclusion' principle; consequently, that is, their carrying capacity ultimately gets exceeded.

Because of absence of property rights over global commons property – alternatively, open-access resources – they tend to be over-exploited and degraded even up to the point of extinction. There is no 'exclusion' principle in the use of open-access resources, in the sense that, for instance, emitting GHGs into the atmosphere is done freely (without any price of access) by all countries or by all individuals or by all firms on planet Earth. But the existence of zero user fees or charges to exploit Earth's atmosphere encourages its excessive exploitation far beyond its carrying capacities – a problem reflected in global warming and climate change.

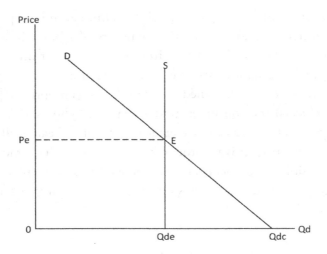

Figure 1.3 Consumption of an environmental resource

Consider Figure 1.3 (after Handwick et al., 1994, Figure 13.6, p. 242) where the quantity OQdc of a common-pool resource is consumed at zero price (without any price of access). Assume now that a market price is introduced at equilibrium price OPe; this will reduce equilibrium quantity demanded to OQde < OQdc. An obvious policy message to draw from this simple hypothetical illustration is that, in some cases, the absence of markets for common-pool resources encourages overexploitation (in our example OQdc – OQde = excess exploitation) with the result that the carrying capacity of the resource is exceeded (or else the assimilative capacity of the natural resource as a waste 'sink' is exceeded), thereby giving rise to a (global) negative externality – a problem reflected in global warming and climate change. As noted above, the free-for-all-access to common-pool resources inevitably leads to their over-exploitation and degradation – the tragedy of the commons theory propounded by the British ecologist Garret Hardin (Hardin, 1968).

Hardin's theory drew on the 1833 pamphlet by the English economist William Forster Lloyd (Lloyd, 1833), which explored the problem faced by herders (livestock farmers) sharing a common grazing pasture. Hardin's tragedy of the commons concept states that self-interested individuals acting independently and rationally (aiming to achieve some private economic objective at minimum cost) according to each's self-interest behave contrary to the best interests of the whole group by undermining the collective will to achieve the common good.

The historical background to the global commons theory traces to the British Industrial Revolution. As the latter began to unravel by the late 1700s through the 1800s, cows still would graze on the commons in many English villages (Perkins et al., 2001, pp. 98-9). But the village commons were undivided land subject or open to use by all and everyone in the village especially for grazing livestock at no cost (free of charge). But the amount of grazing pasture was fixed and soil fertility and climate limited the supply of pasture. With more villagers using this fixed grazing resource, its carrying capacity ultimately got exhausted, so that herders were forced to travel further a field to find pasture, with increased costs for each herder. This was to the disadvantage of the whole village community, rather than to the individual herders who undermined the grazing capacity of the commons, in the first instance.

1.5.1 Uncontrolled Atmospheric Greenhouse Gas Emissions and Degradation of Earth's Atmosphere

The dilemma of the commons as described above is quite applicable to Earth's atmosphere – a renewable environmental resource[8] available to all countries and to all individuals unlimited by fees or regulation. The inevitabl outcome of this situation is ultimate degradation or destruction of Earth's atmosphere – a situation currently manifested in global warming and climate change caused by human-induced atmospheric emissions of greenhouse gases (GHGs). Open-access to Earth's atmosphere seems to have depleted its capacity to self-generate. Because there is zero user cost attached to the use of Earth's atmosphere as global commons – countries are free to draw from it to meet their needs (e.g. all countries are free to draw on Earth's carbon dioxide for plant photosynthesis; all humans are free to draw on Earth's oxygen to sustain live, etc) and to add to it to get rid of their wastes (all countries are free to dump their GHGs, etc) there is a tendency to exploit Earth's atmosphere far beyond its carrying capacity – a problem evident in ozone depletion. As we shall show later, ozone layer depletion represents a global negative externality, whose costs are borne by the entire world community in the form of ultraviolet (UVB) radiation that have adverse health and environmental impacts.

1.6 Dynamic Factors Influencing the Quality of Earth's Environment

Our analysis, so far, does suggest that increase in human activities – industrial, agricultural, transportation, etc – will inexorably result in environmental degradation. That is, economic development will inevitably lead to destruction of the environment. There is a certain neo-Malthusian flavour to this hypothesis, invoking, as it does, the ideas of the 18th century classical economist Thomas Malthus (1766 – 1834)[9], who argued that rapidly growing human populations would exhaust Earth's capacity to feed itself and based his conclusion on the thesis that human populations expand in such a way as to overtake the development of available land to grow enough food to sustain the expanding human populations, until rising death rates and falling birth rates harshly would reduce high population birth rates. This Malthusian trap thesis remains influential today in neo-Malthusian development circles, though current focus has shifted from land and agriculture to all natural capital and the global environment (e.g. Aligica, 2009). The hypothesis that human activities will inevitably over-run Earth's carrying capacity becomes tenable if technology, tastes, and investments to improve environmental quality remain static or fixed. Economic development has shown, however, that the overall effects of human activities on Earth's environment are continuously changing, influenced by the dynamic interactions of diverse economic, social, demographic and technological influences and processes.

Figure: 1.4 (after World Bank, 1992, Figure 1.4, p. 39) shows the four dynamic forces and processes that are hypothesized to influence the quality of Earth's environment: scale of human activity; composition of economic activity (e.g. share of manufacturing, agriculture, transportation, etc. in gross domestic product); efficiency of economic activity, measured in terms of resource consumption per unit of gross domestic product; and environmental damage per unit of gross domestic product, measured in terms of consumption or use of ecological or natural capital per unit of gross domestic product.

It seems thus clear that the size of economic activity and population growth so much emphasized in neo-Malthusian perspectives are just factors among the whole web of variables that shape Earth's environmental quality. Resource-use efficiency referring to the capacity of the production system to reduce input use per unit of output (without compromising the quality of goods produced), for instance, will reduce pressure on demand on Earth's environment as source of inputs (see Figure 1.2) – as, for instance, when the transportation system reduces fossil fuel consumption per unit of goods/passengers through, for instance, use of fuel-efficient vehicles.

There is, also, the influence of resource substitution referring to ability to replace scarcer (and, hence, more expensive) resources with the more abundant (and, hence, cheaper) resources – e.g. shifting away from fossil-fuel energy sources (petroleum products, coal, etc.) to solar energy, wind energy, etc.). Finally, clean technology and management per unit of input or output – as in the use of lead-free gasoline in automobile transportation, or dietry manipulation of livestock feed, which seeks to reduce the carbon/nitrogen inputs into the system of livestock production to reduce enteric emissions of methane, etc. Economic policies, environmental policies and investments in environmental protection will all work to ensure that economic agents appropriately or clearly recognize the true value of environmental resources.

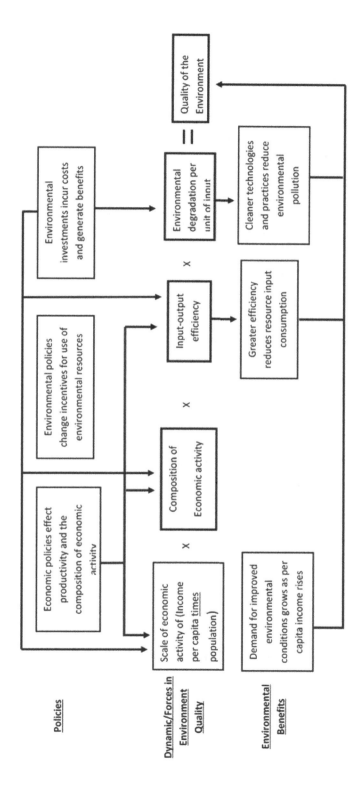

Figure 1.4 Economic Activity and Quality of the Environment (after World Bank 1992, figure 1.4, p. 39)

As noted already, efficiency gains resulting from economic policies are expected to reduce demand on Earth's environment as source of inputs as economic development proceeds apace (as gross domestic product expands or as scale of economic activity increases); on the other hand, environmental policies – e.g. fuel taxes intended to reduce use of personal cars (and, hence, atmospheric greenhouse gas emissions) can reinforce efficiency in resource use and produce incentives for adopting environmental friendly technologies such as fuel-efficient automobiles.

It is clear, therefore, that there is no apparent conflict as such between environmental quality and the scale of economic activity and population growth contrary to the neo-Malthusian standpoint. On the contrary, with proper policy incentives to protect the environment, the apparent conflict between economic expansion and environmental quality can be broken – that is, improvement in environmental quality can be achieved simultaneously as economic development proceeds apace. This is further illustrated in Figure 1.5, which shows that introduction of policy incentives and adoption of cleaner and more efficient technologies can – and do, indeed – lead to improvement in

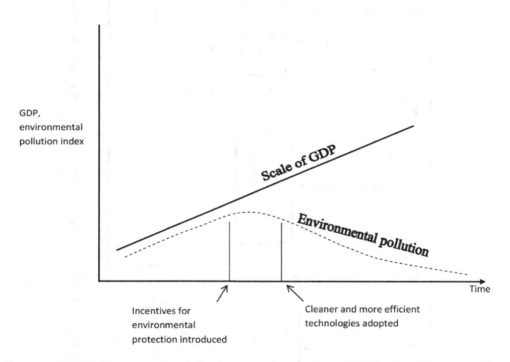

Figure 1.5 GDP Expansion and Decline in Environmental Degradation Given Policy Incentives to Protect the Environment (after World Bank 1992, Box Figure 1.6, p. 40)

environmental quality as economic development proceeds apace. Of course, environmental degradation (as represented in atmospheric greenhouse gas emissions, oil spillages and various types of environmental pollution) is always and everywhere linked to human activity; the important point, however, is that the adverse consequences for the environment arising from human activity can be minimized through adoption of appropriate policies and environment-friendly technologies. We return to these issues in the empirical chapters (14-16) dealing with strategies, policies and institutions to mitigate the impacts of global warming and climate change.

1.7 How To Deal With The Externality Problem

As noted earlier, externalities are important in determining the efficient use of resources; their presence inevitably results from human activities where, typically, human agents seek to maximize their own private gains, so that marginal private costs (MPC) and marginal social costs (MSC) necessarily diverge. This discrepancy between MPC and MSC is the source of negative externalities and, hence, inefficiency in resource use, and can be removed or minimized by policy interventions: specifically, the key to removing an inefficiency due to an externality is to 'internalize' the externality referring to when the producer of the externality treats all social costs/benefits caused by the externality as private costs/benefits. In this way, the producer of an externality bears the true social costs and earns the benefits of his/her activity. Where and when an externality has been internalized, a social optimum in the use of the resource in question is said to obtain; economic theory provides analysis of the ways in which society can achieve this objective.

1.7.1 The Tax-Subsidy Solution

The principle of allowing pollution to occur but imposing a price or cost on polluting agents or taxing them derives from Arthur Cecil Pigou (Pigou, 1932), who pioneered the distinction between private costs and social costs as well as the notion of externalities as putting a wedge between private and social costs – an idea hitherto ignored or neglected in neoclassical equilibrium economics that was built on the premise of existence of perfectly competitive market conditions. Pigou explained that the neoclassical equilibrium economics positing that formation of costs and incomes under perfectly competitive markets guaranteed social optimum was made untenable by two pervasive conditions that characterize modern capitalism, namely, monopoly and externalities; for Pigou, the essence of an externality

> "… is that one person A, in the course of rendering some service, for which payment if made, to a second person B, incidentally, also renders services or disservices to other persons (not producers of like services), of such sort that a payment cannot be exacted from the benefited parties or compensation enforced on behalf of the injured parties" (Pigou, op. cit., p. 183).

Pigou pioneered the socalled tax-subsidy solution to internalizing externalities: the idea that externalities should be corrected by government policy interventions in the form of imposing taxes on negative externalities and granting subsidies on positive externalities to adjust and supplement the operations of the private market. On this basis, Pigou is acknowledged to have evolved the concept of social costs to account for not only the direct private costs, but also the costs imposed on society or the community which fail to be captured by the private market processes. Pigou's work did serve as the starting point for a "new economic theory of welfare" whose aim is the maximization of social welfare (Osadchaya, 1983).

The concept of externalities was to acquire a strategic importance in economic analysis, especially in neo-Keynesian and early development (structuralist) literature that admitted the need for government intervention in the economy. The rationale for government intervention put forward by these two schools of economic theory was based on the argument that government policy interventions – e.g. social spending on education, health, etc., income redistribution effected through fiscal instruments, etc. – create positive externalities. Pigou specifically advocated that the state use taxes and subsidies to adjust and supplement the operation of the market mechanism by improving the structure of the distribution of resources, the social product and consumer demand.

By the 1970s Pigou's 'new economics' began to attract policy attention, influenced by a rejection in policy circles of a unidimensional approach to well being based simply on per capita income. The 'quality of life' approach posits, instead, a multidimensional approach to well being, among which is the quality of the physical environment. Current concern with greenhouse gas emissions, polluted environments, etc. – that is, with social costs not captured or reflected in market prices – are modern illustrations of Pigou's separation of divergences between marginal social and private costs (Osadchaya op. cit.).

1.7.2 Environmental Taxes and Legislation

By the end of the 1990s developments in climate change resurrected interest in environmental taxes; two policy instruments have dominated the policy literature: taxation of fossil-fuel consumption and emission trading schemes (OECD, 2008; Fullerton et al., 2008; Jha, 2010), to which we return in chapter 15. Apart from these two essentially market-based strategies, there is the legislation or 'command-and-control' approach belonging in the wider area of legal rules and regulations guiding the activities of economic agents. This may involve, for instance, introduction of controls by specifying minimum environmental standards on air quality, or imposing complete ban on use of specific inputs, etc. Raising the price of fossil fuel products (petroleum products, coal, natural gas, etc), whose combustion is known to be the major source of atmospheric GHG emissions, has been found to constitute a sure means to mitigate climate change – indeed, the simplest and most cost-effective strategy (see Jha, 2010, chapter 22; Field and Field, 2009, chapters 12-13). When a tax is approximately levied on fossil fuels, the ensuring market price will cover the full or social costs of the fuel involved, including the costs the damages inflicted on the environment by the ensuring atmospheric GHG pollution, which would otherwise go unpaid by the polluting agents and, instead, be shifted to society or the community at large, or to future generations. By imposing a tax on the polluting agents, the external costs become thus internalized by the polluting agents – that is, the costs of polluting the environment become fully borne by the private agents causing the pollution or damage (the negative externality). Recall Figure 1.1 analysed earlier in this section: the gap between MPC and MSC disappears.

Besides, fossil fuel taxes are intended to provide economic agents the incentive to shift from consuming products that degrade the environment – e.g. GHG emissions – to existing 'clean goods' and 'clean technologies'. Pollution taxes are, generally, meant to raise the prices of products which create pollution as they are manufactured, or disposed of – e.g. lubricants; chemical (inorganic) fertilizers; pesticides, including insecticides, herbicides, fungicides, and all other biocides; non-returnable containers; mercury and cadmium batteries; 'feedstock' chemicals; packaging materials; etc. By levying a tax, the demand for such products will be reduced, which will induce the producers (firms) to take account of the external costs that their production activities impose on society (see also Solsbery and Wiederkehr, 1995).

Carbon taxes have been popular, particularly in the European Union (EU). It has been criticized, however, for the simple reason that it does not – and cannot, indeed – guarantee that CO_2 emissions would decline by a certain amount; a carbon tax "represents certain pain for uncertain gain" (The Economist, 2015, 28th November, p. 15).

Cap-and-trade schemes, which specify the quantity of carbon that can be emitted, handout, or auction permits to pollute up to that limit. Polluters can buy and sell permits in socalled carbon markets.

The problem with carbon tax and cap-and-trade schemes is that not every country wants to join the effort – the free rider problem. But reducing carbon emissions is a perfect example of a global positive externality: the benefits come as a public good available and accessible to all countries of the world at zero charge, which undermines efforts at convincing all countries and individuals to volunteer to reduce CO_2 emissions via taxes and legislations (see Shiller 2015; also, Wagner and Weitzman, 2015).

The *command-and-control approach*, also known as the legislation approach, belongs in the wider field of legal rules and regulations guiding the activities of economic agents about the environment. Thus, this approach attempts to introduce direct controls, which may involve specifying minimum standards, or imposing complete ban or use of specific inputs. In some specific cases, legislation may require the installation of specific types of anti-pollution equipment: for instance, in the European Union; (EU) automobile firms are now required to install (as from the early 1990s) exhaust fume systems known as catalytic converters[10] that reduce air pollution from automobiles and to develop fuel-efficient engines. Yet another example may be cited from the United States, where the Environmental Protection Agency (EPA) has already proposed legislation on carbon dioxide emissions, which would, in practice, ban new coal-fired plants after 2013 unless fitted with carbon capture and storage (CCS) systems.

To be effective, environmental legislations setting minimum standards, apart from setting up inspectorates and associated bureaucracies to monitor and enforce compliance, must ensure that the monitoring agencies possess adequate knowledge of what the optimal level of pollution ought to be on the product(s) being monitored. For the standard setting approach to be completely effective, a necessary condition is that the inspectorates must possess knowledge of the marginal benefits and marginal costs curves to be able to determine the optimal level of output and associated level of pollution. This is quite unlikely to obtain in practice, both for reasons of technology and information (data) constraints. Besides, when standards are set across the board for all firms, the process does not consider of the marginal cost differences among firms, a vital information for reducing pollution associated with individual firms.[11]

1.7.3 Coase Bargaining Solution

Ronald Coase (Coase, 1960) in his classic study, *The Problem of Social Costs*, called attention to an alternative to governent tax-subsidy solution to the externality problem. He pointed out that direct voluntary bargaining between affected parties can ease the internalization of an externality if property rights to the externality are well defined and if there are zero transaction costs.[12] When property rights are well defined for an externality, a market for that externality is created, and government intervention to tackle the problem created by the externality may no longer be required, Coase argued. So, the Coase solution is used to demonstrate that a solution to the externality problem is the allocation of property rights. For example, suppose an entrepreneur wishes to start a production activity that emits noxious fumes that pollute the neighbourhood. It is unfair to allow him to start this activity as this ignores the health concerns of the neighbourhood; equally, it is unfair to prohibit him from carrying out this activity as this infringes on his rights to carry out a legitimate activity. Social efficiency requires that the entrepreneur should be allowed to carry out his economic activity only if the profit he obtains from it exceeds the discomfort (in terms of health and environmental pollution) it causes the neighbourhood. This efficient outcome can be achieved by giving the entrepreneur the right to carry out his production, but allowing the neighbourhood inhabitants to bribe him not to carry out the activity, an option the entrepreneur will exercise if the necessary bribe is large enough (to cover the profits he would obtain were he allowed to produce). Alternatively, the neighbourhood could have the right to enjoy an unpolluted environment, but could allow the production to be carried out for a fee. It does not matter who has the initial prerogative – both arrangements will lead to the economic activity being carried out only when the neighbourhood pollution is sufficiently small. The policy of allowing pollution to occur – GHG emissions through fossil-fuel combustion to occur while imposing taxes on fossil fuels to try to reduce demand / consumption for fossil fuels – is an application of the Coase bargaining solution to externality.

1.7.4 Merger Solution

Where one firm generates an externality for another, it may be possible to internalize the externality through a merger of the two firms to form a single firm. Consider two competing firms, Y and Z, where Y generates a negative externality for Z, which essentially means that Y's marginal social cost (MSC) exceeds its marginal private cost (MPC), as shown in figure 1.6. The dd curve represents the demand curve for firm Y's output. Prior to merger, Y will be producing output Oq, which does not account for the external cost which it imposes on Z. Post-merger, the combined management of Y and Z will reduce the level of output of firm Y to Oq_1, the Pareto optimal level. This is so because what was prior to merger an external cost to firm Y has become a private cost to the larger merged firm and must, therefore, be taken into account in determining the profit-maximizing output.

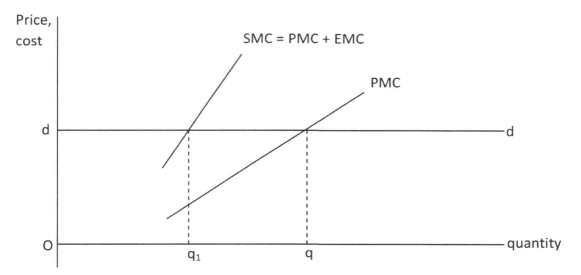

Figure 1.6 The Merger Solution for Externality

1.8 Conclusion

This chapter has dealt with some of the conceptual issues with which to explain global warming and climate change. Economists explain global warming and climate change as a case of global environmental degradation and, hence, constituting a global negative externality that imposes costs on the world community rather than on the individuals, firms and governments who caused the environmental degradation, in the first instance. Global warming and climate represents a global negative externality because: first, it is caused by the production and/or consumption choices of private individuals, firms and governments pursuing their private objectives; and, second, the effects of global warming and climate change transcend national boundaries. As shall be shown in the empirical chapters the rise in average global surface temperatures has led to the melting of the polar ice caps causing widespread flooding in many parts of the world. Yet another example is the use of chlorofluorocarbons (CFCs) which has led to the depletion of the ozone layer – a natural ecosystem in Earth's atmosphere protecting humans and other biological organisms from the harmful effects of ultraviolet rays from the sun. The problem of atmospheric pollution leading to climate change arises from the peculiar nature of Earth's atmosphere as global commons – a natural resource available all individuals and countries of the world unlimited by fees or regulation. The result is ultimate degradation or destruction of Earth's atmosphere caused by human-induced atmospheric greenhouse gas concentrations.

End Notes

[1] A period in Earth's evolution during which ice had advanced towards the Equator and a general lowering of temperatures; the last major ice age, that of the Pleistocene Period (sometimes known as the Ice Age), ended about 10,000 years ago (Oxford Dictionary of Science, 2005, p. 413).

[2] Fossil fuels are energy sources from coal, crude oil (petroleum) and natural gas; they are socalled because they are formed from the remains of organic matter (plant, animals, microbes, etc) that lived in the geological era referring to the time that covers Earth's history from its origin, estimated to be some 400 million years ago, to the present (Oxford Dictionary of Science, op. cit., p. 333). Coal, for instance, is known to originate in the remains of plants that grew in swamps or other moist environment in the geological past.

[3] Budyko's studies are in Russian and most of these studies are yet to be translated into English.

[4] Socalled United Nations Second Development Decade; the *First* spanned the 1960s.

[5] 'Give us the money or the forest gets it', is said to be the 'blackmail' from the developing world received by the United Kingdom Environment Secretary Elliot Morley (See The Economist, 23rd April, 2005).

[6] Externalities, because they arise from the activities of others in the neighbourhood or come as spillovers from the activities of third parties, are sometimes describd as 'third party effect', 'neighbourhood effects' or 'spillovers', etc.

[7] See 'Introduction' – *End Notes*, no. 6.

[8] The literature distinguishes between *renewable* and *non-renewable* environmental resources based on the criterion whether the resource in question can or cannot replenish itself or its stock within a timeframe meaningful to the human mind. Thus a renewable resource (also an infinite or perpetual resource) is one that can replenish itself at a sufficient rate for sustainable economic extraction in a meaningful timeframe – e.g. biological or organic resources (fish, timber, wildlife, etc) as well as inorganic or nonliving resources (e.g. solar energy, hydro power, air, etc). We return to environmental resources in chapter 12.

[9] His most well known works are: *An Essay on the Principle of Population* (1798) and *Principles of Political Economy* (1820).

10   As the exhaust passes through this device (catalytic converter), a chemical catalyst made of platinum-coated beads oxidizes most of the volatile organic compounds (VOCs) to carbon dioxide (CO_2) and water (H_2O). VOCs include materials such as gasoline, paint solvents, and organic cleaning solutions which evaporate and enter the air in a vapour state, as well as fragments of molecules resulting from the incomplete oxidation of fuels and wastes. VOCs are prime agents of ozone formation.

11   For more insight, see Jha (2010) esp. chapter 22.

12   Costs associated with conducting economic activities in an imperfect market – e.g. if perfect information is lacking on where/how to procure inputs and/or sell outputs, etc prices tend to be rather high in imperfect markets due to high transaction costs. However, in practice transaction-costs free market are rarely encountered.

CHAPTER 2

EARTH'S ENVIRONMENT, GLOBAL WARMING AND CLIMATE CHANGE

2.1 Introduction

Understanding global warming and climate change requires some knowledge of how the various spheres of Earth's environment are linked one to the other and how changes in one sphere affect others. This chapter seeks to provide insight in this issue.

2.2 Spheres of Earth's Environment

Environment in our present context refers to the natural world in which humans, animals, plants and microbial organisms live and reproduce themselves. Thus understood, environment includes: the nature of living space (sea or land, soil or water); the chemical constituents and physical properties of the living space; the climate; and the complexes of other organism's present – e.g. microbes. It is this physical world or natural environment occupied by living organisms (humans, animals, plants and microbial organisms) that is being degraded by human-induced GHG emissions.

The scientific literature demarcates Earth's environment into four distinct spheres: three open non-living (abiotic) spheres, namely, **atmosphere** (air), **hydrosphere** (water) and **lithosphere** (land), interacting with the fourth sphere, **the biosphere**. These four spheres, illustrated in Figure 2.1, continually exchange matter – all the gases, liquids and solids in both the non-living and living sphere.

The **atmosphere** is constituted by the whole mass of gases that is gravitationally pulled to Earth, with an average composition, by volume, of 79% nitrogen, 20% oxygen, 0.03% carbon dioxide, and traces of rare gases. The atmosphere is the thin layer of gases separating Earth from outer space. The **hydrosphere** is water in all its various reservoirs: oceans and seas; rivers; groundwater; snow and ice; etc. The **lithosphere** is Earth's crust: the soil, rocks and minerals. The **biosphere** is the living systems supported and sustained by the services and life-support functions supplied by the three non-living spheres. While it appears that these four spheres exist, each is separate entity, in reality the four spheres are united in a continuous process of exchange of matter – all the gases, liquids and solids in both the non-living and living spheres – as indicated by the double-edged arrows in Figure 2.1.

Indeed, Earth's environment can be conceived as a continuous, ever-lasting process of exchange of matter between the non-living and living spheres – a process of atoms moving from the non-living spheres (atmosphere, hydrosphere, lithosphere) into living organisms (the biosphere, as humans, animals, plants, microbes) and returning to the non-living spheres (Wright and Nebel, 2004, p.54)

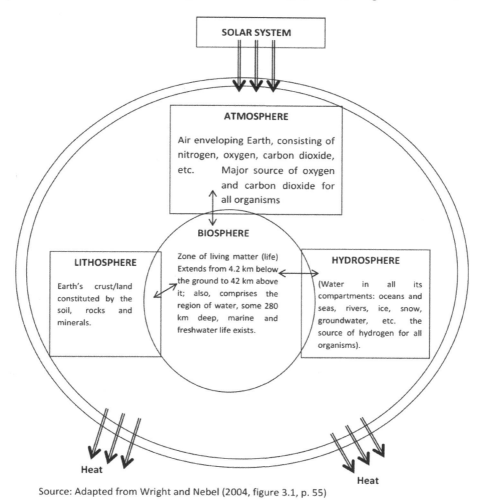

Source: Adapted from Wright and Nebel (2004, figure 3.1, p. 55)

Figure 2.1 Spheres of Earth's Environment

2.3 Earth's Atmosphere and Weather

As noted already, Earth's atmosphere is constituted by collection of gases that is gravitationally pulled to Earth, with an average composition, by volume, of 79% nitrogen, 20% oxygen, 0.03% carbon dioxide, and traces of rare gases. The scientific literature divides Earth's atmosphere into the troposphere and stratosphere[1].

The **troposphere** is the lowest layer of the atmosphere; it extends up to 16 kilometers (km) in the tropical latitudes and 8 km in the higher latitudes. Containing practically all the water vapor and clouds in Earth's atmosphere, the troposphere is the location and source of weather: the day-to-day variations in temperature, air pressure, wind, humidity, and precipitation (e.g. rain, snow, hail) occur here. The troposphere gets colder with altitude, except for local increase of temperature with height (altitude) or temperature inversion (Mayhew, 2009 p.273). Substances entering the troposphere- including pollutants- may be changed by chemical reaction and washed back to Earth's surface by precipitation – e.g. acid rain resulting from the emission into the atmosphere of sulphur dioxide and various oxides of nitrogen because of fossil fuel combustion and from automobile exhausts, respectively.

The **stratosphere** lies above the troposphere. The stratosphere is a layer with which temperature increases with altitude, up to about 64 km above Earth's surface. This temperature increase is due, primarily, to the fact that the stratosphere contains ozone, a form of oxygen absorbing high-energy solar radiation, allowing only a small fraction (about 1%) to reach Earth's surface – a factor determining Earth's climate and changes thereof. When the ozone layer gets depleted increased solar radiation reaches Earth's surface, with consequent harmful effects, to which we return in chapter 5.

As just noted, the daily changes in temperature, air pressure, wind, humidity, and precipitation, determine the weather pattern in a region; in turn, the weather patterns in a region over a long-term period constitute the climate. There is an atmosphere-ocean-land system constituting 'an enormous weather engine', fueled by the Sun and strongly affected by Earth's rotation:

> "Solar radiation enters the atmosphere and then takes a number of possible courses… some is reflected by clouds and Earth's surface, but most is absorbed by the atmosphere, oceans, and land, which are heated in the process. The land and oceans can then radiate some of their heat back upward as infrared energy. Some of this back- radiated heat, is transferred to the atmosphere" (Wright and Nebel, op. cit., p. 511).

By this process, air masses become warmer at Earth's surface and expand, becoming lighter.

2.4 Climate and Climate Change

As noted above, climate, narrowly defined, refers to average weather, the long-term average temperatures and precipitation (e.g. rain, snow, hail) characterizing a given region. More rigorously defined, climate refers to the statistical description in terms of mean and variability of relevant quantities and parameters over a period ranging from months to thousands or millions of years. The scientific literature defines the standard period for averaging these variables to be 30 years (as defined by the World Meteorological Organization, WMO); the relevant quantities are usually surface temperature, precipitation and wind. In sum, climate, in a wider sense, is the state of the climate system (consisting of four major components: the atmosphere, the hydrosphere, the lithosphere, and the biosphere, and interactions between them). The various global climate regimes 'created' in the first instance the different types of ecosystem complexes - e.g. tropical rainforest —which represent the adaptations of plants, animals, and microbes to the prevailing long-term weather patterns, or climate, of a region.

Temperature and rainfall, as noted above, are dominant parameters of climate. They define dominant vegetation, and animal life. Climate change, therefore, occurs following significant alterations in temperature and rainfall regimes to the extent that such alterations lead to significant effects, also, on ecosystems. But a given climate will support only those animal and plant species that find the temperature and rainfall levels optimal or at least within their ranges of tolerance; population densities (of plant and animal species) will be greatest where climatic conditions are optimal, decreasing as any conditions depart from the optimum (Wright and Nebel, op.cit., p. 43).

Climate change refers to the change in the state of the climate that can be identified (e.g. by using statistical tests) by changes in the mean and/or variability of the properties of the climate variables (e.g. temperature), and that persists for an extended period – typically for 30 years, as pointed out above. Climate change may originate in natural internal processes or external forcing, or in persistent anthropogenic changes in the mix of atmospheric GHGs etc. The United Nations Framework Convention on Climate Change (UNFCCC) defines climate change as: 'a change of climate which is attributed directly or indirectly to human activity that alters the composition of the global atmosphere and which is in addition to natural climate variability observed over comparable time period'. This UNFCCC definition makes distinction between climate change arising from anthropogenic activities that alter the atmospheric composition of GHGs on the one part, and on the other climate variability caused by natural forcing.

Internal causes of climate change include: changes in the distribution of land and ocean; continental drift (the theory that continents which are now separate were once united in a super continent); changes in the atmosphere-surface-ocean system; volcanic activity; etc. Although volcanicity is a possible mechanism of climate change, under present rates of eruptions it is difficult to envisage volcanic activity independently of other factors in causing significant and lasting global climate changes (Mayhew, 2009; p. 82).

Earth's surface is three quarter covered by ocean water – hence, planet Earth is often described as 'a water planet'. But the oceans play a dominant role in determining Earth's climates; they are the major source of heat entering the atmosphere: the evaporation of ocean water supplies the atmosphere with water vapor and when the latter condenses in the atmosphere, it supplies the atmosphere with heat (latent heat of condensation, referring to the quantity of heat absorbed or released when water changes its physical state or as it cools into vapor). The oceans, also, play a vital role in climate because of their innate heat capacity – the ability to absorb energy when water is heated. Thus, the well-known ameliorating effect of oceans on coastal-land climate regimes is a consequence of this energy absorbing property of oceans. Finally, through the movement of ocean currents the oceans convey enormous quantities of heat from hot equatorial regions to higher latitudes - e.g. the Gulf-streams, which keep Western Europe warm. We return to this theme in chapters 6 and 8.

2.5 Global Warming and Global Climate Change: Greenhouse Effect

Global warming refers to the unusually rapid increase in average global temperatures origination in increased emissions of greenhouse gases (GHGs) now known to have significant source in human activity (anthropogenic climate change). A greenhouse gas is any gas that contributes to the process known as greenhouse effect referring to a process which causes incoming heat from the Sun to become trapped in Earth's atmosphere.

To explain greenhouse effect, consider the way the interior of an automobile heats up when it is sitting in the Sun with its windows shut. The heating occurs because sunlight penetrating through the glass windows is absorbed by the interior materials of the automobile, including the seats, as light energy and converted to heat energy, which, in turn, is given off as infrared radiation. Unlike sunlight, the infrared radiation is trapped inside the automobile and so cannot escape the interior of the automobile. This trapped heat energy causes the automobile interior air temperature to rise much higher than the surrounding outside air temperature, which is the same process that keeps a greenhouse warmer than the surrounding environment.

At the global level carbon dioxide, water vapor, methane, nitrous oxide, and ozone in Earth's atmosphere play a role analogous to the glass in a greenhouse – hence they are termed greenhouse gases (GHGs). They lock or prevent infrared radiation from escaping from Earth into space. Light (solar) energy comes through the atmosphere and is absorbed by Earth's surface materials and converted to heat energy at Earth's surface; the infrared heat energy radiates back upwards through the atmosphere and into Earth's outer space. The GHGs naturally constituting the troposphere absorb some of the infrared radiation radiating it back towards Earth's surface; other GHGs (nitrogen and oxygen) in the troposphere do not[2].

As pointed out already, the GHGs act like a heat blanket, insulating Earth and retarding or slowing down the escape of infrared energy (heat) into space[3]. But for this insulation Earth's average surface temperature would be 21°C colder, which would make Earth uninhabitable[4]. Wright and Nebel (op.cit., p. 517) conclude thus:

"…our global climate is dependent on Earth's concentration of greenhouse gases. If these concentrations increase or decrease significantly, our climate will change accordingly".

As it has turned out, atmospheric GHG concentrations have actually increased significantly since the 1700s. This is responsible to the global climate change that is acknowledged to be the major global environmental challenge presently facing the international community.

2.6 Anthropogenic Greenhouse Gases (GHGs) and Global Warming

The known anthropogenic GHGs are displayed in Table 2.1

- **Carbon dioxide (CO_2)**, from fossil fuel combustion – principally from coal-fired power plants, and automobile exhausts and deforestation – a point suggested long ago in the 1800s by Swedish Scientist Arrhenius. Every kilogram of fossil fuel combusted results in the emission of about 3 kilograms of carbon dioxide. Currently, each year sees some 6.6 billion metric tons of fossil-fuel carbon combusted, adding some 24 billion tons of carbon dioxide emissions to Earth's atmosphere.

Table 2.1 Anthropogenic GHGs in Earth's Atmosphere

GHG	Average concentration 100year ago	Approximate current concentration (ppb)	Average residence time in atmosphere (years)
Carbon dioxide (CO_2)	288,000	370,000	120
Methane (CH_4)	848	1,800	12
Nitrous Oxide (N_2O)	285	312	120
Chlorofluorocarbon and Halocarbons	0	1.2	5-100

Water vapor (H_2O)	n.a	n.a	n.a
Soot (black carbon)	n.a	n.a	drops out within weeks

Note: ppb= parts per billion

n.a = not available

Bracketed figures are respective chemical formula

Source: Wright and Nebel (2004, Table 21-22, pp., 520).

- **Nitrous oxide:** This GHG is also known as dinitrogen oxide. Although known not to be common in Earth's atmosphere, nitrous oxide has been identified to be the more potent GHG than carbon dioxide and it hang around much layer (see Table 2.1). The upshot is that, over the course of a century, its ability to warm planet Earth is almost 300 times that of an equivalent mass of carbon dioxide (see also the Economist, 11th April, 2009). Other oxides of nitrogen (NO_X), such as nitrogen monoxide (NO), are pollutants. They contribute to acid rain, which result from the emission of various pollutant gases, in particular sulphur dioxide and various oxides of nitrogen. Other agricultural activities that emit nitrous oxide include the use of chemical fertilizers; but nitrous oxide is made by bacteria that live in soils and water, whose raw material is from the nitrogen-rich fertilizers that are a key input in the cultivation of the high-yielding varieties (HYVs) of the Green Revolution (mainly rice, wheat, corn or maize). Finally, accumulation of nitrous oxide is particularly dangerous, because its long average residence time in the atmosphere (120 years; See Table 2.1) makes the gas a problem in not only the troposphere, which it is a contributor to global warming, but also the stratosphere, where it contributes in ozone layer destruction.

- **Methane:** This is the third most important GHG, a product of microbial fermentative processes; its main natural source is wetlands (land intermittently or periodically water logged, including salt marshes, tidal estuaries, marshes, and bogs). Known anthropogenic sources include livestock (methane is produced in the stomach of ruminants), landfills, coal mines, natural gas production and transmission (pipeline losses)[5], rice cultivation, and manure. (Steinfeld et al., 2006, Heinemann, 2010; Gill et al., 2010). When methane reacts with other gases in the atmosphere it is gradually destroyed; on the other hand, methane is being added to Earth's atmosphere faster than it can be broken down. As Table 2.1 shows, methane atmospheric concentration is the most rapid among other GHGs; its atmospheric concentration since the Industrial Revolution of the 1700s and 1800s has doubled. Both methane and nitrous oxide absorb more heat per molecule than carbon dioxide; however, the latter's concentration is much higher (100–1000 times higher, respectively) and therefore has more overall effect on the enhanced greenhouse effect. Their residence times as well as concentrations play important roles on the enhanced greenhouse effect.

- **Chlorofluorocarbons (CFCs) and other Halocarbons:** Anthropogenic sources constitute the sole origin of CFCs. Like nitrous oxide, CFCs are long-lived, being chemically unreactive and stable at high temperatures; they contribute both to global warming in the troposphere and to ozone layer depletion in the stratosphere. CFCs are used as aerosol propellants, refrigerants, solvents and fire retardants, and in manufacture of rigid packing foam. But CFCs have a much higher capacity (10,000 times) to absorb infrared radiation than do carbon dioxide. Because of its role in ozone layer depletion CFCs were the target of the Montreal Accord of 1987 banning its use; the result is that the concentration of CFCs in the troposphere seems to have leveled off as from the late 1990s, though given their very stable (unreactive, chemically) nature, CFCs will continue to exert their global warming impact for decades.

- **Water Vapor:** This is the most abundant GHG, and plays an important role in the greenhouse effect. Through the hydrologic cycle (evaporation and precipitation), water undergoes rapid turnover in the lower atmosphere or troposphere. Its residence in the atmosphere however is so little (days rather than centuries) that it fails to be well mixed and then its effects on temperature are short lived and its spatial or geographical coverage limited.

- **Soot:** Recent scientific research has added soot to the list of GHGs. Also known as 'black carbon', soot is known to stay in the atmosphere for a short time: whereas CO_2 is long-lasting-120 year residence time in the atmosphere and an inevitable product of fossil-fuel combustion, soot drops out of the atmosphere within weeks. Current scientific evidence concludes, however, that soot is the second-most damaging GHG after carbon dioxide and about twice as bad for climate change as had been thought until now[6]. Soot, as currently present in Earth's atmosphere, has a warming effect of about 1.1 watts per square meter of Earth's surface (10/m²). An earlier study by the United Nations Environment Programme (UNEP) put the black carbon (soot) effect at only 0.3-0.6 10/m². The higher this figure, the worse the warming. Black carbon is found to be especially damaging to frozen regions, because when soot falls on snow and ice it increases the amount of light and heat they absorb, which helps to explain why the Arctic ice has been melting faster than anyone had expected. Current scientific evidence hypothesizes that warming is likely to be especially marked in the high latitudes of the northern hemisphere: Northern Canada, Alaska, Northern Europe and Siberia. By changing regional precipitation patterns, black carbons affect monsoons (the sudden wet season within the tropics, but, more explicitly, a seasonal shift of air flows, cloud, and precipitation systems), of which the Asian monsoons are the largest.

2.7 Global Cooling Factors

At the same time, however, there exist in Earth's atmosphere factors and processes that lead to global cooling effects. e.g. on average, clouds cover 50% of Earth's surface and reflect some 21% of solar radiation away to space so-called planetary albedo – and it prevents warming from occurring; volcanic activity (such as the mount Pinatubo volcano in the Philippines in 1991) that spewed some 20 million tons of particles and aerosols into Earth's atmosphere and contributed to a significant drop in Earth's average temperature 'as radiation was reflected and scattered away' (Wright and Nebel, op.cit., p. 517)[7]. Finally, anthropogenic sulphate aerosols (from ground-level pollution) have significant cooling effect by cancelling out some of the greenhouse gas warming effect. Most climate models reckon that aerosols – such as those from sulphates – cool the atmosphere by about 0.3 – 0.5°C (0.54 – 0.9F) (See the Economist, 30th March, 2013, pp. 70-1). The apparent underestimation of aerosols' cooling effect in conventional climate science models might help to settle one of the major controversies in climate science: the lack of a more direct correlation between atmospheric GHG concentration and global atmospheric temperature over the last several decades. Climate change models predict significant higher temperatures than have actually taken place; this has permitted sceptics to argue that global warming is all but 'hot air' (Wright and Nebel, op. cit., p. 524; see also The Economist, 30th March, 2013).

2.8 Conclusion

Earth's environment is constituted by four spheres linked one to another. These four spheres exchange matter – all the gases, liquids and solids in both the non-living and living spheres. Consequently, whatever happens in one sphere has spillover effects on the others.

End Notes

[1]   The description relies on Wright and Nebel (2004, chapters 3 and 21); see also htt//wiki.answer.com/Q/ which gases_are_gr) Retrieved 9th September 2012.

[2]   This greenhouse effect was first discovered by French Scientist Jean-Baptiste Fourier in 1827.

[3]   See also Wright and Nebel, op.cit., especially Figure 21.9, p.514.

[4]   See also Solomon et al., 2008; Karl, 2003; Le Treate et al,. 2007; Mayhew, op.cit., pp. 222, 226; Oxford Dictionary of Science, 2005, p. 370.

[5]   Methane is the main constituent of natural gas (about 99%).

[6]   See **Journal of Geophysical Research,** 15th January 2013.

[7]   On the other hand, however, volcanoes are known, also, to 'change circulation patterns in the atmosphere, which can then warm the climate indirectly, partially affecting direct cooling' (The Economist, 30th March, 2013, p.70).

CHAPTER 3

ANTHROPOGENIC (HUMAN-INDUCED) CAUSES OF GLOBAL WARMING AND CLIMATE CHANGE

3.1 Introduction

This chapter begins the empirical part of the present study; thus, it examines the human activities through which Earth-heating greenhouse gases (GHGs) known to cause current global warming are emitted into the atmosphere. The final section of the chapter surveys the current controversies on "climate sensitivity": rising atmospheric concentrations of GHGs have been found by climate scientists to be responsible for global warming though; however, how much warmer Earth's sea and land surface temperatures will heat up for each doubling of GHG concentrations in the atmosphere is yet to be scientifically firmly established. So, there is a certain hiatus between the predictions of climate science models and the actual behaviour of Earth's climate system over the decades, which requires explanation.

3.2 The Industrial Revolution: Watershed in the Enhanced Greenhouse Gas Emissions

Global warming and climate change, as already noted, is the term that has come to describe observed upward trend over the centuries in Earth's average sea and land surface temperatures caused by human-induced concentrations of GHGs in Earth's atmosphere. Scientific evidence shows that the temperature changes in Earth's climate system observed since the 1800s – in particular, since the mid-1900s – differ fundamentally from trends observed over 10s of 1000s of years. Greenhouse gases have significantly increased in their concentration in Earth's atmosphere, beginning since the Industrial Revolution of the late 1700s through the 1800s – a period a Nobel prize economist,

Simon Kuznets (Kuznets, 1966) labels the beginning of 'modern economic growth'. This enhanced accumulation or concentration of atmospheric GHGs accounts for much of the observed warming of Earth's climatewhich in climate science, is called the 'enhanced greenhouse effect', which is quite different from the 'natural greenhouse effect' occurring in the natural changes in the gaseous composition of Earth' atmosphere that ensure the latter's equilibrium climate behaviour. As explained earlier, certain atmospheric gases – socalled greenhouse gases (carbon dioxide, methane, water vapour, etc.) – absorb the infrared radiation (heat) from the sun, which is transformed into kinetic and potential energy. Eventually these molecules then radiate heat back into the atmosphere as infrared radiation; some of this heat is absorbed by other GHGs and some is absorbed by Earth's surface and the cycle of absorption, conversion and emission repeats continuously as the natural greenhouse effect. It is this natural greenhouse effect that shows the loss of heat to space, keeping Earth's atmospheric temperature warmer than it would be without the GHGs.

The rate at which solar energy is absorbed by Earth is approximately balanced by the rate at which it is emitted back into space, thus keeping Earth's climate system in what climate-scientists describe as a state of equilibrium, and a stable temperature. In this state of equilibrium existing during the centuries prior to the Industrial Revolution, the natural greenhouse effect maintained the average surface temperature of Earth's climate system at about 15°C. So, the natural greenhouse effect is socalled because it is caused by GHGs naturally present in Earth's atmosphere that ensure Earth's equilibrium climate behaviour.

As noted above, atmospheric concentrations of human-induced GHGs started to increase significantly following the Industrial Revolution unraveling in Great Britain (mainly England) by the late 1700s through the 1800s. The Industrial Revolution later diffused into Continental Europe (Germany, France, Scandinavia, etc.), North America, and Japan by the late-1800s and early 1900s. Somewhat later in the early decades of the 1900s, the Industrial Revolution began to diffuse into Eastern Europe and the former Soviet Union; and in the 1960s and 1980s it spread into the socalled newly industrialized countries (NICs) of East Asia and Latin America.

The Industrial Revolution in its various phases has been closely linked to a cluster of fossil fuels, starting with coal in the 1700s and 1800s. Each succeeding phase of the Industrial Revolution has seen significant increases in fossil-fuel produced GHG emissions. But the Industrial Revolution has been described as, especially, an 'energy revolution' (Jacob, 2007; Wrigley, 2011). In particular, the Industrial Revolution marked the transition to large-scale fossil-fuel combustion (mostly coal). In pre-Industrial Revolution times, coal was only a minor energy source (in Britian); the energy scene was dominated by human and draught power, accounting for roughly 50% of the energy total, and wood supplied the balance. Already by the late 1800s, upwards of 50% British energy supplies came from coal; and by the early 1900s, this had reached 90%. As the Industrial Revolution diffused into the European Continent and North America, large coal deposits began to be exploited, mostly in Northern Europe and in Appalachia in the United States.

In the 1900s coals was joined by other fossil fuels, namely, petroleum and natural gas (Smil, 1994; Williams, 2006). The largest oil fields were discovered between 1927 and 1958 in the Persian Gulf region, and petroleum supplies began to develop in the 1940s and 1950s. In the United States, the first natural gas pipelines were constructed starting in 1945, and natural gas was soon widely used for heating; by 1947, the consumption of petroleum and natural gas exceeded that of coal, inspite of the continued supplies of coal particularly for electricity generation.

Due to the high energy efficiency of petroleum and its availability many nations had moved, directly, from wood to petroleum – thus by-passing coal as industrial energy source (contrary to the Euro-American experiences), even where coal was available in these countries. Globally, fossil fuel supplies increased exponentially, beginning in the 1800s: coal supplies increased 100 times between 1810 and 1910, and 5 times during 1910-1990; crude oil supplies grew 300 times between 1880 and 1990; naturally gas, 1000 times over the same period.

Even though in the high-tech world of the 1990s onwards, coal-based energy sources are no longer fashionable and coal-based technologies are being phased out or scaled down (a reaction to coal's reputation as the 'dirtiest' fuel) – in contrast to the Industrial Revolution centuries – yet coal is far from being an energy source confined to history. Currently, coal-fired power plants generate some 40% of global electricity supplies, and this proportion is predicted to increase, especially given that China, the world's second largest and fastest growing economy, is highly dependent on coal-based energy. Besides, other developing countries are equally dependent on coal. But in the developing world, generally, the objective of achieving industrial take-off in the manner of the Euro-American world and the NICs of East Asia in which coal was the cheapest energy source (and widely available) is deemed to outweigh the environmental damage associated with coal as the 'dirtiest fuel'.

3.2.1 The Industrial Revolution as Pandora's Box

Wrigley (op. cit.) described the British Industrial Revolution as a Pandora's Box[1]. But the Industrial Revolution, whose defining technological feature came in the innovation of fossil-fuel-based mechanical technologies, most importantly the steam engine invented by James Watt in 1769 and initially powered by wood and later coal, offered human society 'the escape route' from the severe constraints placed on long-term economic growth by dependence on animate energy sources and organic fuel (e.g. wood). The same Industrial Revolution has, at the same time, unleashed the 'malign forces' of environmental degradation originating in massive concentrations of GHGs in the atmosphere through fossil-fuel combustion.

Table 3.1 Historical and Current Atmospheric Concentration of GHGs

GHG	Average concentration 100 years ago (ppb)	Approximate current concentration (ppb)	Lifetime (residence in atmosphere) (years)	Approx contribution of greenhouse effect (%)
Carbon dioxide (CO_2)	288,000	370,000-400,000	120	9-26
Methane (CH_4)	848	1,800	12	4-9
Nitrous oxide (N_2O)	285	312	120	n.a.
Chlorofluorocarbon (CFCs) and halocarbon	0	1.2	5-100	n.a.
Water vapour (H_2O)	n.a.	Most abundant GHG	n.a.	36-70
Aerosols and Soot (black carbon)	n.a.	n.a.	Drops out within weeks	n.a.
Ozone (O_3)	n.a.	n.a.	n.a.	3.7

Note: ppb = parts per billion
n.a. = not available
Respective chemical formulae are bracketed.
Source: Wright and Nebel (2004, Table 21-22, p. 520); Schmidt (2005); Russel (2007).

Table 3.1 shows that atmospheric CO_2 concentration was stable at 270-288 parts per billion (ppb) (the natural bound) for a long time prior to the Industrial Revolution. Thereafter it moved beyond the 'natural bound' to current levels put variously at 395 and 400 ppb. Following the Industrial Revolution rising levels of GHGs in Earth's atmosphere led to increased radiative forcing from carbon dioxide, methane, trospospheric ozone, CFCs and nitrous oxide. Subsequent analysis highlights the relative contribution of the various human-induced GHGs to global warming.

3.3 Fossil-Fuel Combustion and GHG Emissions

The bulk of GHG emissions originate in fossil-fuel combustion (Table 3.2); Table 3.3 shows the main sources of fossil fuel combustion.

Table 3.2 Main Sources of Fossil-Fuel Combustion

Source	Contribution (%)
Liquid fuels (e.g. gasoline, fuel oil)	36
Solid fuels (e.g. coal)	35
Gaseous fuels (e.g. natural gas)	20
Cement production	0.3
Industrial gas flaring and at well sources	< 1
Non-fuel hydro carbons	< 1
International bunker fuels	04

Source: Raupach et al. (2007)

Table 3.3 Relative Carbon dioxide Emissions from Various Fuels (Mass of Carbon dioxide Emitted per unit of Energy from Various Fuels)

Fuel	(pounds) Carbon dioxide (CO_2) million Btu	(kilograms) Carbon dioxide (CO_2) million Btu
Natural gas	117	53.07
Liquefied petroleum gas (lpg)	117	53.07
Propane	139.05	63.07
Aviation gasoline	152.6	69.20
Automobile gasoline	157.2	71.30
Kerosene	159.4	72.30
Flared natural gas	120.6	54.7
Tires/ tire derived from fuel	189.54	85.97
Wood and wood waste	195	83.83
Coal (sub-bituminous)	214.3	97.20
Coal (lignite)	215.4	97.70
Petroleum coke	251.60	114.12
Coal (anthracite)	228.60	103.70

Note: Btu = British thermal unit, is a traditional unit of energy required to raise the temperature of 1 pound (=0.45 kilogram) of water by 1°F. Btu is now defined as 1055.96 joules. Coefficients may vary slightly from other sources due to estimation methods and time.

Source: USEIA (2016)

Fossil fuels are energy sources used by humans derived from coal, crude oil (petroleum) and natural gas; they are socalled because they are formed from the remains of organic (biological) matter – plants, animals, microbial organisms, etc. – that lived in the geological past (100s of millions of years ago, to the present (Oxford Dictionary of Science, 2005, p. 333). It is believed dead organic matter metamorphoses into fossil fuels over geological time.

Coal, for instance, is known to be formed by the remains of plants that grew in swamps or other moist environments in the geological past; as the vegetable decomposed, it formed layers of peat, which were subsequently buried – e.g. by marine sediments as the sea level subsided. Under intense pressure complemented by consequent high temperatures the peat changed into coal – socalled coalification, involving a progressive transformation of the original peat material to produce the various 'ranks' of coal: in ascending order of carbon content: lignite (brown coal), sub-bituminous coal, bituminous coal, semianthracite coal (which has carbon content of 86 – 92%), and anthracite coal (hard and black coal, with carbon content of 92-98%).

Most coal deposits were formed during the Carboniferous and Permian geological eras (286-360 million years ago); more recent coal deposits occurred during the early Jurassic and Tertiary eras (144 - 1.8 million years ago (See Appendix 4, p. 884 Oxford Dictionary of Science, op. cit.). Petroleum (crude oil) is, like coal, formed from the remains of organic matter, and is often found along with natural gas.

Fossil fuels have all a high carbon or hydrogen content, their fuel value relying on the exothermic oxidation of carbon to form water. Much more important for the present study is that fossil-fuel combustion not only releases carbon dioxide into Earth's atmosphere, it releases various other GHGs, namely, carbon monoxide, methane, nitrous oxide, etc. that cause the enhanced greenhouse effect. Besides, these gases are known to become transformed into harmful acidic compounds upon undergoing chemical changes in Earth's atmosphere – e.g. sulphuric acid, carbonic acid, etc., which in turn return to Earth's surface as acid rain (one of the key industrial pollution problems of the industrial world – see Stutz and Warf, 2007, Figure 4.28, p. 140).

Different fossil fuels are found to emit different amounts of carbon dioxide in relation to the energy they produce when combusted (Table 3.3). The scientific literature provides formula for comparing pollution emissions across fuels: the amount of carbon dioxide emitted per unit of energy output or heat content. The amount of energy produced when a fuel is burned is mainly determined by the carbon and hydrogen content of the fuel (heat is produced when carbon and hydrogen combine with oxygen during combustion).

Natural gas ranks lowest among fossil fuels in terms of carbon dioxide content; coal ranks highest – hence, it is termed the 'dirtiest fuel'. But natural gas is primarily methane, which has higher energy content relative to other fuels, and thus it has a relatively lower carbon dioxide-to-energy content. Water and various elements – e.g. sulphur and non-combustible elements in some fuels – reduce their heating (energy) values and increase their carbon dioxide-to-heat contents.

3.4 Land-Use Change as Source of GHG Emissions

Other major sources of GHG emissions originate in land-use change referring to a change in the use or arrangement of land by humans, which may lead to a change in land cover, which, in turn, may have impact on evapotranspiration, sources and sinks of GHGs, or other properties of the climate system (Steinfeld et al., 2006; Heinemann, 2010; Gill et al., 2010). Land-use change as a source of GHG emissions has received considerable attention in the climate policy literature in recent decades, the bulk of the latter focusing on deforestation (Kummar, 1992; Kummar and Turner II, 1994 and references). Other dimensions of land-use change, apart from deforestation, include livestock production, fire burning, etc. We now proceed to highlight the GHG emission intensity of these three dimensions of land-use change.

3.4.1 Deforestation

Deforestation refers to the **permanent** destruction of a forest in order to convert the land to other non-forest uses- e.g. housing, road construction, ranching, etc. The term is often used, though wrongly, to describe any activity where all trees in an area are removed. However, where all trees are removed in uniformity with sustainable forestry practice, as is generally done in industrialized countries, this is described as 'regeneration forestry': the growth of new trees to replace those harvested for purposes of commercial logging or other economic purposes (Angelson and Kaimoritz, 1999). An estimated 18 million acres (7.3 million hectares) of forest, roughly the size of Panama in Central America, are reported lost each year to deforestation. Although there is little doubt about the rapid pace of deforestation world-wise, in the developing countries, it is not quite clear the precise rate and extent. But consistent and reliable data on deforestation is known to be quite difficult to assemble, both because of difficulties of measurement and what is meant by deforestation itself.

The literature is replete with debates on how to demarcate the various types of forest to gain understanding on the rates and causes of deforestation in the various forest ecosystems- e.g. rainforests, dry forests etc.; besides, as already noted, it is still being debated what really is meant by deforestation. Adams (2009 especially chapter 9) has relevant references on these debates. The debates intensified in the 1980s onwards, when the developing countries were engulfed in the external debt crisis and various strategies, including agricultural export developments, were floated to attempt to overcome the debt crisis, but whose outcome was exacerbation of the deforestation problem (eg Lopez, 1998). Nevertheless, however, the general pattern of deforestation seems broadly accepted. The Millennium Ecosystem Assessment (MEA, 2005) reported that global forest cover had declined by 50% in the last 300 years (that is, beginning in the 1700s), and 29 countries had lost 90% of their forest cover. Also, broad regional variations in pattern of forest exploitation seem clear and accepted. Logging for export timber for the European and other international markets is important in Southeast Asian deforestation, particularly in Malaysia, Indonesia, Papua New Guinea and the Philippines. In South America logging and ranching are the driving forces; however, in the Brazilian Amazon commercial logging began to displace ranching as key source of deforestation in the 1980s onwards. In sub-Saharan Africa characterized by a unique human ecology vis-à-vis South America and Southeast Asia, shifting cultivation practices, fuelwood extraction and charcoal collection are the main sources of domestic energy have driven deforestation.

3.4.1A Deforestation and Ecosystem Balance

Forests represent one of the major terrestrial ecosystem complexes (to which we return in chapter 12); as such they are dynamic entities subject to periodic or occasional disturbances that disturb their equilibrium – referring to the balance between forests (as biological organisms) and their physical environment – but are, nonetheless, capable of recovering from such disturbances provided their self-reproductive capabilities do not become destroyed. For instance, a drought (a local or regional lack of precipitation such that the ability to engage in water-dependent agricultural and livestock activities is seriously impaired) could constitute a short-term variability in ecosystem processes, which could lead to changes in ecosystem functions (e.g. forests regulate local or regional temperatures, precipitation and other biologically mediated climatic processes). Long-term changes in ecosystem environment do also shape ecosystem functions – e.g. drought conditions decades back can still leave their imprints on current ecosystem environment.

Ecosystems – e.g. tropical rainforests – are controlled by external and internal forces and processes. External forces, most notably climate (rainfall and temperature) control the overall structure of ecosystems but remain themselves uninfluenced by the ecosystem themselves. But the rainfall and temperature regimes determine the biomes (the ecological zone defined by the type of plant life that dominates) in which the ecosystem is embedded. On the other hand, internal forces (e.g. plant and animal life, microbial organisms) not only control ecosystem processes and functions, but are also controlled by them. The most important of the internal elements controlling ecosystems is human influence; unlike other internal controlling elements, the cumulative impacts of the human influence on ecosystem are large and strong enough to influence processes like climate (rainfall and temperature). Specifically, global warming, on the scale and trend it has assumed since the late-1700s, is a human-induced factor originating in fossil fuel emissions, deforestation, etc. and is a key factor influencing Earth's climate system.

The proposition that ecosystems – e.g. forests – are dynamic equilibrium systems, thus, are systems in long-run balance or stability – assumes, however, that the reproductive capabilities of ecosystems are not undermined or overburdened by human-induced activities such as when agricultural activities, logging, etc overburden the natural capacity of a forest ecosystem to naturally replace or maintain itself through reforestation.

As suggested above, forests as an ecosystem can sustain a certain amount of use or exploitation and still retain their viability; however, a point could be reached at which increasing use of a forest begins to undermine its natural capacity to regenerate or replace itself. At that point deforestation or over-use or degradation has set in. An important consideration here is the carrying capacity (CC) of a forest ecosystem: the maximum human population that the forest ecosystem can support on a sustainable basis. If this population is well below the CC of the forest ecosystem in question, then allowing that population to grow will increase the number of reproductive human population and, thus, the yield that can be harvested from the forest ecosystem. However, as the population of users approaches the CC of the forest ecosystem, new users must compete with the older ones for the resources of the forest ecosystem.

The problem of exceeding the CC of forest ecosystems does indeed occur because in most developing countries forests represent a common property resource (CPR) – an ecological resource with open access to all and sundry at zero charge (free). Because there is zero user fee to exploit CPRs, there is a tendency to abuse them or exploit them beyond their CC or natural capacity to regenerate, which, in turn could result in environmental degradation – what in the academic literature is known as the tragedy of the commons (analysed earlier in chapter 1). Indeed, rainforest deforestation in several regions of the developing world represents a clear case of the tragedy of the commons.

Why the tendency to overexploit or deplete forest ecosystems? The literature identifies underlying causes in market failures, government economic policies, and poor or inadequate knowledge of the ecological functions of forests.

- **Market failure** is, perhaps, the most commonly cited factor; it is proposed that the interplay of market forces, deemed grossly imperfect, can hardly produce outcomes that are deemed optimal from the standpoint of society. In the case of deforestation (a clear environmental degradation issue), there do arise very significant divergencies between private gains (benefits) – referring to the use-value derived by logging firms, for example, - and the costs inflicted on society from the destruction of forest ecosystems by the private users, but which fail to be reflected in the cost functions of private logging firms and individuals – the market failure problem. This can arise from three distinct sources. First, there is the free-access or common-pool character of forest ecosystems in developing countries whereby there exist no enforceable, or, at best, very weak, enforceable mechanisms to exclude anybody from using forest ecosystem resources, which results in their degradation (the deforestation problem). Rural households extracting fuel-wood from open-access forestland, private individuals logging for timber at zero fees in the tropical rainforests of the Amazon basin in South America, the rainforests of Western and Central Africa, the jungles of Southeast Asia, etc. could generate the same outcome: ultimate deforestation of the rainforests.

- **Government price policies** can, and do indeed, have adverse side effects on the use of forest ecosystem resources. Price controls and subsidies in agriculture, infrastructure (e.g. roads and urban housing projects, etc.) – these distort the prices (costs) of the exploitation of forest resources and, hence, leading to deforestation. Overly high rates of deforestation in developing countries have been blamed on government policies – specifically, policies that underprice the value of forest timber concessions offered to logging companies increase the incentive to extract timber at a high rate; on the other hand, uncontrolled private access to communal forest lands reduces the incentive to conserve timber stocks.

- **Poor knowledge of the benefits of the forest ecosystems** gives rise to suboptimal and unsound policy choices manifested in offering 'perverse incentives' which induce behaviours that lead to deforestation. Scientists point out that ecosystems will undergo 'irreversible collapse' when their CC is exceeded or certain thresholds of change are reached. However, knowledge of such thresholds is, at best, poor among scientists themselves, and completely zero among private firms, private individuals and government bureaucrats, although it is of vital importance in formulating forest conservation policies.

3.4.1B Dynamic Human Factors Shaping Deforestation

What are the human causes of deforestation? The general literature suggests half a dozen or so clusters of human-cause or anthropogenic variables underpinning deforestation: population growth, technology, affluence/poverty, political economy (social structure interacting with public policy), political structure, and beliefs/cultural attitudes (Stern et al., 1992). However, the most researched among these six variables are the first three: population, affluence, and technology. Local and regional experiences show varying significance for these three variables or no association at all (e.g. Kummar, 1992; Kummar and Turner II, 1994, on the Philippines), which has led researchers to incorporate other variables like political economy, beliefs, etc. (Flint and Richards, 1991, on Southeast Asia; Allen and Barnes, 1985 on developing countries). The hypothesis that population growth and associated growing human activities will, inexorably, lead to deforestation becomes tenable if technology, tastes, and policies to improve environmental quality remain fixed. Indeed, it is the nature of underlying economic institutions, including pricing policies, that determine whether and to what extent economic activities will result in deforestation or depletion of forest ecosystems.

The literature suggests that the scale of human activity and population growth are just among the dynamic factors that shape environmental quality / and by implication, quality of the forest ecosystem; the other dynamic factors include resource-use efficiency referring to the capacity of the production system to reduce input consumption per unit of output, which will reduce pressure on demand for resource inputs – as, for instance, when the agricultural system reduces land demand per unit of agricultural output through, for instance, shift away from the shifting cultivation practice characteristic of peasant agriculture in sub-Saharan Africa to permanent cultivation involving intensive cultivation of land – as is practiced in industrialized agriculture. Briefly, it is not always correcting to argue that global loss of forest cover (deforestation) is always associated with population growth and rising economic activity. The reality is that several regions of the world – e.g. Western Europe, North America and Japan – have experienced increase in forest cover in the 20th century with rising population and per capita income (Williams, 1990).

3.4.1C Global Stocks of Forest Ecosystems

The world currently has about 10 billion acres of forest; 3% of this was lost annually between 1990 and 2005, but the net rate of loss has declined since 2000. Growth in northern – hemisphere (temperate) forests has helped offset tropical deforestation though, but there is no agreement on the extent to which increases in temperate forests offset the loss of carbon sinking in tropical forests. As of 2009, some 40% of world forests were located in ten top countries: Russia, Brazil, Canada, United States, China, Australia, the Congos (Republic of Congo or Congo-Brazzarille, and DR Congo or Congo-Kinshasa), Indonesia, Peru, and India. Russia habours the largest forest endowments of any country on planet Earth equivalent to 12 million square kilometers of boreal forest (known as **taiga** in Russia) which is larger than the Amazon rainforest in South America (Gore, 2009). Russia's forests habour some 55% of the global stocks of conifers and represent 11% of Earth's biomass. Russia loses, on the other hand, an estimated 20,000 square kilometers of its forests to deforestation each year roughly at par with the annual rates of deforestation in the Brazilian Amazon basin; and because of extremely cold winters, Russian deforestation becomes a significant contributor to climate change as it takes longer time for forests to regenerate (WWF, 2007, November).

On the other hand, almost 90% of Russia's tundra and up to 75% of taiga in Siberia and Russian Far East "remain close to their natural state" due to permafrost and cold. Nevertheless, as already noted, Russia remains a key actor in global carbon emissions: it is ranked 6th in global GHG emissions; it produces 2.8% of total emissions resulting from land-use, and forestry; Russia often experiences massive forest fires (e.g. in Siberia in 2003), which release huge GHG emissions into the atmosphere; current thawing of permafrost in the polar region due to global warming could also potentially increase GHG emissions as a huge account of carbon stored in Russian forests is locked in peat within the permafrost 'one of nature's best defences, against climate change'.

3.4.1D Effects of Deforestation

- **Impact on the Global Carbon Cycle:** The number 1 problem caused by deforestation is the impact on the global carbon cycle. The atmospheric gas molecules that absorb thermal infarred radiation are known as greenhouse gas (GHGs), as explained earlier in chapter 2. If GHGs are in large enough quantity, they can force climate change-as seems to be happening currently. While oxygen (O_2) is the most abundant gas in Earth's atmosphere, it does not absorb thermal infrared radiation as GHGs do. Carbon dioxide (CO_2) is the most abundant GHG; in 2012 CO_2 accounted for some 82% of all GHGs in the United States, according to the United States Environmental Protection Agency (USEPA). Forest trees are pivotal in the functioning of the carbon cycle; they act as the 'sink' for carbon; 300 billion tons of carbon, which is 40 times the annual GHG emission from fossil fuel stored in trees.

Deforestation not only reduces the amount of carbon stored up in trees, it also releases carbon dioxide into Earth's atmosphere. But when trees are felled and burned or are left to rot and decay, they release the stored carbon: the 2010 Global Forest Resource Assessment says deforestation releases nearly 1 billion tons of carbon into Earth's atmosphere each year. Deforestation is the second most important human-activity source of atmospheric carbon dioxide emissions, amounting to 6-17% (Van der Werf et al., 2010).

Water vapour is another GHG that is affected by deforestation. The impact of deforestation on the exchange of water vapour and carbon dioxide between the atmosphere and the terrestrial land surface is the biggest concern about the climate system. Changes in their atmospheric concentration can directly shift the climate system. According to the United States Academy of Sciences deforestation has decreased global water vapour flow from land by 4%; this can disrupt the natural weather pattern and change current climate models.

- **Adverse Impact on Rights of Forest People:** Forest loss in many ways adversely affects the rights and needs of forest people, not necessarily on environmental quality. Platforms and pressure groups like the World Rainforest Movement and Survival International have driven the debate on forests that serve not the functions of environmental sustainability, but human rights (e.g. Byron and Arnold, 1999). Deforestation, it is argued, will destroy the environment from which forest people derive their livelihoods.

- **Reshaping of Earth's Biosphere and Disruption of Hydrologic Cycle:** Finally, and closely related to the destruction of the ecosystem is the argument that sustained deforestation can – and does indeed – lead to a reshaping of Earth's Biosphere in a significant way, adversely affecting the functioning of the hydrologic cycle, to which we return in chapter 6. Specifically, with existence of forests and other ecosystems, there is little runoff; rather, precipitation is intercepted by vegetation and infiltrates into porous topsoil – a process that serves as "the life-blood" of the natural ecosystems that constitute the biosphere (Wright and Nebel, op. cit., p. 221). But the evaporation transpiring in these ecosystems not only sustains the latter, but also recycles the water to local rainfall, some of this water pecolates down to recharge the groundwater reservoirs, which, in turn, release water through springs, streams, rivers, etc. As forests become lost to deforestation (or land becomes over-grazed), the natural pathway of the hydrologic cycle is put off balance; it shifts from infiltration and groundwater recharge to runoff, as the water discharges into streams or rivers almost immediately – a major cause of flooding.

3.5 Tropical Rainforest Deforestation

As suggested above, tropical rainforest deforestation is largely a phenomenon associated with developing regions of South America, Asia and Sub-Saharan Africa. The United Nations Food and Agriculture Organization (FAO) estimates that some 1.3 million hectares of forestland are destroyed each year, some 80% of this due to increased demand for farmland largely in the developing world. Recent literature has, however, observed a shift in the drivers of deforestation in the developing world. Whereas during the late 1800s through the first two decade of the 1900s – the period of European colonial incorporation of parts of Asia and Sub-Saharan Africa – deforestation was driven by the vent-for-surplus model of agricultural development. Specifically, the opening of the African and Asian economies to external trade, provided by their integration into the industrializing European economies by the turn of the 1900s, is posited as having provided the hitherto 'static economies' with a 'vent' or channel to exploit their idle or unutilized (surplus) capacities in agricultural land and peasant labour, channeling those idle resources into export production for European markets. Export crop production, especially rubber, oil palm, cocoa, coffee, groundnuts and cotton, were developed through destructon of virgin forests to plant new crops. Timber exports, on the other hand, depended on extracting logs located mainly in the 'high forest' zones of the tropical rainforests. Apart from the influence of export agriculture, there was the influence of state-sponsored modernization projects like transmigration in Southeast Asia (e.g. Indonesia), to which we return.[2] By the postwar II decades onwards, deforestation became largely driven by industrialization, including mining and mineral extraction, large-scale cattle ranching and commercial agriculture (agri-business, especially in Latin America) (e.g. Rudel, 2005).

Rates and causes of deforestation have, indeed, varied across countries and regions of the developing world, though. Globally, however, deforestation is estimated to involve 13.7 million hectares annually; only some 50% of this is compensated by forest regeneration. Upwards of 25-30% of GHGs emitted into Earth's atmosphere each year – about 1.6 billion tons – originates in deforestation (Fearnside and Lawrence, 2004). The United Nations Food and Agriculture Organization (FAO) estimates that some 1.3 million hectares of forestland are destroyed each year, some 80% of this due to increased demand for farmland (Moran, 1993; Broecker, 2006, Field, 2006).

Table 3.4 displays country estimates of tropical rainforest loss due to deforestation, of which Brazil, Indonesia, DR Congo, Malaysia, and Paraguay top the list. It may be relevant to note that all three major tropical regions of the world (South America, Sub-Saharan Africa, and Southeast Asia) are represented in the list of top-5 rainforest deforesters. Brazil tops the list in terms of total deforested tropical forest between 2005 and 2014; the country lost, on average, 2, 498, 603 hectares of forest. Between 1990 and 2005 (not contained in Table 3.4) Brazil was reported to have lost 42, 330, 000 hectares of forest, roughly the size of California in the United States.

Rainforest deforestation especially is shaping global and regional climates in significant ways, contributing to global warming, and is often cited as a key causative factor of the enhanced

Table 3.4 Current Estimates of Tropical Forest Loss (Hectares)

Country	Rank	Forest Loss (2014)	Average Loss (2005 – 2014)
Brazil	1	2, 262, 241	2, 498, 603
Indonesia	2	1, 490, 457	1, 506, 965
DR Congo	3	1, 100, 880	633, 262
Malaysia	4	493, 385	445, 252
Paraguay	5	305, 650	360, 058
Bolivia	6	220, 470	270, 797
Myanmar	7	259, 443	173, 978
Madagascar	8	318, 465	162, 911
Cambodia	9	123, 779	136, 682
Peru	10	183, 544	160, 822
Colombia	11	165, 507	203, 500
Mexico	12	130, 717	194, 813
Laos	13	191, 032	139, 211
Mozambique	14	163, 345	169, 403
Tanzania	15	161, 899	138, 070
Tropics			**2, 393, 499**

Source: Butler (2012)

greenhouse effect (Fernside and Lawrence, op. cit.; Fearnside, 2000; Moutinho and Schwartzman, 2005). However, the quantity of tropical rainforest deforestation is still being debated; also, the estimates of annual carbon dioxide emissions from deforestation vary according to sources (see, for instance, Schimel et al., 2001; Achard et al., 2002; Houghton, 2005). Given this, the amount of GHG emissions accounted for by tropical forest conversion in human-induced GHG emissions remains disputed.

The tropical rainforest constitutes the oldest terrestrial ecosystem on planet Earth; it harbours immense range of flora and fauna; so, deforestation has caused destruction of potentially useful plant and animal species leading to biodiversity loss, to which we return in chapter 12. More importantly, for this chapter, tropical rainforest deforestation reduces oxygen from photosynthesis, while smoke from burning biomass increases the quantity of aerosols (particles suspended within the atmosphere (air), such as dust, organic matter, smoke, etc.) and carbon dioxide in the atmosphere. But trees are 50% carbon in content; when they are felled or burned, their carbon content created via photosynthesis is recycled back to Earth's atmosphere, which, in turn, increases the carbon dioxide levels and, hence, contributing to the enhanced greenhouse effect.

The GHGs that are emitted from deforestation are: carbon dioxide, methane, nitrous oxide, and carbon monoxide (though not a GHG, reacts chemically with hydroxyl radicals in the atmosphere to produce the concentration of methane). Research findings explain that most emissions of methane and nitrous oxide do not originate directly from deforestation, but from subsequent land-use change activities- e.g. livestock production, paddy rice and biomass burning account for 22%, 15%, and 10%, respectively, of the global human-induced emissions of methane (Prather and Ehhalt, 2001). Similarly, most nitrous oxide emissions originate in agricultural activities derived from deforestation, in particular nitrous fertilizers that are heavily consumed in modern farming. Further to the emission of GHGs, deforestation, especially biomass combustion, also releases aerosols into the atmosphere, which cools the latter's temperatures and, hence, acting as a negative GHG.

The overwhelming direct cause of deforestation of the rainforest ecosystem is agricultural activities in the following proportions: subsistence farming 48%; commercial farming 32%; logging 14%; fuelwood extraction 5% (UNFCCC, 2007). However, these proportions differ in the context of individual countries; besides, there is no agreement in the literatue on whether industrial logging contributes to global warming (Angelson and Kaimovitz, 1995; Lawrence, 1999), but there is the likelihood that 'regeneration harvest' or sustainable forestry practice in industrial logging to sustain steady supplies of trees (timber) over the long-run period serves to mitigate global warming. As noted above, rates and causes of deforestation differ across regions of the world. Let us illustrate, drawing on the South American, Southeast Asia and Sub-Saharan Africa experiences.

3.5.1 Deforestation in South America[3]

This region of the world has featured most prominently in studies on deforestation and its impact on global warming and climate change. But South America has the world's largest rainforest ecosystem in the Amazon tropical rainforest. The Amazon rainforest borders eight countries; it has the world's largest river basin and the source of 20% of Earth's river water; it is home to more plant and animal species than any other terrestrial ecosystem in the world – perhaps 30% of the world's species are found here.

Available statistics from the FAO and other scientific sources – e.g. Margalis, 2004; Fearnside, 2005; Kirby et al., 2006 – reveal that South America has had the highest deforestation in the world; this has occurred mostly in the Brazilian Amazon rainforest. Brazil is rated to have had the highest deforestation rate in the world and by the onset of the 21st century (early 2000s) had the largest area of forest land removed annually (see also Table 3.4). Since the 1970s, over 600,000 km² of the Amazon rainforest have been destroyed; by 2012, the Amazon was found to measure approximately 5.4 million km² – amounting to just 87% of the Amazon's original state, which suggests that some 13% of Brazil's Amazon Rainforest had been converted to non-forest uses in the past 40 years or so, mostly into pasture for livestock production, ranching, etc.

South America's deforestation accelerated over the 1970s and has occurred mostly along Brazil's Trans-Amazonian highway; also, in the Brazilian Coastal Atlantic Forests – described as one of the most degraded ecosystems in all Latin America (Stutz and Warf, 2007, p. 139). The first two highways, the Redovia Belem-Brasilia 1958 and the Cuiaha-Porto Velho 1968, were opened prior to the late 1990s. The two highways are said to be "at the heart" of the "arc of deforestation" in the Brazilian Amazon but the highways have attracted enormous increase in human settlements and the settlers have had significant impacts on the rainforests (William, 2006), often in an adverse way.

Most of the deforestation in South America is driven by the forces of commercial agriculture, cattle ranching and land speculation (e.g. Myers and Tucker, 1987; FAO Newsroom, 2005; Redo et al., 2012). Throughout South America ranching to produce cattle beef exports is one of the main drivers of deforestation (FAO Newsroom, 2005). Brazil produces 20% of the global meat trade (FAO, 2008). Cattle ranchers are invariably, also, land speculators "who burn huge tracts of rainforest for pasture; this is widespread in the Brazilian Amazon, but, also, in Central America (Costa Rica, Honduras, EL Salvado, etc) to meet beef import demand by United States hamburger restaurant business as well as European consumers. According to the Centre for International Forestry Research (CIFOR), between 1990 and 2001, the percentage of Europe's processed meat imports from Brazil alone grew from 40% to 70%, and by 2003 Brazil's cattle production growth "was largely export driven". (CIFOR, 2007). Brazil's deforestation drivers are mining; logging; subsidies for cattle ranching; investment in infrastructure (mainly roads); hydroelectricity; land tenure etc. issues; high prices for meat and grains in world markets; etc. Eleswhere in South America outside the Amazon rainforest basin, the driving forces tend to increase considerably: demand for agricultural land either directly due to high population pressure or induced by government policies (eg, Nicaragua); in Mexico, the expansion of beef and cash crops trade encouraged and permitted by subsidies; in Bolivia, schemes to resettle people supported by government on the foothills of Andes (Achart et. al., 2002).

Estimates put "large-scale agriculture and pasture" contribution to South America's deforestation at 80% during 1990 – 2000 (Butler, 2012). The Latin American land tenure system, **latifundio-minifundio**[4], encourages deforestation. To return to the Brazil story, in the early 1960s a Brazilian land law was enacted supporting private acquisition of Amazonian forestland by developers: specifically, if a person could show effective cultivation for a year and a day, then that individual could claim legal right to that land; that singular act paved the way for the rush to clear huge areas of Amazonian rainforest for cattle ranching as developers sought to gain a financial profit from land with which they were provided. As stated in the constitution of Brazil, clearing land for crops or fields is considered an 'effective use' of land and is one of the channels acquiring ownership over land (Kirby et al., op. cit.).

The clearing of new forests in the Amazon Rainforest peaked in 2004 (at 27,772.5km^2 per year), declining to 6,234.1km^2 in 2011; it rose rapidly during 2000 through 2004 (Forero and Eilperin, 2011). The decline as from 2004 was a result of policy initiatives to reduce GHG emissions from deforestation (see also Nepstad et. al., 2009; 2014).

In the Brazilian Amazon clearing for mechanized cropland has acquired a significant force in Brazilian Amazon deforestation, apart from ranching. Among the key crops is soybean, of which Brazil is a leading global producer and exporter. Yet another activity that has affected deforestation is logging; both legal and illegal. Whether legal or illegal, logging contributes to deforestation: logging creates a lot of damage to the forest, because for every tree harvested, 5-10 other trees are logged, to transport the logs through the forest; also, a falling tree causes considerable collateral damage in the form of destruction of a lot of other small trees in the forest as well as disturbing or destabilizing habitats.

3.5.1A Deforestation and Drought in the Amazon Basin

Drought in the Amazon Rainforest Basin has been blamed on deforestation (see, for instance, Saatchi et al., 2013). Extensive deforestation in the Amazon Basin seems to have reshaped the Amazon Rainforest biosphere and associated ecosystems in a significant way, adversely affecting the functioning of the hydrologic cycle. Specifically, with sustained deforestation, as has been reported in scientific studies and media, precipitation is no longer intercepted by vegetation leading to water infilterating into porous topsoil – a process that 'provides the life-blood' of the natural ecosystems that constitute the biosphere. But the evaporation taking place in these ecosystems – e.g. freshwater inland lakes, springs, rivers, streams, forests, etc. – not only sustains the ecosystems themselves, but, also, recycles the water to local rainfall; some of the water pecolates down to recharge the groundwater reservoirs, which, in turn, releases water through springs, streams, etc. As forests became lost to deforestation, as has been happening in the Amazon Basin over decades, the natural pathway of the hydrologic cycle becomes destabilized – a key outcome is drought.

In 2005, parts of the Amazon Rainforest Basin experienced the worst drought in a century. This has been blamed on the extensive deforestation that has destabilized the hydrologic cycle in the basin. Beginning in 2005, more than 70 million hectares of rainforest experienced an extensive and severe drought (see **The Independent** (UK), July 23, 2006). Again, in 2010, the Amazon experienced yet another severe drought affecting approximately 3 million square kilometers of rainforest compared to 1.9 million square kilometers in 2005.

The Brazilian droughts draw attention to the vulnerability of the natural ecosystems to climate change. Climate scientists have long found that the hydrologic cycle is very sensitive to climate change (e.g. Fowler and Hennesy, 1995; Held and Soden, 2006; Susuki, 2013). Scientific studies and media reports provide some evidence, that deforestation and drought are pushing the Braziliam Amazon towards a 'tipping point' where the rainforest would begin to experience irreversible extinction and turned into savanna or even desert, with catastrophic outcome for the global climate.

Ecologists argue that the continued deforestation of the Amazon Rainforest is a crucial factor in the drying up of a basin that has already lost some 20% of its forest cover (Saatchi et al., op. cit.); but 50% of the rainfall comes from the trees recycling water through evaporation, which, in turn, creates more rain. So, if the trees are lost to deforestation, as seems to be hoffeuing in Amazonia and elsewhere in the rainforest ecosystems, "you lose the rainfall". As stressed in the literature, deforestation in the tropical rainforest regions of the world is shaping the global climate system in significant ways, contributing to global warming and climate change (see also NASA, 2004).

By the end of the 1980s, deforestation in the Brazilian Amazonia had evolved into a global issue occupying the centre-stage in negotiations on the role of the tropical rainforest ecosystem complexes in carbon storage to tackle climate change (see Adams, op. cit., especially chapter 9). The problems involved not only the loss of biodiversity and disruption of ecosystem balances, to which we return in chapter 12, but also the enormous amounts of GHGs emitted by combustion of forest trees and the loss of a valuable natural carbon sink.

This issue was a major element in the debate over the successor to the post-Kyoto climate regime (to which we return in chapter 16), particularly at the United Nations Climate Change Conference in Bali, Indonesia, in December 2007. Interest has centred on two problems: first, to re-establish cleared forests, funded by developing markets in carbon; and, second, to preserve standing forest for the carbon sequestered in its ecosystem (e.g. Stier and Siebert, 2002; Bonnie and Schwartzman, 2003). The justification to evolve strategies based on reduced emission from deforestation and degradation (REDD) is hinged on the fact, that deforestation (whatever the sources or causes) generates more atmospheric caron dioxide emissions than the fossil-fuel-dependent global transport industry. So, preserving forests and keeping their trees standing "locks up carbon, maintains biodiversity and provides the energy-guzzling industrialized countries with a cost-effective way to offset their carbon without changing their lifestyles" (Adams, 2009, p. 245).

Central America provides yet another unique illustration of how commercial agriculture and cattle ranching have driven deforestation in South America. During the period 2001-2010 deforestation took up the following proportion of the forest cover in: Belize 63%; Costa Rica 46%; Panama 45%; Hinduras 41%; Guatamala 37%; Nicaragua 29%; and El Salvado 21% (Redo et al., 2012). Deforestation in Central America has deep historical roots, tracing to the Ancient

Maya civilization characterized by an agrarian culture of clearing large expanse of forestland for agriculture often surpassing capacity of forests to regenerate naturally. On this ancient Mayan culture was superimposed Spanish colonization in the 1700s and 1800s, which introduced plantation agriculture along the latifundio pattern of ownership to be followed in the 1900s by the "forcing of Europe's money economy on Latin America" (Myers and Tucker, 1987). The latter introduced the production of primary exports, which, in turn, created the need for large tracts of cleared agricultural land to produce these exports – e.g. sugar, which required clear-cutting of land and large quantities of firewood to process sugar, (Myers and Tucker, op. cit.). The 1960s saw cattle ranching to produce beef exports to United States and Europe.

3.5.2 Deforestation in Sub-Saharan Africa

By the beginning of the 2000s, African forests constituted 17% of the global stock, covering over 630 million hectares or about 20% of the continent's land mass (UNEP, 2008; FAO, 2005). Tropical rainforests take up the bulk of Africa's forests: 528 million hectares of the 630 million hectares of forests (or roughly 84% of the continent's total forests and 30% of the world's total.

A. Deforestation Hotspot: Congo Basin and West African Rainforests

Sub-Saharan Africa has its tropical rainforest deforestation hotspot in the Congo Basin Rainforests and the West African Rainforests. Spanning 3.7 million square kilometers (km^2), the Congo Basin Rainforests are surpassed in size and extent only by the Amazon Basin Rainforests analysed earlier; they encompass eight countries in Central Africa: Burundi, Cameroon; Central African Republic; Democratic Republic of Congo (DR Congo); Equatorial Guinea; Gabon; Rwanda; and Republic of Congo (more popularly, Congo-Brazzaville).

Table 3.5 Top 10 Forested African Countries (2005)

Country	hectares (1000s)	% of land cover
DR Congo*	133,610	58.9
Sudan	67,546	28.4
Angola*	59,104	47.4
Zambia	42,452	57.1
Tanzania	35,257	39.9
Central African Republic*	22,755	36.5
Congo-Brazzaville*	22,471	65.8

Gabon*	21,775	84.5
Cameroon*	21,245	45.6
Mozambique	19,262	24.6

* Congo-basin countries.
Source: AfricaFiles (http://www.africafiles.org)

Six of the top 10 forested African countries lie within the Congo Basin Rainforests (see table 3.5). Over 55% of the Basin lies in DR Congo; and all of Congo-Brazzaville lies within the Basin. An estimated 75 million people inhabit the Congo Basin Rainforest area, with an estimated roughly 2 million people added to this population annually. With an estimated population density of some 20 person per km², the Congo Basin Rainforest Zone emerges sparsely populated though. On the other hand, the Congo Basin Rainforests contain rich ecological species of fauna and flora surpassed only by the Brazilian Amazonia. Huge expanses of the Congo Basin Rainforests remain yet unexplored.

The West African rainforests are not as vast, dense and unexplored as those of the jungles of Southeast Asia (e.g. Malaysia) or the Brazilian Amazonia or even the Congo Basin Rainforests. The West African Rainforests extend over an area of 388,600 km² varying in depth from 80 km to 240 km from the Atlantic Coast and include the wetlands or mangrove rainforests, of which the Niger Delta mangrove rainforests remain the most notable. A vast flood plain built by a vast accumulation of sedimentary deposits brought down by the Niger River as it flows from its source in the Fouta Djallon highlands in the west-central region of Guinea down to the Gulf of Guinea, the Niger Delta mangrove swamps are among the largest in the world (Muoghalu, 2007).

The Congo Basin rainforests hold 35 billion of the 290 billion tons of the world's forest-based carbon and supply 30% of world's oxygen (Dlamini et al., 2015). At the global level, the Congo Basin Rainforests are described as planet Earth's 'second lung' serving as the counterpart to the rapidly shrinking Amazon Basin Rainforests of South America. Bu these two tropical rainforest ecosystem complexes constitute a huge carbon 'storage tank' sequestering, carbon that could otherwise become unleashed on Earth's atmosphere as carbon dioxide emissions – the key source of global warming. Given their enormous carbon storage capacity, the Congo Basin rainforest countries stand to gain from current REDD (Reducing Emissions from Deforestation and Forest Degradation) schemes that offer financial incentives to keep forests intact, to which we return in chapter 16.

Sub-Saharan Africa's tropical rainforest ecosystems also affect rainfall in the North Atlantic and West Africa (Conway 2009). In the 1970s, extensive deforestation of the West African tropical rainforest and grassland (savanna) ecosystems was hypothesized in several studies to be the cause of droughts in the African Sahel[8]. Africa's Sahel zone is perched on the southern edge of the Sahara

Desert or the northen edge of the savanna grasslands flanking both sides of Africa's equatorial tropical rainforests. We return to drought and desertification in Africa in chapters 10-11.

B. Patterns of Sub-Saharan African Deforestation

Sub-Saharan Africa is reported to be losing over 4 million hectares (9.9 million acres) of forests annually- two times the global average! It needs to be pointed out, however, that there is little consensus yet on the extent and rate of forest cover in the different countries of the region, arising from differences in definition of what constitutes the different types of forests. Generally, a forest is any area of vegetation in which the dominant plants are trees; tropical forest includes rainforest in which trees from the dominant plants and annual rainfall is high (over 200 cm) and is restricted to equatorial regions, such as the Amazon basin (examined earlier), the Congo basin and West Africa, and Southeast Asia.

There is, besides, some ambiguity on the concept of deforestation, as well as what really constitutes deforestation, which has led to estimates on the rates and extent of deforestation to differ quite widely (e.g. Allen and Barnes, 1985). This problem shows most significantly in the contradictory data on the extent of forest cover and forest cover loss in tropical African countries. These differences arise, in part, from the fact that in tropical Africa large tracts of land are cleared permanently of forests and turned over to wholly different forms of land use – e.g. urban housing, tree crop plantations (rubber, oil palm, cocoa, coffee, etc.). This is quite often superimposed on the age-long land-use associated with shifting cultivation in peasant agriculture. Lekowitz (2006), for instance, points out that forest cover in Cameroon – a deforestation hotspot (Mertens and Lambin, 2000) – exhibits this problem: there are contradictory data estimates on whether deforestation has fallen sharply, leading to socalled 'forest transition', or whether it has increased over time.

Earlier studies on African deforestation tended to be informed by a neo-Malthusian perspective, whereby rapid population growth was singled out as the culprit. For instance, the World Bank in its 1992 **Development Report** emphasized the population factor:

> "Rapid population growth in these areas had led to the mining of soil resources and to stagnation and declining yields. In some circumstances, especially in rural Africa, population growth has been so rapid that traditional land management has been unable to adapt to prevent degradation. The results are overgrazing, deforestation, depletion of water resources, and loss of habitat" (World Bank, 1992, p. 27).

Later studies, however, show that it is not rapid population growth as such that is responsible for the degradation of forestlands in Sub-Saharan Africa (e.g. Lopez, 1998). On the contrary, the problem originates, fundamentally, in the fact that technological innovations fail to keep up with the demands of a rapidly growing population. But in almost all parts of sub-Saharan Africa where population densities are high – e.g. Southern Malawi, Southeast Nigeria, Sierra Leone, etc., farming is being intensified through shorter fallows rather than through the use of more productive technologies such as high-yielding varieties (HYVs) in seed and plant, suitable chemical fertilizers, irrigation, etc.

Yet, other single-factor explanations using cross-national data on forest loss identified, apart from population growth, also rural poverty (lack of economic options), and actions of commercial logging firms, smallholders, etc. (e.g. Rudel and Roper, 1997). By the beginning of the 2000s single-factor explanations became increasingly unconvincing; consequently, multi-factor analysis became popular, in which political economy, social and political processes, history, geographical and environmental factors are considered (e.g. Geist and Lambin, 2002; Lambin et al., 2001).

- **Exceptional Human Ecology.** This apparently new perspective is captured in the notion of sub-Saharan Africa's exceptional human ecology; there is thus the proposition that Africa's exceptional human ecology produces a deforestation dynamic and pattern quite distinct vis-à-vis from those of South America and Southeast. By sub-Africa's exceptional human ecology is meant the region's human populations with their unique social systems (e.g. communal land tenure) and land-use practices (e.g. shifting cultivation), technology, economic policy trajectories, etc. – all these mesh with the equally unique ecosystems and biophysical terrains in a kind of reinforcing connections to produce an exceptional deforestation scenario.

Sub-Saharan Africa's exceptional human ecology means that distinctly different socioeconomic and ecological forces drive deforestation in the region. Specifically, deforestation in sub-Saharan Africa is driven by the following forces; shifting cultivation practices by peasant households; the communal tenure that views forests as commons; fuelwood extraction by rural households with severely limited access to alternative sources of energy; charcoal production by rapidly expanding peri-urban populations that lack access to wage employment opportunities in the urban economy; government policies aimed at increasing export capacity in agricultural commodities to earn foreign exchange to pay off external debt, etc. In contrast, deforestation in South America and Southeast Asia is driven by forces linked to markets and commercial considerations: commercial logging; plantation agriculture to produce for external markets; industrialization and associated urbanization, etc.

Though, not as significant as in the South American or Southeast Asian (see next section for Southeast Asia) cases, nevertheless, logging looms large in Africa's deforestation; its modern history traces to the early decades of the 1900s, when European colonial merchant firms began to penetrate tropical Africa's interior in search of raw materials, including tropical hard woods.

The most sought-after species have been the termite-resistant tropical woods: iroko (*chlorophora excelsa*); teak (*tectona grandis*); abora (*gmelina arborea*); ebony (*diospyros species*); afara (*terminalia species*); and opepe (*nauclea diderrichii*), etc. Forest timber extracted from the tropical rainforests and cut into logs constituted one of the earliest items in the Sub-Saharan Africa's external trade with Europe; otherwise, extracted timber meant for domestic markets were sawn into plants over pits dug in the forests.

By the end of the 1990s Chinese firms were replacing European firms in the demand for Africa's timber resources. Available statistics on logging and the commercial exports of raw tropical timber reveal that more than 3.5 million cubic metres of raw tropical logs were exported from Africa in 2006, much of it illegally; the main destination of African exports in this product has shifted from the European Union (EU) to China and other Asian countries (Globaltimber.org.uk).

- **Poverty: Key Element In Africa's Human Ecology.** The poverty factor is, arguably, the defining element of Africa's exceptional human ecology, and it is the factor that drives most other variables in sub-Saharan Africa's deforestation dynamic. In Sub-Saharan Africa, the population living in poverty or below the poverty line (subsisting on less than US$1/day) increased from 184 million in 1985 to 216 million in 1990 and was expected to exceed 300 million by the early 2000s. This rapidly expanding population of the poor is a reflection of one key problem: the bulk of the population earns a living on subsistence farming. The technology of subsistence agriculture is shifting cultivation, which in turn reflects the total absence of an appropriate technology to increase agricultural yield per hectare of land cultivated. In this context, peasant farming households have little choice outside encroaching on pasture or woodlands to increase the hectarage cultivated to attempt to increase agricultural output (Niklitshek, 1990). As noted above, while large plantations, ranches and export-based agriculture drive deforestation in South America, for instance, sub-Saharan Africa's is driven by forces linked to subsistence agriculture and associated shifting cultivation – which reflects the poverty of the population.
- **Forestlands as Commons or Communal Property.** The fact that in Sub-Saharan Africa forestlands are treated as commons can be explained in terms of market failure (Pearce and Brown, 1994). But it has outcome for deforestation; and, hence, also global warming. The commons property feature of forests and most land resources in rural Africa undermines incentives towards reforestation of harvested forests. But rural residents, and peasant households, generally, lack the tenure security to assure that they will be able to benefit from their reforestation efforts. Besides, there is the more obvious fact that the high levels of poverty endemic in rural Africa undermine availability of capital required to invest in reforestation to guarantee future supply of trees. Closely related to this is sheer ignorance about the value of reforestation or planting trees as a strategy to reduce atmospheric carbon

dioxide concentrations to fight global warming. As pointed out earlier, rural households extracting fuelwood from open-access forestland are hardly aware of the environmental damage their activities entail.

- **Policy Failures.** This variable may, also, complement market failures and ignorance on the usefulness of reforestation in Africa's deforestation dynamics. For instance: in the 1980s onwards, in the wake of the structural adjustment policies (SAPs), criticisms grew on the environmental degradation apparently caused by changing incentive structures engendered by relative price shifts. The gist of these criticisms is that many sub-Saharan African countries had reacted to the external debt shocks of the 1980s by exploiting land and forest resources in an unsustainable manner. In other words, policy reforms apparently aimed to correct biases and distortions against exports, especially in agriculture, had induced degradation and overexploitation of forests in the form of: overlogging to increase timber exports, conversion of forestlands to food and tree-crop plantations, etc. In a study on "the tragedy of the commons in Cote d' Ivoire agriculture" Lopez (1998) concluded that the large losses of forests and the considerable reduction in fallow periods observed in Ivorien agriculture implied a considerable loss of natural capital (see also Glickman and Teter, 1991; Reed, 1992; Cleaver, 1994).

- **Ill-organized Forest Management.** Closely related to the problem of policy failure is that management of tropical forests in sub-Saharan Africa is ill-organized, if not totally unorganized. Nigeria's experience may serve to illustrate this hypothesis. Outsidee the 'forest reserves' occupying just about 29% of the 'high forests' in 1980, which are exploited on concessions granted to large timber firms (to extract timber and do replanting to protect certain timber species) there is little effective control of timber exploitation, though forest laws do exist (but see Dlamini et al., 2015). This has led to indiscriminate logging – both legal and illegal. Besides, the increasing demand for new forestland by rural farmers, particularly in the southern rainforest belt, has led to 'killing off' of forest trees by firing and uprooting – slash-and-burn practices typical of peasant farming – to the extent that in many parts of southern Nigeria what remains of once thick rainforests is a 'derived' forest bushland.

- **Civil Wars and Political Instability.** This factor adds yet to another dimension to Sub-Saharan Africa's deforestation problem. They complement poverty to fuel tropical Africa's deforestation. Indeed, 'blood timber' has featured most prominently in recent armed conflicts in Sub-Saharan Africa – specifically, in DR Congo, Sierra Leone, Liberia, etc. By far the most publicized is the Liberian civil war, in which Dutch businessman Gus Kouwenhoven featured prominently in the timber-for-arms trade during 2000-2003 (see Black, 2006). The 'blood timber' funded the purchase of weapons for former Liberian President and Warlord Charles Taylor. The 'blood timber' involved some of Europe's biggest timber firms, including Swiss-German Danzer, Danish and Dutch DLH Nordisk, Dutch Wijma, Greece-based Shelman, and German Feldmayer Group, etc. These firms continued purchasing timber from Kouwenhoven despite increasing evidence of the link Leebucea his timber trade and weapons smuggling in violation of United Nations arms embargo.

- **Mineral-driven Economic Growth, Dutch Disease and Forest Transition.** Several Sub-Saharan African countries have large mineral extractive sectors. Sectoral growth booms in the mineral enclaves are observed to generate the Dutch disease. The Dutch disease hypothesis posits that mineral-extraction-induced economic growth sets off cascades of economic side effects that may have: retarded agricultural expansion, accelerated urban expansion, and probably slowed down the destruction of rainforests (see Wunder, 1992; 2003a, b; Rudel, 2013).

B1: Forest Transition in the Congo Basin?

The Dutch disease syndrome is used to explain 'forest transition' in the Congo Basin tropical rainforests. The wetter Congo Basin countries – Southern Cameroon, DR Congo, Gabon, etc. – are found to exhibit lower rates of deforestation, partly because of increasing tax receipts from oil and mineral industries in the basin that spurred rural-to-urban migration, agricultural declines and increased food imports, especially cereals. Researchers (e.g. Rudel, 2013) have begun to speculate that the Congo Basin countries "may be experiencing an oil and mineral fuelled forest transition" (ibid). Deforestation and forest degradation have been found to be minimal in the Congo Basin relative to trends in other tropical rainforest regions e.g. Brazilian Amazon and Southeast Asia. Africa contributed only 5.4% to the global loss of tropical rainforest during 2000 – 2005, compared to Indonesia's 12.8% and Brazil's 47.8%. However, deforestation and forest degradation accelerated post – 1990s (see Megevand et. al., 2013, figure 0.2), associated with expansion of agriculture (largely subsistence) and fuelwood extraction and charcoal production.

The forest transition concept was proposed by Mather (1992); it is a generalization about the ways in which the extent of forest cover changes as economies undergo industrialization and associated urbanization (see also Rudel et al., 2010; Rudel, et al. 2005). Forest transition, like an earlier concept of a demographic transition proposed by the American demographer Warren Thompson describing population change over time – specifically, transition from high birth and death rates to lower birth and death rates as a country or region moves from a pre-industrial to an industrialized economic system, provides a framework explaining how deforestation and other land-use changes are impacted on by industrialization and associated urbanization. Regions and places experience forest transition when forest cover loss slows down or ceases and forest regeneration sets in, which occurs under two circumstances, sometimes overlapping (Rudel et al., 2005).

The first is where and when structural change (e.g. industrialization and associated urbanization) has created enough non-farm income outlets to induce out-migration of labour from farm employments, which relieves pressure of land for farmland, which in turn induces the spontaneous regeneration of forests in old farms. This is the pattern that evolved for the industrialized world (Northwestern Europe and North America). Until the early part of the 1900s, deforestation was rising in the latter. As the Industrial Revolution and associated structural change took effect in these countries, the interaction of market forces, government forest policies and other sectoral policy interventions as well as their effective implementation transformed deforestation into sustainable forestry practice, whereby there is growth of new trees to replace those harvested for purposes of commercial logging. Briefly, in these countries there has evolved, generally, sustainable forestecosystem management or regeneration forestry dictated and enforced by forest practice standards. Similar processes and observed for some middle-income countries that have experienced an Industrial Revolution – e.g. the East Asian newly industrialized countries (NICs), China, Pueto Rico, Mexico, etc (see Adam, 2009, especially pp. 249-51).

The second is where and when a scarcity of forest products prompts governments and landowners to initiate a programme of afforestation and plantation development on former grasslands (e.g. Farley, 2007). In both contexts, the forest regeneration would lead to positive outcome for carbon capture as well as soil conservation.

In the developing world, generally, in particular Sub-Saharan Africa, degradation and deforestation processes are still in their upswing phases. But the economic, political, legal and institutional preconditions and infrastructure, including market mechanisms, to arrest and slow down the processes are yet to evolve in sub-Saharan Africa, generally. Specifically, the strengthening of property rights, logging firms' establishment of user rights, land tenure and privatization of forest resources hardly exist for any sub-Saharan African country.

The forest transition currently observed for the Congo Basin countries – e.g. Southern Cameroon, Gabon, etc. – hardly fits the above two scenarios. On the contrary, what has evolved in these countries is deagriculturalization of the economy underpinned by the Dutch disease syndrome. This has led to a significant reduction in demand for forestlands for agricultural uses – a primary real cause of deforestation in sub-Saharan Africa. The forest transition occurring in the Congo Basin countries could then be described as following a perverse pattern: they are not the by-product of an industrialization that creates alternative non-farm employments, which pull labour off agriculture permanently; neither are they underpinned by an agrarian technical change that permanently reduces the share by agriculture in the economically active population (EAP) – these, as already noted, are the processes that underpinned forest transition historically (in Europe and North American) and currently (in parts of Asia and Latin America).

The rapid pace of urbanization observed for Sub-Saharan African countries (see United Nations, 2014) averaging 1.1% annually (second only to Asia's 1.5%) is not a by-product of industrialization or structural change. On the contrary, what is transpiring here, generally, could better be describd as "the urbanization of societies without industrialization, "whose result is absence of well paid non-farm employments in urban sub-Saharan Africa" (Rudel, 2013).

In Sub-Saharan Africa, generally, given high rates of rural-urban migration and urbanization, deforestation has tended to shift in intensity and extent; current hotspots are the peri-urban regions and transport corridors between the large urban centres, which often became a magnet for new population concentrations drawing in farmers, informal service purveyors, tradesmen, producers of charcoal, etc. – who start a new cycle of deforestation of surrounding forestlands (see Malaisse, 1985; Marien, 2009; Chidumayo and Gumbo, 2010). Indeed, 'runaway deforestation' around Africa's major cities is driven by escalating demand for fuelwood and charcoal by urban households; approximately 90-95% of all wood extracted from African forests goes into fuelwood and charcoal production, the bulk consumed in the cities where the rising cost of commercial fossil-fuel energy (kerosene, cooking gas, etc.) has driven middle-income households to shift demand, increasingly, towards readily available biomass alternatives, especially fuelwood (Maconadine et al., 2009). Of course, large variations in this proportion do exist among Africa's urban centres: for instance, this proposition rises as high as over 90% for Kinshasa and Brazzaville in the Congos and falls as low as less than 30% in Libreville (Gabon). In the latter high government subsidies on cooking gas and national electricity network financed by earnings from mineral exports have tended to reduce deforestation significantly (see also Wunder, 2003).

3.5.3 Deforestation in SouthEast Asia

Southeast Asia can be classified into two major ecological zones: the continental zone including Thailand, Vietnam, and Myanmar, and the Peninsular, and insular zone, including Indonesia, Malaysia and the Philippines (Hayami, 2001). Major river deltas characterize Southeast Asia – e.g. the Chao Phraya in Thailand, Irrawaddy in Myanmar and Mekeng in Vietnam – and tropical rainforests. Before the 1860s, when ocean transportation technology linked this region with Industrial-Revolution Europe, the populaton of Southeast Asia thrived on rice farming in small valleys or shifting cultivation in upland forests, with many of the major river deltas and tropical rain forests unused for agricultural production. When the region became linked to West European markets for tropical products upon colonization in the 1800s, this unused land began to be exploited Deltas were converted into paddy fields for commercial rice production; rain forests into plantations for export cash crops, including timber, rubber, coffee, cocoa, palm produce, etc; which, in turn, sowed the seeds of deforestation in the region and other forms of land-use change linked to GHG emissions. On the other hand, the river deltas and tropical rainforests of Southeast Asia provided the basis for Hla Myint's (1965, 1971) vent-for-surplus theory of economic development, which proposes that international trade links provide an opening for exploiting unused natural resources hitherto commanding little commercial value and channeling the latter into exportables that earn foreign exchange.

With an area of approximately 4,000,000 km^2 (1.6 million square miles) as of 2013, some 625 million people lived in Southeast Asia, more than 254 million of this in Indonesia[5]. Within the latter, the island of Java has the bulk of the population: some 143 million, which makes it the most densely populated large island in the world.

Southeast Asia is facing severe deforestation, which has implications not only for habitat loss, (See New Scientists, 2003), but also for regional and global climate. The Food and Agriculture Organization (FAO) estimates that during the 1990s through 2005, forest clearance in Southeast Asia had led to a rapid reduction in regional forest expanse (FAO, 2009). This is illustrated by the fact that during the half decade, 2000-2005, Southeast Asia's forest extent changed at a negative rate averaging -1.3% annually, a trend that was predicted to continue into the 2020s, with strong implications for regional and global climate, in particular regional energy and hydrologic cycle and water budgets: with forest cover significantly reduced, this will affect, among others, the amount of available soil water for plant transpiration (e.g. also Wert and Avissar, 2005).

Southeast Asia's rainforest is the third largest in the world (the Congo Basin rainforests in Central Africa are the second largest). The 'slash-and-burn' activities in the region most pervasive in the peatlands of Sumatra and Borneo in Indonesia, constitute one of the underlying causes of rapid deforestation and habitat loss in Southeast Asia. This practice often results in occurrence of haze pollution; the worst known incidence to date occurred in 1997 and 2006; international press reports explain that the haze is largely a result of illegal agricultural fires due to slash-and-burn practices in Indonesia (especially from the provinces of South Sumatra and Rau in Indonesia's Sumatra island, and Kulimantan in Borneo).

Fire is established to be a tool in land clearing in Southeast Asia, especially in the rainforest peatlands, but it is known to be the cheapest and fastest method to clear land in preparation for planting. After a peat swamp forest has been cleared and drained, the peat soil remains unsuitable for planting crops, because peat soil is nutrient-poor and acidic. But fire not only neutralizes the soil acidity, it helps to remove peats and plant diseases and the resulting ash serves as fertilizer. A peatland describes an area where organic material – e.g. leaves and wigs – had accumulated naturally under waterlogged conditions over 10s of 1000s of years. Peatland can be up to 20 meters deep; in Indonesia, there are 265,500 km^2 of peatland, occupying some 14% of its land area; in Malaysia there as 26,685 km^2, occupying 8.1% of the land area (Jooster, 2009). Much of the peatland in Southeast Asia has been drained for human activities – e.g. agriculture, forestry, urbanization, etc. (ASEAN, 2011). However, excessive drainage of peatland has resulted in the top layer of peat drying out, and the material so dried up becomes highly susceptible to burning in the dry season.

In Southeast Asian deforestation, the recurrent pattern is that of large-scale logging for exports, followed by agricultural expansion (e.g. Kummar, 1992; and Kummar and Turner II, 1994). A joint Indonesia-UK study (Indonesia-UK Study, 1999) suggested that some 40% of the logging was illegal, valued more than $365 million. More recent estimates on legal logging against known domestic consumption plus exports indicate that 88% of Indonesian logging is illegal. Malaysia serves as the key smuggling route for exporting illegal wood products harvested from Indonesian forests (Environmental Investigation Agency and Telapack, 2004). A UNEP-Interpol study in 2012 states that illegal logging accounts for upwards of 30% of the global logging trade and contributes to more than 50% of tropical deforestation in Southeast Asia, Central Africa and the South American Amazon Basin (UNEP-Interpol, 2012). Southeast Asian logging, as elsewhere in South America and tropical Africa, is driven by international demand for tropical woods. For Southeast Asia, particularly, this is a region whose forests have a high ecological and commercial value and have been logged heavily for exports beginning since the 1800s.

In addition, agriculture has expanded in concert with logging through both spontaneous settlements after logging and government planned agricultural projects and population resettlement programmes – e.g. Indonesia's transmigration programme, which was first initiated by the Dutch colonial government in the early 1800s. The objective was to resettle landless people from the densely populated areas of Indonesia in the less populated areas – specifically, to move people permanently from the densely populated island of Java, but also from Bali and Madura, to the less populated ones, including Papua (ended in 2015), Kalimautan, Sumatra, and Salawesi.

Under the Dutch colonial administration, the transmigration programme peaked in 1929, when more than 260,000 contract coolie workers were brought to Sumatra's east coast, 235,000 of them from Java alone. After independence from the Netherlands in 1949, the Sukarno government continued the programme, now expected to include other areas of the archipelago such as Papua. At its peak in 1979-1984 more than 500,000 families (some 2.5 million people) were resettled under the transmigration programme. But the 1980s saw the programme funded by the World Bank, the Asian Development Bank, and several Western governments motivated or attracted by the anti-communist disposition of post-Sukarno regimes in Indonesia (e.g. Goldman, 2006). By the beginning of the 2000s, in the aftermath of the Asian financial crisis, the programme was scaled down due to reduced funding.

Transmigration has been fingered in Indonesia's deforestation discourse – especially for driving deforestation of sensitive rainforest areas: migrants were often resettled in entirely new "transmigration villagers", constructed in regions that had been relatively unimpacted by human activity, which often resulted in resources being used up and lands being overgrazed, resulting in deforestation.

3.6 Fire Burning

Fire burning produces carbon dioxide, methane, etc. through combustion of biomass (the total mass of all the organisms of a given type and/or in a locality – e.g. biomass of trees) and organic materials (individual living bodies, including plants, animals, microbial organisms). Van der Werf et al. (2010) report that during 1997-2001, 44% of carbon dioxide emissions produced through fire burning originated in forest fires in grasslands and savannas, with smaller contributions from tropical deforestation and degradation fires (whereby chemical components are combusted to transform them into simpler compounds) 20%; tropical woodlands 16%; forest fires, mostly in the extratropics 15%; agricultural waste burning 3%; and tropical peat fires (combustion of a mass of dark brown or black, partly decomposed plant material, formed in the wet tropical rainforests and mangroves, where temperatures are low enough to slow down the decomposition of plant residues) 3%.

As suggested above, fire burning in grasslands[7] has had the most significant impact on global warming and climate change. Savannas consist of a continuous layer of grass interspersed with scattered trees and shrubs, and cover some 10 million square kilometers of tropical Africa (Cahoon et al., 1992). African savanna fires may produce a little over 30% of global emissions from biomass burning, almost all originating in human activities. Africa's tropical savannas flank both sides of the continent's equatorial forests. Associated with grass as dominant plant species and combined with insufficient rainfall to support extensive growth of trees (which are also known to be degraded by grazing livestock), African savannas are vulnerable to wildfires, whose emissions are known to be transported over the mid-Atlantic, South Pacific and Indian Oceans (e.g. Levine, 1991). In contrast to the savannas, Africa's tropical equatorial rainforests are less less easily fired, due largely, to heavy rainfall. A key feature of African savanna fires is that the climate factors tend to support fires as a widespread and integral part of its functioning. Often referred to as the 'Fire Continent', climate factors are known to be the driving force of fire ecology, of which Africa is well endowed: there is distinct wet and dry seasons; and lighting as a natural ignition source, takes advantage of the dry savanna vegetation which turns into highly flammable plant fuels during the harmattan months in West Africa (end of November to mid-March).

Both biomass combustion and wind-borne dust also produce large quantities of aerosols; indeed, aerosols (both fossil-fuel and industrial processes generated) exert complex influences on climate: both cooling and warming effects. In cooling effects, aerosols reflect away solar radiation; and in warming effect, they trap heat and thus add to the greenhouse effect. Dust can either reduce or stimulate rainfall: in low clouds, water attaches to dust particles and prevents droplets from becoming heavy enough to fall; in high clouds dust particles over wetter regions may provide surfaces for ice crystals to form around them, resulting in greater rainfall (See, for instance, Mahowald and Kiehl, 2003).

3.6.1 Peat Fires in Southeast Asia

October 15th, 1997 **The Washington Post** reported on Indonesia of a very smokey peat burning, its fire emission "equivalent of 13-40% of the mean annual global carbon emissions from fossil fuel" (Mooney, 2015). Later, analysts and commentators likened Indonesia's peat emissions to the Arctic permafrost emissions – built up over vast stretches of time; the carbon contained in Indonesia's peat fires is also a new addition to the atmosphere's GHG concentrations. Indonesian peat fires have their critical ignition factor in El Nino. The latter drives drought conditions in certain parts of Southeast Asia, including Australia, which make forest peats dry and susceptible to severe fire outbreaks (Yulianti and Hayasaka, 2013).

Studies focusing on Kalimantan Island, Indonesia reveal repeated fire incidence, especially under El Nino conditions, which may not be unrelated to the rapid deforestation rate due to logging, agricultural developments such as palm oil plantation, rice development based on draining of swamps, etc. More than 63% of swamp land was found to be peatland; when swamp draining was ended in 1999, vast drained peatland areas were left exposed to peat fires. Between the late 1960s and first decade of the 2000s – a period of about 40 years – the total forest area for Kalimantan Island decreased from 414,700 km^2 to 248,450 km^2 – a decrease of 40% in the total original forested area. Much like other fires in Indonesia, the greater number of the Kalimantan fires originate in human activities; once started, the latters' fire behaviour becomes controlled by natural factors: precipitation (rainfall), wind and dryness of fuel (specifically, coal in this context). Peat, it ought to be noted, has a high carbon dioxide and can burn under low moisture conditions; once ignited – often by wildfire penetrating the subsurface, - it burns slowly, smoldering unnoticed for a very long time, indeed.

By the late 1990s, peat and forest fires in Indonesia were estimated to have emitted between 0.81 to 2.57 Gt of carbon[8], equivalent to 13-40% of the amount released by fossil fuel combustion, and greater than the carbon uptake of the biosphere. It is speculated that Indonesia's forest fires account for observed increase in carbon dioxide levels since the late 1990s. Ironically, this is a relatively known source (Harris and Sargent (2016). Indonesia ranks first among other countries such as Brazil for land-use change emissions. If these are accounted for, Indonesia would rank in the third position in global GHG emissions.

An international scientific survey of peat bogs has calculated that the latter contain more carbon than the world's forests, heaths and grasslands together, and, perhaps, as much as planet Earth's atmosphere (see Radford, 2015). As noted earlier, peat can smolder underground for years, so it is another potential factor in global warming calculations (as is the peat material buried under the Arctic ice sheets, to which we return in chapter 7).

Peat is simply leaf litter that never completely became decomposed, which had made ancient peatlands (as found in temperate or cold climates – e.g. Arctic, - where temperatures are low enough to slow down the decomposition of plant residues) become distinctive ecosystems. In this context, peatlands constitute a community of plants and animals linked by a flow of materials through the non-living (abiotic) as well as the living (biotic) sections of the environment.

Peatlands cover just about 2-3% of Earth's land surface but contain 25% of Earth's soil carbon. In the high latitudes of the northern hemisphere, they cover about 4 million square kilometers (km²) and store about 500-600 billion tones of carbon. In the tropics peatlands cover 400,000 km² and store 100 billion tones of carbon (Radford, op. cit.) In its natural or pristine form, a peat bog is unlikely to burn: the peat exists because the leaf litter is embedded in a water-logged soil or environment, which prevents it from fully decomposing and drying into a flammable element. On the other hand, dry peat burns easily, causing some of the largest fires on Earth – e.g. the tropical peat fires of Indonesia, which by 1997 alone were estimated to have emitted 2.5 billion tones of carbon dioxide into Earth's atmosphere.

3.7 Livestock Production and Greenhouse Gas Emissions

Livestock production accounts for 18% of GHG emissions that cause global warming; it is the largest direct source of anthropogenic methane CH_4 and nitrous oxide N_2O (Heinemann, 2010; Gill et al., 2010; Reynolds, 2013). GHGs produced from livestock production, including their lifetime (residence) in Earth's atmosphere and global warming potential (GWP), are displayed in Table 3.6.

Table 3.6 GHGs Produced by Livestock Production and Global Warming Potential (GWP)

GHG	Lifetime (average residence time in atmosphere) (Years)	Global warming potential (GWP)	Approx. contribution to greenhouse effect
Carbon dioxide (CO_2)	Up to 100 years	1	9 – 26
Methane (CH_4)	12	23	4 – 9
Nitrous oxide (N_2O)	120	310	n.a.

Source: Extracted from Table 3.1.

Ruminant livestock such as cattle, buffalo, sheep and goats, pigs, etc. contribute the major proportion of the total agriculture-related emissions of methane; also, they are the major contributor to all GHG emissions in agriculture – as high as 80% (IPCC, 2001; Steinfeld et al., 2006). Ruminant livestock emit methane as part of their normal digestive processes (Sejian et al., 2011; Sejian and Naqvi, no date; Johnson et al., 2002). Emissions of CH_4 from animal facilities primarily consist of animal respiration and enteric fermentation; in addition, emissions originate in manure management (including storage and application to crop fields and pasture). As already posited, methane is the third most important GHG, a product of microbial fermentative processes; its main natural source is wetlands (land intermittently or periodically water logged, including salt marshes, tidal estuaries, marshes, peat logs, etc). Better studied anthropogenic sources of methane include livestock production (e.g. Johnson et. al., 2002; Sejian et. al., 2011; Gerber et al., 2013; Sejian and Naqvi, no date); other sources are urban refuse land fills, coal mines, natural gas production and transmission (natural gas is 99% methane), rice paddies and manure.

Nitrous oxide, also known as dinitrogen oxide, though not known to be common in Earth's atmosphere, has been identified to be the more potent GHG than CO_2 and has the same residence time as CO_2. Nitrous oxide is more than 310 times more potent than CO_2 (1 kg of N_2O = 310 CO_2); the upshot is that, over the course of a century, its ability to warm planet Earth is a little over 300 times that of an equivalent mass of CO_2 (The Economist, 11th April, 2009). Other oxides of nitrogen (NO_X) such as nitrogen monoxide (NO) are pollutants contributing to acid rain resulting from the emission into the atmosphere of various pollutant gases, in particular sulphur dioxide and various oxides of nitrogen, which originate from fossil-fuel combustion and from automobiles exhaust fumes, especially.

More relevant to this section are the other agricultural activities that emit nitrous oxide; these include the use of chemical fertilizers. But nitrous oxide is made by bacteria that live in soils and water, whose raw material is from the nitrogen-rich fertilizers that are a key input in the cultivation of the high-yielding varieties (HYVs) of the Green Revolution, mainly rice, wheat, corn or maize. Finally, accumulation of nitrous oxide is particularly dangerous, because its long average residence in the atmosphere (120 years) makes the gas a problem in not only the troposphere, where it is a contributor to global warming, but also the stratosphere, where it contributes to ozone layer depletion.

Ruminant livestock are distinguished by presence of rumen, a special digestive organism, in the body (Oxford Dictionary of Science, op. cit., pp. 720-21). Rumen is the second of four chambers that constitute the stomach of ruminants, a sub-species of hoofed mammals comprising the sheep, cattle, goats, deer, antelope, etc., characterized by a 4-chamber stomach. Swallowed food passes from the first chamber, the **reticulum**, to the **rumen**, where food is digested by cellulose and other enzymes secreted by symbiotic anaerobic microorganisms living in the rumen.

Ruminant livestock have quite unique ability to digest fibrous and low-grade plant material (roughages), apart from being a major producer of methane. Enteric fermentation in rumen is quite useful for humans; however, much more important for the present study is that enteric fermentation in rumen also produces methane through bacterial breakdown of feeds known as methanogenesis. Livestock release methane into Earth's atmosphere through exhaling or ruminating through mouth or nostrils. Methane emissions globally from the digestive processes of ruminants is about 80 million tons/year and considered to be the single largest source of anthropogenic methane emission (IPCC, 2001).

Sejian and Naqvi (op. cit.; Figure 1) identify factors influencing methane yield in livestock production in the type of feed (dietary factor) as well as inflow processes within the rumen itself – e.g. inflow of saliva, rumin pH[9], etc. Another source of methane is manure from confined livestock operations, most often stored in solid or liquid form before being applied to agricultural land. Increasingly, however, manure is composted before land application or anaerobically digested to produce methane as bio-fuel (Sejian and Naqvi, op. cit.).

As already posited, methane is the most emitted GHG from livestock production, ranging up to 44% of the global livestock-related GHGs; the remaining part is almost equally shared between nitrous oxide (29%) and carbon dioxide (27%). Livestock supply chains emit GHGs as follows:

- 2 Gt CO_2 equivalent of CO_2 per annum, or 5% of anthropogenic CO_2 emissions;
- 3.1 Gt CO_2 equivalent per annum of CH_4, or 44% of anthropogenic CH_4 emissions; and
- 2 Gt CO_2 equivalent per annum of N_2O, or 53% of anthropogenic N_2O emissions.

Emissions of hydrofluorocarbons (HFCs) are marginal on a global scale (Gerber et al., 2013). Emissions by species of livestock identify cattle as the main contributor, with 4.6 Gt CO_2 equivalent representing 65% of the livestock sector's emissions; pigs, poultry, buffalo and small ruminants have much lower emission levels. Table 3.7 displays relevant data on estimates of GHG emissions by species of livestock. Cattle, beef and dairy combined, produce 4623 million tones CO_2-equivalent of GHG emissions by

Table 3.7 Global Estimates of GHG Emissions by Livestock Species

Species	GHG Emissions (million tones CO_2 equivalent)
Beef cattle	2495
Dairy cattle	2128
Pigs	668
Buffalo	618
Chickens	612
Small ruminants	474
Other poultry	72
Total	**7067, or approx. 7.1 Gt CO_2 equiv**

Source: Gerber et al. (2013, Figure 2, p. 16)

Table 3.8 Global Livestock Production and GHG Emissions from Livestock (by Region of the World)1

Region	(Million tons CO_2 – equiv)
Latin America & Caribbean	1300
East & Southeast Asia	1050
East Europe	140

North America	650
Oceania	150
Russian Federation	100
South Asia	650
Sub-Saharan Africa	310
Near East & North Africa	310
West Europe	610

[1]The data are authors' approximations based on FAO Figure 6 in Gerber et al., op. cit., p. 21
Source: Gerber et al., op. cit., Figure 6, p. 21

**Table 3.9 Global Emissions of GHGs from Livestock
Supply Chains by Category of Emissions**

Category of emission	% total
Enteric methane CH_4	39.1
Manure management methane CH_4	4.3
Manure management nitrous oxide N_2O	5.2
Indirect energy carbon dioxide CO_2	0.3
Direct energy carbon dioxide CO_2	1.5
Applied & deposited manure	16.4
Fertilizers nitrous oxide N_2O	7.2
Feed: rice, methane CH_4	0.4
Feed, carbon dioxide CO_2	13.0
Soybean carbon dioxide CO_2	3.2
Pasture expansion carbon dioxide CO_2	6.0

Source: Gerber et al., op. cit. (Figure 4, p. 17)

Livestock or 65.4% of the global GHG emissions by livestock. On regional basis, Latin America and Caribbean, has the highest level of GHG emission (Table 3.8) driven by the region's high level of development of ranch-based livestock production, which dates back to the colonial period. Indeed, Latin America stands out as a livestock producing region; most livestock types are found throughout the region, but cattle seem to predominate driven by the region's abundant endowments of grassland ecology and pasture both in tropical Latin America (e.g. Brazil, Mexico, Venezuela, etc.) and temperate Latin America (e.g. Argentina, Chile, Uruguay, etc.), which encourages ranch-based livestock production. Table 3.9 provides insight into global emissions of GHGs from livestock supply chains by category of emmissions, which show the dominance of enteric methane, followed by applied and digested manure.

As we have shown, beginning since the industrial era – the mid-1700s onwards – human activities have added significant amounts of GHGs to Earth's atmosphere (estimated to exceed 400 billion tones), mainly through fossil-fuel combustion and clearing of forests. Also, livestock production has been a significant source of anthropogenic nitrous oxide and methane. According to estimates by the **Inventory of US Greenhouse Gas Emissions and Sinks 1990 – 2014** between 1990 and 2014 GHG emissions from agriculture, including land-use change and livestock production grew by a 100 million metric tones Gt CO_2-equivalent: that is, from a little above 600 metrics million to 700 metric million Gt CO_2-equivalent. How much has Earth's climate warmed relative to observed rising concentrations of atmospheric GHGs? The next sub-section 3.8 highlights the key issues in socalled climate sensitivity debate – a major theme in the climate change literature.

3.8 Natural Processes of CO_2 Emissions

Apart from anthropogenic sources of CO_2 emissions, there are also, natural processes which are highlighted below:

- **Ocean-atmosphere exchange** is the highest source, contributing roughly 43%. The oceans contain dissolved CO2 which is released into the atmosphere at the sea surface. Annually the ocean-atmosphere exchange generates some 330 billion tonnes of CO_2 emissions.
- **Plant and animal respiration** contribute about 29%. CO_2 is produced as a by- product of the chemical reaction that plants and chemicals use to produce the energy they require, a process creating about 220 million tonnes of CO_2. Plants and animals use respiration to generate energy, which is used to drive basic activities like respiration and growth.
- **Soil repiration and decomposition** accounts for roughly 29%. Many organisms that live in the soil use respiration to produce energy – e.g. decomposers which break down dead organic matter – during which they release CO_2 as a by-product amounting to 220 billion tonnes of CO_2 emissions annually.
- **Volcanic eruptions** constitute a minor source of CO_2 emissions, accounting for ust 0.03% of natural emissions. Among the materials released during volcanic eruptions are magna, ash, dust and gasesincluding CO_2. Annually, volcanic eruptions generate about 0.15-0.26 billion tonnes of CO_2 emissions.

Anthropogenic CO_2 emissions are much smaller than natural emissions but (anthropogenic sources) upset the balance in the carbon cycle that existed prior to the Industrial Revolution. The amount of CO_2 emissions generated by natural sources is completely offset by Earth's natural carbon sinks – e.g. forest trees take up CO_2 during photosynthesis; oceans absorb CO_2, etc. – these natural sinks had, indeed, sustained the equilibrium in Earth's carbon cycle before the destabilizing influence of the CO_2 emissions of the Industrial Revolution.

3.9 Climate Sensitivity: How Much Have Anthropogenic GHG Atmospheric Concentrations Really Contributed to Global Warming?

Climate sensitivity is conventionally defined as the equilibrium surface temperature increase for every doubling of atmospheric CO_2 concentrations. Empirical evidence shows that anthropogenic GHG emissions have been on the rise, starting since the Industrial Revolution centuries, the 1700s and 1800s. On the other hand, however, it is not quite certain, empirically, that rising atmospheric GHG concentrations have generated (or will bring) a significant or/even proportionate increase in Earth's average temperature.

The questions often asked in the climate science literature are: To what extent is Earth's temperature sensitive or responsive to rise in atmospheric GHG concentrations? Is Earth's temperature, after all, displaying the level of sensitivity to atmospheric GHG concentrations as postulated in climate science models? By how much do Earth's temperatures get warmer given each doubling of atmospheric GHG concentrations?

Mainstream climate science represented by IPCC models employs socalled equilibrium climate sensitivity to describe the temperature rise/change after allowing all feedback mechanisms to work themselves out (but does not account for emissions of CO_2 through changes in vegetation and melting of ice sheet that do, indeed, affect levels of CO_2 concentrations and, hence, also, Earth's temperature). Recall that changes in vegetation-specifically deforestation-do affect CO_2 concentrations through photosynthesis (whereby plants assimilate carbon dioxide and give out oxygen). With climate change and its adverse effect on vegetation (e.g. destruction of rainforests), CO_2 absorption through 'natural sinks' declines which increases atmospheric CO_2 concentrations. Also, melting ice sheets will release methane gas trapped in Arctic ice sheets and glaciers, which increases GHG atmospheric concentrations.

Increases in CO_2 emissions, from whatever sources, give rise to global warming at a constant rate, according to conventional climate science models: for each doubling of CO_2 atmospheric concentration we obtain roughly 1°C of global warming-socalled climate sensitivity. So, the rise of CO_2 concentration, from pre-Industrial Revolution levels of 228 ppm to 560 ppm would thus warm Earth's temperature by 1°C. However, this global temperature level has hardly been attained.

Two factors work to counteract the theorized linear relationship between temperature rise of 1°C and doubling of CO_2 concentrations. First, rising CO_2 levels directly influence such phenomena as amount of water vapour and clouds that amplify or diminish the temperature rise, which, in turn, affects equilibrium sensitivity directly. This means, therefore, that doubling CO_2 concentrations may not result in a 1°C increase in global temperatures. Second, effects of presence of soots and other aerosols in the atmosphere 'add to or subtract from the effect of CO_2'. Specifically, soots have a warming effect on atmospheric temperatures, and aerosols a cooling effect.

Whereas there is a consensus among climate scientists on these two issues, there is little or none at all as regards the size of the change that is predicted to arise from them. For instance, the IPCC, which represents the conventional theoretical and empirical position on climate science, provides estimates of about 3°C plus or minus 1°C or so. IPCC (2007), for instance, posits that:

> "The equilibrium climate sensitivity … is likely to be in the range 2°C to 4.5°C with a best estimate of about 3°C and is very unlikely to be less than 1.5°C. Values higher than 4.5°C cannot be excluded".

Other studies employing quite different approaches from IPCC's arrive at different estimates. An unpublished report by the Research Council of Norway (cited in The Economist, 30th March, 2013) concludes that there is a 90% probability that doubling CO_2 emissions will increase global temperatures by only 1.2 – 2.9°C, with the most likely figure being 1.9°C, which is well below IPCC's estimates cited above. Another study by Julia Hargreaves of the Yokohoma-based Research Institute for Global Change (also cited in ibid.) suggests a 90% probability of the actual change lying within the range 0.5 – 4.0°C, with a mean of 2.3°C.

The conclusion to be drawn from recent climate change developments – specifically, the 'flat' trend in global temperatures even as atmospheric CO_2 concentrations rise sharply, is that these climate developments need better explanation than current climate science can provide. But these developments mean that Earth's climate is less sensitive to GHG emissions than existing climate science models predict; that there are other factors present in Earth's atmosphere that moderate global temperature that existing climate science is yet to explain – such as the presence of aerosols, natural variability, etc.

A major conclusion to be drawn from the above review is that Earth's climate is not as sensitive to atmospheric GHG concentrations as conventional IPCC climate models predict or theorize. As **The Economist** points out, the explanation to recent climate developments

> "… cannot rest on models alone. There must be other explanations – and, as it happens, there are: individual climate influences and feedback loops that amplify (and sometimes moderate climate change" (The Economist, 30th March, 2013, p. 70; bracketed words in original).

The Economist goes on to conclude:

"Despite all the work on sensitivity, no one really knows how the climate would react if temperature rose ..." (ibid., p. 71).

So, there are "clouds of uncertainty" as regards how Earth's climate reacts to changes in atmospheric GHG concentrations. The conclusion to be drawn is that, rather than linearity, there is nonlinearity in the relation between GHG emissions and changes in Earth's average temperature; indeed, there is no simple or definite proportional relation between GHG emissions and changes in Earth's average temperature. But the climate system contains many nonlinear processes, which result in a climate system with a potentially very complex behaviour, which may lead to abrupt climate change.

End Notes

[1] In classical Greek mythology, Pandora was created by the Greek god Zeus as punishment for Prometheus for stealing fire from the sun to animate his man of clay. Zeus proposed Pandora as a wife to Prometheus and gave her a jar instructing that she should present it to Prometheus. Pandora was ignorant of the jar's actual contents. Pandora, instead, married Prometheus's brother Epimetheus, who ignored a warning about impudent behavior and opened the jar, and in so doing released into the world a host of previously unknown and malign forces.

[2] See, for instance, MacAndrews (1978); Hardjono (1989); Rigg (1991; and Fearnside (1997).

[3] South America in our present context is used interchangeably with Latin America, which includes, Central America.

[4] The 'latifundio-minifundio' system is dualistic in nature, characterized by relative few large commercial estates known as *Latifundios*, which are over 500 hectares and numerous small properties known as *minifundios*, which measure under 5 hectares and are mainly subsistence-oriented smallholdings and are generally formed by indigenous and peasant households. However, the historical origin of the latifundism traces to Ancient Rome and the Roman Empire and was introduced into South America through Spanish colonization.

[5] Indonesia ranks the 4th most populous country in the world.

[6] See, for instance, BBC News, 16 September, 2015; and Agence France-Presse 17 September, 2015. See also Heil and Goldammer (2001).

[7] There are many names for grasslands: in the United States, *prairies*; in South America, *pampas*; in Central Eurasia, *steppes*; and in Africa, *Savanna*. What they all have in common is grass as their naturally dominant vegetation. In grasslands, generally, there is insufficient regular rainfall to support forest growth, but not so deficient as to form a desert. It is found that most grasslands are located between forests and deserts – e.g. the West African Savannas are located between the tropical rainforest belt West Africa and the Sahara Desert. Tropical grasslands – e.g. the African Savannas – are warm year-round, but usually have a distinctive day and rainy season; similarly, temperate grasslands have two seasons: a growing reason and a dormant season; during the latter season no grass can grow because temperature are below freezing point or too cold.

8   When scientist analyse atmospheric carbon dioxide concentrations they use the term ppm (parts per million), but, when analyzing carbon dioxide being released into the atmosphere, they refer to it as gigatonnes of carbon (Gt C). Whereas ppm is a mass or stock phenomenon, Gt C is a kind of flow phenomenon: carbon dioxide, as it cycles through Earth's spheres (See Chapter 2, Figure 2.1), often changes from one form to another; rather than remaining carbon dioxide, it is stored as carbohydrates, oils, carbonates and various other organic materials – socalled carbon fluxes in the scientific literature.

9   pH means "potential hydrogen"; a measure of the level of acid or alkali in a solution or substance (in this particular context rumin). In the pH range of 0 to 14 a reading of below 7 shows an acid and of above 7 shows an alkali.

13 For insights on Latin American livestock development up to the mid-1980s see Jarvis (1986).

CHAPTER 4

REGIONAL SOURCES OF ANTHROPOGENIC GREENHOUSE GAS EMISSIONS

4.1 Introduction

Among the key issues in international climate change negotiations is how to distribute the cost or burden of mitigating global warming and climate change among countries and regions of the world fairly and equitably. This, however, would require detailed knowledge of who have contributed most to anthropogenic GHG emissions both historically and currently, and directly and indirectly. Such knowledge is important if we are to know precisely those countries or set of countries without which no global agreement on climate change will stick.

4.2 Different Methods to Compare National Contributions to Global GHG Emissions

Different approaches have been evolved for gaining relevant insights on who have contributed most to global GHG emissions and, hence, also bearing responsibility for climate change[1]. These include: approaches that focus on **current** emissions; **historical** emissions (which consider long-term cumulative contributions or contributions over long-term time horizons); and the **carbonfootprint** of consumption (which plugs in role of imported goods). Carbon footprint is historically conceived as the totality of the greenhouse gas emissions originating in the activities of an individual, household, event, organisation (e.g. an industrial firm), product (e.g. 8-valve ML Mercedez car), etc. expressed as carbon dioxide equivalent (CO_2e). To arrive at a carbon footprint would, however, require enormous mass of data, which makes this type of task extremely difficult; besides, it would be necessary to discount for carbon dioxide that originates from natural sources, which will also pose difficulties in terms of its practicality.

It is, perhaps, for this reason that a large range of definitions exist for carbon footprint. East (2011) has suggested that, though extensively employed in public discourse, the carbon footprint concept is yet to became adequately defined in scientific literature; he goes further to explain that the term has became popular as a widely used "buzz word" to further stimulate consumers' growing concern for issues relating to global warming and climate change:

"… by describing anything from the narrowest to the widest interpretation of greenhouse gas measurement and reduction. In general, distinctions in the literature are primarily focused on two key issues: units of measurement and scope of measurement" (East, 2008).

Wright et al. (2011) suggest the following more-or-less practicable definition for carbon footprint:

A measure of the total amount of carbon dioxide (CO_2) and methane (CH_4) emissions of a defined population, system or activity, considering all relevant sources, sinks and storage within the spatial and temporal boundary of the population, system or activity of interest, calculated as carbon dioxide equivalent (CO_2e) using the relevant 100-year global warming potential (GWP 100).

As empirical statistics have established, GHG emissions originate in various natural sources and through various human activities: transportation, construction, agriculture (crop, livestock, ranching, logging, production and consumption of food, services, etc.). To simplify reporting, GHG emissions are often reduced in terms of the amount of CO_2, or its equivalent of other gases emitted. It has been established, for example, that the average carbon footprint of the average United States household ranges around 50 tons CO_2e per year, and the single largest source of emissions is from driving (gasoline consumption), followed by housing (electricity, natural gas, waste, construction), then food (mostly from red meat, dairy and seafood, etc). Given that the respective approaches to comparing national contributions to global GHG emission is likely to give a different picture, it would, hopefully, provide a holistic picture if we simply highlighted results from the various approaches.

4.2.1 Current CO_2 Emissions

Most studies use current emission data to compare national and regional contributions, which is obtained by summing up all the fossil fuels combusted and cement produced in each country and converting that into CO_2 equivalent. Data in Table 4.1 are based on current emissions for the top10 global emitters. Table 4.1A provides a picture on emissions based on conditions in 2014. An important fact from Table 4.1A is that, the developing regions outside China are marginal contributors in current global GHG emissions: The Middle East and North Africa, South America, Sub-Saharan Africa, Central America and Caribbean, and Oceania combined contribute less than 14% to current global GHG emissions.

However, when we consider 'net emissions' – that is, gross emissions from all GHG sources **minus** the removal of emissions from the atmosphere by carbon sinks – the picture would change a little. Emissions and sinks related to land-use are not accounted for in table 4.1A. However, as we saw in chapter 3, changes in land-use can be a significant source of GHG emissions. Estimates indicate that net global GHG emissions from land-use changes were over 8 billion metric tons of CO_2 equivalent (FAO, 2014). This amounted to some 24% of total global GHG emissions. In regions such as the United States and Europe, land-use practices (e.g. forest regeneration practices) have the net effect of absorbing CO_2 partially offsetting the emissions from fossil-fuel combustion. On the other hand, land-use change – e.g. deforestation – which is known to be high in developing countries, can affect the atmospheric GHG concentrations by changing how much carbon flows out of Earth's atmosphere into carbon sinks.

However, there are still uncertainties in the measurement of net carbon emissions; besides, there is no agreement over how much carbon sinks should be assigned to different regions and over time (e.g. UNFCCC, 2011). If, for instance, we focus just on more recent changes in carbon sinks, this would favour those regions that have deforested earlier such as North America and Europe. A significant feature in land use in the developing world in recent decades is high rates of deforestation and, hence, high losses in forest sinks; this is particularly high in Sub-Saharan Africa, South America (Brazil, in particular) and Southeast Asia (Indonesia, in particular).

Table 4.1 Top-10 Global CO_2 Emitters for 2011

Country	Fossil fuels burned (million mt)	% of world
China	9697	28.6
United States	5420	16.0
India	1967	5.8
Russia	1829	5.4
Japan	1243	3.7
Germany	810	2.4
South Korea	609	1.7
Canada	555	1.6
Indonesia	490	1.4
Saudi Arabia	464	1.4

Source: Clark (2011); citing sources in **The Netherlands Environmental Assessment Agency**

Table 4.1A Global CO$_2$ Emissions from Fossil-Fuel Combustion and some industrial processes for 2014.

Country	% of total emissions
China	30
United state	15
EU 28	9
India	7
Russia	5
Japan	4
Other	30
Total	**100**

Note: Emissions and sinks related to land use change are not included.
Source: Extracted from Boden, Marland and Andres (2017)

One very important development in current anthropogenic emissions of CO$_2$ is that the regional centre has shifted from the industrialized United States and West Europe to Asia – specifically, China and India, two countries currently undergoing rapid industrial transformation. There has occurred globally, since the beginning of the 2000s, acceleration of CO$_2$ emissions, averaging more than 31% per annum relative to 1.1% during the 1990s, driven by emissions originating in China (The Economist, August 10th, 2013). Every year China is known to construct some 60 gigawatts of power-generation capacity, estimated almost equal to Britain's current existing capacity, about 80% coal-based, the "dirtiest energy source". Table 4.2 contains China's fossil fuel related CO$_2$ emissions in 1998-2004.

Table 4.2 Fossil Fuel-related CO$_2$ Emissions in China, 1998-2004 (ml metric tons of CO$_2$)

Fossil fuel	1998	2001	2004
Coal	2,363 (80%)	2472 (77.5%)	3809 (81%)
Natural gas	47 (1.6%)	64 (2%)	83 (1.8%)
Petroleum	531 (18.1%)	653 (20.5%)	816 (17.2%)
Total from all fossil fuels	2,940	3,190	4,707

Notes: bracketed figures are % share in total fossil-fuel CO$_2$ emissions.
Source: United States Department of Energy / Environmental Information Administration, 2006. % shares are authors' estimates.

In 2011 China overtook the United States as the global leader in electricity generation (The Economist, 5th January, 2013, p. 50) largely based on coal. Table 4.2 shows that China's carbon footprint, coal-based CO_2 emissions have been on the increase. China's continued increase in coal-related CO_2 emissions could undermine international initiatives to reduce CO_2 emissions such as the Kyoto Protocol. Within this same time frame, China's coal plants, rather than reduce CO_2 emissions (not reported in data in Table 4.2), had in fact increased them by 1,926 million tons – over four times the proposed reduction.

The Indian scenario is like China's, more-or-less: India's energy consumption is rising rather rapidly, driven by rapidly expanding industrial capacities; India's share of global energy-related CO_2 emissions was 5.8% in 2011 (Table 4.1). As shall be shown, in per capita terms, however, India's CO_2 emissions remain the lowest among the countries listed in Table 4.4 below. India's power sector's coal consumption is growing at about 6% annually; if that trend is sustained, India, could, according to IEA projections, overtake the United States as the world's second-largest coal consumer (after China) before 2020.

4.2.2 All Greenhouse Gas Emissions

The previous analysis focused solely on CO_2 emissions from burning fossil fuels, thus ignoring other anthropogenic GHGs and non-fossil-fuel sources of CO_2 – e.g. deforestation, bush fires, livestock production, etc. which were treated in chapter 3. When we plug in these other GHG sources, the picture will change significantly, with countries like Brazil and Indonesia with enormous deforestation problem shooting up in the ladder. As of 2005, rough estimates of the 10-top GHG emitters are presented in Table 4.3.

Table 4.3 Top-10 Global Emitters of GHGs, 2005

Country	Million metric tons of GHGs	% of world
China	7,216	16.4
United States	6,931	15.7
Brazil	2,856	6.5
Indonesia	2,046	4.6
Russia	2,028	4.6
India	1,870	4.2
Japan	1,387	3.1
Germany	1,005	2.3
Canada	808	1.8
Mexico	696	1.6

Source: Clark (2011)

Again, China occupies the top position. However, important developments here, as already stated, are that: Brazil, which did not appear in Table 4.1, shot up in Table 4.3 as number 3; Indonesia, which took position 9 in Table 4.1 moves up to position 4 in Table 4.3; Saudi Arabia and South Korea, which appeared in Table 4.1, disappear completely from Table 4.3; etc.

Returning to China, that country emits more GHGs than any country in the world presently, because it has a large population of 1.4 billion compared with 250 million for the United States and European Unon (550 ml.). However, much of China's pollution comes from producing goods for other countries (See section 4.2.5.) A study reported in The Economist (28th November, 2015), which uses data from Michael Grabb of University College, London, controls for GHG emissions created in China by producing goods for export markets; the result is worth being summarized. Once the pollution that goes into traded goods is assigned to countries consuming those goods, the average Chinese person pollutes the planet "less than does the average European and much less than the average American", and is catching up, though (The Economist, 2015, 28 November, p. 9).

China was responsible for upwards of 75% of the net coal-based power-generating capacity added world-wide during the period 2000-2014. Apart from China's coal-based power stations producing GHGs, there is also pollution originating in domestic coal-based heating and from textile mills; here coal is burned, inefficiently, in boilers, which

"… has fouled the air around Chinese cities, turning them into … 19th century Manchester" (The Economist, 2015, 28 November).

This situation tends to be worse around China's coastal cities, where industrial development has progressed at higher pace; and here China has built some of the most polluting power stations in the world.

4.2.3 Emissions Per Capita

Comparing nations can be misleading, when their population sizes and other size variables, (e.g. GDP, geographic size, etc.) are not plugged into the analysis. So, it becomes necessary, if we are to obtain a much more relevant picture, to consider emissions or per capita basis (Table 4.4). On this basis the United States leads the world, with roughly 17 mt of CO_2 per capita, compared with China's 5.13 mt. In fact, as our data show, China and India make bottom of the list of the countries in Table 4.4; the dominant countries following the United States are Canada, Russia and South Korea, in that order. Note that the data in Table 4.4 relate to energy-related CO_2 emissions. In the United States electricity generation takes up to 30% of all GHG emissions; of this about 67% originates in fossil-fuel combustion, mostly coal[2] and natural gas. Transportation is next to energy production in United States GHG emissions.

Table 4.4 Top-10 Annual Energy CO_2 Emitters, 2009

Country	% of global total annual emissions	Mt of GHG per capita
United States	17.9	16.9
Canada	1.8	15.4
Russia	5.3	10.8
South Korea	1.8	10.6
Germany	2.6	9.2
Japan	3.8	8.6
United Kingdom	1.6	7.5
Iran	1.8	7.3
China	23.6	5.1
India	5.5	1.4

Source: International Energy Agency, 2011

4.2.4 Cumulative (Historical) Emissions

Because global warming and climate change results from the cumulative build-up of GHGs in Earth's atmosphere over the long-term period and not emissions in any particular year or short-term span, examining the cumulative sum of a region's or country's historical emission is one indicator that can truly capture the contribution of a particular country or region has made to the global warming and climate change problem. As has been stated earlier, country-level estimates of CO_2 emissions date as far back as the Industrial Revolution period – mid-1700s and 1800s. Also, given that CO_2 and other GHGs are known to have long residence in Earth's atmosphere – specifically, carbon dioxide has 30-95 years, nitrous oxide 120 years, etc. – historical emissions are just as important or even much more relevant, when it comes to analysis of country-contributions to anthropogenic climate change.

Data in Tables 4.5 to 4.8 provide the necessary historical insights. As these data show, the United States tops the list in all the tables. It would be necessary to note,

Table 4.5 10-Top Historical Emitters, 1850-2007

Country	Million metric tons of GHGs	% of world
United States	339,174	28.9
China	105,915	9.0

Russia	94,679	8.0
Germany	81,194	6.9
United Kingdom	68,763	5.8
Japan	45,629	3.87
France	32,667	2.77
India	28,824	2.44
Canada	25,716	2.2
Ukraine	25,431	2.2

Source: World Resources Institutes

Table 4.6 Cumulative CO_2 Emissions, 1950-2000 (With and Without Land-Use Change and Forestry)

	CO_2 from fossil fuels (% of the world)	CO_2 from fossil fuels and land-use change (% of the world)
United States	27	17
European Union	22	16
Russia	9	10
China	8	7
Indonesia	1	6
Brazil	2	6

Source: World Resources Institute (http:/www.wri.org/navigating_numbers_chapter 6.pdf)

Table 4.7 Cumulative CO_2 Emissions, 1850-2002

Country	% of World	Rank
United States	29.3	(1)
European Union – 25	26.5	(2)
Russia	8.1	(3)
China	7.6	(4)
Germany	7.3	(5)
United Kingdom	6.3	(6)
Japan	4.1	(7)
France	2.9	(8)
India	2.2	(9)

Ukraine	2.2	(10)
Canada	2.1	(11)
Poland	2.1	(12)
Italy	1.6	(13)
South Africa	1.2	(14)
Australia	1.1	(15)
Mexico	1.0	(16)
Spain	0.9	(20)
Brazil	0.8	(22)
South Korea	0.8	(23)
Iran	0.6	(24)
Indonesia	0.5	(27)
Saudi Arabia	0.5	(28)
Argentina	0.5	(29)
Turkey	0.4	(31)
Pakistan	0.2	(48)
Developed Countries	76	
Developing Countries	24	

Source: World Resources Institute (http://www.pdf.wri.org/navigating_numbers_ chapter6.pdf)

Table 4.8 Cumulative CO$_2$ Emissions: Comparison of Different Time Periods

	1850-2000 (% of the world)	1990-2000 (% of the world)
United States	29	24
European Union – 25	24	17
Russia	8	7
China	6	14
Japan	4	5
India	3	4

(a) Include emissions from fossil fuels and cement manufacture

Source: World Resources Institute (http:/www.pdf.wri.org/navigating_numbers_ chapter6.pdf) however, that a lot of changes have occurred since the 1st decade of the 2000s when data in these tables were issued, with respect to China's and India's GHG emissions. As stated earlier, by the end of the 1990s, global GHG emissions moved from its traditional centre of world industrialization in Western Europe and North America to the newly industrializind countries – specifically, China and India.

4.2.5 Consumption-based Accounting of CO_2 Emissions

By the end of the 1900s, a new approach to CO_2 emissions accounting was evolving in what became known as consumption-based accounting of CO_2 emissions [e.g. Peters, (2008), Hertwich and Peters (2009)]. As has been shown, CO_2 emissions from fossil-fuel combustion are the primary cause of global warming and the most researched. Much attention has been devoted to the carbon dioxide emissions directly emitted by each country with relatively little attention paid to emissions associated with the consumption of goods and services in each country. Consumption-based CO_2 emissions differ from the conventional production based CO_2 inventories because of inclusion of imports and exports of goods and services that, either directly or indirectly, create CO_2 emissions.

Research results – e.g. Davis and Caldeira (2010) – reveal that in 2004, for instance, 23% of global CO_2 emissions, or 6.2 $GtCO_2$ equivalent were traded internationally, largely as exports from China (see also Guan et al., 2009) – and other emerging economies (e.g. India) to economies of developing countries. The dominant global feature seems to be the export of CO_2 emissions embodied in goods from China (and other emerging economies – e.g. Thailand, Indonesia, Mauritius, etc.) – to consumers in the United States, Japan, and Western Europe. For China, in 2004 alone, 1.4 $GtCO_2$-equivalent emissions were linked to consumption in other countries. Emissions imported to the United States exceed those of any other country or region, largely embodied in machinery, electronics, motor vehicles and parts, chemicals, rubber, plastics, etc. However, these imports seem to be offset by considerable United States exports of similar goods. The consumption-based CO_2 emissions help to shift the responsibility for current high pace of CO_2 emissions from emerging countries – e.g. China, India, etc – to the developed countries, whose prosperity was not only founded on two centuries of fossil fuel emissions but also in some cases is now being maintained by emissions produced by developing countries (see also The Economist, 2015, 28th November).

4.3 Conclusion

China and India are the emerging global leaders in anthropogenic GHG emissions. By 2010 China overtook the United States as the world's largest energy-related CO_2 emitter. China has been projectd to account for much of the increase in energy-related CO_2 emissions during 2006 – 2030 (**Finance & Development,** March, 2008, p. 16)[3]. These analyses do suggest, indeed, that global policies to tackle CO_2 emissions to mitigate the impact of climate change should take the United States, China, Russia and India on board; as well, their primary sectoral focus should be energy and transportation.

End Notes

[1]   The section depends on insights in Clark (2011).

[2]   Some 56% of United States electricity generation is from coal-fired power plants (see also The Economist, 5th January 2013, pp. 50-52).

[3]   China and India are projected to provide about 60% of the global increase in energy-related CO_2 emissions during 2006-2030.

CHAPTER 5

SYMPTOMS OF GLOBAL WARMING AND CLIMATE CHANGE IN OZONE LAYER

5.1 Introduction

The ozone layer is one of Earth's natural systems; it is located in the stratosphere, which caps the lower atmosphere or the troposphere. As explained earlier (Chapter 2, section 2.3) the stratosphere is a layer with which temperature increases with altitude, up to about 64 kilometers above Earth's surface. This temperature increase is due, primarily, to the fact that the stratosphere contains ozone, a form of oxygen O_3 absorbing high-energy solar radiation, allowing only a small fraction (about 1%) to penetrate Earth's surface – a factor determining Earth's climate system and changes thereof. When this protective ozone layer gets depleted, as seems to be occurring currently due to climate change, increased solar radiation beyond that required to keep Earth's temperature within the natural bound, penetrates Earth's surface, with consequent damaging effects for humans and other biological organisms.

Like other natural systems in Earth's environment – e.g. oceans and ocean currents, glaciers and ice caps, coral reefs, tropical rainforests, etc – the ozone layer has had its chemical properties significantly changed by global warming and climate change. Specifically, the ozone layer has been depleted largely as a result of huge concentrations of anthropogenic nitrogen oxides produced from aircraft emissions and, more importantly, chlorofluorocarbons (CFCs) and bromofluorocarbons. An important consequence of ozone depletion is a rise in solar ultraviolet (UV) radiation received at Earth's surface, whose biologically harmful impacts constitute a serious negative externality – a global 'bad'.

5.2 Ozone and Ozone Layer Depletion[1]

Ozone, as already noted, is a form of oxygen (O_3); it is thus a greenhouse gas (GHG), though a minor one (Kiel et al., 1997; Schmidt et al., 2010). The ozone layer (ozonosphere) is an ozone-rich band of Earth's atmosphere. Located at 10-20 kilometers above Earth's surface, the ozone layer serves to shield the biosphere from the harmful ultraviolet B (UV–B) radiation, to which we return below. The ozone layer, however, is found to be at its most concentrated between 20 and 25 kilometers above Earth. Briefly, ozone is mainly found in two regions of Earth's atmosphere: about 90% resides in a layer beginning between 10 and 17 kilometers above Earth's surface and extending up to about 50 kilometers, a region of the atmosphere known as the stratosphere; hence, ozone in this layer is commonly described as the ozone layer. The remaining ozone (some 10%) resides in the lower atmosphere, the troposphere – commonly known as the smog zone. It is, however, found that the thickness of the ozone layer varies seasonally and geographically: it is thinnest at the equator, which is believed to account for the high equatorial incidence of skin cancer (NOAA, 2013).

Two French physicists Charles Fabry and Henri Buisson discovered the ozone layer in 1913; its properties were later explored in detail by Oxford University meteorologist and physicist Gordon Dobson, who developed a simple spectrophotometer (the Dobsonmeter) for measuring stratospheric ozone from the ground. Dobson's world-wide network of ozone-monitoring stations, which were founded between 1928 and 1958, are known to operate to the present day.

In the 1980s scientists found that ozone layer depletion was occruing over both the Arctic and Antarctica, recording up to 50%. Earlier in the 1970s, scientists found that ozone levels had been depleted by as much as 60-70% from their pre-1975 levels (GEP, 2009). It was to be established later by climate scientists that the chemical properties of Earth's atmosphere have been undergoing fundamental change and at a rapid pace on a global scale as a result of centuries-scale GHG concentrations in the atmosphere. Specifically, anthropogenic accumulation of chlorine in the atmosphere was found to have destabilized an otherwise "balanced process of ozone production and destruction":

> "And the source of the chlorine turned out to be a variety of manufactured chemicals, which, released at ground level, slowly migrated up to higher altitudes. The culprits are substances called **halocarbons**, chemicals composed of carbon atoms in combination with atoms of chlorine, fluorine, iodine, and bromine. The primary halocarbons are called **chlorofluorocarbons** (CFCs)… Another subgroup is the halons… which act similarly to chlorine in breaking down ozone molecules". (Field and Field, 2009: 424; emphasis in the original, bracketed word added).

Scientists explain that while there are natural sources for all these chemical species such as those originating in woodfire and volcanic activity or marine algae, the concentrations of chlorine and bromine are of recent origin: the large emissions of anthropogenic nitrogen oxides produced from aircrafts and, more importantly, chlorofluorocarbons (CFCs) and bromofluorocarbons.

It is explained, further, that the 'ozone hole' is not a 'hole' in the true meaning of the term, but, rather, a region in the ozonesphere of reduced ozone (O_3) concentration that periodically changes its size, shape and density. Popular conception, however, tends to confuse 'ozone hole' and global warming, believing the 'ozone hole' to be the major cause of observed rapid increases in Earth's surface temperatures. Current scientific opinion informed by coupled general climate models [CGCHs] suggests, however, that the 'ozone hole' might have indirect effect and, hence, a slight global warming influence, but because of its effect on winds, not temperature (Watts, 2013).

5.3 Role of CFCs In Ozone Depletion

As pointed out above, chlorofluorocarbons (CFCs), species of chemicals found mainly in spray aerosols that have been used by the industrialized countries in industry for much of the past 50 to 60 years (until they were banned in 1996 by the Montreal Protocol)[2] are the primary culprits in ozone layer depletion. A chlorofluorocarbon (CFC), as the term suggests, is an organic compound that contains only carbon, chlorine and fluorine. Many CFCs have been widely used as refrigerants, propellants (in aerosol applications) and solvents. CFCs were discovered way back in the 1930s[3] as a replacement for the refrigerants then in vogue; when they were introduced, attention seemed to have focused exclusively on their industrial benefits so that little or no notice was taken regarding their environmental pollution effects. But as noted earlier, it was only later in the 1980s that ozone depletion was detected by scientists- that is, some 50 years later! But scientific evidence was often lacking (as at that early period) that CFCs could have long-term adverse environmental impacts. It was later found that the very stable nature of these gases allows them to migrate rather slowly in the atmosphere, drifting up through the troposphere, where they begin a process of ozone layer depletion.

CFCs have a high lifetime (residence duration in Earth's atmosphere, averaging 100 years). When they reach the stratosphere (where ozone layer is located) they become exposed to UV radiation, which causes them to break down into substances that include chlorine, which, in turn, react with oxygen in ozone (note that ozone itself is a form of oxygen, O_3) and break down the ozone molecule. Scientists have established that one atom of chlorine can break down more than 100,000 ozone molecules.

The possibility of ozone depletion was first theorized by scientists in the late 1960s as innovations of the supersonic air transport began to evolve. Scientists were already long aware that nitric oxide (NO) can catalytically react with ozone (O_3) to produce ozone O_3 molecules; however, nitric oxide molecules produced at ground level was found to have properties that cannot permit it to migrate to the stratosphere.[4] It was not until the arrival of commercial supersonic jet aeroplanes (which cruise at altitudes much higher than conventional aeroplanes) that the potential for nitric oxide to react with stratospheric ozone was considered possible. By 1974 Sherwood Roland and Mario Molina had discovered that CFCs could be photolyzed by high energy photons in the stratosphere, a process that could release chlorine radicals that would catalytically react with ozone (O_3) to destroy the ozone molecule itself.[5] Table 5.1 contains a summary of the various ozone-depleting substances (ODS), of which CFCs have the highest potential.

Table 5.1 Ozone-Destroying Substances (ODSs)

Compound	Symbol	Typical Uses	Ozone-depleting Potential[a] (ODP)	Global warming Potential[b] (GWP)
Chlorofluorocarbons	CFCs	Commonly used in refrigeration, aerosol spray propellants, solvents and foam-blowing agents. Have relatively long atmospheric lifetime of 45-100 years; so the chlorine from one CFC molecule can do significant damage to the ozone layer	0.6 – 1	4750 – 14,400
Hydrochloro – fluorocarbons	HCFCs	Also commonly used for refrigerants, aerosol propellants, foam manufacture, and air conditioning. Used as a transitional substance from CFCs to ODSs alternatives	0 – 0.2	124 – 14,800

Methyl bromide	$CH_2 Br$	A toxic chemical commonly used to remove insects, rodents, weeds and fungi infestation from agricultural fields, grain elevators, mills, etc.	0.6	5
Halons		Compounds mostly commonly used in fire extinguishers	3 – 10	1,640 – 7,140
Carbon tetrachloride	CCL_4	Used as a raw material to produce chemicals, including ODSs; also, widely used as cleansing agent, in fire extinguishers, and even as pesticides.	1.1	1,400
Methyl chloroform	CH_3 CCL_3	Used as solvent and degreasing agent; also, an ingredient in consumer products – e.g. household cleaners, paints, glues, and aerosols sprays.	0.1	146

[a]Relative amount of degradation to ozone layer the compound can cause, with trichlorofluorocarbon fixed at an ODS = 1.0
[b]100 year GWP relative to CO_2 (GWP of CO_2 = 1.0)
Source: GEF (2013).

5.4 Environmental and Health Damages Linked with Ozone Depletion

As already noted, ozone layer depletion has one obvious negative externality effect: the function of ozone layer as a shield protecting Earth's biosphere from harmful UV radiation is compromised. In the early 1970s, as noted above, scientists discovered that anthropogenic GHG concentrations in Earth's atmosphere have been transforming the chemical properties of Earth's atmosphere in ways that destroy the amount of stratospheric ozone, thus allowing more UV radiation to penetrate Earth's surface. This, in turn, has been responsible for a number of environmental and health damages on humans, animals, plants, terrestrial ecosystems, and biogeochemical cycles. Scientists classify ultraviolet (UV) radiation in the following ranges:

- **UV-A (320 – 400) nanometer (nm)**[6] is the longest wave length range; it is not harmful in normal doses and is used clinically in the treatment of certain skin ailments – e.g. psoriasis; also, to induce vitamin D formation in patients that are allergic to vitamin D.
- **UV-B (290 – 320) nanometer** causes reddening of the skin followed by pigmentation (tanning); excessive exposure can cause severe blistering.
- **UV-C (230 – 290) nanometer** has the shortest wave lengths and is particularly damaging; it is thought to cause skin cancer and the risk of contracting the latter is thought to become increased by ozone layer depletion.

Radiation at the longer UV wavelengths (320-400nm) called UVA plays an essential role: formation of vitamin D in the human skin; and a harmful role of causing sunburn on human skin; and cataracts (a clouding of the eye lenses (EPA 2010). Solar radiation at shorter wavelength (290-320 nm) falls within the UVB 'band'; it causes damage at the molecular level to the fundamental building block of life: deoxyribonucleic acid (DNA). The latter readily absorbs UVB radiation which changes the shape of the molecule in one of several ways: e.g. the protein-building enzymes can be damaged, or the DNA distorted so that it does not function properly. However, living cells evolving in the presence of UVB radiation have developed capacity to repair DNA, which makes the latter somewhat resilient to damages by UVB.

We highlight below five categories of health and environmental degradation impacts known to be linked to ozone depletion.

- **Human health** has been confirmed by laboratory and epidemiological studies to be harmed by UVB radiation in the form of skin cancer by causing mutation of DNA and suppressing certain activities of the human immune system[7]. Studies show that a sustained 1% depletion of the ozone layer will lead to a 2-3% increase in incidence of non-melanoma type of skin cancer; also, it causes cataract (a clouding of the eye lenses). The World Health Organization (WHO) estimates that: between 2 and 3 million non-melanoma skin cancers are diagnosed each year, but are rarely fatal and can be surgically removed; approximately 130,000 malignant melanomas occur globally each year, substantially contributing to mortality rates in fair-skinned populations; some 66,000 deaths occur annually from melanoma and other skin diseases; etc. (Lucas et al., 2006). Globally, some 12-15 million people become blind from cataracts each year, of which upwards of 20% are suspected to originate in UVB exposure. Finally, a growing body of medical evidence suggests that UV radiation may lead to a suppression of cell-mediated immunity and thereby enhance the risk of infections diseases and limit the efficacy of vaccination (ibid.).

- **Plants** have been affected in their physiological and developmental processes; specifically, agricultural crops have exhibited some inhibition of growth and photosynthesis when exposed to elevated UVB radiation, but some plants, including rice cultivars, soybeans, winter wheat, cotton and corn (maize) show considerable capacity to adapt and repair. There is some evidence of indirect changes caused by UVB radiation such as changes in plant form, distribution mechanism of nutrients within plants, timing of developmental phases, etc., which may be sometimes more important than damaging effects of solar radiation. But such have potential to make plants susceptible to plant diseases and biogeochemical cycle, for instance.

- **Ecosystems**, both aquatic and terrestrial, are adversely affected by UVB radiation (El Sayed et al., 1996), caused by reduced productivity of vegetative plankton, which has an important place in aquatic food web. Because UVB radiation affects organisms that move nutrients and energy through the biosphere, there is the speculation that changes in these activities of the organisms will change biogeochemical cycles – e.g. by reducing the populations of phytoplankton would affect the global carbon cycle (given that phytoplankton store huge amount of carbon in the oceans). The impact of UV radiation on agriculture and marine systems is yet to be scientifically established. However, speculative evidence shows that: (i) agricultural crops have demonstrated some inhibition of growth and photosynthesis when plants are exposed to elevated UV radiation, but some plants, including cultivars of rice, show considerable capacity to adapt and repair; and (ii) marine systems may be adversely affected caused by reduced productivity of vegetative plankton which has an important place in aquatic food chain. The Montreal Protocol signed in September 1988 initiated a series of multilateral agreements for phasing out the production and use of CFCs and some 96 chemicals considered harmful to the ozone layer, to which we return in chapter 16.

- **Biogeochemical cycles**, the pathways for transporting and transforming matter within the four spheres of Earth's environment (biosphere, hydrosphere, lithosphere, and atmosphere), are components of the broader cycle governing the functioning of planet Earth. The latter is a system open to electromagnetic radiation from the Sun and outer space, but is virtually closed system with regard to matter. So, matter that Earth was constituted from the time of its origin is transformed and circulated from one location of Earth to the other in line with the law of conservation of matter, namely: matter cannot be created nor destroyed; rather, it can be transformed into various forms, including the transformation between matter and energy. Briefly, biogeochemical cycles facilitate the transfer of matter from one form to another and from one location (geographical space) to another location on Earth. To return to the effects of UVB radiation on biogeochemical cycles, elevated solar radiation could affect terrestrial and aquatic biogeochemical cycles, thus altering both sources and sinks of greenhouse and chemically-important trace gases – e.g. CO_2 and possibly other gases including ozone – which could contribute to biosphere-atmosphere feedbacks that disrupt or, otherwise, reinforce the atmospheric buildup of those gases.

- **Materials**, when exposed to elevated UV radiation undergo accelerated degradation – e.g wood used extensively in building construction. UVB radiation affects adversely the mechanical properties of materials, undermining the useful life (Andrady et al., 1998, 2003). The outdoor service life of common plastic materials is limited by their susceptibility to solar ultraviolent radiation. Of the solar wavelengths the UVB component has been found to be particularly efficient in bringing about photodamage in naturally occurring materials – e.g. rubber, wood used in agricultural production and construction industry. Any depletion of the ozone layer and resulting increase in UVB component of terrestrial sunlight will tend to decrease the service life of these materials.

Ozone layer depletion and the health and environmental degradation it imposes on the world community clearly illustrate the peculiar nature of global warming and climate change as a global negative externality, a 'global bad', that imposes costs on the international community as a whole. Indeed, the history of the ozone layer depletion illustrates the emergence, persistence, and evolution of the fate of atmospheric pollution as both a national and global practical issue (Morrisette, 1989), to which we return in chapter 16.

5.5 Conclusion

Atmospheric pollution, precisely human-induced emissions of CFCs, has been found to damage Earth's ozone layer (ozonesphere) contributing to the threat of global warming and climate change. Earth's protective ozone – stratosphere ozone – is known to be depleted largely as a result of huge accumulation of anthropogenic nitrogen oxides produced from aircraft emissions and, more importantly, CFCs and bromofluorocarbons. An important consequence of ozone erosion is a rise in solar ultraviolet (UV) radiation received at Earth's surface, whose biologically damaging impact (e.g. non-melanoma skin cancers, which primarily affects fair-skinned individuals) began to increase rapidly.

End Notes

[1]   This section depends on insights in: Wright and Nebel, 2004, pp. 511-513, 528-534; Field and Field, 2009, especially chapter 20; USEPA (United States Environmental Protection Agency) (http:/www.epa/ozone/science/effects); Allen (2001); Oxford Dictionary of Science, 2005, pp. 840-841.

[2]   They are being replaced with other products such as fluorocarbons (HFCs).

3   By Thomas Midgley Jr. (1889-1944), an American mechanical engineer and chemist. Midgley was a key figure in a team of chemists, led by Charles F. Kettering, who developed the tetraethyllead (TEL) additive to gasoline as well as some of the first chlorofluorocarbons (CFCs). See also Midgley and Henne (1930).

4   Specifically, the life time (residence in atmosphere) is too short.

5   A process scientists call the Rowland-Molino theory of ozone depletion.

6   Manometer = billionth of a metre, which is shorter than wavelengths of visible light (400-700nm).

7   Sunburn (erythema) is, perhaps, the best known acute effect of excessive UV-B exposure.

CHAPTER 6

CLIMATE CHANGE AND THE HYDROLOGIC CYCLE

6.1 Introduction

The hydrologic cycle (also called the water cycle) is one of Earth's natural systems. Climate and water on planet Earth are intimately linked; water influences the climate and is, in turn, influenced by the climate. Climate models predict climate change variables in temperature, precipitation, sea level, river flow, soil moisture, evapotranspiration, groundwater, etc. Also, climate change will alter future global stock of freshwater supply in several aspects: availability, quality, destructive potential (e.g. flooding, hot-spots), which raise issues of adaptation challenges.[1]

It has been established that global warming and climate change is speeding up the hydrologic cycle referring to the rate at which water evaporates and falls again as rain or snow, the circulation of water between Earth's atmosphere, lithosphere (land) and hydrosphere (Schlesinger and Bernhadt, 2013). This speeding up of the hydrologic cycle seems to make wet regions (e.g. the tropics) more sodden or yet wetter and humid, and arid regions (e.g. deserts), even drier; it brings longer droughts between more intensive periods of rain.

The speeding up of the hydrologic cycle has three important implications for water use. First, it changes the way plants grow: e.g., trees react to downpours with a spurt of growth; in the longer drought that follows, the extra biomass then dries up so that if lightening does strike, forests burn more spectacularly; similarly, crops grow too fast, then wilt (as drought sets in). Second, it increases problems of water management; large floods overwhelm existing controls, as happened in 2013 in several parts of the world – e.g. northern India and Central Europe in the spring of 2013. (European Floods, 2013), and Nigeria's Niger-Benue river confluence around Lokoja (Dukiya and Galhot, 2013), etc. In addition, global warming melts glaciers and causes snow to fall as rain; since snow and ice are natural regulators, storing water in winter and releasing it in summer, 'countries are swinging more violently between flood and drought' (The Economist, 11th April, 2009, p. 55).

6.2 Processes in the Hydrologic Cycle

Earth's surface is three-quarters covered by water – hence, planet Earth is often described as 'water planet'. On the other hand, water as an environmental or natural resource, is supplied and distributed to all parts and spheres of Earth's environment via the hydrologic cycle, - the 'pilgrimage of water' as water as molecules move their way from Earth's surface to the atmosphere and back again via a set of biological and geological (and meteorological) processes[2]. A gigantic system, indeed, the hydrologic cycle is powered by the Sun; it is, thus, a continuous, perpetual process of exchange of moisture between the hydrosphere (seas and oceans), the atmosphere (air) and the land (lithosphere). Without the hydrologic cycle, life on planet Earth would cease (as without air)[3]. The **Oxford Dictionary of Science** (2005, p. 407) describes the hydrologic cycle thus:

> "The circulation of water between the atmosphere, land, and oceans on the earth … Water evaporates from water bodies on earth to form water vapor in the atmosphere. This may condense to form clouds and be returned to the earth's surface as rainfall, hail, snow, etc. Some of this precipitation is returned to the atmosphere directly through evaporation or transpiration by plants; some flows off the land surface as overland flow, eventually to be returned to the oceans via rivers; and some infiltrated the ground to flow underground forming groundwater storage".

The amount of water on Earth remains fairly fixed over time but its division into the various forms, namely, ice, freshwater, salt water and atmospheric water (or vapor) varies determined by a whole range of climatic factors. On the other hand, water moves from one reservoir to another caused by the physical processes of evaporation, condensation, precipitation, infiltration, runoff and subsurface flow; in so doing, water is transformed into the different forms identified above. The global hydrologic cycle has six major reservoirs or places where water resides, as shown in Table 6.1. There is a huge disparity in the distributive shares by the various reservoirs, the largest share being the oceans (97.4%). This has profound implications for climate change, to which we return in chapter 8.

Table 6.1 Distributive Shares by the Various Reservoirs of Water on Earth

Reservoir	Distribution share (appox. %)
Oceans	97.4000
Marine atmosphere	00.0008
Terrestrial atmosphere	00.0003

Surface water	00.0200
Groundwater	00.5900
Snow & ice	01.9800

Source: 'Modeling the Global Water Cycle'
http://www.geosc.psu.edu/_dmb53/DavesSTELLA/water/global%20w

Another important process is glacier melting: ice in glacier flows slowly from places of accumulation to the edges, where it may melt. The bulk of Earth's glacier is stored in the polar regions of Antarctica and Arctic (Greenland). As the polar glaciers melt here the water flows directly to the oceans and seas raising their water levels. This is a factor contributing to sea level rising (SLR), to which we return in chapter 9.

6.3 Environmental Degradation Stemming from Direct and Indirect Impacts of Climate Change on the Hydrologic Cycle

A large share of the environmental degradation facing human societies currently stems from direct or indirect impacts of climate change on the hydrologic cycle. These impacts can be categorized into three (Wright and Nebel, 2004, p. 221):

- **Changing Earth's surface** occurs when, through human activity, there is the direct loss of forests and other ecosystems to various human enterprises, which in turn diminish the goods and services these ecosystems provide. For instance, with existence of forests and other ecosystems, there is little run-off; rather, precipitation is intercepted by vegetation and infiltrates into porous topsoil – a process that provides the life-blood of the natural and human-created ecosystems, humans, animals and plants. But the evaporation taking place in these ecosystems not only sustains the latter, but also recycles the water to local rainfall; some of the water percolates down to recharge the groundwater reservoir, which, in turn, releases water through springs, streams, rivers, etc. As forests become lost to deforestation or land is overgrazed, the natural pathway of the hydrologic cycle is thrown off balance: it shifts from infiltration and groundwater recharge to runoff, as the water runs into streams or rivers almost immediately – a major cause of flooding (see Section 6.7). Wright and Nebel (op. cit.) cites an example from the extreme flooding in Bangladesh (a very low-lying country only a few-meters above sea level): the Himalayan foothills in India and Nepal have been seriously deforested; due to sediment deposited from upriver erosion, the Ganges river basin has risen 5-7 meters in recent years.

- **Polluting the hydrologic cycle.** As we have shown, the hydrologic cycle involves the entire biosphere – the Earth's sphere where life (humans, animals, plants, microbes) is found. Therefore, whichever wastes (products of metabolism that are not required for further metabolic processes and are therefore excreted from the body of organisms) are introduced, they are inevitably introduced into the hydrologic cycle. For example, smokes or fumes exhausted or evaporated into the atmosphere will come back in the form of acid rain. Specifically, acid rain is the popular, non-technical, language for atmospheric deposition of acidic substances (dioxides of sulphur and nitrogen), which originate from burning of fossil fuels and from automobile exhaust fumes, respectively. It occurs as precipitation having a pH ('potential hydrogen', a scale introduced by Søren Sørenson in 1909 to express the acidity or alkalinity of a solution) value of less than about 5.9, which has adverse effects on the fauna and flora on which it falls. Dioxides of sulphur and nitrogen dissolve in atmospheric water to form sulphuric and nitric acids in rain, snow, or hail (wet deposition); otherwise, the pollutants are deposited as gases or minute particles (dry deposition). Acid rain has been implicated in the destruction of European forests (particularly in Germany, Poland, and Czech Republic); it is a key environmental problem in industrial countries (Stutz and Warf, 2007).
- **Withdrawing water supplies for human use** comes in the forms of: irrigation and other agricultural uses (70%); industry (20%); and direct human consumption (10%). There are, of course, variations in this regard across regions of the world, depending on natural precipitation and level of economic development (for instance, in Africa and Asia, agriculture takes more than 80% and industry less than 10%). A problem facing human society is tendency to extract amounts of water that exceed the regenerative capacity of the hydrologic cycle – either in the form of overdrawing surface water or underground water, with serious environmental consequences. In several parts of the world, surface and groundwater has been overdrawn, with serious environmental and ecological consequences. The most dramatic results of overdrawing water to date are the drying up of the Aral Sea, an inland freshwater body in South-Central Russia, and Lake Chad in West Africa, to which we return.

6.4 The Global Water Shortages and Fisheries Depletion

Water represents a perfect example of a renewable ecosystem resource that is showing signs of exhaustion due to over-exploitation and degradation of the natural potential of the hydrologic cycle to replenish the natural water flow in many parts of the world. Globally, freshwater is abundant though; each year an average of more than 7000 m³ per capita of freshwater is known to enter rivers and aquifers (deposits of rocks, such as chalk, that yield economic supplies of water to wells or springs as a result of their porosity or permeability). However, such water has been found to not always arrive where and when it is needed. A World Bank study in the early 1990s found that twenty-two countries already have renewable water resources of less than 1000 m³ per capita – a level commonly accepted to indicate that water stress has reached a crisis point. An additional eighteen

Table 6.2 Availability of Water by World Regions

Region	Annual Internal Renewal Water Resources		% population living in countries with scarce annual per capita resources	
	Total ('000 cubic kilometers)	Per capita ('000 cubic meters)	< 1,000 cubic meters	1000-2000 cubic meters
Sub-Saharan Africa (including South Africa)	3.8	7.1	8	16
East Asia and Pacific	9.3	5.3	< 1	6
South Asia	4.9	4.2	0	0
Eastern Europe and former Soviet Union	4.7	11.4	3	19
Other Europe	2.0	4.6	6	15
Middle East and North Asia	0.3	1.0	53	18
Latin America & Caribbean	10.6	23.9	< 1	4
Canada and United States	5.4	19.4	0	0
World	40.9	7.7	4	8

Source: World Bank, 1992, Table 2.1, p. 48

countries are found to have less than 2000 m³ per capita on average, which may be taken as 'dangerously little in years of short rainfall' (World Bank, 1992, p. 48).

The Middle East and North Africa (MENA) and Sub-Saharan Africa (SSA) harbor most of the countries with limited renewable water resources; these are regions found to harbor countries that consume more than 20% of their renewable water supply each year (Table 6.2). Other regions with water scarcity problems are northern China, west and south India, and Mexico. Cities in these regions are growing rather rapidly well above the global average, which has pushed up demand for water as a 'basic need' (World Bank, 1992, pp. 48-50).

In China, for example, fifty cities were reported by the beginning of the 1990s to be facing acute water crisis: their renewable water supplies are falling below the level at which societies generally experience water deficits. Further, some 1.7 billion people, some 30% or so of the population of the developing world as a whole by the early 1990s, live in countries facing water stress. Limited access to water is known to pose a severe constraint on the development prospects of countries, and conflicts over water use and distribution are known to constitute common sources of international conflicts – as, for instance, between Egypt and Ethiopia over the waters of the Nile River; Israel and its Arab neighbors over the waters of the Jordan River; etc.

In several parts of the world surface freshwater reservoirs – e.g. rivers, lakes, etc – have been overdrawn to develop irrigation facilities; while such projects have provided livelihoods for millions, they have generated considerable negative environmental spillovers. Arguably, the world's most dramatic example of an aquatic ecosystem that has been overexploited and degraded to near extinction is the Aral Sea, an inland freshwater body in south-central Russia. One of the four largest lakes in the world before its degradation, with an area of 68,000 km^2, the Aral Sea steadily began to shrink in the 1960s as the rivers (Ama Darya and Syr Darya) flowing into the inland Aral Sea were diverted into irrigation development for cotton production in Soviet Kazakhstan and Uzbekistain. By 2007 the Aral Sea had already lost some 90% of its original size; by 2014 satellite photographs revealed that parts of the original Aral Sea have, infact, completely dried up for the first time in modern history turning into what is now called Aralkam desert (Miklin and Aladin, 2008).

Nearer home in West Africa, Lake Chad is reported to have shrunk 70 km from its original shores in the past five decades, partly as a result of climate change and constant droughts in the West African Sahel that have led to the desertification of Lake Chad (to which we return in chapters 10 and 11), and partly as a result of diversion of water for irrigation purposes, to which we return in the present chapter.

6.5 Overdrawing Groundwater

Groundwater (or subterranean water) refers to all water that occurs below the surface of the ground, as opposed to that at the surface, but excluding underground streams. Groundwater provides the largest reservoir of freshwater available to humans, who have increasingly turned to this water reservoir to augment supplies of high-quality fresh water. In using groundwater, however, humans are tapping a renewable but not unlimited resource, its sustainability ultimately depending on balancing withdrawals with rates of recharge (Wright and Nebel, op. cit., p. 227).

Scientific studies find that in some dry regions of the world, the groundwater found currently is actually 'ancient water' that accumulated millions of years ago, when the climate in those regions was wetter, and that current rates of recharge are about zero. So withdrawing groundwater in such pockets of "ancient water" is described as "mining fossil water" – similar to mining fossil minerals (e.g. coal or crude oil) from reservoirs that will ultimately be exhausted regardless of rates of exploitation (ibid., p. 227).

Apart from the problem of low rates of groundwater recharge, the simplest sign that groundwater rates of use is exceeding recharge manifests in a falling water table (the level below which the ground is saturated – thus the upper surface of the groundwater). This is found to be a global problem. For instance, in the Great Plains of the United States incorporating the states of Texas, Oklahoma, New Mexico, Colorado, Kensas, Wyoming, and Nebraska, the withdrawal rates of groundwater to supply irrigation needs, has been found to amount to about 2.8 billion cubic meters per year, two times higher than the recharge rate, which has led to a drop of the water table to 30-60 meters and is lowering at 1.8 meters a year (Wright and Nebel, op. cit., pp. 227-9).

6.6 How Sensitive is the Hydrologic Cycle to Climate Change?

As pointed out already, the hydrologic cycle is very sensitive to global warming and climate change (Held and Soden, 2006); indeed, much of the effect of climate change tends to be felt through its effect on precipitation (rain and snow) (Dore, 2005; Suzuki, 2013). The circulation of water between Earth's atmosphere, land, and oceans is enhanced through the warming up of global atmospheric temperatures, with great implications for the frequency, intensity and duration of hydrologic events, namely precipitation, floods, drought, etc. (Fowler and Hennesy, 1995). On the other hand, changes in hydrologic extremes – e.g. floods, monsoons, droughts, etc. – in response to global warming could be more significant than changes in hydrologic mean conditions such as mean precipitation.

For example, as the lower atmosphere (troposphere) gets warmer, evaporation will intensify, resulting in an increase in the amount of moisture circulating throughout the lower atmosphere, which, in turn, will lead to the increased frequency of intense precipitation events mainly over land (as the latter warms up faster than the ocean) creating low pressure into which moisture-laden winds from the ocean flow. However, because of warmer temperatures, more precipitation will occur as rain rather than snow. The northern latitudes experience earlier arrival of spring-like conditions resulting in earlier peaks of snow-melt and resulting overflow of water bodies (rivers, inland lakes, etc.). On the other hand, warmer temperatures have led to increased drying of the land surface in some regions, resulting in increased incidence and severity of drought – as in the West African Sahel, India, etc. We return to this theme in chapter 10.

From 1900 through 2002, for example, changes were observed to have occurred in the hydrologic cycle due to a confluence of natural variations and human forcing. During this period drought worsened in Sub-Saharan Africa and Southern Africa, Eastern Brazil, and Iran. Over the same period, in contrast, Western Russia, South-Eastern regions of South America, Scandinavia, and Southern United States experienced less severe drought.

The following trends are the emerging hydrologic events caused by climate change (Dore op. cit.). First, there is increased variance of precipitation everywhere both in frequency and intensity. In the United States, for instance, during the 1900s precipitation increased in frequency by about 10%, reflected mainly in the heavy and extreme daily precipitation events (Karl and Knight, 1998). Second, wet regions become wetter, or may experience changes in the intensity of precipitation – such as moving from a damp (wet) climate to one defined by a mixture of floods and droughts – changes which impact severely on the natural world or vegetation as, for instance, in desertification in the African Sahel, drought in parts of the Amazon rainforest, etc (Cox et al., 2000; Houghton et, al., 2001; Radford, 2002). The following developments predicted for the Amazon have begun to unravel:

- In 2005, parts of the Amazon (southern and western) began to experience the worst drought in a century. United States NASA scientists using data collected on the Amazon basin found that, beginning in 2005, more than 70 million hectares of pristine, old-growth forest experienced an extensive and severe drought (**The Independent** (UK), July 23, 2006).
- In 2010 the Amazon experienced yet another severe drought affecting approximately 3,000,000 km² of rainforest compared to 1,900,000 km² in 2005. Even though the total rainfall levels gradually recovered after the 2005 drought, the damage to the rainforest canopy persisted to the start of the 2010 drought (Saatchi et al., 2013). These droughts draw attention to the vulnerability of natural ecosystems to climate change (WWF, 2006).

Third, increased mean (average) atmospheric water-vapor has enabled storms to generate more precipitation. Since the 1930s or so precipitation amounts have changed in various regions of the world in different ways, increasing generally at the middle-to-higher latitudes, often in excess of 10%. This trend has occurred greatest near the cold regions for two reasons: one, global warming has been most felt in the polar regions, and warmer water tends to hold more water vapor; and, two, global warming has led to extensive glacier retreat and sea-ice melt, which would allow more evaporation from open water (Li et al., 2013)[3].

Fourth, significant increase in precipitation has occurred in some regions of the world at the same time it has decreased in some others. The West African Sahel, for example, has been plagued by drought in the last 40 years or so. Fifth, there are changes in regional climate, including greater warming over land, with most warming occurring at high northern latitudes, and least over the southern ocean and parts of the North Atlantic Ocean. This has resulted in the model prediction that snow cover area and sea ice extent will decrease and the Arctic 'largely ice-free' by the 2030s (IPCC, 2007; Wang, 2009). Sixth, systematic changes are occurring in ocean currents (Bryden et al., 2005; IPCC, 2012), to which we return in chapter 8. Seventh, there has occurred an increased intensity of storms linked to atmospheric fronts in the northern hemisphere in the past few decades.

6.7 Floods

As pointed above, a key problem arising from changes in the hydrologic cycle is increased incidence and intensity of flood events. Flood from a strict hydrological sense refers to a rise, usually brief, in the water level in a river or stream or lake to a peak from which the water level recedes at a slower rate (Mayhew, 2009, p. 184). The episodic behavior of a river that may qualify as a 'flood event' is when the flow of water in a river or stream constitutes a distinct progressive rise, culminating in a crest, together with the recession that follows the crest[4].

A key element in the above definition is that flood is a rise in the water level, usually brief, that results in its spilling over and out of its natural or artificial confines or reservoirs into land that is normally dry. Flood is thus a temporary rise of the water level, as in a river or lake or along a sea coast that spills over onto adjacent dry land. This does not, however, explain or provide a theory of flood. Such a theory is suggested in Mayhew (op.cit., p. 184): flood occurs when peak water discharge exceeds channel capacity, which may be caused naturally by intense precipitation, snow-melt and ice-melt, the rifting of barriers such as ice dams, the failure of artificial structures, deforestation and urbanization which reduces infiltration and interception and by land drainage and the straightening and embankment of rivers. Specific developments appear to illustrate this theory.

Extreme flooding in Central Europe in 2013 began after several days of heavy rain in late May to early June, affecting primarily southern and eastern Germany, Bohemia region of Czech Republic, and to a less extent Switzerland, Slovenia, Hungary, etc. The flood crest progressed down the Elbe and Danube drainage basins and tributaries leading to high water and flooding along their banks (European Floods, 2003). Dukiya and Gahlot (2013) explain that the floods in the Niger-Benue confluence come as a result of the monsoon rain occurring in July through September in West Africa. This monsoon rain produces 'a surge' that expands the flood plains of the Niger River to as high as 25000 km^2 but which shrink to as low as 4000 km in dry periods. Complementing the monsoon factor is a 'conflict between man and environment': specifically, land-use (especially urbanization) and land-cover have been poorly managed in the drainage basin and river courses of the Niger River, which give rise to silt-laden floodwater cascading down the Niger River and overflowing its banks.

Researchers at the University of Pennsylvania showed that sea level rise (SLR) was a factor in flooding during hurricane Sandy in New York in 2012 (Kemp and Benjamin, 2013). The Kemp-Benjamin study looked at seven major hurricanes in New York's history, starting way back in 1788 through 2012 (Sandy), would have been 22 inches (= 30.8mm) than it was.

In the tropical latitudes of Asia especially, stronger tropical storms and monsoon rains may increase the flood risk. Monsoon is traditionally defined as a seasonal reversing wind accompanied by corresponding changes in precipitation. Current usage conceives Monsoon as seasonal changes in atmospheric circulation and precipitation associated with the asymmetric heating of land and sea (Mayhew, op. cit., p. 332). Monsoon involves large-scale sea breezes which occur making the temperature on land significantly warmer than that of the ocean. These temperature imbalances arise because the land and oceans exhibit significant differences in capacity to absorb heat (with oceans exhibiting high capacity). Monsoons, or the most severe form of monsoons, usually occur in South Asia[5].

6.8 Conclusion

The hydrologic cycle is very sensitive to global warming and climate change; indeed, much of the effect of climate change tends to be felt through its effects on precipitation (rain and snow). The circulation of water between Earth's atmosphere, land, and oceans is facilitated through the warming up of global atmospheric temperatures – speeding up of the hydrologic cycle – with great implications for the frequency, intensity and duration of hydrologic events, namely, precipitation, floods, drought, etc. On the other hand, changes in hydrologic extremes – e.g. floods, monsoons, drought, etc – in response to global warming could be more significant than changes in hydrologic mean conditions such as mean precipitation.

End Notes

[1]   Water Impacts of Climate Change. EPA http://www.water.epa.gov/scitch/climatechange/ water-impacts-of-climate-changecfm.

[2]   See 'Modeling the Global Water Cycle'. http://www3.geosc.psu.edu/_dmb53/Daves STELLA/water/global%2010.

[3]   '…water provides the life-blood of the natural and human-created ecosystems that sustain us with essential goods and services' (Wright and Nebel 2004, p. 221).

[4]   http://www.kidlat.pagasa.dost.gov.ph/genmet/flood/def_nature.html

[5]   On India, for instance, see. http://en.wikipedia.org/wiki/climate-of-india. North India Floods 2013.

CHAPTER 7

SYMPTOMS OF CLIMATE CHANGE IN POLAR GLACIERS, ICE CAPS AND MOUNTAIN SNOW

7.1 Introduction

Glacier retreat, melting ice caps, and mountain snow loss provide one of the most visible and sensitive evidence of global warming and climate change. A glacier is a persistent body of dense ice exceeding a surface area of 0.1 km² constantly moving under its own gravity which forms where the accumulation of snow exceeds its ablation (melting and sublimation) over many years, often running into centuries. Glaciers form only on land surfaces and are distinct from the much thinner sea ice and lake ice that form on water bodies. Glacier ice is contained within vast ice sheets in the polar region (Antarctica and Arctic), but glaciers may also be found in mountain tops on all the continents, and on a few high-latitude oceanic islands. Within the tropical and sub-tropical latitudes, between 35° north and 35° south, mountain glaciers are found only in the Himalayas, Andes, Mt. Kenya[1] and Kilimanjaro in East Africa, and other mountains in Mexico, New Guinea and on Zard Kuh in Iran.

Glaciers provide the largest reservoir of freshwater on Earth, supporting some 33% of planet Earth's population; in the temperate, alpine and seasonal polar climates, many glaciers store water as ice during winter or colder seasons, releasing it in the form of melt-water during the warmer summer weather thus creating a water source vital for plant, animals and human use when other water reservoirs are either lacking or scant. Because glacial mass is affected by changes in precipitation, mean temperature, and cloud cover – indeed, elements of long-term climate change – glacial mass changes have been identified to belong among the most sensitive indicators of climate change – a point made earlier – and are major sources of variations in sea level, to which we return in chapter 9.

Global warming and climate change causes variations in both temperature and precipitation (snowfall), which result in changes in glacier mass balance. Glacial balance refers to the difference between accumulation and ablation. A glacier exhibiting negative mass balance shrinks in its mass or retreats; as well, a glacier with sustained positive mass balance expands in its mass or adds to its spatial extent and will advance to reestablish equilibrium mass balance. Given current global warming trends, nearly all glaciers have lost their mass balance (Gardner and 16 others, 2013). Glacier sizes expand and contract determined by both natural variability and external forcing; variability in temperature, precipitation and englacial and subglacial hydrology; the process of water flow in and under glaciers determine the development of any glacier during any particular season.

7.2 Glacier and Sea Ice Retreat

Glacier retreat has been on since 1850, affecting the availability of fresh water for irrigation, domestic use, etc., and, in the longer term, sea level. A global glacier inventory has been compiled since the 1970s. The technologies for this inventory compilation have evolved from use of aerial photographs and maps to deployment of satellite images. On the other hand, the inventory compilation has focused on 100,000 glaciers covering a total area of approximately 240,000 km². Estimates, though preliminary, reveal ice cover amounting to 445,000 km². Available evidence provided by the world Glacier Monitoring Service (GMS) shows that glaciers, globally, have been retreating significantly over the decades, with the pace accelerating since the 1980s due largely to global warming.

Further evidence for rapid climate change over the last three to four decades comes both in the extent and thickness of glacial sea ice referring to frozen seawater that floats on ocean surface[2]. When sea water freezes as temperature falls, it floats on ocean surface. Arctic sea ice, in contrast, is 'seasonal ice' – that is, it melts away and reforms annually.

7.3 Glacier and Sea Ice Retreat in Selected Regions of the World

We now highlight glacier retreat in different regions of the world – selectively, of course.

- **In Europe** we focus on the Alps and Pyrenees. Though the glaciers of the Alps have attracted the attention of researchers than in other European mountain ranges, research shows that in most of Europe glacier retreat is occurring in a sustained manner. In 2010, ninety-five (95) Swiss glaciers were studied, 86 were found to have retreated from their terminal points in 2009, six (6) were found to have made no retreat, and three (3) had advanced[3]. Other researchers find glaciers across the Alps to be retreating faster than in previous decades – this is true of the Swiss, French and Italian Alps. For the Pyrenees as a whole, 50-60% of the glaciers has retreated: for instance, important losses have occurred in the extent and volume of the glaciers of the Maladeta massif during 1981-2005.

- **In Asia** the most prominent mountain glaciers are those of the Himalaya and Tibetan Plateau. Glaciers in the Mount Everest region of the Himalaya are all in retreat. The retreat of the Gangotri Glacier, one of the largest glaciers in the Himalaya, has been going on since 1780, accelerating after 1971 (cited in Pidwiny, 2012). The Tibetan Plateau is known to contain the world's third largest store of ice; the glaciers are retreating at a higher rate than in any other part of the globe. Citing various research results on Earth's 'Third Pole', **The Economist** (11th May, 2013 p. 78) concludes that "Tibet's permafrost has been disintegrating rapidly for the past two decades". Though the amount of ice on the Tibetan Plateau and its surrounding mountains, such as the Himalaya, Karakoram and Pamirs, is a lot smaller than that at the polar region, it is still huge. The area's 46,000 glaciers cover 100,000 km^2 – about 65% of the area of Greenland ice cap; another 1.7% km^2 is permafrost, which can be up to 130 meters deep – equivalent to 7% of the Arctic permafrost. Unlike the ice at the polar region, the fate of the ice on the Tibetan Plateau affects millions of people directly: about 1.5 billion people in 12 countries live in the basins of the rivers of Asia's water tower (ibid).

- **In North America** the glaciers are primarily located along the spine of the Rockies in the United States and Canada, and the Pacific Coast Ranges extending from northern California to Alaska. Virtually all glaciers in this region are in retreat, accelerating since the 1980s; some have disappeared completely. The North Cascades glaciers illustrate the North American experience; here, all 47 monitored glaciers are retreating and four – Spider Glacier, Lewis Glacier, Milk Glacier, and David Glacier – have disappeared completely since 1985. As of 2005, 65% of the North Cascades glaciers monitored are in disequilibrium and will not survive the continuation of the present climate regime[4].

- **Sub-Saharan Africa** lies in the tropical and sub-tropical climate regimes, where glaciers covers are restricted, confined to Kilimanjaro, Mount Kenya and the Ruwenzori Ranges. Apart from earlier processes which saw glacier cover on the summit of Kilimanjaro retreat by 75% and the volume of glacier ice decline to 80% less than it was in the early 1900s, in the one and half decades, 1984-1998, one section of the glacier had receded 300 meters, caused by a combination of increased sublimation (loss of snow caused by sunshine acting directly on the upper layers of the snow) and decrease in snowfall. Mount Kenya glaciers have lost at least 45% of their ice mass since the mid-1900s. The United States Geological Survey reports that by 1986 only eleven of eighteen glaciers atop Mount Kenya remained; the total area covered by glaciers was 1.6 km^2 in 1900, and by 2000 only some 25%, or 0.4 km^2 remained[5]. In the Rumenzori Ranges located largely in DR Congo photographic evidence indicates that during the period 1955-1990, glaciers receded about 40%.

- **South America.** A 1992-1998 observation of Chacaltaya Glacier in Bolivia and Antisana Glacier in Ecuador indicated that between 0.6 and 1.9 meters of ice was lost per year in each glacier; Chacaltaya Glacier sustained a loss of 67% of its volume and 40% of its thickness over the same period. Research indicates, also, that since the mid 1980s, the rate of retreat for both glaciers has accelerated. In Patagonia on the southern tip of the South American Continent, the large ice caps have retreated 1 km since the early 1990s increasing to 10 km since the late 1990s – these rates of glacier retreat surpass those in other regions of the world.

- **Oceania.** Developments on the ice caps of the equatorial mountains of New Guinea illustrate the experience of this region. The ice cap of 470 meters Wilhelmina Peaks, which reached below 4400 metres in 1909, disappeared between 1939 and 1963, the Mandala Juliana ice cap in the 1990s, and the Idenburg Glacier in 2003. Currently, only the remnants of the once continuous ice cap of Mount Carstenz are left.

- **Polar Regions.** About 99% of the freshwater ice of the world is in the great ice sheets of polar and sub-polar Antarctica and Greenland. The polar ice sheets are continent-size in scale, and 3 km or more in thickness; like rivers flowing from an enormous lake, numerous outlet glaciers channel ice from the margins of the polar ice sheet to the ocean. In Iceland, the northern Atlantic island nation, most of the glaciers retreated rapidly during the warm period of the 1930s up to the 1960s; as a result of the rapid global warming that resumed in the 1980s onwards, most Icelandic glaciers began to retreat after 1990. In Canada, the Arctic islands, which contain the largest area and volume of land ice on Earth outside of the Greenland and Antarctica ice sheets, have experienced a sharp increase in mass loss in response to global warming (reflected in warmer summer temperatures), losing 92 Gt per year between 2007 and 2009. In Antarctica most of the world's freshwater is stored in the great ice sheets that cover that continent, most of which has melted.

- **Sea Ice Loss:** Further evidence for rapid climate change over the last 3-4 decades comes both in the extent and thickness of global sea ice. Sea ice is frozen seawater that floats on ocean surface. When sea water freezes as global temperatures fall, it floats on ocean surface. Arctic sea ice persists year after year; Antarctica sea ice, in contrast, is 'seasonal ice' – that is, it melts away and reforms annually. The extent and thickness of sea ice, and the fraction of open water within the ice park can respond very rapidly profoundly to changes in weather and climate.

7.4 Causes and Predicted Impacts of Ice Melting

As already stated, scientific explanation of the 'basic cause' of polar ice melting/warming is, as elsewhere, the result of an increase in heat-trapping GHGs: because of a rise in solar ultraviolet (UV) radiation (as Earth is shedding less solar heat), Earth is warming – a physical effect predicted in 1896 by Swedish scientist Svante Arrhenius. Scientists predicted that changes in regional climate, including greater warming over land, with most warming at high northern latitudes and least warming over the Southern Ocean and parts of the North Atlantic Ocean, will result in snow cover area and sea ice extent decreasing and the Arctic being "largely ice-free in September 2037" (IPCC, 2007). Systematic changes are also detected in rainfall patterns and in ocean currents. This is how **The Economist** magazine dramatizes the melting of the Arctic North:

"A heat map of the world, color-coded for temperature change, shows the Arctic in sizzling maroon. Since 1951, it has warmed roughly twice as much as the global average. In that period the temperature in Greenland has gone up by 1.5°C, compared with around 0.7°C globally. This disparity is expected to continue. A 2°C increase in global temperatures – which appears inevitable as greenhouse gas emissions soar – would mean Arctic warming of 3 – 6°C. Almost all Arctic glaciers have receded. The area of Arctic land covered by snow in early summer has shrunk by almost a fifth since 1966. But it is the Arctic Ocean that is almost changed. In the 1970s, 80s and 90s the minimum extent of polar pack ice fell by around 8% per decade. Then, in 2007, the sea ice crashed, melting to a minimum of 4.3 sq km …, close to half of the average for the 1960s and 24% below the previous minimum, set in 2005. This left the north-west passage, a sea lane through Canada's … Arctic Archipelago, ice-free for the first time in memory" (The Economist, 16th June, 2012, pp. 3 – 4).

The melting of polar ice caps is predicted to release methane gas trapped in the frozen ice peats of the tundra of northern Canada, Eurasia and northern Europe. As global temperatures rise, the frozen tundra is bound to thaw, releasing trapped methane. As the latter is a powerful GHG, this could accelerate the pace of global warming. Other predicted impacts of glacier melting include sea level rise (SLR), alterations in ocean currents and thermohaline circulation, to which we return in chapters 8 and 9, respectively.

7.5 Conclusion

Glaciers provide the most sensitive indicators of global warming and climate change, constituting one of the most visually compelling examples of recent climate change. Globally, glaciers are showing evidence of continuous melting and retreat – a process shown to follow increases of atmosphere GHGs. On the other hand, the melting of polar ice is predicted to release methane gas trapped in the frozen ice peats of the tundra, which could accelerate the pace of global warming.

End Notes

[1]   Mount Kenya lies across the equator, 140 km north of Nairobi; the mountain is 5200 metres high, with permanent snow and ice, which is now threatened by climate change.

[2]   http://www.inside.org/cryosphere/sotc/seq_ice.html

[3]   Swiss Glacier Monitoring Network 2011.

[4]   See P.M. Pelto, North Cascade Glacier Climate Project (Recent Global Retreat Overview): http://nichols.edu/DEPARTMENTS/glacier_retreat.htm.

[5]   http://www.en-wikipedia.org/wiki/Retreat_of_glaciers_since_1850.

CHAPTER 8

SYMPTOMS OF CLIMATE CHANGE IN THE OCEANS

8.1 Introduction

Oceans are defined as continuous bodies of water encircling planet Earth. The world's oceans are demarcated into five principal bodies of water with relatively free interchange among them: Pacific, Atlantic, Indian, Arctic and Southern, with the Arctic and Southern Oceans sometimes subsumed under the Pacific, Atlantic and Indian Oceans. The oceans constitute the largest reservoir of water on Earth, supplying most (97:4%) of the water for the hydrologic cycle; as well, they are the main source of heat entering the atmosphere (Schlesinger and Bernhardt, 2013). For these reasons, developments within the ocean system have profound implications for global warming and climate change.

A vital point to note, however, is the two-way causal relationship between the oceans and climate change: climate change affects the oceans and the oceans, in turn, affect the climate system. Due to climate change, as the oceans get warm this too has effect on the ocean floor. Because of GHGs, such as CO_2, this will have an effect on the bicarbonate buffer of the ocean – that is, the concentration of bicarbonate ions that keeps the ocean's acidity balance between pH[1] ranges of 7.5-8.4, to which we return below.

Oceans occupy 70% of Earth's surface and absorb over 90% of the temperature due to global warming – thus suggesting that, but for the oceans, global temperatures would be a lot warmer than they are presently. Despite ocean waters' high heat capacity, this heat that is radiated into the oceans by GHGs in the atmosphere causes water molecules to expand, which creates more water volumes in the oceans leading to sea level rise (SLR), to which we return in chapter 9. Apart from thermal expansion, melting glaciers and polar ice sheets – such as the one on Greenland – lead to huge volumes of water pouring into the oceans, adding to SLR. Lastly, through the movement of ocean currents, the oceans play the highly important role as conveyors of heat: enormous quantities of heat are conveyed laterally through water, from the hot tropics to the temperate latitudes – e.g. the Gulf Stream, which keeps Western Europe warm, to which we return.

8.2 Global Warming and Ocean Ecosystems

As suggested above, most of the warming caused by climate change is going into the oceans, where a lot of ecosystem changes are also occurring. Scientific studies reveal the following facts regarding where global warming is going: ocean 93:4%; atmosphere 2.3%; continents 2.1%; glaciers and ice caps 0.9%; Arctic sea ice 0.8%; Greenland ice sheet 0.2%; Antarctica ice sheet 0.2% (Cook, 2011).

Rapidly rising GHG concentrations are driving ocean systems towards conditions not seen for millions of years, with an associated risk of fundamental and irreversible ecological transformation (Cook, op. cit.). Changes in biological function in the ocean caused by anthropogenic climate change go far beyond death, extinctions and habitat loss: fundamental processes are being altered, community assemblages are being reorganized and ecological surprises are likely (Hoegh-Guldberge et al., 2011).

8.2.1 Ocean Acidification

A key symptom of climate change in the oceans is acidification: the effects of GHG emissions, in particular CO_2, on the oceans may well be significant. As explained by United States National Oceanic and Atmospheric Administration (NOAA), the basic chemistry of ocean acidification has three concepts:

- More CO_2 in Earth's atmosphere means more CO_2 in the oceans.
- Atmospheric CO_2 is dissolved in the ocean, which becomes more acidic, producing carbonic acid (a weak acid), which changes the seawater chemistry.
- Resulting acidity in the chemistry of the ocean disrupts the ability of plants and animals in the seas to make shells and skeletons of calcium carbonate meanwhile dissolving shells already formed.

Scientific research reveals that oceans absorb some of the excess CO_2 released by anthropogenic processes, which helps to keep planet Earth cooler than it would have been otherwise – i.e. had the CO_2 remained in the atmosphere. It is this additional excess CO_2 being absorbed by the oceans that results in acidification of the oceans (as explained above). It is explained that ocean water is 30% more acidic now than in pre-industrial times, depleting carbonate ions – the building blocks for many marine organisms[2].

In addition, concentrations of carbonate ions are now observed to be lower than at any time during the last 800,000 years, which damages ocean biological diversity and ecosystem functioning[3]. Because current change in CO_2 concentrations tends to be rapid, this gives many marine organisms too little time to adapt to changes in marine conditions. Other related problems include more acidic dead zones (areas where there is too little oxygen in the sea to support life) and decline of important coastal plants and forests – e.g. mangrove forests that play an important role in carbon absorption through photosynthesis[4].

8.2.2 Coral Reef and Climate Change

Around the globe coral reefs are dying off due to global warming and climate change. A good example is the effect of global warming on coral reefs and mangroves. The El Niño event of 1997-1998 often cited as a consequence of global warming[5], brought record-high sea-surface temperatures to many tropical coasts; extensive coral bleaching (wherein coral animals lose their symbiotic algae) resulted in the death of some 15% of global reef corals population during 1998. Wright and Nebel (2004, p. 306) citing results from studies by marine scientists observe that repeated EL Niño episodes could permanently wipe out coral reefs over vast areas of the shallow tropical oceans, which would result in an enormous biodiversity and economic value loss[6].

El Niño refers to a disruption of the equatorial Pacific, East-West Walker Circulatory Cell (one of the world's most prominent and important atmospheric systems, closely linked to the mean-state of the equatorial Pacific Ocean). The gradient between the low pressure of the warm, western tropical Pacific and the high pressure of the coral, eastern tropical Pacific decreases, weakens the easterly trade winds, and allows warm surface water to move eastwards.

Coral reefs are offshore ridges, mainly of calcium carbonate, formed by the secretions of small marine animals. Corals are found in shallow waters over 21°C and require abundant solar energy (sunlight), so that the water must be mud free, and shallow. Fringing reefs lie close to the shore; barrier reefs lie further from the shore, in deeper water. Coral reefs are known to be the most biodiverse marine ecosystems, estimated to harbour nearly one million species globally (Mayhew, 2009, p. 105). With rapid pace of anthropogenic GHG emissions leading to ocean warming, acidification, and sea level rise (SLR), the health of coral reefs is declining at the global scale; on the other hand, due to overfishing, nutrient enrichment, and coral diseases, coral reefs are being damaged at the local scale (Huegh-Guldberg, 1999).

8.3 Ocean Currents and Climate Change

The currents in the world's oceans originate in varying temperatures associated with the changing latitudes of planet Earth; given that the atmosphere is warmed most near the equator, the hot air near Earth's surface is heated, causing it to rise and suck in cooler air to take its pace, which creates so-called circulation cells. This ultimately causes the air to be significantly colder near the polar region than at the equatorial latitudes. It is the wind patterns associated with these circulation cells that drive surface ocean currents; they end up pushing the surface water to the higher latitudes where the air is now cold. It is through the sinking, this up-swelling that occurs in the lower latitudes and the driving force of the winds on surface ocean water that the ocean currents all combine to circulate water all throughout the world's oceans.

8.3.1 The Atlantic Thermohaline Circulation

The thermohaline circulation (THC) pattern dominates ocean currents. Because of its innate heat capacity and its role as a conveyor of heat, the ocean has a strategic role in climate and climate change. The adjective thermohaline derives from **thermos** – referring to, or derived from, temperature – and **haline** referring to salt content or the degree to which water contains dissolved salts, usually expressed in parts per thousand (ppt), factor which combine to determine the density of sea water. The THC is sometimes called the ocean conveyor belt, the great ocean conveyor, or the global conveyor belt.

The THC phenomenon acts as a giant complex conveyor belt moving ocean water masses from the surface to deep oceans and back again; according to the density of the masses (Wright and Nebel, 2004, p. 516). Wind-propelled surface currents such as the Gulf Stream travel pole-wards from the equatorial Atlantic Ocean, cooling as they encounter otherwise cooled Arctic air currents, eventually sinking at high latitudes (forming North Atlantic Deep Water, NADW). Wright and Nebel (op. cit.) describe the working of the THC in this excerpt:

"A key area is the high-latitude North Atlantic, where salt water from the Gulf Stream moves northward on the surface and is cooled by Arctic air currents. Cooling increases the density of the water, which then sink to depths of up to 4,000 on the North Atlantic Deep Water (NADW). This deep water spreads southward through the Atlantic to the southern tip of Africa, where it is joined by cold Antarctic waters, to spread northward with the Indian and Pacific Oceans as deep currents. The currents gradually slow down and warm, becoming less dense and welling up to the surface, where they are further warmed and begins a movement of surface waters hack again toward the North Atlantic. This movement transfers enormous quantities of heat toward Europe, providing a climate that is much warmer than the high latitudes there would suggest. This circulation pattern operates over a period of about 1,000 years for one complete cycle is vital to the maintenance of current climatic conditions" (p. 516; Figure 21.8).

The THC plays a strategic role in supplying heat to the polar latitudes, and thus in influencing the quantity of sea ice in the latter, although more heat transport outside the tropics are effected through the atmosphere than in the ocean. Changes in the THC are hypothesized to influence Earth's radiation budget significantly. The term Earth's radiation budget refers to the amount of incoming energy (the total rate at which the energy enters Earth's atmosphere) and outgoing energy (the total rate at which energy is spent). Insofar as the THC determines the rate at which deep waters are exposed to the ocean surface, it is also probably a key factor determining the atmospheric concentration of CO_2. As pointed out earlier, the THC transfers enormous quantities of heat towards Europe "providing a climate that is warmer than the high latitudes there would suggest" (Mayhew, op. cit., p. 516).

8.3.2 Postulated Shutdown or Slowdown of the THC

This is being hypothesized as the effect of global warming and climate change. Specifically, global warming resulting in thawing of Arctic ice sheets and retreat of glaciers could add enormous quantities of fresh water to the North Atlantic Ocean region, resulting in salinity changes that could shut down the THC, potentially triggering localized cooling in the North Atlantic and leading to cooling, or lesser warming, in that region, especially in the British Isles and Nordic countries. However, THC shutdown could have other major environmental consequences apart from cooling of northern Europe – such as increase in flooding and storms, collapse of plankton stocks, warming of rainfall changes in the tropical latitudes or Alaska and Antarctica, etc.

It is not quite clear how the THC shutdown or slowdown could happen though; or how its effects could come about. There is some evidence, however, that this conveyor belt has been disrupted in the past, which changed climate patterns drastically; one mechanism possibly affecting this is the appearance of unusual quantities of fresh water in the north Atlantic, which lowers the density of the water and thereby preventing much of the sinking normally taking place in the North Atlantic region. Wright and Nebel (op. cit.) explain that North Atlantic marine sediments show evidence of the period invasion (six times in the last 75,000 years) of icebergs from the polar ice cap that supplied the huge amounts of fresh water as they melted – called Heinrich event[7].

8.4 Conclusion

The effect of climate change in the oceans has been found to be a two-way causal relationship. Climate change affects the oceans (through increased GHGs emissions such as CO_2, which influence the bicarbonate buffer of the oceans). Due to climate change, as the oceans get warmer, this too has effect on the ocean floors – addition of GHGs, methane especially, to the environment, which in turn accelerates global warming. The ocean, because of its innate capacity and role as a conveyor of heat, has a strategic role in climate and climate change – e.g. the thermohaline circulation (THC) acts as a giant complex conveyor belt moving ocean water masses from the surface to deep oceans and back again – thus, from the warmer equatorial Atlantic Ocean to the cooler high latitudes (North Atlantic). The THC plays a strategic role in supplying heat to the polar latitudes, and thus in influencing the quantity of sea ice in the latter. Insofar as the THC determines the rate at which deep waters are exposed to the ocean surface, it is also probably a significant contributor determining the atmospheric concentration of CO_2. On the other hand, global warming resulting in thawing of Arctic ice sheets and retreat of glaciers has been postulated to add enormous quantities of freshwater to the North Atlantic Ocean region, resulting in salinity changes that could shut down the THC, leading to cooling, or lesser warming, in the north Atlantic region.

End Notes

[1]   pH stands for 'potential hydrogen'; it is a scale introduced by Søren Sørenson in 1902 as a scientific common measurement for expressing the acidity or alkalinity of a solution; The lower the number, the more acidic the solution with 7.0 as the border between acidity and alkalinity (See Oxford Dictionary of Science (2005), p. 628). Ocean acidification is the process of decrease in the pH of ocean water due to uptake of anthropogenic CO_2.

[2]   Global Biodiversity 2010.

[3]   Ibid, p. 58

[4]   Robert Diaz, Virginia Institute of Marine Research (http://www.youtube.com/watch: v = OJEWPO M 115 C.

[5]   See also Latif and Keenlyside (2009).

[6]   See Shah (2014).

[7]   See http://en.wikipedia.org/wiki/Heinrich_event.

CHAPTER 9

CLIMATE CHANGE AND SEA LEVEL RISE

9.1 Introduction

Sea level rise (SLR) is a specific aspect of the process of global sea level change; the latter is a phenomenon that has taken place continuously over the millennia caused by a combination of several factors in the global environment that operate on a great range of time scales: from hours (tide[1]) to millions of years (ocean level changes due to tectonics and sedimentation). On the time scale from decades to centuries, some of the most significant factors influencing the average levels of the sea originate in climate and climate change processes (see below).

Described as an 'invisible threat' that emerges gradually, in contrast to the much more easily perceptible effects of climate change such as heat waves, flooding, tornadoes, etc., sea level rise remains, arguably, the most intensely studied symptom of climate change. IPCC models project that during the course of the current century (the 2000s), SLR will accelerate but these projections discount uncertainties in climate-carbon cycle feedback, and do not include the full effects of changes in ice sheet flows. Other scientific sources conclude that sea levels rose at an average rate of 1.7 ± 0.5 mm yr^{-1} during the 1900s (20th century). They estimate further future sea level rise of between 0.18 and 0.59m for the 2000s (21st century) as climate change proceeds inexorably (Mayhew, 2009, pp. 445-6).

9.2 Factors Contributing to Sea Level Rise

There are two broad contributing factors in SLR. The first is thermal expansion: as ocean water warms, it expands – a physical law of thermal expansion in liquids, which holds that when a liquid (e.g. water) expands, its volume expands (illustrated in the sea rise phenomenon). Ocean water reacts to global warming slowly though, but persistently. The second is from contribution of land-based ice due to increased melting of polar glaciers and ice sheets. Polar exploration using satellite measurements provides evidence of how Earth's ice sheets are changing: as global temperatures have risen, so have rates of snowfall, ice melting and glacier flow. Data from satellite measurements reveal that Antarctica and Greenland are each losing ice and glacier mass overall estimated to average 125 gigatons per year of ice – enough to raise sea level by 0.35 millimeters per year. Thus, Antarctica and Greenland combined contribute some 12% to the present rate of SLR of 3.0 mm per year. Much of the loss from the polar ice stocks is found to be a result of the flow of ice stocks to the ocean from ice streams and glaciers, a process which has accelerated in recent decades triggered by global warming effects in the polar region. These are processes that are predicted to continue over the 21st century (the 2000s) and would rapidly counteract the snowfall gains predicted by climate science models.

About 20,000 years ago, during the last glacial maximum when the average global temperature averaged 4-7°C colder, global sea level was reported to be 120 meters lower than its current level; in contrast, much earlier, 3,000,000 years ago during the Pliocene[2], Earth's climate was 2-3°C warmer and the seas were 25–35 meters higher than currently. Aside from variability over time, sea level is not spatially even nor is change in sea level uniform, as some areas witness levels rising faster than others. Further, despite the global trend in SLR, in some areas the mean sea level (MSL) has been observed to be currently falling[3].

9.3 Sensitivity to Sea Level Rise

For many atoll island states such as Maldives, Seychelles, etc – most of which are located in the Indian and Pacific Oceans and are known to be sensitive to fluctuations in relative sea level – SLR is a threat to their very existence. But these countries have low adaptive capacity[4] to sea-level rise, heavily dependent, as they are, on fragile environmental goods and services, such as coral reefs and fisheries. Generally, SLR in atoll island states is known to contribute to saltwater intrusion, long-term loss of land, and damages to ecosystem, agriculture and livelihoods. Table 9.1 contains a list of thirty-eight small island states (SIS) threatened by SLR.

Table 9.1 List of Small Island States (SIS) (United Nations Members)

1.	Antigua and Barbuda	20.	Federated States of Micronesia
2.	Bahamas	21.	Mauritius
3.	Bahrain	22.	Naura
4.	Barhados	23.	Palau
5.	Belize	24.	Papua New Guinea
6.	Cape Verde	25.	Samoa
7.	Comoros	26.	São Tomé and Principe
8.	Cuba	27.	Singapore

9.	Dominica	28.	St. Kitts and Nevis
10.	Dominican Republic	29.	St. Lucia
11.	Fiji	30.	St. Vincent and the Grenadines
12.	Grenada	31.	Seychelles
13.	Guinea Bissau	32.	Solomon Islands
14.	Guyana	33.	Suriname
15.	Haiti	34.	Timor-Lesté
16.	Jamaica	35.	Tonga
17.	Kiribati	36.	Trinidad and Tobago
18.	Maldives	37.	Tuvalu
19.	Marshall Islands	38.	Vanacita

**Source: http://www.un.org/special_rep/ohrlls/sid/list.htm
Retrieved 20th September 2013.**

Similarly, low-lying deltas – e.g. the densely populated Nile delta and Ganges and Brahmaputra – are threatened by rising sea-levels. Calculations by climate scientists estimate that within the next 8-9 decades local sea level in the Nile and Bangladesh deltas, respectively, could be as much as 3.3 to 4.5 meters higher than at present, which could lead, at the higher calculated ranges, to Egypt and Bangladesh losing 26-34% of their currently habitable land. In Asia particularly millions of people live in low-lying amas in the path of typhoons of expected increasing frequency and intensity or otherwise at greater risk of ocean or river flooding. Citing IPCC sources, Todaro and Smith (2009, p. 494) identify as at risk socalled Asian megadeltas: the Huanghel Yellow (China); Changjiang/Yangtze (China); Pearl (China); Red (Vietnam); Mekong (Indo-China); Chao Phraya (Thailand); Irrawady (Burma); Ganges-Brahmaputra (India and Bangladesh); and Indus (Pakistan) river systems. We now proceed to highlight the degree of sensitivity of SLR by some countries and regions of the world.

- **Bangladesh**, a South Asian nation and among the world's poorest developing countries, is facing actual and potential threat by SLR. The Bangladeshi population is already severely affected by storm surges, with catastrophic events in the past causing damages up to 100 km inland. These catastrophic damages are expected to rise sharply as SLR accelerates with global warming: estimates by UNEP have projected that by the year 2030 some 16% (22,000 km^2) of the land area, and 15% (34 million) of Bangladeshi population could be threatened by SLR. Bangladesh's turbulent weather events (floods, hurricanes, etc.), particularly in its low-lying Ganges-Brahmaputra delta, illustrate the connections between climate change and SLR and the vulnerability of coastal, low-lying alluvial regions to extreme weather events. Bangladesh is the world's largest delta of the Ganges-Brahmaputra-Meghna river systems. Floods, droughts, cyclones etc. are frequent natural hazards with large visible influence on the human populations and agricultural productions (e.g. Huq et. al., 1999). The perennial plight of Bangladesh and other low-lying coastal nations of the world prompted UNEP to focus attention on the longer-term issue of possible future of SLR and its socioeconomic consequences.

- **Maldives** is situated south of India's Lakshadweep islands, and about 600 km south-west of Sri Lanka. Twenty-six corallines are spread across the top of an under-sea volcanic ridge for 960 km, running from south to north; some of the larger atolls are 50 km long and 30 km wide or just about 1500 km^2. The 1,190 islands that constitute the rest of Maldives are no larger than 50km (The Economist, 19th December, 2006, p. 97). Maldives is only about 12 meters above sea level at its highest point; like all other atoll nations, SLR is threatening the very existence of Maldives (The Economist, 19th December, 2006; Astaiza, 2012). Maldives, the flattest country on Earth, is likely to experience worsening environmental stresses from SLR such as periodic flooding from storm surge. The island is projected to experience SLR on the order of 0.5 meter and to lose some 77% of its land area around the year 2100; if SLR is, instead, 1 meter, the island could be almost inundated by about 2085 (Woodworth, 2005; Anthoff et. al., 2008).

- **Kiribati** located in the central tropical Pacific Ocean lies about half way between Hawaii and Australia, and is made up of 32 low-lying atolls and one raised island Banaba. The rest of the land in Kiribati consists of the sand and reef rock islets of atolls or coral islands rising only one or two meters above sea level. Two small uninhabited Kiribati islets, Tebua Tarawa and Abanuea, disappeared under water in 1999. The IPCC predicts that sea levels will rise by about 50 cm by 2100 due to climate change and a further rise is bound to occur, which suggests the likelihood that within a century Kiribati's arable land will become subject to increased soil salination and will be largely under water (see The New York Times, 2016, July 2).

- **Seychelles** is a 115-island country spanning an archipelago in the western Indian Ocean, some 1500 km off the African Indian Ocean Coast, northeast of the island of Madagascar. Seychelles is ranked 9th among the island nations threatened by climate change. About half of Seychelles islands are granite in origin, with narrow-coastal strips and central ranges of hills rising to 900 m; the other half are coral atolls. Rising sea surface level and changes in ocean chemistry threaten to damage the coral reef system and mangrove forests which which are a natural productive barrier for the coastal plateau (where 90% of the population lives). Both shield the islands against soil erosion and serve as breeding grounds and natural habitats for fish (Seychelles News Agency, 2014).

- **Torres Strait Islands** are constituted by a group of at least 274 small islands lying in Torres Strait, the waterway separating far northern continental Australia's Cape York Peninsula and the island of New Guinea. The islands are distributed across an area of some 48,000 km². The islands are threatened by rising sea levels, especially those islands rising less than one metre above sea level. Posing the greatest danger are storm surge and high tides. Sea level is projected to rise 0.8 meters over the next 100 years. The United Nations declared 100 residents of Tegua, part of the Torres Strait Islands, the first climate change refugees in 2005.

- **Solomon Islands** are located east of Papua New-Guinea, and have a population of a little over 500,000, with 992 islands constituting the island chain. Satellite data indicate SLR near the Solomon Islands of about 8 mm per year since 1993 – much larger than the global average of 2.8-3.6 mm per year, which may be partly related to natural fluctuations taking place year to year or decade to decade caused by phenomena such as the EL Niño-Southern Oscillation. SLR is expected to persist in the Solomon Islands, based on the IPCC emissions scenarios: low, medium, and high, for time periods around 2030, 2055, and 2090. By 2030, based on a high emission scenario, SLR is projected to be in the range of 4-15 cm[5] (see IPCC Fifth Assessment Report, 2014).

- **Micronesia**, made up of 607 mountains islands and low-lying coral atolls located 'three-quarter of the way between Hawaii and Indonesia', is being eroded away by rising sea levels: 'a small one meter rise would make the island uninhabitable' Micronesia may disappear entirely – and quite possibly within the life-time of today's teenagers' (see Astaiza, 2012).

- **Palau** consists of eight principal islands and more than 250 smaller ones, located some 750km southeast of the Philippines and north of New-Guinea. Its coasts are being eroded, and its farmlands tainted by seawater, and its valuable reefs threatened. Sea level rose 120 mm in the 1900s and the United Nations estimates they could rise by that much this century (2000s), and may be even more if the polar ice melt speeds up.

- **The Carteret Islands (also known as Carteret Atoll on Kilinailau Islands/Atoll)** are Papau New-Guinea islands located 86 km north-east of Bougainville in the South Pacific. The atoll has a maximum elevation of 1.5m above sea level. Like many atolls throughout the Pacific Ocean, the Carteret Atoll is very low-lying and its main constituent, the coral, needs to be covered in water most of the time. It was widely reported in November 2005 that the Carteret Islands have progressively become uninhabitable, with an estimate of their complete submersion by 2015, caused by SLR associated with global warming. Others are suggesting that the Carteret Islands are sinking, not the sea rising, caused by tectonics[6].

- **Tuvalu** consists of six true atolls and three reef islands and has its highest point less than 5 meters above sea level, but most of it is less than a meter above sea level. Located midway between Hawaii and Australia, Tuvalu is the third-least populous country on Earth.

Because of the low elevation (highest elevation is 4.6m above sea level), which gives Tuvalu the second-lowest maximum elevation of any country (after the Maldives), the islands that constitute Tuvalu are threatened by current and future SLR.

9.4 Conclusion

Among the most certain effects of climate change is rising sea levels caused both by thermal expansion of ocean water and by partial melting of the vast sheets of ice in the polar region. Already the mean global sea level has risen by between 10 and 25 centimeters by the beginning of the 2000s (21st century); the IPCC forecasts an additional rise between 8 and 88 centimeters by 2100. Small island states – e.g. Maldives – stand threatened in their very existence by a rising ocean; as well, low-lying alluvial regions such as the heavily populated delta of the Ganges and Brahmaputra Rivers. Many of the world's most important cities are built on coastlines. Such cities can only avoid being destroyed by rising sea levels by building expensive protective infrastructures. Finally, rising sea levels threaten the existence of a variety of biologically rich economically important ecosystem such as mangrove tropical forests, coral reefs, wetlands, etc.

End Notes

[1]   Tides result from the regular rise and fall of the water level in Earth's ocean result from the gravitational pull of the moon and sun on Earth (which also affect land masses, but the response of the water is greater and much more visible). The forces and processes are complex; but see Mayhew, 2009, p. 502; **Oxford Dictionary of Science** 2005, pp. 818 – 9).

[2]   Pliocene Epoch refers to the period in the geological time scale extending from 5.332 million to 2.588 million years before present (BP). It was a period of global cooling after warmer Miocene Epoch (23.03 to 5.3 million years ago), when tectonics contributed to formation of the mountain ranges – e.g. the Andes of South America, the rifting in East Africa, etc. (http://www.ucmp.berkeley.edu/tertiary/miocene.php).

[3]   http://www.wunderground.com/climate/SeaLevelRise.asp?MR=I.

[4]   Adaptative capacity in SLR context can be approached in three ways: by decreasing the probability of incidence of SLR by construction of flood barriers along coastlines; or by providing facilities that enhance communities' or individuals' ability to cope with SLR, etc. Adaptation capacity differs significantly both across countries and societies, and within the latter among households, determined by differential resource endowments in finance, infrastructure, technology, networks, etc.

[5]   Pacific Climate Change Science Programme (PCCSP) http://www/sprep.org/attachments/ climate_change/ SI_change_change_policy.pdf.

[6]   http://en.wikipedia.org/wiki/Carteret_Island.

CHAPTER 10

DROUGHT AND CLIMATE CHANGE

10.1 Introduction

Drought and desertification are two closely related environmental problems. Their climate causes did not become a major international issue until the 1972-1974 Sahel drought in West Africa led to a debate in the United Nations resulting in the 1977 United Nations Conference on Desertification (UNCOD) in Nairobi organized by the United Nations Environment Programme (UNEP). The global interest became further promoted by the persistence of drought in the West African Sahel and Horn of Africa in the 1970s through the 1980s (Lamb, 1979; Mabbutt, 1984; Warren,1993; and Sivakhuman and Ndiang'ni, 2007). Also, the drought of 1992 in Southern Africa, another in the West African Sahel in 2005, and in the Horn of Africa and northern Kenya in 2006 – all these developments reinforced the hypothesis that drought and climate change are intimately linked. Droughts have been frequenting because of global warming and are expected to become more frequent and intense in Africa, Southern Europe and Middle East and most of the Americas, Australia and Southeast Asia (Dai, 2011).

10.2 Different Concepts of Drought

There are basically three to four definitions of drought found in the literature, based on meteorological, agricultural, hydrological and socioeconomic criteria.

Meteorological drought obtains when there are severe precipitation shortages resulting in a disruption of ecosystem functioning measured, for instance, in inability or reduced capacity to supply those services that matter for human and animal survival such as forage, food, fuelwood, biochemical, etc. What is severe precipitation shortage, however, remains relative and can only be measured in the context of a specific region and its average precipitation. Once that average precipitation is not attained, this is bound to affect the ecosystem in ways specified above. So, what qualifies as meteorological drought in the equatorial Brazilian Amazon ecosystem, for instance, where the rainfall ranges around 2000-3000 mm annually would differ from conditions in the West African Savanna ecosystem where annual precipitation is less than 1000 mm[1]. Briefly, meteorological drought is conceived based on degree of dryness, in comparison to a normal or average amount, and the duration of the dry period, which implies that meteorological drought must be region-specific, given that the atmospheric conditions that result in precipitation shortages tend to be highly region-specific. The following historical instances of definition of drought have been reported[2]:

- Great Britain (1936): fifteen consecutive days with daily precipitation less than 0.25 mm.
- United States (1942): less than 2.5 mm of rainfall in 48 hours.
- Libya (1964): when rainfall is less than 180 mm.
- Bali (Indonesia) (1964): a period of 6 days without rain.

Agricultural drought links various aspects of meteorological drought to agricultural impacts, focusing on shortfalls in precipitation that affect agricultural production or the ecology, including differences between actual and potential evapotranspiration, soil-water deficits, reduced groundwater or reservoir levels, etc. Agricultural drought can arise independently from any change in rainfall levels when soil conditions and erosion triggered by poorly planned agricultural activities cause shortages in water supply to the crops. So, a good definition of agricultural drought should account for the susceptibility of crops during different stages of crop development. For instance, deficient topsoil moisture at planting stage may harm germination, leading to low plant populations per hectare and a reduction in crop output. Agricultural droughts show up in failures in crop and livestock production (Mishia and Singh, 2011; Ding et al., 2011).

Hydrological drought occurs as a result of reduction in precipitation leading to shortages in water reserves available in sources such as aquifers, lakes and reservoirs fall below the statistical average. Hydrological drought, by this definition, tends to arise more slowly, because it involves water in natural reservoirs that is used but not replenished and can, therefore, be triggered by more than just a deficiency in precipitation. Good examples here may be drawn from the Kazakhstan experience in Central Asia, when water was diverted from the Aral Sea for irrigation projects to develop cotton during the Soviet era (Miklin and Aladin, 2008); also, from the shrinking of Lake Chad in West Africa in the past five decades or so caused by a combination of climatic factors and diversion of water for irrigation (see Onuoha, 2008; Mayhell, 2001; Goa et. al., 2011).

Socioeconomic drought refers to the impact of precipitation shortages on socioeconomic activities, including both direct and indirect impacts. Socioeconomic drought associates the supply and demand of an economic good with elements of meteorological, hydrological, and agricultural drought, but differs from the latter types of drought in that its occurrence depends on the processes of supply and demand.

Drought, generally, is a climate-related phenomenon; it is a period when "normal" precipitation within a particular region fails to obtain. It is one of those external shocks that ecosystems and economic systems experience. During drought ecosystems (and the socio-economic systems that are sustained by them) are adversely affected, but survive, and can return to their former state when the drought is over. This is quite different from desertification and dessication referring to a much longer dry period, long and sufficiently intense to lead to permanent change in ecological and/or human communities. On the other hand, how long it takes for an ecosystem or community to recover from a drought depends, inter alia, on policy interventions, availability of capital, technology, etc (Warren, 1996).

10.3 Fundamental Causes of Drought

The fundamental causes of drought trace to changes in certain elements of climate that combine to support precipitation. Most importantly, generally, rainfall is related to the amount and dew point (determined by air temperature) of water vapor carried by regional atmosphere, coupled with the upward forcing of the air mass containing that water vapor. Drought occurs if these combined factors fail to support precipitation volumes sufficient to reach Earth's surface. This can be brought about by high level of reflected sunlight (high **albedo**), and above average prevalence of high pressure systems, winds carrying continental, rather than oceanic air masses (i.e. reduced water content); and ridges of high pressure areas from behavior which prevent or restrict the developing of thunderstorm activity or rainfall over certain region.

Reoccurring drought in Australia, for example, has been explained as originating in oceanic and atmospheric weather cycles such as the EL Niño-Southern Oscillation (ENSO); similarly, drought in north-east Spain is tied to the North Atlantic Oscillation System. Anthropogenic factors – e.g. over-farming, excessive irrigation, deforestation, and erosion – all factors that adversely affect the ability of the land to capture and hold water – also are drought causing factors, though these tend to be restricted in their coverage.

Extensive deforestation can – and does, indeed – lead to a reshaping of the biosphere in a significant way, adversely affecting the functioning of the hydrologic cycle (Wright and Nebel, 2004, p. 221). Specifically, with existence of forests and other ecosystems, there is little runoff; rather, precipitation is intercepted by vegetation and infiltrates into porous topsoil – a process that "provides the life-blood" of the natural ecosystems that constitute the biosphere (Wright and Nebel, op. cit.). But the evaporation taking place in these ecosystems not only sustains the latter, but also recycles the water to local rainfall; some of the water percolates down to recharge the groundwater reservoirs, which in turn release water through springs, streams, rivers, etc. As forests become lost to deforestation or land is overgrazed, the natural pathway of the hydrologic cycle is thrown off balance: it shifts from infiltration and groundwater recharge to runoff, as the water runs into streams or rivers almost immediately – a major cause of flooding.

The natural causes of droughts can be traced to changes in certain elements of climate that combine to support precipitation; these have had their impacts aggravated because of increased water demand, population growth, urban expansion, and environmental protection efforts in many regions of the world.

10.4 Regions of the World Prone to Drought

As noted earlier, regions of the world known to be drought-prone with associated desertification include: The Great Horn of Africa; the West African Sahel, including the Darfur region of Sudan; India; Pakistan; Bangladesh; Nepal; and Myanmar (formerly Burma) and China. Approximately 2.4 billion people are known to inhabit the drainage basin of the Himalayan Rivers incorporating parts of India, China, Pakistan, Bangladesh, Nepal and Myanmar. These are regions prone to floods followed by droughts. In India, in particular, drought affecting the Ganges can have significant consequences, as the Ganges provides drinking and irrigation water for well over 500 million human populations. The problem is that the fast meltdown of Tibetan and Xinjiang glaciers – the major source of Asia's biggest rivers – due to climate change is seriously threatening the survival of major rivers, including the Yangtze, the Mekong, the Yellow River, the Indus and the Ganges. With the rapid melting of the glaciers, in the long run 'the glacier water will decrease, and droughts will follow'.

The North American West Coast drained by water from glaciers in the mountain ranges of the Rockies and Sierra Nevada are potentially threatened by drought. This is due in part to global warming triggering losses of the Sierra Nevada and Colorado River basin snow park. The North American West Coast incorporates Southern California, a region that has a desert climate and is prone to prolonged drought with historical roots tracing back to the Dust Bowl drought of the 1930s and 1940s. On the other hand, climate change has exacerbated the drought conditions through its effect on the hydrologic cycle – a problem complemented by water management policy mistakes. Specifically, the Colorado River System, which supplies a large share of Southern California's water needs (for irrigation; urban water needs, etc.) has had its water persistently extracted at a rate that exceeds the natural flow (that is, the rate of withdrawal exceeds the rate of recharge), so much so that the Colorado River System 'sometimes fails to reach the Gulf of California' (Wright and Nebel, op. cit., p. 226).

In 2005, parts of the Amazon rainforest basin underwent the worst drought in a century. Scientific studies and media reports provide evidence to the effect, that deforestation and drought are pushing the Amazon basin towards a 'tipping point' where the rainforest would experience irreversible extinction and turned into savanna or desert, with catastrophic consequences for the global climate[3]. Ecologists argue that the continued deforestation of the Amazon rainforest is a crucial factor in the drying up of a basin that has already lost nearly 20% of its forest cover (Saatchi et al., 2013); but 50% of the rainfall comes from the trees recycling the water through evaporation, which, in turn, creates more rain. So, if the trees are removed, as is happening currently in the Amazon basin, 'you lose the rainfall'. As noted earlier in chapter 3 deforestation in the tropical rainforest regions is shaping global climate in significant ways, contributing to global warming; but deforestation is a key cause of enhanced GHG effect.

East Africa, including the Great Horn of Africa, has faced drought since the 1980s[4]. The 2009 drought was the worst in East Africa since 2000, and possibly since 1991, stoking conflict; it engulfed the pastoral areas of northern Kenya, southern Ethiopia and south Somalia, resulting in the death of livestock on a massive scale. The African Sahel, a semi-arid transition zone between the Sahara Desert to the north and wetter savanna grasslands of sub-Saharan Africa and stretching from the Atlantic Ocean to the West to the Indian Ocean, is one of the world's most drought-prone regions, and also a region of conflict often fueled by decades of drought (Brooks, 2004). In the North Darfur and Kordofan regions of Sudan, an arid region where drought is an inherent feature and lying between isohyet 100 mm and 600 mm, a mere 100 mm decline in mean annual precipitation could result in disaster (hunger and death) for the human population and livestock alike. Here a combination of drought, desertification and overpopulation are among the causes of the conflict.

East Africa, arguably, is the most conflict-ravaged region of Sub-Saharan Africa; it was a focus of geopolitical rivalries for well over 100 years – from the days of British colonial expansion through the Cold War decades to the recent 'Global War on Terror' (Mobjörk and Van Baalen, 2016). But the region's strategic location guarding entrance to the Red Sea and its oil and mineral interests have attracted world power rivalry for over 150 years (ibid.).

10.4.1 Droughts In Sub-Saharan Africa: East Africa and the African Sahel

A. East African Droughts

East Africa has been subjected to drought conditions of various intensity and duration beginning since the 1980s. Studies show that by the last three decades of the 20th century (the 1900s) up to the beginning of the 21st century (the 2000s) rainfall decreased over eastern Africa; that precipitations in Eastern Africa show high degree of spatial and temporal variability. Based on data reported in Gemeda and Siina (2015) and summarized in table 10.1, the various East African countries experienced drought events over the 1983-2008, which affected over 100 million people. In Ethiopia, arguably the most drought-ravaged African country, more than 40 million people were affected by drought.

In East Africa, as elsewhere in Sub-Saharan Africa, droughts have structural causes that have deep roots in climate factors and socioeconomic forces. In recent decades climate change factors have attracted both academic and international policy attention in the attempt to explain the region's droughts: while IPCC reports often suggest that the Horn of Africa would get wetter with climate change (similar to the West African Sahel since the beginning of the 2000s, to which we return below), academic research results suggest that global warming will exacerbate drought in the region.

Table 10.1 East African Droughts Over 1980-2008

Country	Years	Population affected (million)
Kenya	2008	1.4
	2005 – 06	3.5
	2004	2.3
	1999 – 2002	23.0
	1997 – 98	1.6
	1994 – 95	1.2
	1991 – 92	2.7
Ethiopia	2008	6.4
	2003 – 2004	12.6
	1997	1.0
	1989 – 94	6.5
	1987	7.0
	1983 – 84	7.8
Sudan	2000 – 2001	2.0
	1991 – 92	8.6
	1987	3.5
	1983 – 85	8.4
Eritrea	2008	1.7
	1999 – 2003	2.3
	1993	1.6
Somalia	2008	3.3
	2000 – 2001	1.2
	1987	0.8

Source: Compiled from Gemeda and Siina (2015, table 1, p. 257).

The climate of East Africa varies from arid desert to tropical monsoon conditions; it is mainly influenced by large scale seasonal atmospheric patterns as well as proximity of the Indian Ocean (similar to the influence of the Atlantic Ocean on West Africa). Although cooler temperatures are experienced in the Ethiopian, Kenyan and Tanzanian highlands, temperatures remain relatively high throughout the year for much of East Africa.

As for most parts of Sub-Saharan Africa, mean temperatures across East Africa have risen by 1-3°C beginning since the 1960s, the highest increases registering in central regions located inland from cooling affects the oceans, particularly in South Sudan where average increases have exceeded 3°C – a rate broadly consistent with the wider African and global trends (Christy et al., 2009). Among the visible indicators of this warming trend has been the decrease of the Lewis Glacier on Mount Kenya, which has lost 40% of its mass since the early 1960s (KENYA MENR, 2002).

In contrast to rising average temperatures, there was notable decrease in rainfall overall; large parts of the region – specifically Tanzania, Kenya, and Southeastern Ethiopia – have seen decreases in rainfall exceeding 100 mm. Overall, there is significant decreasing trends in overall precipitation (Omondi et al., 2014).

For Ethiopia – Sub-Saharan Africa's most drought-prone country – drought is reported to be the most climate related risk. This is found to be more frequent and severe in the arid and semi-arid parts than elsewhere in Ethiopia (Amsalu and Adem, 2009; Degefu and Bewket, 2014). But increases in temperature do affect the soil and surface water resources by affecting the atmospheric moisture holding capacity and rate of actual evaporation and evapotranspiratuon (NMA, 2007; Conway and Schipper, 2011).

In Kenya drought frequency has increased as failure of the rains has come to occur once every year rather than every 2-3 years as previously. In Uganda drought is concentrated in the Eastern sub-regions such as Karamoja and Toso (e.g. Egeru, 2012).

In East Africa, as elsewhere in Sub-Saharan Africa, climate change is affecting pastoral mobility patterns often leading to conflict. Pastoralists earn their livelihoods mainly by herding livestock and rely on spatial mobility as a way of coping with the harsh climate conditions in East Africa. Changes occur in the environment imposed both by climate-related environmental change and by non-climate factors – e.g. community disputes over resources, international territorial disputes, etc. Drought remains, however, the dominant climate-related factor affecting pastoral migration patterns.

"Along their traditional trecking routes, pastoralists negotiate access and follow customary laws that regulate their access to resources. When their routes change, conflicts often arise over water and pasture with groups already present in the area – conflicts that sometimes turn violent. This pattern has been observed across the region, particularly in Kenya, Ethiopia and the Sudans" (Mobjörk and Van Baalen, 2016).

But changing pastoral mobility patterns and migration is often a form of adaptation to climate-related environmental change.

B. Droughts in the West African Sahel

The word **Sahel** is the Arabic term for seashore, edge or fringe. The West African Sahelian zone is an area of extreme difficulty for its very arid and semi-arid. It covers the extreme north of West Africa, forming what might be described as a transition zone between the Sahara Desert to the north and the wetter savanna grasslands to the south and stretching in a west-to-east direction from the Atlantic Ocean Coast to the west to the Indian Ocean Coast to the east. It is a risky venture to fix the exact boundaries of the Sahel though; however, climatologists and geographers use isohyet 100 mm and 600 mm to attempt to demarcate the Sahel from the Sahara Desert to the north and savanna grasslands to the south. Perhaps, a more practical approach is to describe certain ecological properties which distinguish the zone from the rest of the West African Sudanic belt (Dike, 1986, pp. 157-160).

The vegetation is mostly dry savanna in the south merging into thorn-bush steppe and then desert in the extreme north. Crop production is severely limited, and the economy rests almost solely on pastoralism. Due probably to the severe climatic conditions, the human population densities tend to be sparse. In the extreme north of the Sahel where pasturalism predominates, the typical livestock are camels, goats and sheep which survive on patchy vegetation whose availability depends, on the other hand, an irregularly distributed rainfall. The movement of the livestock population tends to lack seasonal pattern in contrast to the transhumance practised further south where rainfall is more regularly distributed and has conditions similar to those obtaining in the rest of the Sudanic savanna.

Most areas of northern West Africa above the 12° parallel lie within the Sahel. Within this zone is the region of the 'millet culture'; the millet crop (also known as sorghum) thrives here precisely because it can grow even if the land is parched, which is, of course the 'normal' rather than 'exceptional' climatic condition. Other grain crops- e.g. rice, sorghum, or guinea corn, and wheat – can be grown but only where there is adequate irrigation water or **fadama** soil. The fadama refers to low-lying farmland flooded during the brief rainy season (July – September). It is perennially arable because of the water table, which permits growing crops during the long, dry season, when it is impossible to grow crops on upland farmland (Turner, 1977).

The African Sahel is one ecological zone very much susceptible to drought and desertification, historically and contemporarily. There were a series of historical droughts beginning in, at least, the 1600s AD and increasing in frequency at the end of the 1800s (Nicholson, 1978, 1996, 2001).

However, three long droughts are identified to have registered dramatic environmental and human impacts upon the Sahel: farmng followed severe droughts in the 1910s, the 1940s, the 1960s through the 1980s; there were droughts in the early 1990s and 2005; the latest droughts occurred in 2010 and 2012.

Briefly, modern Sahelian droughts began in concrete terms in the 1960s and have continued into the 1980s, during which rainfall has fallen below the 1930-1960 mean (average); it abated by the 1990s and by 2003 rainfall was observed to show significant departure from the 1970s pattern reflecting a wetter pattern. During the 1960s through the 1980s, drought-driven famine killed over 100,000 people in the Sahel, left another 1 million or so dependent on food aid, and affected well over 50 million Sahelian populations (Adams, 2009). A key feature of the Sahel is that rainfall is confined to just three months of the year (July – September) or even less, and averages less than 100 mm/year, all of which occurs in a season lasting at the longest three months and in some years barely a few weeks.

Considerable controversy surrounds the relative roles of anthropogenic factors (e.g.deforestation, overgrazing, land-use practices etc) and climate factors (e.g. forcing by regional and global temperature patterns-during the 20th century (1900s)). We proceed to expatiate on these two sets of factors.

- **Anthropogenic causes** were the first to be hypothesized in attempting to explain the Sahelian droughts. The socalled Charney's hypothesis (Charney et al., 1977) argued that reductions in Sahel rainfall were a result of human activity: the systematic and irreversible degradation and desertification of the zone through overgrazing and deforestation and inefficient land-use practices. More technically, it was argued that decreases in the region's vegetation cover and deforestation have led to an increase in the reflectivity or albedo, as dense vegetation yields to bare, sand, and light-coloured soils; that this increase in reflectivity results a reduction in the heating of the ground, which in turn reduces the heating of the atmosphere by the ground surface, resulting in a reduction in the convection that is essential for the formation of rain-carrying clouds.

The view that the Sahelian environment had experienced significant degradation and desertification through land clearing, overgrazing, and inappropriate land-use practices was standard knowledge among observers and researchers in the early 1900s (references in Mortimore, 1998; Stebbing, 1935, 1938). The upper limits of the carrying capacity of grazing pastures were claimed to have been exceeded by the number of cattle grazing on the Sahelian pastures. Variations in annual rainfall amounts and vegetation cover were claimed as evidence for the southward advance of the Sahara Desert. Lamprey (1988), for instance, claimed that the Sahara Desert had advanced by some 90-100 km in the north Kordofan region of Sudan between 1958 and 1975.

- **Climate Change Hypothesis.** The anthropogenic perspective began however, to be abandoned or relaxed in the 1990s onwards, as it began to be hypothesized that large-scale climate-change processes were unfolding, which were significantly transforming weather patterns. But remote sensing studies of the Sahel environment had begun to reveal evidence that the Sahel had not, afterall, experienced systematic degradation and irreversible desertification at the regional scale as a result of anthropogenic or human activity. E.g. Tucker et al. (1986, 1985, 1984) using satellite technology to study vegetation cover produced evidence that vegetation has capacity to recolonize areas that had apparently suffered desertification land degradation, when rainfall permits; that the desert boundary, defined in terms of vegetation cover, changes with rainfall. So, changes in the state of the land surface seem to be driven by climate factors rather than by anthropogenic activity; what was interpreted as desertification in many instances appear to be the natural response of semi-arid landscapes and ecosystems to climate variability (Brooks, 2004).

If desertification is defined as "the transition of a region into dry barren land with little or no capacity to sustain life without an artificial source of water" (Todaro and Smith, 2009, p. 820), then we could conclude that parts of the Sahel have experienced only transient desertification caused by drought and climatic dessication, and this process has had a severe adverse outcome on many of the Sahelian region's human populations. This transient dessication of the Sahel landscape caused by drought is obviously quite different from desertification of the Sahel landscape leading to an irreversible decrease in the land's productive potential or permanent loss of cultivability. Based on studies using remote sensing technology, anthropogenic factors were absolved from blame in the persistent droughts ravaging Sub-Saharan Africa beginning in the early 1900s but becoming more regular and intense in the 1970s onwards. The climate-based evidence proves that the Sahel droughts originated in warming of the Indian and Southern Atlantic Oceans and cooling of the North Atlantic Ocean, and not by over-farming and deforestation as hypothesized earlier. So, modulation of the African monsoon by regional and global-scale patterns of sea-surface temperatures (SSTs) has been found to provide the most plausible explanation for variations in Sahelian rainfall on a multi-year to decadal timescales throughout the 20th century.

Monsoons involve large-scale sea breezes occurring when the land or surface temperature is significantly warmer than the ocean temperature, causing temperature imbalance. Usually the latter occurs because land and ocean exhibit significant differences in heat absorption capacity; the ocean absorbs heat much faster than land can, which makes the latter's environment significantly warmer than the ocean's, which explains why coastal regions, for instance, tend to be cooler than inland regions. As the lower atmosphere (troposphere) over land gets wamer, evaporation will intensify resulting in an increase in moisture circulating in the lower atmosphere, which in turn leads to increased frequency of precipitation events mainly over land. As the latter warms up faster than the ocean it creates a low-pressure belt into which rain-bearing winds flow.

Monsoons have been described in Western and Eastern Africa, Northern Australia, Chile, Spain, and Texas, etc. But the most celebrated remains the Asian monsoons. For western Africa, it is hypothesized that warmer temperatures (caused by global warming) have had the outcome of increased drying up of the land surface, given high rates of deforestation (extensive destruction of forestlands for purposes of extracting timber and/or fuelwood or clearing land for agriculture, urban use, minning, etc.). In West Africa the monsoons arrive in late June; there is a continuous southerly flow of warmer, rain-ladden winds into the West African mainland. This flow is a continuation of the south-easterly trade winds, altered to the south-westerlies as they move northwards across the equator, bring huge precipitation. Subsiding upper air presents heavy precipitation in the Sahel located south of the Sahara Desert proper. The monsoons begin to retreat in September – October; therefore, the north-east harmattan wind, dry and dust laden as they blow across the Sahara Desert, begin to dominate.

It is, also, argued that extensive deforestation in the Western Africa rainforests (treated earlier in section 3.5.2) has reshaped the biosphere in a significant way, adversely affecting the functioning of the hydrologic cycle. How? Specifically, as forests became lost to deforestation or land is overgrazed, the natural pathway of the hydrologic cycle is thrown off balance: the evapotranspiration taking place in the rainforest ecosystems, which not only sustains the latter but also recycles the water to local and regional rainfall, is reduced or lost completely. The deforestation perspective, however, began to be abandoned by the beginning of the 1980s, as it began to be hypothesized that the climate factor is the culprit.

Even so, there is still considerable uncertainty regarding the future trend of climate change and its outcome for the Sahel: will there evolve a wetter or dry Sahel? Computer models of the future direction of climate change often disagree on the scale of future direction of climate change; also, predictions for the Sahel are contradictory about the direction of future climate change; here are some aspects of this uncertainty and confusion (Conway, 2009):

- By the 1980s several computer models were suggesting that changes in the SSTs of the oceans have changed the dynamics of West African monsoon and are therefore response for the droughts. However, it not agreed which ocean – the Indian or North Atlantic has had its SST most affected by global warming.

- Another question is: how will SSTs affect rainfall? Are they going to make the Sahel wetter? While some models predict wetter Sahel, others argue that far from being wetter, the Sahel faces a future of 'dramatic drying' if GHG emissions remain unabated.

Scientists point out that among the obvious constraints on making any reliable predictions on Sahel climate are: first, a lack of reliable data base; and, second, researchers assume a uniform Sahel with homogenous physical and environmental properties. It should be pointed out, however, that different parts of the Sahel face different, quite often counter-veiling influences (to what obtains in other parts). For instance: evidence points to the fact that different parts of the Sahel may be affected differently by the relative influence of each ocean – Northern Atlantic, Southern Atlantic, Indian. So, it seems that different models are giving different weights to forces originating in the different oceans. Currently, the African Monsoon Multidisciplinary Analysis (AMMA) seeks to close the data gap by measuring the factors affecting this complex weather system that brings monsoon rains to the West African Sahel. This will be achieved and coordinated through the following five processes: (i) West African monsoon and global climate; (ii) water cycle; (iii) surface-atmosphere feedbacks; (iv) prediction of climate impacts; and (v) high-impact weather prediction and predictability (Redelsperger et. al., 2006).

10.5 Some Common Consequences of Drought

Drought can have significant environmental, agricultural, health, economic and social consequences.

- **Significant decline in crop yield, production and carrying capacity for livestock** is, perhaps, the most visible consequence of drought, especially in sub-Saharan Africa. Mijindadi and Adegbehin (1991) report that the Sahel drought of 1972-1975 saw groundnut cultivation above the 12° latitude become almost impossible. Indeed the 1972-75 drought inaugurated the decline of Nigerian groundnut exports (Bernus, 1975; Apeldoorn, 1981; Dike, 1986).
- **Shrinking Surface Water Reservoirs.** A good example is Lake Chad in the drought-prone West African Sahel. The mid-1960s saw record levels in the size of Lake Chad (Charney, 1975); the 1970s with onset of the Sahel drought saw severe contraction of the size of Lake Chad 'changing its character to swampy delta at the mouth of the River Chari, with dire consequences for lake-side communities' (Evans, http://www.fao.org). Evans (op. cit.) notes that the falling Lake Chad levels observed since the 1970s demonstrate the effect of a rainfall reduction of 25% on river flow in a semi-arid region where rainfall gradients are steep and small shifts in the atmospheric circulation can result in large rainfall changes. However, unlike Lake Chad, River Nile has remained more-or-less unscathed by the African drought owing to the large over-year storage in Lake Nasser; also, the exceptionally high levels in Lake Victoria have helped to maintain higher White Nile flow (Conway et al., 1996). The latter has inturn helped to compensate for the lower discharges in the Blue Nile.

- **Dust bowls** are a sign of soil erosion in arid regions, which further erode the landscape. The Dust Bowl drought was an environmental disaster that severely affected much of the American and Canadian prairie lands in the 1930s; it was one of the most devastating droughts experienced by the United States in the 20th century. The Dust Bowl drought came in four waves: 1930-31; 1934; 1936; and 1939-1940. The Dust Bowl effect came because of sustained drought conditions compounded by sustained land management policies that created conditions for wind erosion, whereby the top soil, depleted of moisture, became exposed to wind erosion creating great clouds of dust and sand often referred to as "black blizzards".

  The Dust Bowl of the 1930s in the United States illustrates, indeed, the hypothesis that the way humans interact with their environment prior to and during drought can profoundly affect the outcome. Can the various droughts that affect the American West bring another Dust Bowl? Is the Dust Bowl experience likely to be repeated elsewhere in the world? As has been stated, anthropogenic processes on land is one reason why dust is likely to accumulate; climate change is another factor complementing the latter. As global temperatures become elevated as a result of rising GHG emissions, persistent drought in many parts of the world is far more likely resulting in more dust, which in turn opens up cracks in the ground that can furnish additional dust to the hot, dry winds. In the arid and semi-arid American West prone to multiyear drought the potential exists. Researchers from a variety of disciplines – geochemists, climatologists, geographers, etc. – predict that multiyear drought in the American West could bring another Dust Bowl, although there are counteracting influences such as the Pacific Decaded Oscillation (PDO) - a hot-and-cold oscillation in the sea-surface temperatures (SSTs) of the Pacific Ocean and its complex interaction with the EL Niño – La Niña cycle.

- **Dust storms or sand storms** occur when drought hits an area suffering from desertification and erosion, blowing loose sand and dirt from a dry environment. The Sahara Desert and drylands around the Arabian Peninsula have been identified as the main terrestrial sources of airborne dust, with some contributions from Iran, Pakistan and India into the Arabian Sea. The Saharan dust storms are known to have increased approximately ten times since the 1950s, leading to topsoil loss in the Sahel – Niger, Chad, northern Nigeria and Burkina Faso. Levels of Saharan dust coming off the east coast of Africa in June 2007 were found to be five times higher than that for 2006 and are the largest recorded since 1999, which may have cooled the Atlantic Ocean waters enough to slightly reduce hurricane activity in late 2007. Heat from warm ocean surfaces is known to fuel hurricanes, leading to stronger and more frequent storms.

10.6 Conclusion

Drought, referring to extended period of absence of or significant shortfalls in rainfall, is a result of changes in certain elements of climate that combine to support precipitation volumes sufficient to reach Earth's surface. For example, winds carrying continental, rather than oceanic air masses, will lead to lack of precipitation. Anthropogenic factors e.g. over farming, excessive withdrawal of water for irrigation, deforestation (which affect the ability of the land to capture and hold water) etc. have all combined to aggravate drought.

End Notes

[1] http://www.britannica.com/EBchecked/topic/7924/Africa/37158/climate

[2] http://threeissues.sdsu.edu/three_issues_droughtfacts01.html.

[3] See The Independent, July 23rd, 2006; WWF 2006; Saatchi et al. 2013. Adams (2009), especially chapter 9, contains useful insights on deforestation in the Amazon basin and other regions of the developing world and its ecological and socioeconomic consequences.

[4] See Adams, op. cit., especially chapter 8; see also Few et al. 2015 and references.

CHAPTER 11

SYMPTOMS OF CLIMATE CHANGE IN DESERTS AND DESERTIFICATION

11.1 Introduction

Deserts, also known as arid zones or drylands in the climate science literature, describe landscapes or regions of low precipitation: less than 250 millimeters (mm) per year (Mayhew, 2009, pp. 128-9). Approximately 41% of Earth's terrestrial sphere is desert, located in all the continents; Earth's deserts cover some 59.9 million km² (Table 11.1). The polar regions, Antarctica and Arctic, contain the world's two largest deserts (Table 11.2); the rest of Earth's deserts are located outside the polar regions, the largest being the Sahara Desert extending eastwards from the Atlantic Ocean some 4200km to the Nile River and the Red Sea, and southwards from the Atlas mountains of Morocco and the Mediterranian shores the Sahel. On the whole the Sahara desert covers 10% of the African continent.

Table 11.1 Drylands and Their Subsystems

Dryland Subsystems	Area (million km²)	Share of Earth's terrestrial surface (%)
Hyper-arid	9.6	6.5
Arid	15.3	10.4
Semi-arid	22.3	15.3
Dry sub-humid	12.7	8.6
Total = 59.9 million km² (without dry sub-humid) (47.2) million km²		40.6
		(32.0)

Source: World Resources Institute (2005) (http://www.millenniumassessment.org/documents/documents.335.aspx.pdf)

Table 11.2 The World's 10 Largest Deserts (ranked by area)

Desert	Area (km^2)
Antarctic (Antarctica)	14, 200, 000
Arctic (Arctic)	13, 900, 000
Sahara (Northern Africa)	9, 100, 000
Arabian (Middle East)	2, 600, 000
Gobi (Asia)	1, 300, 000
Patagonian (South America)	670, 000
Great Victoria (Australia)	647, 000
Kalahari (Southern Africa)	570, 000
Great Basin (North America)	490, 000
Thar (South Asia: India, Pakistan)	450, 000

Note: bracketed words refer to region or continent of location.
Source: http://en.wikipedia.org/wiki/Desert. Retrieved 25th August, 2013.

The World Resources Institute demarcates drylands into four subsystems (Table 11.1). The driest desert environment is the Atacama located along the Chilean Coast in South America and occupying a region in the rain shadow of Chile's Coast Range:

> "It is virtually devoid of life because it is blocked from receiving precipitation by the Andes Mountains to the east and the Chilean Coast Range to the west. The cold Humboldt Current and the anticyclone of the Pacific are essential to keep the dry climate of the Atacama. The average rainfall in the Chilean region of Antofagasta is just 1 mm per year ..." (http://www.en.wikipedia.org/wiki/Desert).

Most deserts tend to be situated beneath areas of high pressure into which rain-breaking, moisture-laden, winds find difficult to penetrate, which results in these areas experiencing low, scattered rainfall patterns which are, besides, highly variable both seasonally and annually. Because (lack of) water emerges the most important factor in arid or desert ecosystems, changes in regional and global precipitation regimes, even of relatively small degree and short duration, tend to exert significant desertification effects. Apart from short-lived surface water that remains after rainstorms, most water reservoirs in desert regions are underground, including fossil water (or geologically trapped water), which being no longer supplemented by rainfall or the natural hydrologic cycle is a finite, non-renewable resource. The quantity of surface water is, as already suggested, severely limited by the low and variable rainfall, among other factors.

11.2 Desertification

The exact, generally accepted, definition of desertification is yet to be found. Adams (2009) explains that the term desertification itself was pioneered by the French ecologist Aubreville (1949), who described it as an extreme form of "savanization": the conversion of tropical and subtropical forests into savannas because of severe soil erosion, changes in soil properties and invasion of dryland plant species. Another definition by Grove (1977) conceives desertification as the spread of desert conditions for whatever reasons, desert being land with sparse vegetation and low productivity associated with soil degradation, the degradation being persistent or in the extreme irreversible (see also Graetz, 1991). Mayhew (op. cit. p. 129), conceives desertification as a process of land degradation in drylands, induced by climatic and anthropogenic factors; desertification itself undermines the capacity of a community to survive, a situation known to be specifically acute in the Sahel (borders of the southern Sahara characterized by a vegetation of scattered grasses, shrubs, and trees with annual rainfall of 200-400mm, but unreliable).

The United Nations Convention to Combat Desertification (UNCCD) defines desertification as land degradation in arid, semiarid, and dry sub-humid lands; land degradation is, in turn, conceived as a persistent reduction of biological and economic productivity measured in terms of the 'things that ecosystems provide that matter to people' – e.g. forage, food, fibre, fuelwood, biochemical, etc; also, benefits obtained from regulation of ecosystem processes (water purification, etc.) and soil development (conservation, formation), etc[1]. This definition has the advantage that it provides a benchmark for viewing desertification quantitatively in an operational way. However, it has the limitation that it conceives desertification as simply the outcome of land degradation and nothing else or the outcome of human activity. It thus excludes natural or climate change factors, drought or precipitation.

By 1996, the United Nations admitted the climate factor among the various factors it deemed responsible for desertification, including climate variations and human activities (e.g. Warren, 1996). The trigger for the interest in desertification was the Sahel droughts of the 1970s and 1980s. It was reported that: 1 million people had starved; 40-50% of the population of domestic livestock perished; and millions of people become refugees (Graetz, 1991).

11.3 Underlying Causes of Desertification

In general, desertification is a product of two complementary processes: climate factors (climate change, drought, etc.) and unsustainable land management practices in dryland regions – such as overgrazing and expansion of cropped land due to demographic changes[2]. Typically, arid and semi-arid ecosystems are characterized by sparse and highly variable rainfall. Given these features, climatic changes such as those that result in extended droughts have potential to reduce the biological productivity of these ecosystems, which, in turn, leads to poverty, emigration and reduced human well-being. Because dryland regions and environments are used for many human activities – most importantly agriculture, livestock breeding and fuelwood extraction – the activities can trigger the problem of desertification and generate lasting changes to dryland ecosystems. Also, river abstractions for irrigation purposes can – and does, indeed – lead to desertification. Examples may be cited from experiences with large-scale irrigation schemes: paramount examples are the Aral and Caspian Sea region; the Hei and Tarim River basins in Western China; the Senegal River Basin in West Africa (Geist and Lambin, 2002). We may add, also, the Lake Chad region in the West African Sahel (Mayhell, 2001; Onuoha, 2008; Goa et al., 2011). Over the past fifty years or so the hydrologic cycle over most river basins has been subjected to extensive human changes with the construction of reservoirs, land-use changes, river abstractions, groundwater abstractions, inter-basin diversions, etc., which alter river flows and the hydrology of basins.

The Aral Sea, once the world's largest lake, has seen its surface area shrink dramatically as the primary rivers feeding this water reservoir became diverted and tapped virtually dry for agricultural (cotton development) purposes. As the Aral Sea's southern part dried out, its salty bed became exposed; dust storms have increasingly spread the dusty dust on the agricultural lands of the Aral Sea region. Meanwhile, the water making its way back to the Aral Sea is increasingly saline and laden with pesticide and chemical fertilizer pollution[3].

On the other hand, in certain dryland regions, desertification processes operate in absence of human activities. But these are areas human activities may be negligible because of low population density, - such as parts of the African Sahel where natural recurring drought processes complemented by climate change are largely to blame for desertification, a point made in chapter 10. A widely cited study (Nicholson et al., 1998) shows that anthropogenic factors have not produced a progressive southward shift of the Sahara, neither a long-scale exposure of barren, less productive land in the Sahel. Rather, underlying desertification are complex causes: rainfall variability; drought; deforestation.

11.4 Symptoms of Desertification

The more evident symptoms of desertification include: an increase or acceleration in soil erosion by wind and soil; a decline in soil natural stability with an attendant increase in surface crusting and surface runoff and a concomitant reduction in soil infiltration capacity and soil moisture storage; replacement of forest or woodland by secondary savanna grassland – "Savannization" a la Aubréville (1949) – or scrub; an increase in the flow variability of dryland rivers and streams; an overall decrease in species diversity and plant biomass in dryland ecosystem, etc. In many semiarid areas, there is a progressive shift occurring from grassland to shrub-land that works to worsen the soil erosion process. It is pointed out that during the second half of the 1800's, large-scale commercial stockbreeding had evolved spreading over the semiarid drylands of north and South America, southern Africa, and Australia. However, both the kind of imported herbivore and grazing management system failed to adjust to the semiarid environment.

"The resulting disturbance was therefore a "transition trigger" that, combined with drought events, led to a progressive dominance of shrubs over grass (sometimes called "bush encroachment"). The transition from land fully covered by grasses to one covered by scattered bushes creates greater bare soil surfaces, which encourages increased runoff velocity, resulting in higher soil erosion" (**World Resources Institute, 2005**, p. 6; bracketed words and parentheses in original).

11.5 Links Between Climate and Desertification

Both climate and desertification interface at a variety of scales through a complex and still only partially understood series of feedback loops. Climate influences desertification processes through its impact on dryland soils and vegetation. Unlike the organically rich soils of the more humid regions, dryland soils have low organic matter content and are frequently saline and/or alkaline, which renders them highly susceptible to accelerated erosion by wind and water. Empirical studies and satellite imagery to monitor changes in vegetation along the semi-arid zones of the Sahara Desert in Africa in relation to changes in rainfall find the highly elastic response of the vegetation cover to growing-season rainfall: the desert margin vegetation expands or contracts year-to-year influenced by the annual variation in rainfall (see, for instance, Dregne, 1984). During the 1980–1990 period the southern limit of the 200-mm annual rainfall boundary used to demarcate the southern limit of the Sahara Desert were observed to fluctuate considerably; the 200-mm rainfall boundary was based on average vegetation index values; in 1984, the driest year of the 1900s in the Sahel, the Sahel/Sahara boundary was found to be even further south than in previous years. So, it is not clear, given this movement up and down, whether there was any long-term expansion or contraction of the Sahara (Tucker et al., 1985).

In turn, desertification impacts on climate change indirectly during biomass combustion, a common practice in the tropics and sub-tropics, which generates a large volume of atmospheric aerosols and tract gas emission. As we saw earlier in chapter 3, tropical savanna biomass burning is a significant source of global emissions of sooth, nitrogen, carbon and ozone. The total smoke emissions from tropical biomass burning are estimated to generate between 25 and 80 teragrams per year (Tg/year: one (1) Tg = 1 million metric tons) – comparable to estimated smoke emission from fossil fuels (22.5 to 24 Tg/year). Dryland biomass combustion is estimated to contribute 10% of gross emissions from all sources.

Arid and semi-arid regions are sources of crustal-derived aerosols (dust) transported by the atmosphere; atmospheric dust impacts on the surface and atmospheric energy balance in complex ways. First, as pointed out in chapter 2, aerosols in the form of black carbon (BC) can contribute to global warming, directly absorbing incoming and reflected sunlight in addition to absorbing infrared radiation. BC can also deposit on and darken snow and ice, which increases snow's absorption of sunlight and accelerating snow melt (warming aerosols). Also, desert dust is a kind of aerosol that may have a significant effect on climate; this is the type of dust observed streaming out over West Africa from the Sahara Desert in North Africa: so-called 'harmattan haze'; it is highly dehydrating, anhydrous and non-hygroscopic (i.e. does not attract and condense atmospheric water vapor – a process which undermines the process of cloud formation and rainfall). The particles of these dust plumes are minute grains of dirt blown from the desert surface; they are relatively large for atmospheric aerosols and would normally fall out of the atmosphere after a short flight if they were not blown to relatively high altitudes (about 2400 meters) by intense dust storms. Because the harmattan dust is composed of minerals, the particles absorb sunlight as well as scatter it; through absorption of sunlight the dust haze warms the layer of the atmosphere, which (warm air) is believed to inhibit the formation of storm clouds, which in turn suppresses rain. It is for this reason that the harmattan haze is known to further desertification in the West African Sahel, to which we return.

Second, organic carbon can cause cooling by reflecting sunlight (cooling aerosol) – such as volcanic aerosols which form in the stratosphere after volcanic eruptions like Mt. Pinatubo in the Philippines in June 1992. The relative coolness of 1993 is explained as a response to the stratospheric aerosol layer that was generated by the Mt. Pinatubo eruption. The aerosols formed a global layer of sulphuric acid (H_2SO_4) haze; global temperatures dropped by about 0.5°C, and ozone depletion temporarily increased significantly.

11.6 Climate Change and Desertification in the African Sahel

As noted above the African Sahel is the terrestrial ecozone[4] lying between the Sahara Desert to the north and the Sudan savannas to the south. Characterized by a semi-arid climate, the African Sahel stretches across the southern most extent of Northern Africa[5] between the Atlantic Ocean to the west and the Red Sea to the East. Spatially, the African Sahel incorporates parts of (from East to West) the Gambia, Senegal, Southern Mauritania, Central Mali, Burkina Faso, Southern Algeria, Niger, 'Far North' Nigeria and Cameroon, Central Chad, Southern Sudan, Northern South Sudan and Eritrea. The African Sahel spans in all 5,400 km of territory, running in a West-East direction covering an area of 3,053,200 km² of semi-arid grasslands, savannas, steppes, and thorn shrub lands.

11.6.1 When did desertification begin in the African Sahel?

Historical records show that the margins of the African Sahara were wetter in the 1500s through the 1700s, but experienced major droughts in the 1680s and between 1738 and 1756 (Nicholson, 1978, 1996). The end of the 1700s to the late 1800s experienced drier conditions; wetter conditions obtained during 1875 and 1895 – a period when European colonial expansion began in Africa. Nicholson (1996) explains that similar periods of wetter and drier conditions occurred in Southern Africa; rainfall anomalies in 20th century Africa reflect those of the 19th century.

What explains the sudden shift in climate and desert ecological conditions in the Sahara? What explains the sudden transition from vegetated to desert conditions in the Sahara? The first shift is said to have occurred about 5500 years ago, when there occurred sudden transition from vegetated to desert conditions. Wet environmental conditions in the Sahara giving rise to extensive vegetation, lakes, wetlands, etc. – came to abrupt end about 5500 years ago. Climate paleontologists, who study fossils to explain the climate condition and ecologies of the historical past, explaining climate change during this period suggest that the millennial-scale changes in Earth's orbit could have caused the wet conditions that prevailed in the early Holocene[6] and the current dry desert conditions: a 'green Sahara' and 'desert Sahara' (see American Geophysical Union, 1999).

11.7 Desertification as Major International Issue

Desertification has evolved into a major environmental issue, starting since the 1930s. In the 1980s the UNEP had estimated that about 35% of the terrestrial globe was prone to erosion (about 4.5 billion hectares); this land supported some 25% of the world's population (some 850 million). Of this 'terrestrial globe' vulnerable to erosion, 30% was said to be severely or very severely desertified; about 80% of rangelands were affected by 'over use' (Tolba, 1986); and the extent and severity of desertification were observed to be on the rise in arid regions of the world (Mabbatt, 1984). The Brundtland Report (1987) was even more alarmist: 'each year another 6 million hectares of productive dryland turns into worthless desert' (p. 2); and desertification is among the environmental trends that threaten 'to radically alter the planet, that threaten the lives of many species upon it, including the human species' (p. 2).

The climate causes of desertification became a major international environmental concern only in the aftermath of the 1972-1974 Sahel drought which led to a debate in the United Nations, resulting in the United Nations Conference on Desertification (UNCOD) in Nairobi organized by UNEP (Adams, op. cit., pp. 212 – 3). This global interest became further sustained by the persistence of the Sahel and African droughts (in the Horn of Africa and Southern Africa) through the 1970s and 1980s (Mabbut op. cit.; Tolba, op. cit., Warren, 1993, 1996).

As suggested above, at the time of the Sahel drought in the early 1970s little was known regarding climate change as a major factor in the African drought (Lamb, 1979). The persistence of drought events in the Sahel and Horn of Africa in 1984 had reawakened global concern; also, the drought of 1992 in Southern Africa (Hulme, 1995), another one in the Sahel in 2005, and in the Horn of Africa and Northern Kenya in 2006 – all these had combined to reinforce the climate change perspective on drought.

11.8 Conclusion

Deserts describe landscapes or regions of low precipitation: less than 250 mm per year. Most deserts tend to be located beneath regions of high pressure into which moist-laden winds find difficult penetrating resulting in those areas experiencing low, scattered rainfall patterns that are, besides, highly irregular both seasonally and annually. On the other hand, desertification refers to the process of spread of desert conditions for whatever reasons; however, desertification results from two complementary factors: climate factors (climate change, drought) and unsustainable land management practices in dryland or desert ecosystems – such as over-grazing and expansion of cropped land due to demographic changes; fuelwood extraction beyond regenerative capacity of forests; extraction of surface water beyond the recharge potential of the hydrologic cycle. Both climate change and desertification interface at a variety of scales through a complex feedback loops: climate influences desertification through its impact on dryland soils and vegetation; in turn, desertification influences climate through biomass combustion – a common practice in the tropics and semi-tropics, which releases a large volume of atmospheric aerosols and tract gas emissions.

End Notes

[1] See World Resources Institute 2005 (http://www.millenniumassessment.org/documents/ document.355. aspx.pdf.

[2] See http://www.millenniumassessment.org/documents/document.355.aspx.pdf (Ecosystems and Human Well-Being, Figure 1.1)

[3] NASA Earth Observatory; http://earthobservatory.nasa.gov see also Miklin and Aladin 2008.

[4] Ecozones delineate large areas of Earth's surface within which organisms have been evolving in relative isolation over long historical periods separated from one another by geographic features – e.g. oceans, high mountain ranges, deserts, etc – that constitute barriers to migration. As such, eco-zone designations are employed to indicate general groupings or organisms based on their shared biography (http://en.wikipedia. org/wiki/Terrestrial_ecozone).

[5] Defined by the United Nations to include: Algeria, Egypt, Libya, Morocco, Sudan, Tunisia and Western Sahara; also, a number of Spanish territories (Ceuta and Melilla, the Canary Islands and the Portuguese Madeira Islands.

6   The **Holocene** refers to the most recent geological epoch, geological age we are currently in; it started evolving about 11, 550 years ago. The **Holocene** was preceded by the **Pleistocene**, when most of our species' evolution took place; the Pleistocene began 1.8 million years ago. All human civilization began during the Holocene; historians put the first evidence of human civilization in 9,500 BC, only 100 years after the beginning of the Holocene (http://www.wisegeek.com/what-is-the-holocene.htm).

CHAPTER 12

CLIMATE CHANGE AND ECOSYSTEMS

12.1 Introduction

In this chapter, we explore the symptoms of global warming and climate change in ecosystems. Climate change is known to cause significant changes in the properties of ecosystems and the resources and functions they supply, which have implications for human welfare. But humans rely on Earth's ecosystem resources for survival and welfare.

Current economic literature explicitly emphasizes four to five interrelated points in analysis of ecosystem resources. First, they constitute a unique, special type of economic goods, generating a flow of benefits to humans (as producers and consumers) over time. Put differently, ecosystem resources serve both as production inputs (intermediate goods) and final consumption items. Second, most ecosystem resources are renewable in the sense that they grow according to some biological laws – e.g. fisheries and timber replenish themselves; otherwise, they are reproduced and replenished by natural processes or forces – e.g. water, via the hydrologic cycle, or ozone through biochemical process in the atmosphere. Third, many ecosystem resources exhibit the characteristics of 'global public goods': accessible to all at no cost, which lends them open to overexploitation and degradation often to the extent of extinction in many instances. Fourth, in contrast to the renewable resources are nonrenewable resources for which there exist no natural processes of replenishment: once used they are gone forever (e.g. fossil fuel reservoirs). Fifth, ecosystem resources constitute natural capital goods created by biogeographical processes – which contrasts with the conventional concept of capital goods as the result of human action (saving and investment), and represent Earth's ability to meet human needs, whether through providing food (e.g. fish, fruits, etc) or raw-materials (e.g. timber, minerals) or providing vital services (e.g. maintaining the hydrologic cycle; ozone layer shielding us from solar ultraviolet radiation; forests controlling flooding, absorbing pollutants, etc.).

Ecosystem resources began to attract academic and policy attention only as from the 1980s. Prior to that period, the economic literature took little interest or recognition of the importance of ecosystem resources as an essential factor in economic development, the key driver of the latter being conceived only in rapid accumulation of (industrial) physical capital and, by the 1970s, human capital, and lately, by the 1980s, social capital[1]. But early attempts to admit ecosystem resources into economic analysis were clearly hampered by three problems on the part of economists: first, their myopic understanding of what is meant by environmental or ecosystem resources "beyond the obvious ones of timber and fish" (**The Economist**, 23rd April, 2005); second, their limited knowledge of the economic benefits and values provided by Earth's natural environment; and third, the obvious difficulty of putting 'cash values' or market prices on environmental goods such as, clean air to breath, soil formation, assimilation and breakdown of pollutants, etc., which are not supplied through the market system.

Natural scientists, biologists and ecologists, geographers and economists have, in recent decades, produced abundant literature on evidence that Earth's natural environment supplies a wide range of economic goods, services and benefits; this literature reveals a great deal more than we used to know about how Earth' physical environment is constituted and functions, what spheres deliver which services, and in what quantities, and the actual and potential impacts of the exploitation of the various spheres of Earth's environment on human welfare. Ecologists have investigated organisms in the context of the community and physical environment of which they form a part; discoveries made in ecology have provided insights into how human activity induced climate change affects Earth's natural environment and the outcomes e.g. biodiversity loss. Current concern, however, is not that climate change affects biodiversity but that rapid climate change affects ecosystems and species ability to adapt and so biodiversity loss increases, which, in turn, risks human security – e.g. major changes in the food chain upon which humans depend; water sources may change, recede or disappear completely; medicines and other pharmaceutical resources humans rely on may be harder to access as the plants, animals and microbial organisms they are derived from may have their reproductive capabilities undermined or such organisms may disappear completely or become extinct.

This is how the United Nation's **Global Biodiversity Outlook** (2010), summarizes the concern posed by climate change:

> "Climate change is already having an impact on biodiversity, and is projected to become a progressively more significant threat in the coming decades. Loss of Arctic sea ice threatens biodiversity across an entire biome and beyond. The related pressure on ocean acidification, resulting from higher concentrations of carbon dioxide in the atmosphere is also already being observed. Ecosystems are already showing negative impacts under current levels of climate change … which is modest compared to future projected changes … In addition to warming temperatures, more frequent extreme weather events and changing patterns of

rainfall and drought can be expected to have significant impacts on biodiversity" (UN **Global Biodiversity Outlook**, 2010, p. 56).

12.2 Conceptualizing Ecosystems and Ecosystem Resources

The ecosystem concept describes a community of plants, animals and microbial organisms within a particular physical or natural environment that is linked by a flow of materials through the non-living (abiotic) as well as the living (biotic) sections of the system (Mayhew, 2009, p. 151). Thus, the concept includes consideration of the ways plant and animal populations and microbial organisms interact with each other and Earth's physical environment (air, land and water) to reproduce and perpetuate the entire grouping.

Thus, an inland freshwater lake, or a tropical rainforest, or a wetland or mangrove swamp, etc. each with its plant (flora) and animal (fauna) species in a particular physical space, constitutes an ecosystem system. Nutrients pass between the different organisms (animals, humans, plants, microbes) that constitute an ecosystem such as when carbon dioxide CO_2 is absorbed by rainforest trees, which are then consumed by humans and other animals, which are then consumed by other organisms, etc. Pioneered in the 1930s by British ecologist Arthur Tansley (Tansley, 1935)[2], the ecosystem concept permits us to capture the fact of the complex interrelationships between and among the living and non- living spheres of Earth's environment. Knowledge of ecosystems permits us to appreciate the reciprocal relationships between the living organisms (humans, animals, plants, microbes) and their physical environment, and the conditions, circumstances and influences that underpin and determine their continued reproduction.

Ecosystem resources, then, refer to the whole complex of factors or items – living and nonliving – supplied by a particular physical environment and consumed by the organisms occupying that environment to sustain and perpetuate their existence. This definition of ecosystem resources suggests that the concept itself incorporates, also, spatial needs – such as a place on the intertidal rocks or a hole in a tree or soil for animals to live or hide from predators; recreational facilities for humans – e.g. beaches, mountain ranges, recreational parks, botanical or zoological gardens, etc. Also, non-living factors that vary in space and time, but are never used up or made available to other species (e.g. certain temperature ranges, wind direction or pattern, salinity, etc.) qualify to be included among ecosystem resources. Thus, when such 'non-living factors' become disturbed or are no longer available in their optimal levels there will begin to occur biodiversity loss; otherwise, the organisms will begin to shift their ranges. IPCC 2007A, for instance, reports of marine ecosystems that a warming of 2°C above 1990 levels would result in mass mortality of coral reefs, that 4°C increase in global temperature by 2100 (relative to 1990-2000 level) may lead to many freshwater species becoming extinct[3]. Another study reports that pine forests in British Columbia, Canada, have been devastated by pine beetle infestation, which has expanded unhindered since 1998 at least in part due to the lack of severe winters since that time (Kurz et al., 2008).

The degree to which each non-living factor is available, or otherwise lacking or high or low, profoundly affects the ability of organisms in the specific ecosystem to survive and reproduce themselves. So, which non-living factors are available or absent, and in what quantities determine which species may or may not survive in specific region or area; in turn, which organisms do not survive is the key determinant of the **nature** of a given ecosystem.

Ecosystem resources may be conceived from yet another perspective: nature's gift to humans supplied by biological, chemical and geophysical processes. Thus, ecosystem resources differ fundamentally from human-made resources that are the result of saving and investment or are created by human activity or anthropogenic processes.

12.3 Ecosystems: Services and Functions

Various definitions of the concept of ecosystem services and functions exist in the literature, of which three commonly used ones may be cited for the present purpose: (i) the conditions and processes through which natural ecosystems and the species that constitute and define them sustain and fulfil human life (Daily, 1997a, 1997b); (ii) the benefits humans derive, directly or indirectly, from the functioning of ecosystems (Constanza et al., 1997); and (iii) the benefits humans derive from ecosystems (MA, 2005). All three definitions suggest broad agreement as to the general idea of ecosystem services: benefits from Earth's natural world that sustain and fulfil human existence.

Tables 12.1 and 12.2, respectively, summarize the major terrestrial and aquatic ecosystems, including their dominant parameters, animal and plant live, and geographical or spatial distribution globally. Table 12.3 summarizes the various ecosystem services and functions.

Table 12.1 Major Terrestrial Ecosystem Complexes

Ecosystem	Climate and Soil	Dominant Vegetation	Dominant Animal Life	Geographical Distribution
Deserts	Areas of very low rainfall, sometimes specified as below 250mm/yr; or where evapo-transpiration exceeds precipitation. Soils are thin and porous, as climate is too dry to permit chemical weathering and humus formation	Widely scattered thorny bushes and shrubs; cacti, etc.	Rodents, lizards, snakes, numerous insects, rots, hawks, small birds.	North and Southwest Africa; parts of Middle East and Asia; Southwest USA, Northern Mexico.
Grasslands	Seasonal rainfall, 250-1500 mm/yr; fires frequent, soils rich and often deep.	Grass species; bushes and woodlands in some areas.	Large grazing mammals; wild horses, lions, termites.	Central North America; Central Asia; Subequatorial Africa; and South America; much of South India, Northern Australia.
		Non-seasonal, annual average temperature 28°C; rainfall frequent and heavy, averages over 2375 mm/yr; soils thin and poor in nutrients. Within this ecosystem complex are found variants such as:		

Tropical rainforests	**Tropical Mangrove Swamps.** Where prop-roots trap sediments from the ebb and flow of tidal currents gradually extending land seawards. The mangrove rainforests of the Niger Delta (in Nigeria) are the largest in the world, covering some 11,700km². **Tropical Montane Forests.** In mountainous regions of the tropics, where rainfall can be heavy and persistent, trees are typically short and crooked, etc. **Tropical Dry Forests.** Characterized by annually dry season. Soils sometimes producing pockets or tropical dry forest.	High density of broad-leafed evergreen trees, dense canopy, abundant epiphytes and vines; little understory.	Enormous biodiversity; exotic colorful insects, amphibians, birds, snakes, etc.	Northern South America, Central America; Western, Central Africa, Southwest Asia; Islands in Indian and Pacific Ocean.
Temperate forests	Seasonal; temperature below freezing in winter; summers warm humid, rainfall from 750-200 mm/yr; soils well developed.	Coniferous trees (Spruce, fir, pine, hemlock), some deciduous trees.	Large herbivores (e.g. male deer); important nesting area for neotropical birds.	West and Central Europe, East Asia, Eastern North, America.

Tundra	Bitter cold except for an 8-to-10 week growing season with long days and moderate temperatures; precipitation low, soils thin and underlain with permafrost well developed in the barren plains of northern Canada, Alaska and Eurasia; Arctic tundra ecosystems are highly responsive to temperature changes on a relatively short time scale; highly sensitive to both environmental fluctuation and climate change, and play a significant role in biospheric feedbacks to global climate.	Low-growing mosses, lichens and seages, etc. Tundra vegetation restricted by the intense winter cold, insufficient summer heat and soils with a thick, peat layer of poorly decomposed vegetation, which is usually underlain by a frozen layer of soil. Climate change may cause tundra soil to dry, which accelerates oxygen uptake, which, in turn, would lead to increased carbon dioxide and methane emissions.	Year-round; arctic hares, arctic foxes; many migrant shorebirds, geese, and ducks, etc.	North of the coniferous forest in Northern hemisphere, extending Southwards at elevations above the coniferous forests.

Source: Compiled from Wright and Nebel (2004, Table 2.3, pp. 42-43); Mayhew (2009, p. 517).

Table 12.2 Major Aquatic Ecosystems

Aquatic System	Major Environmental Parameter	Dominant Plant Life	Dominant Animal Life	Distribution
Lakes and Ponds (freshwater)	Bodies of standing water; low concentration of dissolved solids; seasonal vertical stratification of water	Rooted and floating plants, phytoplankton	Zooplankton, fish, insect, larvae, geese, herons.	Physical depressions in the landscape where precipitation and groundwater accumulate.
Streams and Rivers	Flowing water; low level of dissolved solids; high level of dissolved oxygen.	Attached algae, rooted plants.	Insect, larvae, fish, amphibians, birds, ducks, geese, etc.	Landscapes where precipitation and groundwater flow by gravity towards oceans or lake.
Inland Wetlands (freshwater)	Standing water, at times seasonally dry; thick organic sediments; high nutrients.	Marshes: grasses, reeds, etc Swamps: water-tolerant trees. Bogs: low shrubs, etc.	Amphibians, snakes, numerous invertebrates, wading birds, ducks, geese, alligators, etc.	Shallow depressions, poorly drained, often occupy sites of lakes and ponds that have filled in
Estuaries	Variable salinity; tides, create two-way currents, often rich in nutrients, turbid.	Phytoplankton in water, column, rooted grasses like salt-marsh grass, mangrove swamps-in tropics with salt-tolerant trees and shrubs.	Zooplankton, rich shellfish, worms, fish, wading birds, ducks, geese, etc.	Coastal regions where rivers meet the ocean; may form bays behind sandy barrier islands.

| Coastal Ocean (saltwater) | Tidal currents provide mixing nutrients high | Phytoplankton, large benthic algae, turtle grass, symbiotic algae in corals. | Zooplankton, rich bottom fauna of worms, shellfish; coral colonies, jelly-fish, fish, turtles, ducks, sea lions, seals, dolphins, penguins, whales. | From coastline outward over continental shelf; coral reefs abundant in tropics. |
| Open Ocean | Great depths (to 11000 metres); all but upper 200 m dark and cold; poor in nutrients except in up-swelling regions. | Exclusively phytoplankton | Diverse zooplankton and fish adapted to different depths; sea birds, whales, tuna, sharks, squid, flying fish. | Covering 70% of Earth, from edge of continental shelf outward. |

Source: Wright and Nebel (2004, Table 2.1, p. 29).

Table 12.3 Ecosystem Services and Functions

Ecosystem Service	Ecosystem Function
Gas regulation	Regulation of atmospheric chemical composition.
Climate regulation	Regulation of global temperatures, precipitation and other biologically mediated climatic processes at global or local levels – e.g. greenhouse gas regulation, etc.
Disturbance regulation	Capacitance, damping, and integrity of ecosystem response to environmental fluctuations – e.g. protection, flood, control, drought recovery, and other aspects of habitat response to environmental variability controlled by vegetation structure.
Water regulation	Regulation of hydrologic flows – e.g. provisioning of water for agriculture (e.g. irrigation) or industrial (e.g. milling) processes or transportation.

Water supply	Storage and retention of water – e.g. provisioning of water by watersheds, reservoirs and aquifers.
Erosion control and sedimentation retention	Retention of water within ecosystem e.g. prevention of loss of soil.
Soil formation and nutrient cycling	Soil function processes and storage, internal cycling, processing, and acquisition of nutrients – e.g. nitrogen fixation.
Waste treatment	Recovery of mobile nutrients and removal or breakdown of excess nutrients and compounds – e.g. waste treatment, pollution control, detoxification.
Pollination	Movement of floral gametes – e.g. provisioning of pollinates for the reproduction of plant populations.
Biological control	Trophic–dynamic regulations of populations – e.g. keystone predator control of prey species, reduction of herbivores by top predators.
Food production and raw materials production	That portion of primary production extractable as food and raw materials—e.g. fish, game, crops, fruits as food, timber, fuel, fodder, etc. as raw materials.
Genetic resources	Sources of unique biological materials and products – e.g. medicines, products for materials science, genes for resistance to plant pathogens and crop pests, etc.
Recreation and cultural	Provision of recreational activities (ecosystem, sports, fishing and other outdoor activities); provision of opportunities for non-commercial uses (cultural: aesthetic, artistic, educational, etc. values).

Source: Wright and Nebel (2004), Table 3.3, p. 76.

Many ecosystem resources provide a flow of services and functions to humans as producers and consumers alike. Earth's atmosphere, specifically clean air and ozone layer, is a major contributor to the sustenance of life on Earth, as suggested by the dangers posed by depletion of the ozone layer (treated earlier in chapter 5). Forests, swamps or wetlands supply essential ecological services: they are known to filter and purify water, and act as reservoirs to capture rain and melting snow. Wetlands lie mostly in the tropical and semi-tropical regions, between 30° north of the Equator and 30° South of the Equator, a zone which incorporates much of Asia and the Pacific, most of Africa, and South and Central America.

The economic importance of tropical rivers and their associated wetlands have been studied in the literature. Adams (2009, p.313) citing Moorhead (1988) reports that the Inland Delta of the

Niger River in Mali supports over half a million people, and in the dry season supports grazing for some 1.5 million cattle, 2 million sheep and goats and 0.7 million camels, apart from some 80,000 fishermen. The seasonal grazing resources of the Niger Inland Delta are based on the perennial aquatic grass **bourgou** (*Echinochloa stagnina*) capable of yielding up to 25 tonnes per hectare of forage, and is accessible for livestock grazing once seasonal floodwaters recede (Skinner, 1992). Besides, there are other services provided by wetlands: sustaining regional groundwater levels and as an ecological and economic resource for very extensive surrounding drylands, especially in drought periods (e.g. Lake Chad); flood control; wildlife conservation, etc. (Barbier, 1998).

As scientific understanding of ecosystem services improves, new financial opportunities emerge: for example, the importance of tropical rainforests in protecting the ozone layer (via absorption of CO_2 during photosynthesis) was already becoming apparent by the beginning of the 2000s, which is probably behind the demand by developing countries for monetary compensation from the industrial countries for their forests[4]. Also, current REDD (Reducing Emissions from Deforestation and Degradation) initiatives, if successful, would yield huge financial benefits for developing countries in the tropical rainforest regions of the world e.g. Brazil, Indonesia, and Sub-Saharan African countries (those in the Congo Basin Rainforests).

12.3.1 Ecosystems Balance

Ecosystems are dynamic entities subject to periodic or occasional disturbances that disturb their equilibrium – referring to the balance between organisms and their physical environment – but are, nonetheless, capable of recovering from such disturbances provided their self-reproductive capabilities do not become destroyed. For instance, a drought (a local or regional lack of precipitation such that the ability to engage in water-dependent agricultural and livestock activities is seriously impaired) could constitute a short-term variability in ecological processes, which could lead to changes in ecosystem functions. Long-term changes in ecosystem environment do also shape ecosystem processes: e.g. drought conditions decades (and even centuries) back could still leave their imprints on current ecosystem environment. The frequency and severity of ecosystem disturbances determine how ecosystem processes are affected: for instance, as pointed out already, the frequency and severity of droughts will impact on the hydrologic cycle and, hence, the regulation of water flows and provisioning of water for agriculture (e.g. irrigation) on industrial processes or transportation (e.g. river channels become too shallow to permit passage of certain sizes of boats or ships) or even domestic use. Specifically, ecological disturbances like drought could leave behind shrinking freshwater inland lakes and flood plains with disappearing fauna and flora – as in the case of Lake Chad, to which we return below.

Ecosystems are controlled by external and internal forces and processes. External forces, most importantly climate (rainfall and temperature) control the overall structure of ecosystems but remain themselves uninfluenced by the ecosystems themselves. But the climate determines the biomes[5] in which the ecosystem is embedded. On the other hand, internal forces (e.g. animal and plant life, microbial organisms) not only control ecosystem processes, but are also controlled by them – hence, they (internal processes) are often subject to feedback loops – negative or positive[6]. The most important internal element controlling ecosystems is human beings; unlike other internal controlling elements, the cumulative effects of the human influence on ecosystems are large enough to influence external processes like climate. Specifically, global warming, on the scale and trend, it has assumed since the 1700s, is a human-induced factor (originating in fossil fuel emissions, deforestation, etc.) and is the key factor influencing climate.

Ecosystems are sustained by two basic principles and processes: first, the use of sunlight as their source of energy (See chapter 2, Figure 2.1); and, second, recycling of nutrients in what natural scientists call biogeochemical cycle (also nutrient cycle)[7] whereby the products and by-products of each group of organisms become the food and essential nutrients for the other organisms; thus, there is a cyclical movement of energy and materials within ecosystems. But this cyclical movement of energy and materials is of fundamental importance for two reasons: first, it prevents waste accumulation that would, otherwise, constitute environmental pollution that could undermine, even completely destroy, the life-sustaining capabilities of ecosystems; and, second, recycling guarantees continuous supply of essential elements by ecosystems.

The paradigm that ecosystems are equilibrating systems-thus, are systems in long-run balance or stability-assumes that the two basic principles identified above remain uninterrupted in their workings – e.g. that the recycling capabilities of ecosystems are not undermined or overburdened by human activity such as when fossil-fuel GHG emissions destroy the ozone layer and, hence, disrupting the life-sustaining capability of solar energy, or when the exploitation of rainforests via logging with the exclusive aim of maximizing profits in the short-run leads to the disruption of the carbon storage capabilities of Earth's forests.

The paradigm that ecosystems are equilibrium systems borrows ideas from classical economics; indeed, the idea of ecosystem equilibrium had dominated ecology up until the 1970s (Steward et al., 1992); this paradigm suggested that ecosystems were closed, and self-regulating, so that if disturbed, they possessed internal, built-in, equilibrating mechanisms, which, in turn, gave rise to the idea that there was a 'balance of nature', easily upset by inappropriate human-induced processes.[8]

12.4 Ecosystem Resources: The Renewable and Nonrenewable Distinction

The literature draws a fundamental distinction between renewable and nonrenewable ecosystem resources. This distinction is based on the criterion, namely, whether the resource in question can or cannot replenish its stock within a time-frame meaningful to the human mind.

12.4.1 Renewable Resources

Thus, a renewable resource (also an infinite or perpetual resource) is one that can replenish itself at a sufficient rate for sustainable economic extraction in a meaningful timeframe[9]. Examples here are timber, fish, wildlife, etc. – these are organic or biological resources that can reproduce themselves according to biological laws within timeframes meaningful to the human mind, provided their rates of use or exploitation does not undermine or destroy their regeneration capacities through degradation or overexploitation. Open rangelands regenerate each year; fish breed new stocks to replenish harvested ones; wildlife replenishes its herds; biomass regenerates, etc. – provided, as already posited, their reproductive potentials are not impaired. Provided annual harvests do not exceed the annual growth of the stock, it is possible to exploit renewable resources sustainably (Tietenberg, 2000).

Some inorganic or non-living resources – e.g. wind energy, solar energy, wave energy, water power, geothermal energy, etc. – are considered renewable resources, precisely because their localized replenishment occurs within time-frames meaningful to the human mind; thus, this category of renewable resources is available for use on a continuing basis. Of solar energy, for instance, Wright and Nebel (op. cit.,) observe:

> "How much or how little of this energy is used on Earth will not influence, much less deplete, the Sun's output. For all practical purposes, the Sun is an ever-lasting source of energy" (p. 68).

However, scientists (astronomers) inform us that the Sun will burn out in another 3-5 billion years! Even so, 3-5 billion years is a time-frame that is meaningless to the human mind; it is meaningful only in the context of geological time-frames when Earth's minerals, fossil-fuels and metal-and non-metal minerals are formed.

We should point out, however, that there is certain difficulty in establishing, in practice, whether certain renewable resources qualify as renewable in the strict definition of this term: ability to replenish at a sufficient rate for sustainable economic extraction in meaningful time-frames. In principle, water, for example, is a renewable inorganic resource replenished via the hydrologic cycle (chapter 6), but, in practice, in the absence of good water control and management, short-term exploitation of water can be characterized by over-drawing (in the case of underground water or surface freshwater lakes) relative to rates of recharge, which will likely yield results better likened to mining fossil minerals – e.g. coal or crude oil – than sustainable use.

Whereas a resource such as solar energy is a perpetual resource – infinite in output- this cannot be said of all resources that are, in principle, renewable. The fact is that, as pointed out above, over-exploitation of a renewable resource – such as serious over-fishing of a particular species (an example is often the case of tuna in the Pacific Ocean); or excessive removal of vegetation cover from low-quality soils (such as the case in many parts of sub-Saharan Africa, through the use of 'slash-and-burn' farming techniques or over-grazing by livestock farmers (see Weber and Horst, 2011), or excessive withdrawal of water from inland freshwater lakes and seas (as is the case of the Aral Sea in South-central Russia or Lake Chad in West Africa) can destroy an otherwise renewable resource.

12.4.2 Nonrenewable Resources

Nonrenewable resources are depletable resources – so-called because such resources are completely used up when used at all, and must eventually get exhausted in their supplies regardless of rate of exploitation. Thus, nonrenewable resources are fixed in their supplies (by nature); they do not possess natural capacity to self-generate or to replenish (in contrast to renewable resources) at sufficient rates for sustainable extraction in meaningful time-frames. Perfect examples are fossil minerals (coal, crude oil or petroleum, natural gas, etc) and non-fossil minerals (copper, iron ore, uranium, phosphorus, etc.).

Nonrenewable resources do, however, replenish but only within geological time-frames that are not meaningful to the human mind. For instance, most deposits of fossil minerals currently being extracted were formed in the geological past – some 286-360 million years ago (in the case of coal deposits); more recent ones were formed 144-1.8 million years ago (see, for instance, Mayhew, 2009, p. 164)[10]. Global reserves of coal are estimated to amount to 5.04 billion tonnes, which at current rates of exploitation will be exhausted in 250 years (Clunies-Ross et al., 2009, pp. 292-5). Crude oil has global reserves put at 1.23 trillion barrels-sufficient to last another 100 years; natural gas, often found in association with crude oil, has known global reserves of some 177.4 trillion cubic metres (m^3) – sufficient to last another 50-60 years at current rates of exploitation.[11]

12.5 Special Type of Ecosystem Resource: Biodiversity

The renewable and nonrenewable ecosystem resources analyzed above reside in one sphere or the other of Earth's environment and can be located as visible elements. For instance: water as a renewable resource is in different forms and reservoirs in Earth's hydrosphere; fossil fuels are extracted from the lithosphere; air (ozone) is a component element of the atmosphere; etc. However, there are ecosystem resources that do not reside in anyone substance but in a collection of elements, and so do not reside in one specific compartment of Earth's environment. One such resource readily comes to mind namely **biodiversity**. As ecosystem resource, biodiversity should not be abused or overexploited in the same way we should not overexploit renewable and nonrenewable resources. Yet, biodiversity is threatened by anthropogenic climate change.

Beginning in the 1980s biodiversity began to impress itself upon both academic and policy thinking, perhaps because of the ecological crisis – referring to a human-induced ecological disorder that could lead to the destruction of Earth's ecosystems. On the hand, the ecological crisis is a result of extensive deforestation, increased atmospheric CO_2 concentrations, ocean acidification, etc. But since the beginning of the 1980s, there has occurred extensive deforestation, increasing scale of atmospheric carbon dioxide concentration, ocean acidification, etc., which suggest that the ecological crisis was no longer just a hypothesis but, infact, a reality.

Biodiversity, as the term suggests, is not something that resides in anyone organism or element; on the contrary, it refers to the collection of the diverse living organisms that constitute Earth's biosphere, the composite of the genetic information, species, and ecosystems that provide humans with natural wealth in the form of food, fibre, medicines and pharmaceutical preparations, and inputs into diverse industrial processes; besides, it supplies the raw materials that may assist human communities to adapt to future and unforeseen environmental stresses (World Bank, 1992, p. 59).

The Oxford Dictionary of Science (2005, p. 91) defines biodiversity or biological diversity to refer to:

> "…existence of a wide variety of species (**species diversity**) or other taxa of plants, animals, and microorganisms in a natural community or habitat, or of communities within a particular environment (**ecological diversity**), or of genetic variation within a species (**genetic diversity**)" (emphasis and bracketed words in original).

There are other, if similar, definitions by geographers and environmental economists. Thus, Mayhew's (2009, p. 47) defines biodiversity to refer to:

> "The number and variety of living organisms, from individual parts of communities to ecosystems, regions, and the entire biosphere, including: the genetic diversity of an individual species; the subpopulations of an individual species; the total number of species in a region; the number of endemic species in an area; and the distribution of different ecosystems" (p. 47).

Finally, Field and Field's (2009, p. 205) conceives biodiversity as '… the stock of unique genetic material contained in the millions of animals and plant species worldwide'.

The literature points out that there is greater biodiversity in the tropical regions of the world than at the poles. Certain habitats, particularly tropical rainforests, habour rich species diversity which are currently threatened by anthropogenic activities. Adams (2009, p. 17) citing Palumbi (2001) points out that rising human demands on the biosphere involving continuous annexation of biological processes to attempt to improve productivity has had adverse impacts on biodiversity, while at the same time creating evolutionary trajectories in the species and ecosystems:

"Humans are not simply annexing the earth's productivity, and driving the reduction of living diversity, but also starting to effect evolutionary trajectories in the species and ecosystems…"

So, as posited above, biodiversity is quite unlike other renewable ecological resources (plant or animal or microbial organisms) that can be identified in one item or one geographical location. Rather, it is represented in the variety of living beings that constitute and distinguish Earth's biosphere. The latter describes that sphere or zone of Earth's surface where life or living organisms (humans, animals, plants and microbes) are found (Cloud, 1983). Briefly, all species on Earth, along with all their ecosystems, can be conceived as one vast ecosystem, even as the separate, individual ecosystems constitute their individual units of sustainability.

Scientists do admit, however, that the number of species on Earth has never been precisely ascertained (and may never be precisely ascertained). An estimated 5-100 million have been speculated in the literature (UNEP, 1995; Bishop and Hill, 2014); on the other hand, only about 1.75 million species of plants, animals and microbes have been examined, named, and classified (Wright and Nebel, op. cit., p. 264; see also Hails et al., 2006; United States National Academy of Sciences, 1998). Briefly what we (do not) know currently on biodervisity in regard to number of species is based on "educated cases and opinion of experts". These guessestimates range from 3 million to 100 million species – widely differing estimates, indeed! According to the United States National Academy of Sciences (1998), a typical 10 km² of pristine rainforest may contain as many as 125 species of mammals, 100 species of reptiles, 400 species of birds, 150 species of butterflies, etc. (see also Hails et al., 2006).

12.6 Ecosystem Resources as Biological or Natural Wealth

The actual species of many organisms collectively are responsible for the structure and maintenance of ecosystems; the ecosystems they form represent a kind of wealth-the biological wealth – that sustains human life and economic activity with goods and services (see Tables 12.1, 12.2 and 12.3).

"It is as if the natural world were an enormous bank account of capital assets, capable of paying vital, life-sustaining dividends indefinitely, but, like a bank account, only as long as the capital is maintained" (Wright and Nebel, op. cit., p. 264).

The biota existing in each economy represents a major component of the country's wealth – its natural capital.

Valuing the worth of a nation's ecological resources has brought into the economic development vocabulary the notion of natural capital – which suggests that there is wealth involved in a natural ecosystem and associated biodiversity, which can yield income. First, ecological resources constitute the natural assets of a nation-state in the form of nonrenewable minerals (fossil fuels, metal and non-metal minerals) and renewable resources such as land, timber, rangelands, fisheries, underground water, inland freshwater lakes, beaches, etc. – these are exploited on a continuous basis to meet human needs in their various forms and generate incomes. Second, there are the services performed by natural ecosystems that benefit human life and enterprises, represented in such goods like timber, fibre, and food, and vital services such as waste assimilation and nutrient recycling.

Figure 12.1 provides a conceptual illustration of the total economic benefits of ecosystems using the tropical rainforest ecosystem. Thus, the total economic value of an ecosystem can be broken into two broad categories: (i) use-values (outputs or services that can be consumed directly or indirectly); and (ii) non-use-values (values that confer no current visible material benefits to society) though, but serve to provide stability to ecosystems, apart from representing an important pool of species and genetic material of potential use to human societies.

Figure 12.1 A Conceptual Illustration of the Economic Benefits of Ecosystems

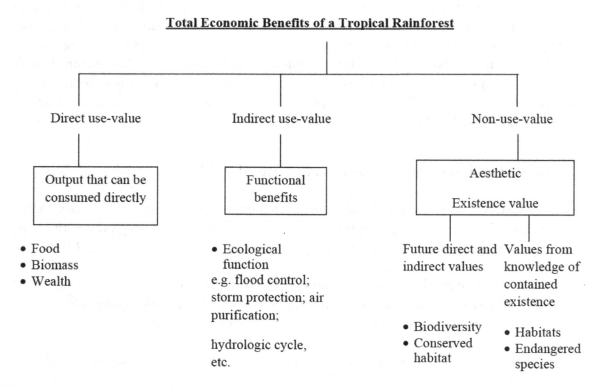

Total Economic Benefits of a Tropical Rainforest

Direct use-value — Output that can be consumed directly
- Food
- Biomass
- Wealth

Indirect use-value — Functional benefits
- Ecological function e.g. flood control; storm protection; air purification; hydrologic cycle, etc.

Non-use-value — Aesthetic / Existence value

Future direct and indirect values
- Biodiversity
- Conserved habitat

Values from knowledge of contained existence
- Habitats
- Endangered species

Source: Adapted from Monasinghe 1993

The direct benefits of tropical rainforests come in the provision of livelihoods for rural populations in developing countries: wild fruits, mushrooms, assorted plants, seeds and naturally growing edible resources, etc – these still represent, indeed, a significant source of nutrition in many countries, especially in rural areas (Cavendish, 1999; Falconer and Arnold, 1989; Falconer, 1990; Chomitz and Kumari, 1998). Apart from serving as a direct source of food, rainforests supply timber, bark, sap, and medicinal plants (Ibe and Nwufo, 2005). The indirect use-values of tropical rainforests come in the ecological services and functions they provide, whose social benefits often exceed their direct benefits: they influence local and regional climates; store carbon or capture dioxide and thereby regulating the amount of atmospheric CO_2; preserve soil cover on site, and in the case of watersheds protect soil downstream from floods; etc. Mangrove rainforests provide an illustration of an ecosystem whose social benefits exceed the direct benefits; the services and functions they render to society as a whole are hardly appreciated, which has led to their destruction in many countries. Mangrove rainforests occur in tropical coastal areas where waters are shallow and river deltas receive suspended sediment (mud) – often termed coastlands.[13] Mangrove prop-roots trap sediments from ebb and flood tidal currents, gradually extending land seawards; mangrove forests commonly consist of several shoreward belts of red, black, and white mangroves which constitute highly productive marine and estuarine ecosystems. Mangroves generate large volumes of degradable waste (leaves, stems, etc.) called **detritus**, the primary energy source for tropical coastal marine ecosystems. Colonies of microscopic life feed on **detritus** and are in turn consumed by estuarine species-shrimp, some fish, and small crustaceans, which serve as forage for birds, predatory fish, and eventually humans.

Other 'free' services are provided by mangroves, including storm protection, erosion control, wastewater cleansing, and areas for educational and leisure activities, as well as many direct products (fuelwood, construction timber, etc.) and indirect products (food from fish, shrimp, birds, etc.). Moreover, mangroves are a renewable resource – reproducing and regenerating themselves at no costs: sustainable yields of food and other items can be harvested on a continuing basis provided the ecological or biochemical processes governing the mangrove ecosystem are not overexploited and destroyed.

The first attempt to estimate the value of natural capital at the global level was made by a team of thirteen natural scientists and economists led by Robert Costanza (Costanza et al., 1997). The reason for their study was that the goods and services supplied by natural ecosystems are hardly captured in market prices, so that it is not easy to place a monetary value on them. Costanza and his team identified seventeen major ecosystem goods and services and their functions for humans; they also identified the ecosystem functions that actually carry out the vital human support and gave examples of each, arguing that it was useless to consider human welfare outside these ecosystem services.

The economic development literature of the 1990s onwards centred on the notion of sustainable development evolved a framework for so-called environmental accounting. The latter seeks to incorporate not only produced capital goods (e.g. machines, plant, infrastructure, etc.) and human capital (knowledge, work experience and skills inhering in a nation's workforce) but, also, natural capital (forests, soils, rangeland, beaches, etc.) (Aronsoon and Lofgren, 2010).

12.7 Anthropogenic Climate Change and Biodiversity Loss

That human-induced climate change is exacting heavy toll on planet Earth's ecosystems and associated biodiversity is no longer in doubt. What is in doubt is the extent of the effect of climate change on ecosystems and the consequences in quantitative terms (Hails et al., 2006; Botkin et al., 2007), which probably explains the poor appreciation by the public at large of the problem of biodiversity loss (Tobey, 1996; Wilson, 1992; Mayhew, op. cit., p. 47). Current literature reports of mass ecosystem extinction – the fastest in human history (see, for instance, Wilson, op. cit.) – which is clearly a result of human activity.

Biodiversity crisis describes observed significant decline in the number and variety of living organisms, from individual parts of the communities to ecosystems, regions and entire biosphere, including: the genetic diversity of an individual species; the subpopulations of an individual species; the total number of species in a region; the number of endemic species in an area; and the distribution of different ecosystems (Mayhew, op. cit., p. 47). Even within scientific circles the full spectrum of biodiversity values and impact of human activity on the stability and resilience of ecosystems are yet to be properly understood.

Scientists argue that, for example, ecosystems undergo irreversible collapse when certain 'thresholds' of damage are reached; but knowledge of such thresholds remains highly theoretical (see below), at best, poor in practice. Estimates on the late 1990s by UNEP (1995) cited in Adams (2009) suggest that up to 5-20% of the estimated 14 million plant and animal species on Earth are threatened by extinction (UNEP, 1995). Wilson (1992, p. 268) sounding rather alarmist, remarks that human-induced climate change has had the effect of increasing previous 'background' extinction rates by at least 100 and 10,000 times: 'we are in the midst of one of the great extinction spasms of geological history'. He (Wilson) calculates that if the annual extinction rate is 0.27%, and the tropical forests contain 50% of all species, then about 0.14% of all species are committed to extinction each year; unless immediate action is taken to restrain the rate of tropical habitat loss, the 2000s will see another major extinction catastrophe.

The ecological crisis has been most visible in (much of the) developing world: Africa and Asia are reported to have lost almost 66% of their natural habitat. Powerful drivers of this process have been identified in: people's desire for better way of life; desperate poverty of rural populations; booming global market for animal, timber and forest resources – all these continue to generate forces that 'draw down biological wealth' in developing countries (Wright and Nebel, op. cit., pp. 276-84). Pollution is another powerful factor. In the industrialized world energy-intensive and other modern technologies continue to emit enormous volumes of GHGs into the atmosphere. As pointed out earlier, anthropogenic GHGs 'are the legacy of the already developed nations' (ibid, 278). We now proceed to provide illustrations of biodiversity loss arising from destruction of ecosystems.

12.7.1 Destruction of Coral Reefs and Mangroves: Symptom of Biodiversity Crisis

The destruction of coral reefs by climate change illustrates, clearly, the biodiversity crisis. Coral reefs are mainly of calcium carbonate, formed by secretions of small marine animals in tropical oceans (mainly in the Indian and Pacific oceans). They thrive most in shallow ocean waters over 21°C and need abundant sunlight, so that the water must be mud free and shallow (Mayhew, op. cit., p. 105). Globally, coral reefs thrive in ocean waters 30°C north to 30°C south of the equator.

Scientific studies report that coral reefs are among the most diverse and biologically productive ecosystems on Earth, harbouring an estimated nearly one million species globally. However, the viability of coral reefs is reported to be in rapid decline, caused by overfishing, nutrient enrichment, and coral diseases, at the local scale, and ocean warming, acidification, and sea-level rise at the global level (Wright and Nebel, op. cit., pp. 306-307; Maes et al., 2013). Schneider et al. (2007, p. 792) warn that a global mean temperature rises of 2°C above 1990 levels would result in mass mortality of coral reefs; of freshwater ecosystems, that 4°C increase in global mean temperature by 2100 (relative to 1990-2000 levels) would result in many species becoming extinct.

These predictions may sound alarmist though; but the devastation of coral reefs on the coast of Belize (in South America) by high sea-surface temperatures during the 1997-98 El Niño lend credence to such predictions. The intensity and frequency of El Niño are thought to be a consequence of global warming (see Wright and Nebel, op. cit.). Extensive coral bleaching – wherein the coral animals lose their symbiotic algae – resulted in the death of 15% of the world's reef corals during the summer of 1998 (ibid., p. 306). Scientific studies posit that some annual bleaching is normal though, related to the high temperatures and light intensities of summer, but the 1998 event seems unprecedented. Belize, home to the longest barrier reef in the northern hemisphere, witnessed temperatures as high as 31.5°C (89°F) in the El Niño event of 1997-98, which devastated most of the coral.

El Niño, as a term applies to climate, originated with fishermen in Ecuador and Peru, who used El Niño to mean the Christ Child as a way to describe a warm current that appears every few years (5 to 8 years) in their fishing areas – specifically, off the eastern coast of South America (in the equatorial part of the Pacific Ocean), characterized by movement of a mass of warm water eastwards towards the west coast of South America (**Oxford Dictionary of Science**, 2005; pp. 286-7; Wright and Nebel, op. cit., p. 509). In normal years the trade winds blow from east to west across the Pacific, effect a difference in sea level and a mass of warm water builds up in the Western Pacific.

This, in turn, creates a warm area of ocean off the east coast of Indonesia, known to record some of the highest rainfall regimes in the world. In El Niño years, there is a reduction in the intensity of trade winds across the Pacific, which allows the mass of warm water in the west to flow across to the east, creating a warm area of ocean off the west coast of South America, which brings rain to Peru but causes drought in Southeast Asia and Australia.

Coral reefs are also being destroyed by eutrophication of coastal waters: when nutrients – especially phosphorus – are deposited on the reefs by currents in the vicinity of developed coastlines, they encourage the growth of macroscopic algae and other submerged vegetation (Wright and Nebel, op. cit., p. 306); as the coral becomes shaded (from sunlight) the coral animals become starved of oxygen, which, in turn, causes the reefs to become brittle and stunted (see also Oxford Dictionary of Biology, 2000, p. 18). Studies report that the algae thrive in the corals because herbivorous turtles and fish that normally graze on the corals have been removed.

Another source of damage traces to the fact that islanders and coastal people in the tropics depend on the reef for fish, shellfish and other edible sea foods. Besides, there is commercial exploitation, encouraged by thriving trade in tropical fish – reported to be worth annually of up to $1.2 billion in Southeast Asia (Wright and Nebel, op. cit., pp. 306-7). Locals are reported to employ illegal fishing practices: cyanide (and dynamite), are used to flush the fish out of their hiding in the coral, a deadly practice which damages the coral severely.

Finally, there is the problem of mangrove deforestation. Mangrove trees have the unique ability to take root and grow in shallow marine sediments, where they protect the coasts from damage due to storms and erosion and form a refuge and nursery for marine fish (Wright and Nebel, op. cit., p. 307). Mangroves are equally under assault from three exploitative activities: coastal development, logging, and shrimp aquaculture (ibid.). It is reported that between 1983 and the first decade of the 2000s, half of the world's 45 million acres of mangroves were cut down – from 40% (e.g. in Cameroon and Indonesia) to up to about 80% (e.g. in Bangladesh and Philippines) (ibid.). The mangrove forests of Nigeria are the third largest in the world, and the largest in Africa; over 60% of this mangrove ecosystem complex is in the Niger Delta and covers some 6000 km². Muoghalu (2007) reports that high rates of deforestation are destroying this ecosystem.

12.7.2 Overfishing and Depletion of Fish Stocks

This is a classic example of the tragedy of the commons. But overfishing is a form of overexploitation whereby fish stocks are driven or harvested to levels below accepted levels. This occurs in ponds, rivers, lakes, open seas, etc. and can result in resource depletion and reduced growth rates of fish stocks.

Overfishing, which can result in upsetting entire marine ecosystems (Scales, 2007), has been documented in several parts of the world, of which the following are the very notable ones often cited in the literature: Western Atlantic Ocean from the earliest days of European colonization of the Americas (Bolster, 2012); the Peruvian Coast anchovy crisis in the 1970s, declining from 10.2 million metric tons of anchovy to 4 million metric tons (Trade and Development Database, 1999); the collapse of codfish off Newfoundland (Kunzig, 1995); and East China Sea (Lu Hu, 2006).

12.7.3 The Lake Chad Experience

Africa is endowed with some 677 inland lakes, holding about 30,000 km^3 of freshwater and yielding 1.4 million tons of freshwater annually. Before its current dramatic shrinking starting in the 1970s, Lake Chad was ranked the fourth largest among Africa's inland lakes and sixth largest in the world. Lake Chad initially spanned 25,000 km^2; by the beginning of the 2000s, it had shrunk to 1500 km^2 – 6% of its original surface area! Satellite images show that Lake Chad has receded 72 km from its original surface area, including flooded areas at peak flood periods.

Lake Chad, located in the semi-arid Sahel, is perched on the southern edge of the Sahara Desert; and straddles four West African countries: Niger, Chad, Cameroon and Nigeria. The human population of the Lake Chad basin is estimated currently to exceed 37 million people; more than 50% of this population is located within the Nigerian side of the lake (Onuoha, 2008). Apart from fishing, livestock farming constitutes a major source of livelihood for the diverse ethnic groups inhabiting the Lake Chad basin; indeed, the latter has for centuries been the 'traditional convergence point' for herdsmen and pastoralists of the western Sudan: Tuareg, Toubou, Feda, Kaemba, Shuwa Arab, Fulani and Waidai from Niger, Chad, Northern Cameroon and Northern Nigeria (Ibrahim, 1989). Lake Chad has served as a vital source of freshwater and other resources for human, livestock and wildlife communities. The flood plains support a rich terrestrial and aquatic fauna; more than 150,000 fishermen live on the lake shores and its islands. The fisheries are of the artisanal category though, which poses difficulty in terms of regulation and control of the fish stocks, which in turn poses potential damage for overexploitation of the over 220 species of fish recorded in the basin.

In addition to the rich fish fauna, the basin harbors enormous bird population comprising many seasonal migratory and resident species. Lake Chad and its islands offer migration routes for birds moving between Africa and Palearctic; at least, 70 species of migratory birds are recorded, though their numbers are reported to have declined relative to the 1960s. In contrast to the fish and fauna, the mammalian fauna is much less rich in species and most of them are getting extinct, facilitated by unregulated hunting activities. The Sahelian large mammalian species found in the Lake Chad ecosystem include: the red-fronted gazelle, dama gazelle, and dorcas gazelle; striped hyena; patas monkey; cheetah; caracal; and the endangered wild dog. Other species include: the African elephant; two specie of otter; hippopotamus; sitatunga, etc.

Coe and Foley (2001) using computer models and satellite data provided by United States' NASA (National Aeronautics and Space Administration) estimate the age of Lake Chad to be 20,000 years – which is quite young in the context of geological time-frame that runs in millennia.

The Lake Chad hydrological basin is located between latitude 6° and 24°N and longitude 7° and 24°E; it spans a geographical basin covering 2,434,000 km² or 8% of the African continent, shared between the following countries: Algeria, Libya, Sudan (which now includes Sudan and South Sudan), Niger, Chad, Cameroon and Nigeria. About 20% of the total area of the Lake Chad Basin, or 427500 km², is under the mandate of the Lake Chad Basin Commission (LCBC) established under the Fort Lamy (now N'djamena) convention and statutes on May 22, 1964 (UNCCD, 2012). Finally, Lake Chad is situated on a plateau at an altitude of about 283 meters above mean sea level; it is drained by numerous rivers, including the Chari-Logone (which provides 90% of the inflow to the lake), Komadugu-Gana or Lesser Yobe Ebeji, Ebeji Mbuli, Botha El Beed, the Yedseram, Ngadolu, Ngadda, Komaduguyobe, Taf-taf and Sebewel.

What can account for the dramatic shrinking of Lake Chad from an original surface area of 25000 km² to just 1500 km² by the beginning of the 2000s? Satellite images taken by the United Nations Environmental Programme (UNEP) show that more than 600 of Africa's 677 inland lakes have shrunk dramatically in the past 4-5 decades, of which the Lake Chad experience is, perhaps, the most studied and the most dramatic.

We have seen that many natural ecological systems have equally experienced dramatic changes similar to the Lake Chad experience due to climate change: e.g. melting mountain snow and ice caps; retreating polar glaciers; warming oceans leading to rising sea levels; etc. So, there is nothing particularly unique in the shrinking of Lake Chad, if considered in the context of other natural ecosystems currently experiencing dramatic changes. However, there is need, still, to explore the following question: Is the dramatic shrinking of Lake Chad a result of natural variation or climate change or is it human-induced? There are atleast four perspectives on this problem: natural climate variation; drought; overdrawing the regenerative potential of the hydrologic system; and population pressure.

A. Natural Climate Variation

This perspective strongly supports climate variation as the key explanatory factor. It is advanced by palaeoclimatologists who study climates of earlier geological eras based largely on the study of sediments that were laid down during these periods and of fossils. These studies explain that the millennia-scale changes in Earth's orbit could have caused the wet conditions prevailing in the early Holocene[14] and current dry desert conditions: a 'green Sahara' and a 'desert Sahara'[15]. It is pointed out, however, that changes in the positions of the continents because of continental drift (the theory that the continents were once joined in a single mass) and plate tectonics (the theory that Earth's surface is made of lithospheric plates, which have moved throughout geological time resulting in the present-day positions of the continents, and which explains the locations of mountain building as well as earthquakes and volcanoes) make such studies rather complex. Nevertheless, however, this perspective provides some useful insights into the changing climates of the Lake Chad area.

Historical records show that the margins of the African Sahara were wetter in the 1500s through the 1700s, but experienced major droughts in the 1680s and between 1738 and 1756 (Nicholson, 1978, 1996). The end of the 1700s through the later 1800s witnessed drier conditions; between 1875 and 1895, the period of European colonial expansion into Africa, wetter conditions were experienced. Similar wetter periods and drier conditions prevailed in Southern Africa, and rainfall anomalies in Africa of the 1900s reflect those of the 1800s (Nicholson, 1996).

It seems that the Lake Chad area, as of the entire African Sahara, was vegetated, even as it alternated between wet and dry conditions. What then explains the sudden shift in climate into desert ecology in the Lake Chad area (and African Sahara)? It is explained that the first climate shift began to unfold about 5500 years ago, when there occurred sudden transition from vegetated to desert ecology. Wet ecology in the African Sahara giving way to extensive vegetation, lakes, wetlands, etc. came to abrupt end about 5500 years ago.

B. Drought and the Shrinking of Lake Chad

This perspective blames drought as the dominant factor in the shrinking of Lake Chad. The Sahel environment in which Lake Chad is embedded is hot and dry, characterized by a highly erratic rainfall regime ranging from 565 mm in 1954 (the highest ever?) to just 94 mm in 1984. Let us note that annual rainfall in the Sahel averages 200-400mm; however, severe droughts, as obtained in the early 1970s, bring this down to less than 100mm.

A study on the hydrological history of the Lake Chad basin in the early 1980s found that the balance between the water intake and evaporation is continuously changing its size and shape (Connah, 1981). Overall, this has been decreasing in the Lake Chad basin since the 1960s, caused by drought. The droughts of the early 1970s (1972-1974) were, perhaps, the most severe in living memory in terms of its toll on human life and livestock and agricultural losses (Nicholson, 1978; Apeldoorn, 1981; Dike, 1986; Mortimore, 1986, 1998; Mijindadi and Adegbehin, 1991; Bloeman, 2011). The 1972-1974 droughts saw the end of the groundnut boom in Nigerian agriculture: as the boundaries of the Sahara Desert shifted further southwards, this made crop production above the 12° latitudes almost impossible (Mijindadi and Adegbehin, op. cit.). As noted earlier in chapter 10, there were droughts in the early 1990s and 2005; the latest occurred in 2010 and 2012. Briefly, modern Sahelian droughts began in the 1960s and have continued into the 2000s, during which rainfall has fallen below the 1930-1960 mean (average).

A key feature of the Sahel is that rainfall is confined to just three months of the year (July-September) or even less, and averages less than 100 mm annually, all of which occurs in a season lasting at the longest three months and in some seasons barely a few weeks. Specifically, the Sahel rainfall has decreased from the wet 1950-1960s to the dry 1970s-2000s, a huge part of which is attributable to climate change – the change in the inter-hemispheric contrast of the Atlantic sea-surface temperatures (SSTs). What factors lie behind the Sahel drought?

Earlier analyses in the 1970s and 1980s blamed anthropogenic factors: the prolonged mismanagement of the savanna grassland ecosystem, coupled with the fragile nature of the savanna ecosystem has stripped open large areas of vegetation thereby making 'the soil susceptible to wind/ water erosion' (Mijindadi and Adegbehin, op. cit., pp. 27 – 28)[16].

A section of the international policy circle bought into this perspective. The UNEP stressed the impact of the Sahel droughts: the impacts and size of the regions affected by the Sahel droughts are unprecedented in hydro-climatic history (UNEP, 2007; IPCC, 2012). According to UNEP, fluctuations in Lake Chad's size are a sensitive indicator of climate change. Over a substantial area of Africa covered by the Sahel within which Lake Chad is located – an area stretching over 5000 km in an west-to-east direction running from southern Mauritania across the entire northern fringes of West Africa into Somalia and the Horn of Africa. The droughts of the 1970s and 1980s left serious environmental degradation impacts on Lake Chad: shrinking lake surface area and decreased flows in the major rivers feeding Lake Chad; falling groundwater tables; disappearance of specific fauna and flora species; reduction in canopy cover because of disappearance of specific plant species; increased soil erosion and loss of soil fertility. Since the 1970s the discharge from the Chari/Logone river system providing 90% of water inflows to Lake Chad has drastically reduced by almost 75%; as a result, the maximum flooded areas of the Lake Chad plains have dropped from 37000 km^2 in the 1950s to 15000 km^2 in the 1990s (see also Niasse, 2005).

A team of researchers at the Massachusetts Institute of Technology (MIT) (cited in Smith, 2000) locate the cause of West Africa's incessant drought in deforestation in the coastal rainforest zones; they conclude that further deforestation in West Africa 'could cause the complete collapse of the West African Monsoon'. This team used a statistical computer model to show that as deforestation proceeded in West Africa's coastal regions, coastal rainfall will no longer be recycled to create inland precipitation. It based its explanation on developments in the 1970s: after three decades of heavy deforestation rainfall over West Africa has been lower than usual.

Monsoon involves large-scale sea breezes which occur when the temperature on land is significantly warmer than that on the oceans, causing temperature imbalance. Usually, the latter occurs because land and ocean exhibit significant differences in capacity to absorb heat: the ocean can absorb heat faster than land can, which makes the land environment significantly warmer than ocean environment[17]. As the lower atmosphere (troposphere) over land gets warmer, evaporation will intensify resulting in an increase in moisture circulating in the lower atmosphere, which in turn, leads to increased frequency of precipitation events mainly over land. As the latter warms up faster than the ocean it creates low pressure into which moisture-laden winds flow.

Monsoons have been described in Western and Eastern Africa[18]. In West Africa, it is hypothesized that warmer temperatures (caused by global warming) have led to increased drying up of the land surface, given high rates of deforestation (extensive cutting down of forests for the purpose of extracting timber or fuel wood or to clear land for mining or agriculture)[19]. In Western Africa, the monsoon comes in late June; there is a continuous southerly flow of warmer, moisture-laden air into mainland West Africa. This flow is a continuation of the south-easterly trade winds, altered to the south-westerlies as they move northwards, across the equator, bringing huge precipitation. Subsiding upper air prevents heavy precipitation in the Sahel located south of the Sahara Desert proper. The monsoon begins to retreat in September-October; therefore, the north-east harmattan winds, dry and dust-laden as they blow across the Sahara Desert, begin to dominate.

Extensive deforestation in West Africa has reshaped the biosphere in a significant way, adversely affecting the functioning of the hydrologic cycle. How? Specifically, with existence of forests and other ecosystems, there is little runoff; rather, precipitation is intercepted by vegetation and infiltrates into porous topsoil – a process that 'provides the life-blood' of the natural ecosystems that constitute the biosphere (see Wright and Nebel, 2004, p. 221). But the evapotranspiration taking place in these ecosystems not only sustains the latter, but also recycles the water to local rainfall; some of the water percolates down to recharge the groundwater reservoirs, which, in turn, release water through springs, streams, rivers, etc. As forests became lost to deforestation or land is overgrazed, the natural pathway of the hydrologic cycle is thrown off balance: it shifts from infiltration and groundwater recharge to runoff, as the water runs into streams or rivers almost immediately – a major cause of flooding.

C. Overdrawing the Regenerative Potential of Lake Chad Hydrologic System

If climate variability and occasional extreme droughts in the West African Sahel negatively affected water availability in Lake Chad, diversion of the waters of the lake for dam construction and increased water use by rapidly human populations contributed to undermining 'the carrying capacity of the lake to replenish itself' (Onuoha, 2008, p. 71). Large and unsustainable irrigation projects and impoundments undertaken by Chad, Cameroon, Nigeria and Niger, which have diverted substantial volumes of water from both Lake Chad and its two-major feeder-rivers-Chari-Logone and Komadugu-Yobe Rivers – constitute significant factors affecting the hydrology of the Lake Chad area. The major facilities which have contributed to the shrinking of the lake are: the construction of both the Yaguou-Tekele dyke (on the Chari-Logone) and the Maga Dam by Cameroon in 1979; a series of dams by Nigeria, such as the Tiga Dam on River Yobe, the Alau Dam on River Ngadda, the Yedersdam Dam on River Yedersdam, and the South Chad Irrigation Project (SCIP); and the MAMDI Polder Project in the Republic of Chad. These dam and irrigation facilities combined account for upwards of 30% of the observed shrinking of the Lake Chad's area since 1960 (e.g. Coe and Foley, 2001). By the end of the 1970s, irrigation was observed to have had a modest impact on the hydrology of the Lake Chad Basin; in contrast, as from the 1980s, the amount of water extracted for large-scale irrigation systems had increased four-fold relative to the amount drawn in the previous twenty-five years, accounting for 50% of the additional decrease in the Lake's size.

The SCIP facility built by Nigeria was aimed at developing wheat production in the 'Far North' of Nigeria. Developed to irrigate 67,000 ha, a special technological feature of SCIP is the cutting and dredging of a 38-km long intake canal from Lake Chad; the water flows into a 21-km long canal from where it is carried to another pumping station from which it can be released into the irrigation system. Due to the shrinking surface area of Lake Chad, the water has largely been unable to reach the intake canal designed to transport water to the irrigation system even in peak flood periods (Birkett, 2000). The shortage of irrigation water is cited as key factor underlying the failure of wheat development in Nigeria (Andrae and Beckman, 1985; Dike, 1990).

D. Pressure on Lake Chad Water Resources By Rapidly Growing Human Population

Beyond the adverse impacts of natural climate variation, droughts, and overdrawing of the regenerative potential of the Lake Chad hydrological system to develop dams and irrigation facilities, pressure on the lake's water resources by a rapidly growing human population constitutes a key factor behind the over-exploitation and degradation of Lake Chad. Even though the Lake Chad Basin Commission (LCBC) was formed way back in 1964 to regulate the exploitation of the water resources of Lake Chad, the status of the lake as a free-access natural resource, accessible to all at no fees has resulted in the over-exploitation and ultimate degradation of the lake's regenerative potential.

For much of Lake Chad's estimated 10,000 years of existence, population growth and human pressure on the resources of the lake was never considered a key factor in the shrinking of the lake's surface area. However, as from the 1970s the impact of this factor began to be felt. Citing UNESCO sources, Onuoha (op. cit., p. 74) put the population of the Lake Chad basin at over 37 million by the beginning of the 2000s. Growing human population of the Lake Chad basin has equally induced growth in the livestock population. The combined effect of these two forces is an added factor in the accelerated over-exploitation and degradation of the Lake Chad basin witnessed since the 1980s. Based on current trends it is predicted that by the year 2025 – that is, a decade from now (2015) – the population of the Lake Chad basin will exceed 45 million, which will put further pressure on the lake's water resources, which, in turn, will lead to further shrinking of its surface area and even its complete collapse as an aquatic ecosystem.

12.8 Conclusion

Climate change is a factor shaping the capacity of ecosystems to supply their goods and services as well as perform their functions. Ecosystems face occasional disturbances in their equilibrium, but are, nonetheless, capable of recovering from such disturbances, provided their self-reproductive capabilities are not destroyed. However, the frequency and severity of ecosystem disturbances determine the way they affect ecosystem functions. Long and reoccurring droughts in the West Africa Sahel beginning in the 1970s, for instance, have seriously undermined the natural capacity of the hydrologic cycle to replenish Lake Chad.

End Notes

[1] This paradigm shift came in the rise of so-called new growth economics or endogenous growth economics hypothesizing that growth and development are the essential outcomes of the saving and investment choices made by economic agents within the economic system (See for instance, Piazza-Georgi, 2002).

[2] See also Willis (1997) and Adams (2009), especially pp. 37-58.

[3] See 'Climate Change and Ecosystems' http:www.en.m.wikipedea.org.

[4] 'Give us the money or the forest gets it' is credited to United Kingdom Environment Minister Eliot Morley; quoted in the Economist, 23rd April, 2005, p. 79, as the 'blackmail' he received from the developing countries.

[5] Refers to 'an ecological zone whose uniformity is defined by the type of plant life that dominates within it, since plant life will often give a strong indication of other ecological features of a zone, such as animal life and soil type' (Mayhew, 2009, p.50). it is explained that because biomes are defined by plant life rather than region or zone, some biomes can stretch around the world tropical grasslands (Savannah), temperate grassland (steppe), hot deserts, etc.

[6] Feedback loops refer to the response within the ecosystem itself to an action or process; **positive** feedback causes further change (e.g. fire and vegetation loss due to deforestation have degraded tropical and humid forest ecosystems); and **negative** feedback causes the situation to revert to the original (e.g. heavy precipitation and high temperatures have led to rapid growth of microbial organisms).

[7] Thus, **Oxford Dictionary of Biology** (2000, p. 71) defines biogeochemical cycle as the cyclical movement of elements between living organisms… and their non-living… surrounding (e.g. rocks, water, air).

[8] Thus, nature was portrayed as homeostatic machine; ecosystems, as if they are some '…machines, full of gears and wheels…' (Botkin,1990, p.12). Nature came to be conceived as a system where equilibrium was maintained.

[9] A time frame meaningful to the human mind may be interpreted to mean such timeframe within which some human or economic activity can be completed – such as a farming cycle, within which a certain crop can be planted, grown and harvested. Human beings, as economic agents, plan their economic activities within timeframes within which their plan objectives can be meaningfully realized – e.g. months, decades.

[10] Fossil minerals are so-called because they are formed from the remains of organic matter (plants, animals, microbes) that lived in the geological past – that is, 1000s of millions of years ago. It is believed that a small fraction – much less than 1% - of dead organic matter accumulates as deposited matter, is removed from contact with atmospheric oxygen, is subjected to intensely high temperatures and pressures, which inhibit decomposition by bacteria, and over geological time, metamorphoses into fossil minerals (e.g. coal, petroleum, gas, etc). Coal, for instance, is a product of the remains of plants that grew in swamps or other moist environment in the geological past; thus, the origin or source of coal is often characterized as lithospheric or terrestrial, signifying its association with continental land masses. See **Oxford Dictionary of Science** 2005, Appendix 4, p. 884 for geological timeframe.

11   Calculations regarding time span or sustainability of non-renewable resources are done as the balance between potential remaining supplies and current demand (consumption). Given that potential remaining supplies may change as new reserves are discovered and current demand are influenced by economic and technological variables, the time spans predicted for nonrenewable mineral quite often shift.

12   Current economic literature categorizes ecological resources into four areas in terms of their values: (i) sources for agriculture, forestry, aquaculture, animal husbandry, and industry; (ii) sources for medicine and pharmaceutical preparations; (iv) sources for recreation, aesthetics, and scientific exploration; and (iv) intrinsic value. Whereas (i)-(iii) represent **instrumental** values – i.e. confer direct and indirect use-values or benefits, (iv) represents **intrinsic** value – appreciated for own sake.

13   The mangrove rainforest of the Niger Delta in Nigeria are among the largest in the world covering some 11,700 km² (Muagholu, 2007).

14   See chapter 11, End Note no. 6.

15   See American Geophysical Union, 1999, June 12.

16   For the literature on drought incidence in West Africa, see the following: Oladipo, 1988; Mortimore 1989, 1998; Birkett, 2000; Smith, 2000; World Bank, 2002; Salkida 2012; UNCD 2012; Hartford 2012.

17   This explains why coastal regions tend to be cooler than inland regions.

18   Other monsoon climates are northern Australia, Chile, Spain, and Texas, but the most celebrated is the Asian monsoon.

19   Globally, Africa is reported to have suffered a net forest loss exceeding 4 million hectares annually during 2000-2004 resulting from conversion of forestland of agriculture and extraction of fuelwood. African forestland declined from 656 million to 635 million hectares in 2000-2006 (Dike, 2007).

CHAPTER 13

CLIMATE CHANGE AND SOCIOECONOMIC SYSTEMS

13.1 Introduction

This chapter highlights the symptoms of global warming and climate change in human systems or socioeconomic systems. A socioeconomic system may be conceived as any structured or patterned or stable relationship between any number of humans or economic agents possessing any degree of common interests (social, political, economic), values or goals. A socioeconomic system as such is delimited by a specific geopolitical space, or occupies a geographical space defined by the boundaries of a state. The notion of socioeconomic system thus suggests that economic activities, conducted within the boundaries of a nation state that regulates the activities of the human agents, are involved, and it is where economic activities that are impacted on by climate change. So defined, the various countries of the world may be defined as representing socioeconomic systems. On the global level, countries may be classified into two broad categories: **developed** (industrialized) and **developing** (less industrialized). These two categories of countries exhibit quite different degrees of exposure, sensitivity, and adaptative capability to climate change (Clunies-Ross, et al., 2009, pp. 305-8; Stern et al., 2007; Stern, 2009, a, b).

13.2 Sensitivity, Adaptability and Vulnerability of Socioeconomic Systems to Climate Change

The impacts of climate change on socioeconomic systems can be analysed and understood in terms of the degree of sensitivity, adaptability and vulnerability. It remains, therefore, to define these concepts relating them to climate change effects.

Generally sensitivity refers to the degree to which a body or system will respond to some external stimulus. In our present context, it refers to the degree to which a socioeconomic system will respond to a change in climate conditions – e.g. the extent of a change in the composition, structure and function of a system when, for instance, there is a change in rainfall or precipitation due to drought; or a rise in average temperatures. Sensitivity of socioeconomic systems to climate change is most direct and most felt in agriculture (crop production, fisheries, forestry, livestock etc.). But agriculture is an activity very much vulnerable to changes in Earth's environmental conditions. However, not every aspect of climate change will have negative outcomes for agriculture: countries and societies in the cold regions – e.g. Russia and the Nordic countries, etc. could benefit from warming temperatures as parts of these countries hitherto too cold for human activity become habitable. For instance, rising temperatures are reported to have led to birds and butterflies to shift their ranges northwards by 200 kilometers in Europe and North America (Hirsch, 2005; Root et al., 2002).

On the other hand, in contrast, climate change has created enabling conditions for undermining the viability of ecosystems, with adverse implications for human welfare, as shown in chapter 12. In many developing countries, the combination of drought and poverty – these are key 'exposure' factors – can further exacerbate exposure to climate change. For example, in the West African Sahel and the Horn of Africa (especially in Ethiopia), where drought is a regular environmental problem, water-storage facilities are very limited (on per capita basis less than 1% of the capacity in the industrialized world where the hydrologic variability is smaller than in the developing world) with adverse health and productivity outcomes.

Adaptability refers to the degree to which adjustments can be affected in the practices, processes, or structures of a system in response to actual or potential changes in climate conditions. Adaptation can be spontaneous or planned, and can be carried out in response to or in expectation of changes in environmental conditions. Adaptative capability referring to capacity to change course promptly and effectively in response to changed environmental conditions differing across human societies and within the latter, across individuals and households, and is a function of level of technological knowledge and financial capability. For this reason, developing countries, generally, possess much lower adaptative capability than developed or industrial countries.

Vulnerability refers to the extent to which climate change may damage or undermine a system's capacity to realize its original performance capacity in some activity – e.g. agriculture; - which, however, depends on a system's sensitivity and ability to adapt to new climatic conditions. Developing countries, generally, have peculiar geographical characteristics. Specifically, developing countries' location nearer or within the tropical climatic environment exposes them more to the effects of global warming than the developed countries. Also, developing countries exhibit greater sensitivity to the negative feedback effects of climate change, and possess weak adaptative capacity to climate change – that is, they possess rather low autonomous capacity to adjust promptly and effectively in response to changed environmental conditions – e.g. flooding, droughts, etc.

13.3 Regional and Country-Specific Symptoms of Climate Change

Cline (2008) posits a model separating the symptoms of climate change in agriculture into two: first, if CO_2 emissions continue to proceed apace or unabated; second, if CO_2 emissions abate. The Cline model shows that by the 2080s there will be a reduction in agricultural yields (output per hectare) of 16% without carbon fertilization (CF) and a reduction of 3% should CF occur. The developing countries are likely to suffer more than the developed ones: whereas the latter will experience outcomes ranging from 6% losses without CF to 8% gain with CF, the former (developing countries) will sustain losses of up to 25% with CF and 10-15% with CF. We proceed below to highlight the actual and potential symptoms of climate change in regions of the world: Africa, Asia-Pacific, South America, North America and Europe.

13.3.1 Africa

As already pointed out, Africa emerges as the continent or geographical region most vulnerable to the effects of climate change, much because of its geography or location largely within the topics. Africa's geographical factor is worsened or reinforced by the its low-level economic development and associated low adaptive capacity. In fact, Africa began to experience the impacts of climate change as early as the 1970s, when droughts became a regular feature of the sub-Saharan African region, particularly in the West African Sahel, and the Horn of Africa. The continent experienced significant increases in average temperatures by 2010, particularly in the Sahel and parts of Southern Africa. IPCC Assessment Report for 2014 predicts the following climate change induced outcomes for Africa.

- 75-250 million of Africa's population will be exposed to water stress and more than 1.8 billion by the 2080s. Already inland freshwater lakes – e.g. Lake Chad – are shrinking.
- Rainfed agriculture could decline by 50% in some African countries by the year 2020. IPCC Assessment Reports predict that wheat output will be hardest hit and may disappear from African agriculture by the 2080s, and that maize – a key grain staple – will fall significantly in Southern Africa. Simulations on maize yields (kg/ha) by Jones and Thornton (2003) using FAO yields for 2000 as baseline predict that yields in South Africa and Nigeria, respectively, will decline from 2029 to 1061 and 1400 to 858 kg/ha. Adhikari et. al. (2015) reached similar conclusions in South Africa. Two grain crops, millet and sorghum, are found to be more resilient to climate changes; root crops such as potatoes and cassava are projected to be lesss effected than the grain crops. For the export crops such as coffee and tea, output will decline due to reduction in suitable production environment. So, climate change is most likely to worsen Africa's food security situation.

- Arid and semi-arid lands will increase by up to 8% with severe socioeconomic implication – specifically, it will undermine efforts towards poverty eradication.

For Sub-Saharan Africa, the mean average temperatures have risen, beginning since the 1970s, by as much as 1-3°C, the highest increases registering in inland regions located far from tmoderating influence of the oceans- e.g. South Sudan, West Africa's Sahel – where average increases are reported to exceed 3°C. In contrast to the rising average temperatures, there is notable decrease in rainfall overall – large parts of sub-Saharan Africa – specifically, East and Southern Africa, and the Sahel – have seen decreases in rainfall exceeding 100mm resulting in drought in some countries: northern Kenya, Ethiopia and Eritria, Zimbabwe, etc.

For Ethiopia, Sub-Saharan Africa's most drought-prone country, drought is reported to be the most climate-related constraint in agriculture. This is found to be more frequent and severe in the arid and semi-arid parts (Amsalu and Adem, 2009; Degefu and Bewket, 2014). But rising temperatures and droughts do affect the soil and surface water resources by affecting the atmosphere's moisture holding capacity and rate of actual evaporation and evapotranspiration.

In East Africa, as elsewhere in Sub-Saharan Africa, climate change is affecting population movements – especially among the pastoral populations, often leading to conflicts. But pastoralists in particular earn their livelihoods mainly by herding livestock relying on spatial mobility as a way of coping against the harsh climatic conditions (see below). Indeed, droughts remain the dominant climate-related factor driving pastoral migration patterns in Sub-Saharan Africa.

The West African Sahel is another drought-prone region. Here the agricultural potential has been significantly reduced by incessant droughts. Most areas of northern West Africa above the 12° parallel lie within the Sahel. This is the region of the 'millet culture' which thrives here precisely became it can grow even if the land is parched, which is, infact, the 'normal' rather than the 'exceptional' environmental condition. Briefly, modern Sahelian droughts began, in concrete terms, in the 1970s and continued into the 1980s during which rainfall has falled below the 1930-1960 mean (average). During the 1970s and 1980s drought-driven famine in the Sahel killed over 100,000 peoples, left over 1 million dependents on food aid and affected over 50 million Sahelian population (Adams 2009; Mortimore, 1989, 1998).

Sub-Saharan Africa has been dubbed "the food crisis epicentre of the world"; this crisis is most severe in the arid and semi-arid drought-prone regions such as the African Sahel and East Africa's arid zones (e.g. Thornton et al., 2007, p. 4), where rainfall variability and associated droughts have been major sources of food production deficits and crises. Ethiopia's experiences in the 1970s through the 1990s in the provinces of Wollo and Tigray, in Harar and Shewa have received the most publicity in world media. It ought to be pointed out, however, that drought is not the only source of famine and food crises in Africa; other causes include a lack of access to modern technological inputs, rural-urban migration, debt burden, etc. (e.g. Biazin and Sterk, 2013).

Drought and Conflict: Drought leads to resource degradation – e.g. it reduces or undermines water availability for humans and livestock as well as pasture for the latter (see, for instance, Baker, 1995). This has great potential to lead to increasing competition and conflict over resources as the latters' supply (availability) and accessibility become significantly reduced. In Ethiopia, for instance, drought has been associated with multiply types of conflict: cross-border, inter-community and community with state authority (e.g. Gebresenbet and Kefule, 2012). In Kenya, there is reduced water availability for domestic crop and livestock purposes (COBRA, 2014), which in some cases had led to violent conflict (CARE ALP, 2013). Besides, high incidence of drought has led to proliferation of boreholes in Kenya, apparently causing groundwater depletion. In some drought-prone dryland zones of Kenya, 58% of the water decreased is met by utilizing groundwater in districts where only about 21% of the area has potential for this ecological resource.

13.3.2 Asia-Pacific Region

This is the most populous region of the world. In the Asia-Pacific region there is manifest evidence of increases in the intensity and/or frequency of many extreme weather events: heat waves; tropical cyclones; prolonged droughts; intense rainfall leading to flooding; tornadoes; snow avalanches; thunderstorms; tsunami; severe duststorms; etc. The region accounts for some 91% of global total death and 49% of global total damage due to natural disasters, including tsunami, earthquakes and volcanic eruptions. Briefly, climate change emerges as the most prominent development challenge facing the Asia-Pacific region.

The IPCC predict temperature increases in the order of 0.5-2°C by 2030 and 1-7°C by 2070; the increases will be much more rapid in northern Pakistan and India and Western China (IPCC Fourth Assessment Report, 2014). The region will be most affected by sea level rise (SLR) of approximately 3-16cm by 2030 and 7-50cm by 2070. The following are the region's key elements in exposure, sensitivity, and adaptive capacity.

- Influences of monsoons, the El Niño – Southern Oscillation and cyclones; much of the region is reliant on monsoon rainfall, which leaves the region vulnerable when the monsoons fail and rainfall becomes significantly reduced. Anthropogenic climate change is bound to affect the climate challenges of the region- e.g. coastal Asia is bound to be affected by tropical cyclones, and the associated high winds, storm surge, and extreme rainfall that often lead to disastrous flooding.
- Besides being heavily exposed to a variety of climate hazards, the vulnerability of the Asia-Pacific region is also affected by the sensitivity of the different countries and economic sectors to these hazards when they do occur. Studies reveal that the region has more of the world's low-lying regions, including small island states – e.g. Sri Lanka, Vanuata, Solomon

Islands, Seychelles etc. – these are more sensitive to the effects of SLR and storm surge than other countries.

- Rapid economic growth in countries such as China and India suggests enhanced adaptive capacity to climate change, thanks to enhanced economic, technological and infrastructure upgrading (ADB, 2009).
- Within the Asia-Pacific region, Southeast Asia depicts a fast-growing region, but with long coastlines, population and economic activity concentrated in the coastal regions. Relying on agriculture, the region is highly vulnerable to the harsh aspects of climate change.

13.3.3 South America

The fourth largest continent with a population of more than 370 million people, South America includes all continental countries of the Americas from Mexico to Chile and Argentina as well as adjacent islands and seas. This is a highly heterogeneous region in terms of climate regimes (ranging from hyper-arid desert climates to humid tropical climates), ecosystems, human population distribution, etc. Discounting deforestation, South America's current global GHG emissions contribution is roughly 4%; however, potential future trends could be large and costly for the region; in addition, the release of carbon dioxide through deforestation could have the potential to alter the global carbon balance.

South America's global climate change role revolves around the vast Amazon basin; as with other continents, South-America is already experiencing some effects of climate change with socioeconomic outcomes: shifts in precipitation and warming temperatures; projected effects include more extreme weather events, species extinctions, water stress, decreased rice and soybeans yields, adverse impacts on coastal regions from SLR. As noted above, the most important direct anthropogenic impact on the Amazon is deforestation (treated in chapter 3). IPCC Assessment Reports document the following impacts:

- All Latin America has been severely affected by climate variability and extreme weather events, including intense rainfall, flooding, drought in the Amazon, and Hurricane Catarina in March 2004 (not to be confused with Hurricane Katrina in 2005 in the United States) – the first known hurricane-sized tropical cyclone to be experienced in the region. Hurricane Catarina affected mostly Santa Catarina and Rio Grande do Sol in Southeastern Brazil inflicting damages worth $350 million (2004 US dollars).
- Shifts in temperature and precipitation; rainfall increased in Southeast Brazil, Paraguay, Uruguay and parts of Argentina; decreased in Southern Chile, Southwest Argentina and Southern Peru.
- Land-use changes, including deforestation, have degraded land, changing weather patterns – e.g. drought in the Brazilian Amazonia. Smoke from burning forests has changed

regional temperatures and rainfall in South Amazonia, apart from causing human health by pollution.

- Future impacts projected by IPCC Assessment Reports are likely to include: accelerated glacial retreat in South Andes Mountains, reducing water availability for hydroelectricity; intense hurricane in the Caribbean; Mexico prone to droughts which are likely to become more regular and intense as climate change proceeds apace. Briefly, a number of large-scale drivers of environmental change have been established to operate simultenously and interacting nonlinearly in South America, most intensely in the Amazon rainforest basin, namely land-use change and climate changes due to global warming and deforestation. These in turn induce higher incidence of extreme climate events and of forest fires, which in turn add to increased tropical forests' exposure and vulnerability. By and large, deforestation in the region is driven by development in the global warming, specifically, global market demand growth in cattle beef, soybean, timber, also, new investments in transportation and energy infrastructure projects, and weak institutions have been found to constitute key drivers in environmental change (eg. Schmitz et al, 2015).

13.3.4 North America

North America is the world's third largest continent and home to approximately 515 million populations by 2015. Stretching from the Central American peninsular to the Arctic, North America has experienced a wide range of effects from climate change, and these effects have been most intense in the Arctic North as the Arctic ice sheets thaw. As we saw earlier in chapter 4, North America is having a large impact on climate change: specifically, since it has produced a greater share of GHG emissions over time than any other continent. Historically, the United States is the global single largest emitter of anthropogenic GHG; currently, it is the second largest emitter after China.

The major symptoms of climate change in this region include: sea level rise (SLR) leading to increases in inundation; storm surge, and flooding as in hurricane Harvey that wrecked harvoc in Houston Texas and hurricane Maria that devastated Puerto Rico in September 2017, shoreline erosion; etc. This will affect the populations living in the coastal regions and coastal ecosystems like salt marshes. On the other hand, North America exhibits the most capacity to adapt to the climate change effects due to its high levels of technological endowments and high percapita income (Chen, 2011). Wildfires are caused by hotter temperatures, occurring mostly in Western United States. Between 1980 and early 2000, an average of 22,000km^2/year occurred in the United States. There are also problems of drying lake surface areas and shrinking river channels etc.

13.3.5 Europe .

Precipitation has, generally, increased in Northern Europe but has decreased in Southern Europe; snow cover is equally decreasing and the extent and volume of Arctic sea ice have been decreasing much faster than previously predicted in climate change models (see IPCC, 2013). Observed climate change impacts, however, vary across Europe, depending on climatic, geographic and socioeconomic conditions. For instance, the climate change impacts in Russian differ significantly from those in France, much as a result of Russia's much larger land mass lying mostly in the high latitudes (see below). Key observed and projected impacts from climate change for the main regions of Europe may be summarized as follows:

- In the **Arctic North,** average temperature rise is much larger the global average. This has a key contributory factor in the observed decrease in Greenland ice sheet and permafrost areas. Permafrost describes soil that has frozen for two or more years; in most Arctic areas permafrost is from a few to several 100 metres thick. Permafrost thawing releases methane which has 25 times the global warming potential (GWP) of carbon dioxide. It is estimated that carbon storage in permafrost globally measures some 1600 gigatons, which is twice the atmospheric pool.
- **Coastal zones** and **regional seas** will experience significant sea level rise (SLR); as well, sea surface temperatures and ocean acidity will increase.
- **North-western Europe** will experience increase in winter precipitation, river flow, and northward shift of species and decrease in energy demand for heating as a result of warming average temperatures.
- In **Mediterranean** Europe temperature rise will be larger than the European average; there will be decrease in annual precipitation, decrease in crop yields, increase in risk of forest fires; etc. (IPCC, 2007).
- **Central and Eastern Europe** will experience warm temperature extremes (heat waves), decrease in summer precipitation, and increased risk of forest fires (IPCC, 2007).
- **Russia** is affected much more intensely by climate change than any country in Europe – indeed, the world. Scientists have posited that the effects of climate change on permafrost thawing in Russia's northern territories could have devastating effects on regional ecological systems due to methane gas emissions from permafrost thawing. Estimated annual net methane emissions from permafrost thawing as at the end of the 1900s for the Northern regions were 51 million metric tons, the bulk of these (some 64%) originating from Russia's Northern regions.

The most well-known feature of Russia's climate system is its very cold winter created by the country's location in the high latitude (40-70°N, vast land mass (covering 9 times zones, reduced from 11 time zones in 2010) and a lack of topographic barriers to protect it from the Arctic winds sweeping across its long, north-facing and often frozen coastline. Satellite measurements for the last 30 years (beginning since the 1980s) show that snow cover have reduced considerably in the Northern hemisphere in spring and summer, due mainly to surface air temperature rise. During the last 40 years, the average temperature in Russia increased by 0.4°C every ten (10) years. IPCC Assessment Reports suggest that climate change may increase the frequency of wildfires; in Russia, this includes the risk of peatland fires (IPCC, 2007).

13.4 Symptoms of Climate Change in Agriculture

As noted above, agriculture is the most vulnerable economic activity in terms of the adverse effects of climate change. But rising global average temperatures are most likely to inflict the most change and, hence, causing the most damaging effects on land. The latter warms quite much more easily and quickly than water in its various forms and reservoirs. Briefly, agriculture depends for its productivity mostly on environmental factors, namely temperature and rainfall.

Precisely because they are heavily dependent on agriculture as an economic activity, the developing countries, generally, are more vulnerable to the effects of global warming and climate change than the industrialized countries. The developing countries possess far less adaptive capacity than the developed countries; most developing countries are in the tropical latitudes, where temp eratures have reached or are close to thresholds at which further increases in temperatures will harm rather than boost or improve agricultural productivity. Further, agriculture has a larger weight in the gross domestic product (GDP) of developing countries, generally, a point earlier pointed out.

How does climate change affect agricultural production? Agronomic research shows that beyond a certain range of temperatures, global warming will reduce yields because cereal crops, for instance- e.g. maize – speed through growth cycles, producing less grain in the process; higher temperatures will interfere with plant ability to obtain and use moisture; and evaporation from the soil accelerates when temperatures rise and plants increase transpiration – that is, lose more moisture from their leaves. Given that global warming is likely to increase rainfall, the net effect of warming temperatures on water availability 'is a race between higher evapotranspiration and higher precipitation. Typically, the race is won by higher evapotranspiration' (Cline, 2008, p.24). As the term implies, evapotranspiration describes the process of release of water vapour from Earth's surface by evaporation and transpiration, which is accelerated by warming temperatures. On the other hand, carbon dioxide (CO_2), the principal greenhouse gas, can also boost agricultural productivity by enhancing photosynthesis in socalled C3 crops: rice, wheat, and soybeans - what crop scientists call carbon fertilization or carbon assimilation C3 plants produce a three-carbon compound during photosynthesis, including most tree and agricultural crops such as rice, wheat, soybeans, potatoes, vegetables. There are, besides, C4 plants which produce a four-carbon compound during photosynthesis, mainly of tropical origin: maize, sugarcane, millet, sorghum (guinea corn); etc.

13.4.1 Food Security and Climate Change

Food security especially figures prominently in the list of human activities and ecosystem services that are most adversely affected by anthropogenic climate change (Watson et al., 2000; IPCC, 2001a; Ecosystem Millennium Assessment, 2005). Food security, generally, describes the condition when all people, always, have physical and economic access to sufficient, safe, and nutritious food to meet their dietary needs and food preferences for an active and healthy life (FAO, 1996). A function of robust food systems that encompass issues of availability, accessibility, and utilization – not just production alone – food security can only be guaranteed by an autonomous capacity to produce, distribute and control food supplies. As suggested above, food security is best guaranteed if the capacity to produce, distribute and control available food supplies resides within the domestic economy rather than residing in external bodies or being dependent on external sources of food supplies such as, for example, commercial imports, food aid, etc.

This is an ideal situation, which is hardly met in practice; worse still, in developing countries various socioeconomic constraints, policy bottlenecks and environmental conditions combine to undermine not only food production, but also food distribution and accessibility. There is a certain consensus in the development literature that while crop yields will be positively affected by elevated carbon dioxide in the absence of radical changes in the elements of climate- e.g. temperature and precipitation- the associated effects of warming global temperatures, altered patterns of precipitation and possibly frequency of extreme weather events (e.g. flooding, droughts, etc.) will likely combine to depress yields and increase risks in agriculture production in many parts of the world, which will lead to a widening of the gap between rich and poor countries (e.g. Cline, 2008). For Sub-Saharan Africa, the mean temperatures have risen beginning since the 1960s by as much as 1-3°C, the highest increase occurring in inland regions – e.g. the Sahel – where, average mean temperature increases are reported to exceed 3°C. In contrast to rising average temperatures, there is notable decrease in rainfall overall in large parts of sub-Saharan Africa, specifically, East and Southern Africa, the Sahel, etc – caused by climate change. But sub-Saharan Africa is directly affected by several aspects of climate change such as rising average temperatures, erratic rainfall conditions both in amount and geographical distribution, deforestation, population migration, etc., changes in climate variability (e.g. drought and desertification), extreme weather events (e.g. flooding). The development literature is replete with debates on climate-change related food security problems in Sub-Saharan Africa (e.g. Ludi, 2009; Rena, 2008). Africa spends $25 billion annually on food imports and receives food aid worth $2 billion annually, with upwards of 30% of its population suffering from 'chronic hunger'. We return to Africa's food crisis (Rena, op. cit.)

13.4.2 Food Availability, Famine and Drought

Famine in developing countries has often been explained as originating in a decline in food availability. In semi-arid regions the most obvious cause of farming was a lack of food availability, which was pinned on drought and environmental degradation – that is, on natural or climate factors.

A neo-malthusian perspective would posit that excessive numbers of people and livestock caused land to be degraded and over-used, reducing soil fertility, vegetation cover and productivity in ways that set the preconditions for collapse of the agricultural system when the next drought occurred. The neo-malthusian perspective has been disputed by Mortimore's (1989, 1998) research on villages in the Sahelian zone of Northern Nigeria, which found that rural farmers here have long since established sustainable systems of land-preserving agricultural practices.

Sen (1981), drawing on the concept of famine and hunger, established that famine and hunger are caused by a collapse in entitlement to food, not in non-availability of food as such; that entitlements derive from trade, production, labour, inheritance or transfer. Sen cites, *inter alia*, the Great Bengal Famine of 1943, when people were seen to starve in front of the doors of a grain warehouse, and, also, the famine in the African Sahel and Ethiopia in the 1970s caused by a breakdown of ability of people to get access to available food supplies. Sen's work was to become a reference point for explaining the underlying causes of the Darfur Famine in Sudan (see de Waal, 1989). Sen argues that diverse factors contribute to acute famine:

> "While many starve in famine, not all will do so: different groups typically do have … different commanding powers over food, and an over-all shortage brings out the contrasting powers in stark clarity" (Sen, 1981, p. 43).

Other studies extended Sen's framework, all in an effort to explain that the one-crop economies of West Africa, which evolved from a need to statisfy European demand for socalled cash crops – e.g. cotton or groundnuts – created conditions in which Sahelian producers were exposed to famine during droughts in the 1970s. Colonial policies reduced the food self-sufficiency of West African populations by diverting production capacities to export crops (Mortimore, 1989); post-colonial policies did little to remedy this problem by, for instance, building up capacities to withstand drought. Instead, what has evolved in most African countries is that people have been exposed to new risks that have eroded their flexibility and adaptability (Mortimore and Adams, 1999). Risk and vulnerability are critical concepts in understanding who is threatened by environmental change – e.g. climate change (Blaikie et al., 1994). The understanding of the food security problem in the context to reduce the impact of climate change in agriculture must start from understanding of both environmental variability and political economy.

Current explanations of famine locate its causes in complex factors – political, economic, climate or natural forces. For instance, Olson (1993), on Sudan, argued that severe reductions in rainfall in 1984 triggered widespread speculation in food, which, in turn, pushed up food prices beyond the reach of ordinary people. At the national level there was enough food, but poor distribution allowed famine to evolve.

13.4.3 Food Accessibility

Accessibility in the present context refers to ability of individuals or communities or countries to obtain food in sufficient quantities and quality (Ludi, 2009). Quality refers to food that meets minimum nutritional standard. In Sub-Saharan Africa individuals and households fail in this regard for social reasons: e.g. high food prices; lack of access to markets; poverty referring to income falling below an established poverty line; employment conditions; educational and social status; property rights, etc. (Oyiga et al. 2011). In Sub-Saharan Africa, given that markets, especially external markets, have become, increasingly, a key source of food supplies, the accessibility problem has come to complement the food availability problem to worsen the food security situation. Quite unlike in other parts of the developing world, where the Green Revolution has helped to improve food supplies leading to falling real prices for food over the past 40 years. For Sub-Saharan Africa especially, the reverse is the case: agricultural stagnation and associated spiraling food prices, complemented by falling real per capita income all have combined to worsen the food accessibility situation.

13.4.4 Food Utilization

Food utilization refers to the individual's or household's capacity to consume and benefit from the food to which they have access (FAO, 2011). But this depends on how available food is used, whether food has sufficient nutrients and whether diet can be maintained. A household may have adequate physical and economic access to food and yet fail to be food secure because it fails to obtain a balanced and nutritious diet (Negin et al., 2009).

The utilization component of food security is generally related to the nutritional aspect of food consumption. Climate change affects this aspect of food security by: changing the yields of important crop sources of micronutrients; by altering the nutritional content of a specific crop; by influencing decisions to grow crops of different nutritional value (http:/www.povertynet.org). Climate change can – and does, indeed – affect the income and capacity of households to purchase a diversity of food items to obtain a balanced diet. A study on Sub-Saharan Africa shows that food prices have tended to rise sharply since the first half of the 2000s, rising by almost 50% during 2010-2011 caused by extreme weather events. Most households have been forced, due to rising food prices, to reduce both the quantity and quality of food they consume, consume less preferred food and allocate food only to certain household members (Oyiga et al., op. cit.)

Finally, climate change limits access to clean water and sanitation facilities – a leading cause of diarrhea-disease. The latter is a significant contributor to child morbidity and poor food utilization by limiting the absorption of nutrients (see Zewdie, 2012). Also, climate change will cause emergence of new pest and disease patterns to evolve, which affect human health – e.g. increased incidence of vector borne diseases in flood prone zones; it could bring about changes in vectors from climate change responsive pests and diseases; and the emergence of new disease patterns could affect both the food chain and population's physiological capacity to obtain necessary nutrients from the food consumed.

13.4.5 Climate Change and Dynamics of Global Food Supply and Demand

Many interactive processes influence the dynamics of global food demand and supply: agro-climatic conditions, land resources and their management are obviously key elements; but there are, also, problems originating in high population growth rates, availability and accessibility of technology and development. It was found that between the 1980s and beginning of the 2000s, for instance, average daily caloric per capita intake had risen globally from 2400 to 2800 calories, thanks to economic growth, technological growth, international trade and globalization of food markets (Fischer et al., 2002). These trends have been especially more visible in rapidly growing China and India – indeed, Asia generally – where dietary changes have been manifested in growing shares of meat, fat and sugar in total food consumption.

Given that there are severe constraints limiting empirical studies on overall symptoms of climate change in agro-climatic and socioeconomic systems, researchers have resorted to partial modeling to assess at least some of the symptoms likely to influence agricultural productivity by climate-change factors, focusing on 'site-specific', regional and/or national short-and long-term assessments of climate change effects (e.g. Rosenzweig et al., 2002; Fischer et al., 2005). The following summarize the results of climate change effects in agricultural resources.

- Northward shift of thermal regions, reducing significantly boreal and arctic ecosystems (60% reduction of current total 2.1 billion hectares). Tropical zones expanding covering Africa and a narrow fringe along the Mediterranean coast.
- Arid zones expand in less developed countries. Currently, almost 1 billion people live in arid lands globally; in Africa alone, there are 180 million.
- Cultivated land predicted to expand in North America and Russia, due to larger planting windows and generally friendlier growing conditions under global warming.
- Rainfed cereal production gains in both developed and developing regions, especially wheat in the 2080s. However, results indicate, in agreement with previous research results that a wide range of outcomes exist for many countries, due to heterogeneity of their agro-climatic conditions.

13.5 Can Technological Change Offset Losses Caused by Climate Change?

There is consensus in the literature that sustained, technological change in world agriculture will raise agricultural yields so much by the 2080s that any losses caused by climate change would easily be offset. Over the past half century or so, world agricultural productivity has, indeed, witnessed a 'great leap forward': between the late-1960s and mid-1970s, there began to occur dramatic increases in cereals output per hectare in several Asian and Latin American countries, driven by technological developments in high-yielding varieties (HYVs) of seeds especially wheat (*Triticum aestivum*) and rice (*Oryza sativa L*), complemented by inorganic (chemical) fertilizers, pesticides and herbicides, and irrigation – a process that became known as the Green Revolution[1].

The Green Revolution was the technological component of the strategy to boost agricultural productivity growth and, hence, sustaining availability, in real terms, of a net agricultural surplus. The Green Revolution first began in Latin America – precisely in Mexico – where new-seed wheat and maize (corn) developed at the International Maize and Wheat Improvement Centre (Spanish acronym: CIMMYT, **Centro International de Mejoramiento de Maiz Y Trigo**) were introduced in large farms by the Rockeffeler Foundation. The Green Revolution was later pushed to Asia in the 1960s, where socalled 'miracle rice' became the initial key crop; later, new varieties of rice, maize and wheat were developed to suit local ecological conditions – e.g. the tropical wetlands of Malaysia, Thailand and Indonesia on the one hand, and the irrigated fields of Taiwan and South Korea. It might be more insightful to highlight the historical background to the Green Revolution and its shift to Asia. The Green Revolution initiatiye was originated by Norman Borlaug, dubbed 'Father of the Green Revolution'. However, the term Green Revolution was pioneered by the former Director of United States Agency for International Development (USAID), William Gaud, who noted the spread of the new seed technologies as containing "the makings of a new revolution":

> "These and other developments in the field of agriculture contain the makings of a new revolution. It is not a violent Red Revolution like that of the Soviets, nor is it a White Revolution like that of the Shah of Iran. I call it the Green Revolution" (Gaud, 1968).

As to its shift to Asia, the historical background was India on the brink of famine in the early 1960s. Norman Borlaug was invited to India; wheat seeds were imported from CIMMYT. Punjah was selected as the first Indian test site; India began its own Green Revolution programme of plant breeding, irrigation development and production of agro-chemicals. India soon adopted the IR8 – a semi-dwarf rice variety developed by the International Rice Research Institute (IRRI) in the Philippines that could produce more grain of rice per plant when cultivated with complementary chemical fertilizers and irrigation. IR8 rice was found to yield about 5 tons per hectare without fertilizer input, and almost 10 tons per hectare under optimal conditions, which is 10 times the yield of the traditional rice variety – thus IR8 was dubbed 'Miracle Rice' throughout Asia. India exploited the IR8 rice breed to expand its rice production capacity. In the 1960s rice yields in India averaged 2 tons/hectare; by the mid-1990s, they had jumped to 6 tons/hectare; simultaneously rice prices were falling: from $550/ton in the 1970s they declined to less than $200/ton in 2001 (Barta, 2007). By the beginning of the 2000s India had emerged a global rice exporter shipping some 4.5 million tons in 2006. For Thailand, in the 1960s rice yields averaged some 2 tons per hectare; by the 1990s, three decades later, yields had improved 3-fold to 6 tons per hectare, which put Thailand in the League of major rice exporters.

Todaro and Smith (2009, figure 9.2, p. 435), citing World Bank sources, explain that cereal yields per hectare in 2005 were nearly triple the 1960 yield in the 'Asian developing economies', thanks to rapid diffusion of Green Revolution technologies; that in about all countries of Asia agricultural productivity have witnessed a 'great leap forward': India, Pakistan, Turkey, Philippines, Malaysia, Thailand, etc. have became net grain exporters.

Table 13.1 carries comparative data on the extent of diffusion of the Green Revolution technologies among the developing regions of the world by the beginning of the 2000s. As noted above, Asia emerges the region of the developing world most penetrated by the Green Revolution technologies; Sub-Saharan Africa the least. For instance: in 2000 South Asia and East Asia and Pacific, respectively, had 78% and 84% of their cereal fields cropped with high yield varieties (HYVs); for sub-Saharan Africa, in contrast, this averaged just 22%.

Table 13.1 Trends in Diffusion of Green Revolution Technologies in the Developing World

(A) Irrigation (share of arable and permanent cropland %)

Region	1962	1982	2002
Sub-Saharan Africa	3	3.5	4
South Asia	20	29.0	39
East Asia & Pacific	23	29.0	33
Latin America & Caribbean	7	9.0	11

(B) HYVs of Cereals (share of cereal area %)[a]

Region	1980	2000
Sub-Saharan Africa	3	22
South Asia	50	78
East Asia & Pacific	42	84
Latin America & Caribbean	24	61

(D) Fertilizer Consumption (kg per hectare or arable and permanent cropland)

Region	1962	1982	2002
Sub-Saharan Africa	<1	13	13
South Asia	<1	45	98
East Asia & Pacific	10	110	198
Latin America & Caribbean	10	48	81

a) Based on estimates for rice, wheat and sorghum
Source: Todaro and Smith (2009, figure 9.4, p. 449).

The comparative data carried in Table 13.1 suggest that even if other developing regions of the world succeeded in using technological change in agriculture to offset the effects of climate change in agriculture, Sub-Saharan Africa clearly lacks that capacity[2]. Yet for Sub-Saharan Africa there is utmost urgency to increase food production through increases in crop yields per hectare.

Between 1966-68 and 2006-08 agricultural output per capita in Sub-Saharan Africa declined by 25%, while it doubled in South Asia and trippled in East Asia (Hunt and Lipton, 2011). Although cultivated area rose by 25% during the same period, average cereal yields just managed to rise from 0.8 to 1.5 tonnes per hectare (t/ha); in sharp contrast, in South Asia and East Asia, respectively, yields climbed from 1 to 2.6 t/ha and 1.5 to 5.4 t/ha.

Yet there are perspectives that reject the Green Revolution solution to Africa's agrarian crisis and associated food deficits. The Green Revolution, it ought to be recalled, led to significant increases in agricultural supplies particularly in Asia and parts of Latin America, and involved the use of HYVs rather than the traditional farmer-saved seed varieties that dominate in rural African agriculture; also, the use of chemical (inorganic) fertilizers and pest-control chemicals. Briefly, the Green Revolution, in general, embraces any technology-based innovation to boost agricultural production, including gene modification.

Current arguments against the Green Revolution are based on opposition to genetically modified (GM) crops being initiated into African agriculture (see section 13.4.7). As is well known, farming in Africa is dominated by smallholder households who produce largely for own consumption, employing techniques dominated by the hoe-and-matchete technology often incorporating selective modern methods. The traditional shifting cultivation practice, itself a method to restore soil fertility, is no longer of much practical relevance given rapid population pressure that has reduced availability of agricultural land in many parts of Sub-Saharan Africa- e.g. Southeast Nigeria, Uganda, etc. This has led to soils being worked with no fallow periods, or, at best, very short fallow periods to restore soil fertility, which, in turn, has resulted in steep decline in soil fertility.

African smallholders, who dominate the agricultural scene, find chemical fertilizers and other inputs of the Green Revolution inaccessible. On the other hand, the traditional soil fertility replenishment inputs – e.g. animal manure, ash, kitchen refuse and residues, etc. – face severe constraints in the availability as the food deficits deepen.

Most farming in Sub-Saharan Africa is rain-fed (see table 13.1), which leaves agriculture vulnerable to the vagaries of environmental conditions (e.g. reoccurring drought incidence), apart from diseases and plant pests which lead to heavy agricultural losses. Individual African governments, generally, have lacked capacity to deal with the myriad problems constraining agricultural growth. Even where gains have been made in agricultural technology, their effects have been slow to trickle down to the level of the smallholders. Nevertheless, however, there have been efforts to stimulate Africa's green revolution, which we highlight below.

- **New Partnership for African Development (NEPAD).** This is latest effort along this path on an Africa-wide platform. Under the auspices of NEPAD an African Fertilizer Summit was held in 2006; among its stated aims was to find develop strategies to dramatically increase African farmers' access to fertilizer. Eleven years on (2006 – 2017) there has been no follow up to the 2006 fertilizer summit. On the contrary, fertilizer subsidies have either been scrapped in many sub-Saharan African countries or, at best, significantly scalled down.
- **Alliance for Green Revolution in Africa (AGRA)** is yet another effort, with heavy emphasis on biotechnology; its aim is to tackle the issues of wider hybrid seed distribution, farmer access to fertilizers and other green revolution inputs, train of more African agricultural scientists/extension workers, etc.

Opponents oppose the Green Revolution initiatives. These opponents originate in a network of African farmer groups, environmentalists and related non-governmental organizations (NGOs), and their opposition centres on the following arguments:

- Fertilizers and other agro inputs pollute the environment – i.e. cause negative externality effects.
- Green revolution inputs are too expensive for the average smallholder to be used on a sustainable basis, much more so now that subsidies have been significantly scaled down.
- Green inputs are hardly produced in African countries, although they produce better yields than the traditional inputs.
- Green revolution agriculture is premised on one-crop, 'monoculture' of modern commercial agriculture; among its costs or disadvantages is that it leads to biodiversity loss (Mawere, 2010) by sidelining traditional seed varieties, which runs the risk of losing seed varieties that may have a lot to offer the farmer and humanity now and in the future, even if their yield potential is less impressive than hybrid varieties (Rena, 2008).

In Asia, the Green Revolution was focused on irrigated wheat and rice (IR8). This needs not be the focus in Sub-Saharan Africa where the main staples are rain-fed maize, cassava, millet, sorghum, yam, sweet potato, plantain and rice. Green Revolution technologies in Africa must be adapted to these diverse staples, most importantly adapting them to the various agro-ecological zones and rain-fed farms.

Africa is heavily dependent on rice to feed its rapidly growing populations – both rural and urban; this rice consumption is not mostly through imports (Africa Rice Center, 2008). One of the ways of realizing a rice Green Revolution is to expand the diffusion of the New Rice for Africa (NERICA) varieties developed by the Africa Rice Center. NERICA varieties have been found to possess traits of traditional rice varieties in Sub-Saharan Africa (*Oryza glaberrima*) characterized by good weed competitiveness and resistance against major African biotic and abiotic stresses and Asian varieties (*Oryza sativa*) characterized by good yields and absence of lodging and grain shattering, and high fertilizer returns. In Uganda, for resistance, the average yield of NERICA rice is found to range around 2.5 t/ha, which is significantly higher than the average upland rice yield of 1 t/ha in Sub-Saharan Africa. Besides, it is found that adoption of NERICA increases the income of adopters significantly. In addition to the advantages, NERICA seeds can be self-produced by local farmers as with other rice varieties (Kijiina et al., 2011).

Even though NERICA varieties seem to hold great prospects for realizing a rice green revolution in the style of India and other Asian countries, their adoption and diffusion rates are still low even in countries where NERICA has been seen to have success – e.g. Guinea (see Dager, 2007).

13.6 The Gen Revolution

By the 1990s the world had reached the threshold of yet another technological revolution in agriculture, now described as the Gen Revolution whereby genetically engineered crops and animals produced from organisms whose genetic makeup has been altered via a process of gene splicing or recombinant DNA, to give the organism a desirable trait – socalled transgenic organisms or genetically modified organisms (GMOs). Wright and Nebel (2004, p. 349) report that the first GMOs to be marketed were: (a) the Flavr Savr™, a tomato that can be vine ripened and subsequently brought to market and kept fresh much longer than the naturally produced one; (b) cotton plants with built-in resistance to insects; (c) numerous crop plants resistant to the herbicide Round-up, allowing farms to employ no-till techniques; (d) genomics has developed sorghum (an important African grain staple) resistant to a parasitic plant known as 'witch weed' infesting many crops in Africa; (e) corn, potatoes, and cotton resistant to insects; (f) rice resistant to bacterial blight disease; etc.

GM revolution portends problems though: genes for herbicide or insect resistance may spread from crop plants to wild plants, constituting possible serious consequences for both agriculture and natural ecosystems – e.g. 'superweeds' will evolve, insect populations could decline (adverse consequences for natural ecosystems); etc. GM crops have developed farthest for use in developed countries, where currently more than 75 million acres (30 million hectares) are cropped. It is argued that farmers may be able to reduce production costs by adopting GMOs, which, in turn, will lead to a closing of the food supply deficits in developing countries (Bren, 2003). Although there is opposition to the Gen Revolution, especially in Western Europe where a number of NGOs, including Greenpeace[3], have been so vocal in their protest, a number of developing countries have introduced selected GM crops into their agricultural systems: in cotton (India) and maize (Egypt);[4] in soybeans, maize and cotton (South Africa); and an estimated 8% of the crop-land of the world currently amounting to some 100 million hectares is reported to be under GM crops[5].

Three groups of problems have been identified associated with GM technology: environmental problems; food safety; and access to the new technology (Wright and Nebel, op. cit., 250-251)[6]. A major environmental concern relates to the pest-resistant properties of the transgenic crops. It is possible that pest incorporated into the GM crop will develop its own resistance to the toxin more rapidly and thus render it ineffective as an independent pesticide; in the event, the transgenic crop loses its advantage. As to the ecological concern: for example, pollen from the cotton plants with built-in resistance to insects that comes from genes taken from a bacterium (so-called Bt = *Bacillus tharingiensis*, the name of the bacterium) disperses in the wind and can spread to adjacent natural ecosystem where beneficial insects may pick it up and die because of the toxin.

The food supply concern arises, for example, from the fact that GM crops contain proteins from different organisms and might trigger unexpected allergic responses in individuals who consume them. Finally, the problem of access to the new technology relates to developing countries. As noted above, GM technology has been developed by multinational biotech agro-industrial firms with profit as their key motive.

> "Farmers are forbidden by contract from simply propagating the seeds themselves and must purchase seeds annually. Farmers in the developing countries are far less able to afford the higher costs of the new seeds, which must be paid up front each year. Aware of the potential for farmers simply to begin to produce their own seeds, researchers developed what is called the **terminator technology**, a transgenic technique that renders any seeds from the crops sterile" (Wright and Nebel, op. cit., pp. 250 – 51 emphasis in original).

13.7 Counter Argument: Technology Cannot Offset Losses Caused By Climate Change

There is a counter argument denying that technological change – both in the earlier form of the Green Revolution and the current Gen Revolution – will offset the losses in agriculture caused by climate change (Cline, 2008). First, it is pointed out that the Green Revolution has lost steam: grain yields, which averaged roughly 3% in annual growth rates in the 1960s through the 1970s, have declined significantly averaging 1.6% by the end of the 1990s (Clunies-Ross et al., op. cit., Table 16.3, p. 460). This argument denies that rising agricultural food prices will provide the required incentives that would reverse the slowing down process observed in the Green Revolution. Rising global food prices have originated partly in the running down of food stocks in response to the effects of bad weather and poor harvests (also caused partly by climate change), partly in rising population growth and rising percapita incomes particularly in Asia (China and India), and partly in rising oil prices (up until late 2014) which raised the attractiveness of diverting grains from food to biofuels. In the United States, for instance, 30% of corn (maize) supplies are reported to be channeled into production of biomass for ethanol production.

Second, the Gen Revolution has not been enthusiastically received, in contrast to the enthusiastic reception accorded the Green Revolution in the developing world in the 1960s and 1970s. Third, even if there is no further slow-down in the Green Revolution, there is likely to be a tight race between rapidly growing food demand and rising output – a race likely to be won by the former (Cline, 2008). It is pointed out that world population is currently exhibiting unprecedented rapid growth underpinned by exceptionally rapid growth rates in developing countries: around 70 million people are added to world population every year; complemented by rising per capita income driven by rapid economic growth in Asia (China and India), rapid population growth is expected to drive up food demand relative to available supply. Current projections show that global food demand will approximately triple by the 2080s from current trends.

There is a certain neo-Malthusian flavour to the argument that technological change will not offset losses in agriculture caused by climate change; that, even if there is no further slow down in technological change in agriculture (or the Green Revolution), growing food demand (driven by rapid population growth and rising per capita income) will outpace rising food output. As just suggested, this argument invokes the ideas of the 18th century classical economist Thomas Malthus, who argued that rapidly growing human population would exhaust Earth's capacity to produce the means of livelihood by using up available agricultural land assumed fixed in supply, until rising death rates and falling birth rates harshly would keep population in check. This Malthusian trap thesis remains influential today, though current focus has shifted from land and agriculture to all natural capital and the global environment. In current, neo-Malthusian thinking technological change is not discounted though; only that it will not be strong enough to offset losses in agricultural growth caused by climate change. In the event, the losses in agriculture will not relent and the gap between food output and food demand will widen (by the 2080s as climate change proceeds inexorably).

Both historical and current evidence fail to align with this neo-Malthusian pessimistic scenario in several major ways. Specifically, tremendous progress in agricultural technology has helped to shift, continually, the production possibility frontiers in world agriculture and, hence, pushing back the threat of famine in populous Asia – specifically, India, Bangladesh, Pakistan, Indonesia, etc. Second, resource scarcities or actual and potential food scarcities have always provided the major incentive to search for substitutes, introduce new technologies, and improve production efficiency in agriculture. Logically, for agricultural supplies, increases in consumption (as currently being witnessed) implies a reduction in available stocks. Economic development experience, however, gives little support to the hypothesis that marketed agricultural supplies are becoming scarcer in an economic sense because potential or actual shortages are always reflected in higher or rising market prices, which provide incentives to discover new sources of supply, improve efficiency in resource use, find substitutes, and make technological innovations. The Green Revolution of the 1960s and 1970s in Asia and parts of Latin America represented the answer by human society to potential or actual food shortages. Human society has not exhausted its innate capability to use innovation to overcome constraints on economic development – both natural and human-made.

The problems facing the global society now and in the medium and longer term cannot be conceived in scarcity of food supplies or agricultural output failing to meet growing demand. The real problems, rather, are three: first, how to distribute growing agricultural surpluses (concentrated largely in the industrialized world) made possible by rapid technological change; second, how to diffuse existing Green Revolution technologies to reach smallholder producers in developing countries (sub-Saharan Africa, in particular) so that they can raise productivity to meet their own immediate food needs and, over time, expand marketed surpluses; and, three, how to ensure that the negative externalities associated with the expansion of commercial agriculture and consumption of new food staples (e.g. GM crops, etc) do not escalate the environmental degradation problem – e.g. destruction of natural habitats or biodiversity loss.

On a global level grain (rice, maize, wheat, etc.) harvests have declined 1% since the peak harvest of 1.88 billion tons achieved in the late 1990s; in per capita terms, grain output has shown decline since 1984, if still much higher than the level of 1950-1974. Even so, there is no shortage of food supplies on a world-wide basis. What has changed is dietary shifts from high starchy foods to high-protein consumption as living standards (per capita incomes) continue to rise in developing countries generally – in particular, China and India.

Even though current global trends in population growth show a slowing down, the dynamics remain highly enough to expect a doubling of the world's population by 2050 or thereabout (World Bank, 1992, p. 26). Most of the growth recorded in world population since the post-world war II decades has originated in populous Asia and Latin America. A rising share of this population will likely aspire to the high consumption standards of the industrial middle classes in Europe and North America, which suggests more intensive demands on Earth's environmental resources and associated pollution, a trend now observed for China particularly but also Africa and Latin America.

13.8 Conclusion

The symptoms of climate change in socioeconomic systems (human societies) are most felt in the sphere of agriculture (crop production, livestock, fisheries, etc.) – the sector of human activities most sensitive to changes in environmental conditions. On the other hand, different socioeconomic systems display different degrees of exposure, sensitivity and adaptative capability about the effects brought about by anthropogenic climate change. Generally, developing countries have greater exposure to the effects of climate change than developed (industrialized) countries; they (developing countries) exhibit greater sensitivity to the negative feedback effects of climate change, as well as possess far lower autonomous capacity to adjust promptly and effectively in response to changes in environmental conditions – whether caused by natural forces or by anthropogenic forcings.

The effects of climate change on socioeconomic systems involve complex interactions among population growth rates, economic growth rates, technological change, geographical factors, etc. Overall, on the global scale, agriculture and food security are likely to be affected adversely by climate change. However, even though technological change will likely offset the losses in agriculture due to climate change, the fact of the widening technology deficits in the developing world in contrast to rapid technological change in the developed world will result in a widening of the development gap between the developing and developed worlds.

End Notes

[1]   See Pearse (1974) on how this concept has been used in the literature.

[2]   See Richards, 1985; Lipton and Longhurst, 1989; Evensen and Gollins, 2003, for constraints on the Green Revolution in Africa.

[3]   Greenpeace was set up in 1971 by a small group of North American activists, who sailed their small boat into the United States atomic test zone near Alaska; McLean and McMillan (2003, p. 232) report that Greenpeace has some 4.5 million supporters (as at 2003?) in 158 countries and is the world's largest international environmental campaign organization.

[4]   **Financial Times** (London), 3rd June, 2008, p. 13.

[5]   **Financial Times** (London), 23rd June, 2008

[6]   See also Smyth et al., 2014.

CHAPTER 14

COPING WITH GLOBAL WARMING AND CLIMATE CHANGE: MITIGATION AND ADAPTATION STRATEGIES

14.1 Introduction

A variety of strategies have been evolved to cope with the environmental threats and challenges posed by global warming and climate change. Although these strategies tend to differ across countries or regions influenced by differences in type, intensity and extent of climate change threats, the resources facing societies and individuals, etc., they can be categorized into two broad types:

- **Mitigation strategies**, which seek to reduce atmospheric concentrations of greenhouse gases (GHGs) and, hence, reducing global temperature rise. Mitigation strategies would include, for example, measures on energy efficiency and land-use change.
- **Adaptation strategies**, which seek to equip human societies with capabilities to function more effectively as Earth's temperatures continue to warm up with rise in atmospheric GHG concentrations.

Mitigation strategies require that humans change their behaviours; specifically, that people adjust the ways they live, or agree to make sacrifices today so that future generations will inherit better living conditions; and to weigh the needs of "third parties" in whatever production/ consumption choices they take. Because of the free-rider problem, however, it is difficult to alter people's behaviour. Adaptation strategies, in contrast, require little in the way of changing people's behaviour; on the contrary, they contain very strong incentives for humans to respond to whatever challenges global warming and climate change throws up; they involve managing the risks, both in terms of society or community and as individuals or members of households, that are associated with global warming and climate change such as flooding, drought, hurricanes and tornadoes, etc. We now proceed to examine more closely the respective strategies.

13.2 Mitigation Strategies

This category of strategies aims to moderate or reduce global temperatures by evolving measures to reduce human-induced GHG emissions; or, otherwise, they seek to introduce technologies to enhance Earth's capacity to absorb CO_2 sequestration in the terrestrial biosphere-socalled geoingeneering. Given that most aspects of the latter (geoingeneering) remain in their theoretical stages or tend to be so costly that they cannot be possibly deployed on the scale required to effect any significant change in GHG emissions[1] we shall necessarily focus on discussing practicable mitigation strategies, which include the following five categories:

- Innovations in fossil fuel technologies.
- Developing biofuels as alternative to fossil fuels.
- Developing "new" technologies in non-carbon energy.
- Improving energy efficiency.
- Land-use change.

What is fundamentally important for mitigation strategies to produce the required results is that all countries of the world and all income classes participate simultaneously, while acknowledging the principle of differentiated capacities and responsibilities[2]. Noble and Watson (2006, pp. 229-233) observe that:

> "The industrial countries alone, despite their greater resources and more advanced technology, cannot reduce their emissions by enough to stabilize atmospheric concentrations, because today's developing countries are industrializing and will soon become major contributors to emissions themselves ... (and) will more than double their total energy consumption between 2000 and 2030 ... and fossil fuels will continue to provide about 85 percent of the total. For their part, although developing countries have the opportunity to build energy-efficient, reduced-emissions economies from the ground up, rather than engage in expensive retrofitting, it is unlikely that these countries will accept – nor should they – a larger share of the mitigation burden than the industrial countries. Cooperation on a global scale will be needed, including transfers of finance and technology from the industrial world to the developing world where opportunities for low-cost mitigation are greater." (pp. 228-9; bracketed word added).

Among the key issues which dominate current climate change negotiations is how to share the burden of GHG mitigation between the developed countries, who have achieved industrialization and are, historically and currently, the major global emitters, and the developing countries that are yet to achieve industrial development. The developing countries seem to argue that the developed countries have exceeded their "quota" in global GHG emissions and should not impose restrictions on the developing countries now attempting to industrialize by limiting their fossil-fuel combustion to drive their industrial and agricultural modernization. Even though all countries of the world seem to agree that climate change constitutes 'the most important issue we face as a global community', effective solution to this problem is limited by serious constraints originating in the obvious difficulty of bridging the protective self-interest of developed countries that have long achieved industrial take-off yet are alarmed at the disastrous consequences of 'drastic climate change', and those of developing countries yet to achieve industrial transition and for whom 'crises of poverty', not climate change as such, are their immediate concern (Vera, 2002; Najam et al., 2003). This evident contradiction between the interest of the developed countries and those of the developing countries is further emphasized by Adams (2009, p. 102), when he reports that "while the north argued the priority of environmental protection and that any measures agreed should be cost effective, the south pushed for development and industrialization, and the principle of historical responsibility". That is, the developing countries (the south), insist that the developed countries (the north) should bear responsibility for past GHG emissions which occurred during their industrial take-off in the mid-1700s through the 1800s by bearing the greater burden of the current GHG mitigation strategies. We shall return to this issue in chapters on international policies on climate change; let us focus, for now, on the five strategies on climate change mitigation identified above.

14.2.1 Innovations in Fossil-Fuel Technologies

This category of mitigation strategies has attracted interest along the following lines:

- **Substitution of gasified coal gas for coal (classified as the 'dirtiest' fossil fuel) to reduce CO_2 emissions.** As we saw earlier, coal emits more CO_2 than any fossil fuel. Technological innovations can, however, mitigate the CO_2 content of coal through gasification through partial oxidation to produce synthetic gas or synfuels[3]. Superclean fuels derived from synthetic gas in poly generation facilities are predicted to be economically competitive. The word 'competitive' in the present context is meant to capture the fact that synthetic gas has been made artificially, and so does not originate in coal which contains CO_2. However, on the other hand, the economic viability of this synthetic gas is said to be predicated on rising oil prices (as in the case of fracking in the United States which experienced a boom during the 1970s through 2014) – which would provide the necessary price incentives for research and development (R&D) to upscale technologies to convert coal into synthetic gas to replace high-price oil. With the rapid collapse of global oil prices post-2014 the price incentives to induce innovations to produce crude oil substitutes seem to have been seriously undermined.

- **Processes to capture and store emitted CO_2 at the site of production,** converting it into liquid CO_2 and pumping it into deep oceans, where the low temperatures and high pressure would preserve it as solid mass; otherwise, it could be injected into depleted oil and gas wells or other geological formations. It seems obvious that, although this would permit continued combustion of fossil fuels with far reduced atmospheric CO_2 concentrations, this could pose environmental risks of its own, apart from being less permanent solution in the sense that the ocean depths would in future become saturated in their capacity to accommodate this type of 'waste' and/or there would not be available enough depleted oil and gas wells.

14.2.2 Developing Biofuels as Alternative to Fossil Fuels

Biofuels, as the term suggests, refer to fuels whose energy content originates in organic or biological matter – e.g. ethanol produced from sugarcane; biodiesel produced from oils or fats through hyprocracking biological oil feedbacks such as vegetable oils and animal fats; biogas (a mixture of methane and carbon dioxide) produced from the anaerobic decomposition of domestic, industrial, and agricultural sewages (done in special digesters, which are widely used in China and India); etc. Scientific studies find that biofuels, generally, have far less GHG emission potentials than fossil fuels (e.g. coal); that burning biofuel instead of fossil fuels will lead to 148% reduction in global warming potential (GWP); besides, total net savings from using biofuels [especially those from socalled conventional biofuels produced from food crops, sugar cane, corn (maize), etc.] have been found to range around 25-82% compared with diesel derived from crude oil.

There is, however, a cloud of controversies on "how-green this form of energy really is". Specifically, it is observed that the climate change benefit of a particular biofuel is a function of the scale and model of production, as well as the type of feedstock that is employed. But growing and processing biofuels employs fossil-fuel-based technologies, including equipment fueled by oil and petro-chemical-based fertilizers and pesticides used, which inevitably increase the GHG footprint of the biofuel being produced[4].

Some food-based biofuels such as maize (corn) and soya are generally more energy intensive (higher in carbohydrates) than others, such as sugarcane and rapeseed, meaning that their GHG emissions are larger. Ethanol and biodiesel are the most commonly produced biofuels; whereas ethanol is used to blend gasoline to enhance octane and cut down carbon monoxide (CO) and carbon-ladden emissions, biodiesel is employed as additive – typically, 20% - to reduce vehicle emissions or in its pure form as a renewable alternative fuel for diesel engine.

Studies disputing the climate change benefits of biofuels argue that the findings on which biofuels seek their justification often discount the GHG emissions originating from land-use change caused by direct farming of biofuel crops (e.g. maize, sugarcane, soy, sweet potatoes, etc.) or the indirect conversion of forestland and grasslands to agricultural use resulting from the need to boost food production that has been displaced by biofuel crops. The Paris-based International Council for Science reports that maize-based biofuels, for instance, produce 93% more GHG emissions than gasoline[5]. But most studies had failed to correctly account for the global warming impact of nitrous oxide (N_2O) produced from farming biofuel crops, which cancel out any advantages offered by reduced emissions of CO_2. As pointed out by various studies, N_2O is made by bacteria that live in agricultural soils and water, and, currently their (bacterias') raw materials is often the nitrogenous chemical fertilizers that constitute key input in modern farming, which has increased manifold beginning since the 1960s in the wake of the Green Revolution. Maize (corn), a key food crop of the Green Revolution, is known to be a significant producer of nitrous oxide (N_2O) emissions, and is one of the main sources of conventional biofuel, as pointed out above.

14.2.3 Developing New Technologies in Non-Carbon Energy

These technologies are targeted at nuclear energy and various forms of renewable energy, which are expected to lower the cost, or improve the efficiency, of these non-carbon emitting forms of energy and, hence, permitting them to substitute for a large proportion of the energy currently supplied by fossil fuels. Apart from the conventional non-carbon energy sources in nuclear power, biomass and hydroelectricity, there are socalled new renewable energy sources in wind, solar (photovoltaic) and geothermal energy. Although these non-carbon, renewable energy sources currently contribute just a little over 13% of world energy supply (see Table 14.1), they are likely to increase their supplies significantly in future especially in the energy-hungry OECD countries and other industrialized economies and, hence, contributing in solving the climate change challenge.

Table 14.1 Sources of Energy (% Global Energy Supply)

Non-renewable (fossil fuels)	%
Oil (petroleum)	34.3
Coal	25.2
Natural gas	20.9
Sub – Total	80.4
Renewable	**%**
Hydro	2.2000
Biomass	4.4000
Tide (wave)	0.0004

Wind	0.0640
Solar	0.0390
Geothermal	0.4100
Sub-Total	<u>13.1134</u>

Source: The Economist, 2nd June, 2007, p. 20. See also The Economist, June 13th, 2015, pp. 59-60.

A. Nuclear Power (Nuclear Energy)

This form of energy uses nuclear reactions to produce steam to turn generators; its source is naturally occurring uranium. The latter is concentrated, enriched, and converted to uranium dioxide – the fuel used in the reactor. The uranium dioxide undergoes nuclear fission (a nuclear reaction in which uranium splits into two parts releasing enormous quantity of energy: mass for mass, uranium generates some 2,500,000 times more energy by fission than carbon does by combustion (Wright and Nebel, 2002, chapter 14; Oxford Dictionary of Physics, 2009, p. 306;). Some of the highly radioactive spent fuel may be reprocessed while the larger proportion must be carefully disposed of, both of which are costly and pose significant health and environmental hazards. Much more relevant for the present study is the low CO_2 emission properties of nuclear power, which can contribute significantly to mitigation of climate change. The following facts provide some decided environmental advantages of nuclear power over coal-fired energy (comparing a 1,000 – megawatt nuclear plant with a coal-fired plant of similar capacity, each operating for a single year) (Wright and Nebel, op. cit.):

- **Fuel needed:** The coal plant would use about 3 million mt of coal, (which if obtained by strip mining, will cause environmental degradation and acid leaching will result; if through deep mining has potential for pit collapses, apart from release of methane gases leading to death of miners and impaired health). The nuclear plant, on the other hand, would require some 30 mt of enriched uranium obtained from mining 75,000 mt of ore, with much less environmental degradation and human cost. The fission of about 0.5 kg of uranium fuel releases energy equivalent to combustion of 50 mt of coal – thus, fueling the reactor with about 60 mt can run the nuclear power plant for up to 2 years.
- **CO_2 emissions:** Nuclear plants emit none; coal mines emit tremendous CO_2 – over 7 million tons into the atmosphere each year.
- **Sulphur dioxide (SO_2) and other emissions:** Some 300,000 tons of SO_2 and other acid-forming pollutants are generated from the coal plant, apart from low levels of many

radioactive chemicals. Nuclear plants release none of these though, but may produce low levels of radioactive waste gases.

- **Solid waste material:** Coal plants generate considerable coal ash requiring careful land disposal – the average coal plant generates about 600,000 mt of coal ash. The nuclear plant produces about 250 mt of highly radioactive wastes requiring careful storage and ultimate safe disposal.

- **Accidents:** Coal pit mining often results in fatal accidents, as happened in Donestkh, Eastern Ukraine in early 2015. Accidents in nuclear plants can range from mine emissions of radioactivity to catastrophic release leading to widespread radiation sickness. In the event of a nuclear accident – such as Three Mile Island in Pennsylvania, United States in March 1979 and Chernobyl, Ukraine in April 1986 – there will occur radioactive fallout (radioactive particles deposited from the atmosphere from a nuclear explosion or from a nuclear accident). Local fallout within 250km of an accident falls within a few hours of the event; tropospheric fallout are particles deposited all over Earth's atmosphere within about a week; and stratospheric fallout may fall anywhere on Earth over a period of years (Wright and Nebel, op. cit., especially pp. 342-58).

As at the first decades of the 2000s, 104 nuclear plants were in operation in the United States alone, generating some 20% of its electricity. As we noted earlier, the United States depends heavily on coal and natural gas for its electricity, which makes it one of the top-10 polluters of the world. Globally, the top-10 countries in nuclear-based electricity generation are: France (75%); Lithuania (73%); Belgium (58%); Bulgaria (47%); Slovakia (47%); Sweden (47%); Ukraine (44%); South Korea (43%); Hungary (38%); and Armenia (36%). France's high dependence on nuclear energy for electricity started to evolve in the early 1970s in the wake of the OPEC-inspired oil shocks that destabilized the energy balance of several West European countries driving them to seek alternatives outside fossil fuels. Because of France's high dependence on nuclear-based electricity generation, that country has an extremely low level of CO_2 emissions per capita from electricity generation (nuclear and hydro produce up to 90% of France's electricity needs). The environmental advantages of nuclear-based electricity vis-à-vis fossil fuels is a factor driving France's and other European countries' – e.g. Belgium – high dependence on nuclear-based electricity, apart from the slow pace of developing alternatives in renewable energy sources, to which we return below. Nuclear energy has gone out of fashion in much of the world, much because of fear of deadly nuclear accidents which always leave long-term adverse health impacts (e.g. Christodouleas et al., 2011). Globally, the share of nuclear-based electricity has declined to 10.8% from a peak of 17.6% in 1996, though some countries – e.g. China, Russia, India, and several Middle East countries – are expanding their nuclear programmes (The Economist, 2015, 28th November, p. 35). The pressure to expand nuclear energy has legitimate reasons though: demand for energy is rising, along with pressure to reduce carbon emissions. As The Economist observes: "… nuclear plants tick both boxes" (ibid.)

B. Biomass Energy

As the term implies, biomass energy or bioconversion is the form of energy derived from biological or organic matter, mainly wood, crops, animal waste, etc. In the developing world, generally, biomass (e.g. wood fuel sourced from forests) is the major energy source for household cooking and heating purposes – supplying more than 90% in many countries.

In the European Union (EU) wood-based energy is found to constitute the largest socalled renewable fuel, accounting for some 50% of Europe's renewable energy consumption: in Poland and Finland, wood meets more than 80% of renewable-energy demand; in Germany, 38% of non-fossil demand is met from fuelwood. Briefly, in all its various forms – from sticks to pellets (used in woodstoves, otherwise called pellet stove, a devise that burns compressed pellets made from wood wastes) to sawdust-wood, etc. – biomass supplies upwards of 50% of Europe's renewable energy. Among the key problems of biomass energy is that this form of energy can only be produced on any large scale through heavy subsidies (in the OECD countries), which makes it an inefficient route to mitigate CO_2 emissions. For example: in Great Britain, it takes £45 sterling in subsidy to produce 1 mwh biomass / wood energy and £225 sterling to save one tonne of CO_2 by switching from gas to wood:

> "And that assumes the rest of the process (in power station) is carbon neutral. It probably isn't" (The Economist, 2013, 6th April, p. 62).

Yet another issue is that:

> "Wood produces carbon twice over: once in the power station, once in the supply chain. The process of making pellets out of wood involves grinding it up, turning it into a dough and putting it under pressure. That, plus the shipping, requires energy and produces carbon: 200kg of CO_2 for the amount of wood needed to provide 1 mwh of electricity" (ibid.).

Scientists have explained that the original idea – carbon in managed forests or according to the principle of sustainable forest management (SFM)[7] offsets carbon in power stations – was not always correct because it was based on assumption of carbon neutrality without considering the type of forest used, how fast the trees grow, whether one was woodchips or whole trees and so on. In support of this view, the European Environment Agency (EEA), an agency of the European Union (EU), explains that the assumption:

"That biomass combustion would be inherently carbon neutral ... is not correct ... as it ignores the fact that using land to produce plants for energy typically means that this land is not producing plants for other purposes, including carbon otherwise sequestrated" (ibid).

It is important to appreciate, as a final note, that rural households' dependence on local woodlands and forests for their fuelwood often cause deforestation. The literature suggests a solution: develop a market in fuel wood, which would encourage rural communities with land to begin to cultivate trees as a cash crop.

"When we have to pay for fuelwood, trees become an important resource that can be put under the stewardship of local communities or private landowners, and a sustainable use of forests can result; then all of the other benefits of goods and services provided by forests are preserved or restored" (Wright and Nebel, op. cit, p. 380).

In many developing countries, as previously shown, a booming informal market in fuelwood has evolved though, but lacking the replanting mechanisms and processes to make it sustainable[8].

C. Hydroelectric Power

Hydroelectric power is generated by a flow of water. For example: a natural waterfall provides an energy source, in the form of falling water, which can be harnessed to drive a turbine (in the case of a hydroelectric facility, a turbo generator), which, in turn, can be coupled to a generator to provide electrical energy. Hydropower technology has a long history, tracing back to ancient civilizations that developed knowledge of how to exploit water power for various purposes – e.g. agriculture, transportation, food processing, etc. Hydroelectric dams, where water flows through channels to drive turbogenerators, are the modern version of this exploitation of water power. Hydroelectric power provides 16-19% of electrical energy supply world-wide and is by far the most important and widely renewable energy source; in some (developing) countries hydropower supplies almost 100% of total electrical energy supplies – e.g. Nepal in South Asia, over 90%; Zambia in Southern Africa, over 60%; Tajikistan in Central Asia, over 70%; etc. Globally, China currently possesses the largest hydroelectric generation capacity, amounting to nearly 900,000 Tw-h/year (terawatt-hours per year, equal to 1 billion kilowatt hours). Table 14.2 shows the top-10 hydroelectric power generating countries in the world by 2012.

Studies show that hydropower is non-polluting and has several advantages over other power-producing

Table 14.2 Top-10 Hydroelectric Power Generating Countries, 2012

Country	Hydroelectric power generation Tw-h/year (terawatt-hours per year (equal to 1 billion kilowatt hours)[a]
China	900,000
Brazil	< 400,000
Canada	400,000
United States	300,000
Russia	200,000
Norway	180,000
India	150,000
Venezuala	100,000
Sweden	100,000
Japan	100,000

[a]Data are rough estimates from a bar chart and may differ from actual data.
Source: United States Energy Information Administration (EIA) {http://www.eia.gov/cfapps/ipdbproject/IEDIndex3.cfm}.
Accessed 8th June, 2016

technologies: fuel is not combusted so there is minimal pollution; water to run the hydroelectric plant is a renewable resource, perpetually supplied through the hydrologic cycle; hydropower plays a significant role in reducing GHG emissions; relatively efficient in operation, with low operations and maintenance costs[9]; the technology is reliable and proven over time; and it is a renewable energy source – rainfall renews the water in the reservoir, so the fuel is almost always available though may fluctuate in supply due to irregularities in rainfall. Nevertheless, however, hydroelectric power does have some negative spillovers: by changing the environment; affecting land-use; displacing human, animal and plant habitats in the dam area; etc.

However, available scientific evidence shows that hydropower is not always carbon neutral; but dams and other water reservoirs can be sources of GHG emissions – e.g. CO_2 (carbon dioxide) and CH_4 (methane) – resulting from the decomposition by bacteria of the biomass that was either submerged due to impoundment, that enters the reservoir from upstream inflows or that grows within the reservoir itself. At present, however, it is not firmly established the extent the GHG emissions from reservoirs contribute to the global GHG emissions[10]. Hydropower reservoirs are known to cover some 3.4×10^5 km^2 and comprise 20% of all reseviors globally, the global GHG emissions from them represent just 4% of the estimated global CO_2 emissions from inland waters – most of these located in the tropical regions (Barros et al., 2011; see also Kosten et al., 2010).

D. 'New' Renewable Energy: Wind, Solar, Geothermal

These socalled new renewable energy sources are known to possess enormous potentials in reducing fossil fuel combustion; though currently they contribute less than 14% to world energy supplies (see Table 14.1), there exist enormous potentials to increase their supplies quite significantly in future, especially in the energy-thirty OECD economies, China and India, and, hence, contributing to climate mitigation. Wind and solar energy have been identified to possess the strongest potentials for rapid expansion.

- **WIND POWER.** Wind power is the use of air currents in Earth's atmosphere to drive machinery, especially to drive electrical generator. Practical land-based wind generators or aerogenerators have potential to generate million of kilowatts of energy per year throughout the world, a potential which current interest in wind power as a renewable energy source is trying to exploit to reduce combustion of fossil fuels to mitigate anthropogenic climate change. The power, P, of wind energy to drive a wind generator is posited to be a non-linear function of three variables; namely, air density (k), diameter of the blades of the wind generator (d), and the average wind speed (v); the model is: $P = kd^2v^3$ (Oxford Dictionary of Physics, 2009, p. 589). With a given air density k, the power of wind energy P will depend on the diameter of the blades of the wind generator d, and wind speed v. Hence, the efficiency of modern wind generator technology revolves on making the blades sleeker so they can catch more wind and move faster.

As an alternative to fossil fuels, wind energy is clean, produces no GHG emissions during operation, and uses little land (as photovoltaic (PV) or solar energy) compared to other renewable energy sources (Fthenakis and Kim, 2009). The most rapid growth has occurred during 1996-2015, when global wind power cumulative capacity increased from a little over 6 Gigawatts to 432 Gigawatts (see also GWEC, 10 February, 2015). Since 2010 more than half of all new wind power installations have originated in China and India. At the end of 2015 China had 145 GW or roughly 34% of wind power installed. Table 14.3 contains the top-10 countries in installed wind power capacity.

Table 14.3 Top-10 Countries in Installed Wind Power Capacity by 2015

Country	MW	Share of world capacity (%)
China	145,362	34.3
United States	74,471	17.6

Germany	44,947	10.6
India	25,088	5.9
Spain	23,025	5.4
United Kingdom	13,603	3.2
Canada	11,205	2.6
France	10,358	2.4
Italy	8,958	2.1
Brazil	8,715	2.1
Rest of the world	58,275	13.7

Source: Global Wind Report, 2014 – Annual Market Update

Much more relevant for this study is the environmental effect of wind energy compared to fossil fuels. IPCC assessments of the life-cycle global warming potential (GWP) of energy source establish that wind turbines have some of the lowest GWP per unit of electrical energy (Guezuraga et al., 2012). While wind farm may take up a large area of land, only a small area of turbin installation and infrastructure is used by wind energy installations.

As to its history, the first accounts of wind power are of windmills being used for power in Persia (modern Iran) around 500 to 900 AD and Crete, Greece to water crops by pumping out water from reservoirs, for refining grain quicker than the mortar-and-pestle technique would have done the job. Wind mills began to evolve in Europe during the Middle Ages – about the late 1200s – employed in grain milling, and become highly developed in Holland, where the original windmill concept (as developed in Persia) was upgraded and revised – e.g. making blades sleeker so they could catch more wind and thus move faster[12]. By the 14th century (the 1300s AD), later-Middle Ages, Dutch windmills were in use to drain areas of the Rhine delta. The 1700s saw the technology cross the Atlantic into the New World and was in use to pump water in the Cape Cod region during the American Revolution (Kurlansky, 2002); it began to be applied to water crops by the mid-1800s, and between 1850 and 1970, more than 6 million windmills were reported installed in the United States.

It was not until the late 1800s when wind power began to be applied to attempt to generate electrical energy: first, in Europe in 1887 (in Scotland, by James Blyth) who built the first modern windmill turbin (see Price, 2005). World War I (1914-1918) saw the development of fossil-fuel technologies based on petroleum to generate electricity – the result was that the windmill as an electrical source died.

Post-1973 witnesses a resurgence of interest in wind energy technology, spurred by OPEC-inspired oil price shocks. During this period, large-scale investments were made in R&D, particularly in the United States, to develop wind energy systems often supported by heavy subsidies from the United States government. By the beginning of the 2000s, fears of fossil fuels depletion and global warming spurred rapid growth in the wind energy industry. As at the end of 2014 over 240,000 commercial-sized wind turbines were reported operating in the world supplying some 4% of global electricity (World Wind Energy Association, 2014).

- **SOLAR ENERGY.** Solar energy is any energy source originating **directly** from the sun's radiation referring to the electromagnetic waves emitted by the sun, of which only 0.0005% is known to reach Earth's surface. It is this 0.005% that reaches Earth's surface that provides energy to make planet Earth habitable. Allen (1958) long ago describes solar radiation as "the sun's most generous gift to the earth. It provides energy to make the atmosphere work…"

The direct ways of exploiting solar energy can be categorized into two: thermal method (solar heating), and non-thermal method (solar cells). Solar heating is a form of domestic or industrial heating that relies on the direct use of solar energy, the basic form of which is a thermal devise in which a fluid is heated by the sun's rays in a collector and pumped or allowed to flow round a circuit that provides some form of heat storage and serves as a form of auxiliary heat source for use when the sun is not shining. In rural sub-Saharan Africa, solar heating is the major method of drying and preserving agricultural produce, drying clothes, etc. Solar cell is, on the other hand, an electric cell that uses the sun's radiation to produce usable electric current. Solar cell technology is currently being exploited on a global scale in the effort to mitigate climate change.

In the industrialized world, there are concerted efforts to exploit solar energy to provide an alternative to fossil-fuel energy sources. The objective here is two-fold: mitigate climate change and attain energy security. In the developing world, generally, the importance of solar energy is only appreciated from the objective of a solution to the 'energy crisis'; the environmental benefits of the 'greeness' of solar energy is not of any major or immediate concern to potential users of solar energy (See, for instance, Ndzibah, 2010, on Ghana).

Solar energy plants deploy one of two technologies: (1) **photovoltaic (PV)** systems, which use solar panels, either on roof tops or in ground-mounted solar farms; and (2) **concentrated solar power (CSP)**, also known as concentrated solar thermal, which harnesses solar thermal energy to make steam that can be converted into electricity by a turbine. The more widely exploited technology is PV system. The latter is a device consisting of solar panels, a battery (which allows light to be supplied at night when there is no sunshine), a charger controller, and an inverter. The lifetime of the solar panels averages 20-25 years, considered the average lifetime of a PV system.

Table 14.4 Top-10 Countries in Installed Solar Power Capacity (MW) in 2015

Country	Installed Solar Power Capacity (MW)	% of World Total
China	43,530	22.5
Germany	39,700	20.6
Japan	34,410	17.8
United States	25,620	13.3
Italy	18,920	9.8
United Kingdom	8,780	4.5
France	6,580	3.4
Spain	5,400	2.8
Australia	5,070	2.6
India	5,050	2.6
World Total	256,000	2.6

Source: IEA (2016, 22 April)

Table 14.5 Top-10 Countries in Solar Energy Power Capacity Per Capita Installed

Country	PV Watt Per Capita Installed
Germany	491
Italy	308
Belgium	287
Japan	271
Greece	230
Australia	215
Czech Republic	198
United States	79
China	32
India	4

Source: IEA (2016, 22 April)

Globally, PVs have exhibited rapid growth, though varying across countries and regions of the world. According to IEA sources China, Germany, Japan and United States, in that order, are currently, the leading countries in PV installed capacity (Table 14.4). However, the countries where PV technologies have penetrated most, measured in terms of solar energy capacity per capita installed, are Germany, Italy, Belgium, and Japan, in that order (Table 14.5). As Table 14.5 shows, China though has accumulated immense PV capacity, comes no where near the level of PV penetration already attained by Germany[13] and most other European countries or even Japan.

Outside South Africa, which is expected to reach PV installed capacity of 8,400 MW by 2030, no sub-Saharan African country has PV capacity of any significance by global standards. However, tremendous potentials exist for expansion of PV capacities in African countries, given that most African countries are in environments that permit a very high amount of days per year with bright sunlight-this is particularly true for countries located on the fringes of deserts and the Sahel. Existing studies on Nigeria, for instance, show the country is endowed with an annual average daily sunshine of 6.25 hours ranging between 3.5 hours in the coastal states bordering the Atlantic Coast and 9 hours in the 'far north' located on the fringes of the Sahara Desert and Sahel (See, for instance, Osueke and Ezugwu, 2011; Osueke et al., 2013; Newsom, 2012). Nigeria's annual average solar energy insolation value is put at 1.804 x 10.15 kwh, which is about 27 times the total conventional energy resources in energy units and over 117, 000 times the amount of electrical power generated in the country in 1998.

The problem is that in most African countries, Nigeria inclusive, development of alternative 'new' renewable energy sources, especially solar and wind, is yet to acquire importance in public policy; neither is the importance of renewable energy sources properly and adequately understood among the public and even policymakers. But there are no viable examples of success in renewables to encourage favourable perception of this alternative source of energy. As one observer put it, what abound in Nigeria's energy history are failed projects, of which solar power installations are among the visible examples.

"... Solar power installations have largely joined the many failed projects initiated by government-testimonies associated with patronage and corruption" (Newson, 2012, p. 7).

Generally, however, high cost is found to constitute a key constraint facing diffusion of the PV technology in sub-Saharan Africa: unlike fossil fuels, solar energy is difficult to store for long periods without large stocks of solar cells and batteries, which are rather expensive relative to the average per capita income in sub-Saharan Africa. There are, however, optimistic forecasts as regards falling costs for producing solar energy, thanks to cheaper techniques of producing silicon wafers and to economies of scale (See The Economist (2015, 13th June, pp. 59-60).

Finally, even though unlike fossil fuels, PV systems produce no GHG emissions when they are operated, they are not GHG-emission neutral when we consider the lifecycle of the PV system – that is, GHG emissions starting in the stage of production to the stage of transportation to markets or regions where they are operated, and finally to the stage when the technology is phased out. Carbon emissions based on the lifecycle of the PV system occur during the manufacture of solar modules. Currently, the latter are largely produced in China (upwards of 50% of global production) where coal-based power plants provide the sole energy source for this production. Compared with coal power plants, PVs emit more CO_2 not during operation but during manufacture or production of the PV cells, whose global centre of production has shifted from Western Europe, North America and Japan to Asia (mainly China, but also Malaysia, Taiwan and Philippines) (Mulvaney, 2014). The description of the production mechanisms below relies on Malvaney (op. cit.).

The mechanics of the manufacture of solar panels is important for appreciating the lifecycle of the PV system and associated chemical pollutions and CO_2 emissions. The vast requirements of solar cells start in quartz, the most common form of silica (silicon dioxide), which is refined into elemental silicon. The mining of the silica puts miners at risk of getting lung cancer: **siliconsis.** The second stage involves refining quartz into metallurgical grade silicon, a substance used mostly to harden steel and other metals, which process consumes a lot of energy with consequent CO_2 and sulphur dioxide (SO_2) emissions. The third stage involves converting the metallurgical-grade silicon into a power form called polysilicon, which creates silicon tetrachloride. Solar-cell firms purify chunks of polysilicon to produce bricklike ingots and then slice the latter into silicon wafers into which are introduced impurities to produce the essential solar-cell architechture that produces the PV effect.

As can be seen, producing solar cells involves processes emitting not only toxic fumes and chemical wastes that pollute the lithosphere and hydrosphere and their interactions with the biosphere, but also uses a lot of energy with associated GHG emissions. Fortunately, because solar cells generate electricity when they are deployed they are said to pay back the original investment in the energy consumed in their production – ranging from 6 months to 2 years-which is measured in terms of kilowatt-hours supplied by the solar cells. However, analysts also judge the impact of the energy consumed in producing a solar panel in the amount of carbon generated in the production of that energy – socalled carbon-intensity value (= kilogramme of CO_2 emitted per kilowatt-hour generated).

It is found that countries that depend largely on coal-based plants to produce their industrial electricity supplies – e.g. China – have the most carbon-intense electricity in the world. Specifically, China is found to have two times carbon-intense electricity compared with the United States electricity system. Because China supplies the bulk of global production of solar panels, (as noted above, upwards of 50%), the carbon print of China-produced solar panels is found to be double that of panels produced in Europe or United States. But because Europe and United States import the bulk of China's output of solar panels for its PV systems, there is **net** GHG emission for solar energy, contrary to popular perception. Mulvaney (op. cit.) observes thus:

> "If the photovoltaic panels made in China were installed in China, the high carbon intensity of the energy used and that of the energy saved would cancel each other out, and the time needed to counterbalance greenhouse-gas emissions during manufacture would be the same as the energy-payback time. But that's not what's been happening … The manufacturing is mostly located in China, and the panels are often installed in Europe or the United States. At double the carbon intensity, it takes twice as long to compensate for the greenhouse-gas emissions as it does to pay back the energy investments."

Mulvaney concludes that concerns about the greenhouse-gas emissions of PV technology will persist as long as manufacture of PV panels is located in carbon-intense electricity environments of Asia; on the other hand:

> "… Powering photovoltaic-panel manufacturing with wind, solar, and geothermal energy will end concerns about the carbon footprints of photovoltaics."

It remains to examine the potential of geothermal energy as means to mitigate GHG emissions.

- **GEOTHERMAL ENERGY.** Geothermal energy derives from heat within Earth's crust that constitutes a potential source of energy; it is contained in the rock and fluid (that fills the fractures and pores within the rocks) in Earth's crust. Geothermal energy is that heat originating from the core of planet Earth to the surface, created by the radioactive decay and continual heat loss from Earth's formation (Turcotte and Schubert, 2002). Temperatures at Earth's core may reach over 4000°C (7,200°F); the high temperatures and pressure in Earth's core cause some rock to melt into molten magma, and solid mantle to behave plastically resulting in positions of mantle convecting upwards since it is higher than the surrounding rock. If the molten magma is sufficiently close to Earth's surface (i.e., 10,000 feet), underground water may have sufficiently heated to produce steam that can be tapped by drilling geothermal wells.

Geothermal energy has been exploited since the beginning of human civilizations. In Paleolithic times, it was exploited for bathing and for space heating in ancient Roman times. In the modern industrial age, it is exploited for electricity and various other purposes. Globally, some 960 MW of geothermal electricity has been installed (as at 2014) in 24 countries, which is expected to produce 67,246 Gwh of electricity (Fridleifsson et al., 2008).

Table 14.6 Installed Geothermal Electricity Capacity (2010)

Country	Installed capacity (MW)	% of national electricity supply	% of global geothermal production
United States	3,086	0.3	29
Philippines	1,904	27	18
Indonesia	1,197	3.7	11
Mexico	958	3.0	9
Italy	843	1.5	8
New Zealand	628	10.0	6
Iceland	575	30	5
Japan	536	0.1	5
Iran	250	n.a.	n.a.
El Salvado	204	25	n.a.
World	10,959.7	-	-

Source: International Geothermal Association (IGA) **News**

Although geothermal energy is available throughout the world as a perpetual energy resource, currently regions of the world where it has been exploited on a significant scale to produce electricity are limited. Table 14.6 contains the top-10 countries with significant installed geothermal electricity, of which the United States leads with 3088 MW produced from 77 power plants. The largest group of geothermal power plants in the world is in The Geysers in California, United States. However, as data in Table 14.6 show geothermal contribution to United States electricity supply is less than 1%. A much more significant role for geothermal electricity is noticeable in the data for the Philippines, Iceland, El Salvado, Indonesia, New Zealand and Mexico.

As a renewable energy resource with infinite or unlimited supply (like solar energy, wind, etc.) geothermal energy is theoretically more than adequate to solve Earth's energy needs. However, the problem is whether this energy resource can be **economically** exploited, which is a function of several factors: technology, fossil fuel energy prices, government policies on subsidies, interest rates, etc.

As just stated, geothermal energy as renewable energy is infinite in supply; any projected heat extraction from geothermal energy does not subtract from geothermal energy available for future use. Scientists establish that planet Earth has an internal heat content approximately 100 billion times current (2010) global annual demand for energy (Fridleifsson et al. op. cit.). By drawing on this infinite resource present generations of humans will not jeopardize the welfare of future generations (See Rybach, 2007).

What about the GHG emissions from geothermal energy production and use? It is established that fluids from deep down Earth's crust carry a mixture of gases – e.g. carbon dioxide (CO_2), hydrogen sulphide (H_2S), methane (CH_4), ammonia (NH_3), etc., which might contribute to global warming, acid rain, and noxious smell if not carefully stored. Existing geothermal electricity plants are found to emit an average of 122kg (269 lb) of CO_2 per MW-hour (MW-h) of electricity. The good news, however, is that this level of emissions is considered a low carbon intensity compared with emissions from fossil fuel plants (Bertani and Thain, 2002).

An implication we draw from our analyses is that the prospects of using development of renewables as a strategy to mitigate climate change are rather limited. But as data in Table 14.1 show, renewables currently supply a little over 13% of global energy. On the other hand, however, though current global energy supplies are preponderantly dominated by fossil fuels and non-renewables which emit the bulk of atmospheric GHGs, the International Energy Agency (IEA) estimates that there exist abundant cheap energy-efficient measures - e.g. new buildings-that can be made 70% more energy efficient than average existing ones; development of super-efficient automobiles, etc. (See Solbery and Wiederkehr, 1995, p. 42).

14.2.4 Improving Energy Efficiency

Technological innovations along this path have, in a large extent, been adopted in the OECD economies, implemented on voluntary basis by firms, households and individuals to reduce energy consumption. These innovations have focused on three sectors: energy production; industrial processes; residential, commercial and institutional buildings; and transportation. Simultaneously, three measures have been adopted: energy conservation (e.g. fuel-efficiency targets on new cars and development of super-efficient automobiles); fuel-switching and cleaner energy (e.g. switch to electric cars in transportation); and promotion of renewable energy (e.g. use of wood-energy for heating in public buildings, etc).

Industry has accounted for the greatest energy-efficiency innovations to reduce GHG emissions; but the sector has accounted for the greatest energy-related CO_2 emissions globally: 43% by the 1990s, though the rate of increase in emissions has tended to decrease over the decades caused largely by "the collapse of the notoriously energy-inefficient heavy industries of the former Soviet bloc" (Noble and Watson, op. cit. p. 232)[14]. Yet another important factor is reforms in China's energy-intensive industries[15], which consume more than 10,000 mt of coal equivalent (tce) per year (See, for instance, Buijs, 2011; Paltsev et al., 2012; Yuan and Zhao, 2016). In 2008 China alone consumed 345.1 billion KWh of electricity more than the electricity generation of Africa, Central and South America, the Middle East and India combined.

Table 14.7 Innovations in Energy Efficiency to Mitigate GHG Emissions

Sector / Measures	Energy-Efficiency and Conservation	Fuel-Switching and Cleaner Energy	Promotion of Renewable Energy
Energy Production and Transportation	- Uses of combined heat and power for electricity production. - Energy audit and efficiency campaigns. - CO_2 reduction goals	- Uses of natural gas and landfill gas, reduction of losses. - Promotion of gas district-heating. - Natural oxide reduction	Use of wind-power, photovoltaic biomass / wood and hydropower for electricity generation.
Industrial Processes	- Corporate efficiency commitments on CO_2 reduction targets for large energy mass. - Energy audit and efficiency campaigns.	- Use of lower carbon fuels, natural gas, landfill gas. - Cleaner production, material recovery and recycling.	Increasing use of renewable energy.
Residential, Commercial, Institutional	- Labeling and efficiency standards for electrical appliances, etc. - Building / home efficiency rating.	- Promotion of natural gas for heating. - Promotion of tree planting in communities and reforestation.	Use of wood-energy for public-building.
Transportation	- Fuel-efficiency targets on new cars. - Global reduction of fuel consumption for road transport. - Development of super-efficient automobiles.	- Promotion of natural gas vehicles. - Alternative fuels, electric cars.	

Source: Solsbery and Wiederkehr (1995) p. 42.

Buildings, including their heating and cooling and other operations, are the next largest source of energy-related CO_2 emissions: 31% globally in the mid-1990s, with an annual average growth rate of about 1.8% during the 1970s through the first decade of the 2000s. Finally, transportation contributed some 22% of energy-related CO_2 emissions, but has exhibited the highest growth rate in emissions: 2.5% per annum. Table 14.7 summarizes the various innovations in energy efficiency aimed at mitigation of climate change.

Energy-efficiency innovations began to evolve in the 1970s in the wake of the energy crisis; the first concerns focused on reducing fossil-fuel demand for heating, power and transport. The 1980s saw policies shift towards energy and environmental regulations, which involved exploring additional policy tools – e.g. taxes – to which we return in chapter 15. As from the 1990s onwards, with increasing global awareness of the dangers posed by climate change and pressure to reduce GHG emissions and stimulated by the commitments contained in the United Nations Framework Convention on Climate Change (UNFCCC), energy-related innovations began to witness a 'come back'.

14.2.5 Land-Use Change

Here opportunities do exist, also, to mitigate atmospheric CO_2 concentrations through storage of more CO_2 in soils and vegetation. As we showed in earlier chapters, the world's rainforests and some other terrestrial ecosystems act as carbon 'sinks'absorbing significant amounts of CO_2 – some 60 gigatonnes (Gt) a year (Noble and Watson, op. cit., p. 233). Given that rising CO_2 concentrations, higher atmospheric temperatures, and increased precipitations stimulate additional plant growth, this would provide a natural feedback process partly mitigating global warming. Anthropogenic effort can equally augment this natural process by, for instance, reducing deforestation (currently known to result in enormous volumes of atmospheric CO_2 emissions) and growing new forests (afforestation) and restoring those that have been destroyed and sustainable forest practices-all these could lead to significant volumes of CO_2 sequestration.

It has been observed that up to 25-30% of atmospheric GHG emissions annually – about 1.6 billion tons – originates in deforestation. The United Nations Food and Agricultural Organization (FAO) estimates that some 1.3 million hectares of forestland globally are destroyed annually, some 80% this originating in increased demand for farmland largely in developing countries (Field, 2006). However, the actual quantity of tropical rainforest deforestation has never been acturately estimated; given this, the volume of GHG emissions accounted for by forest conversion remains a subject of speculation (see, for instance, Achard et al., 2002).

14.3 Adaptation Strategies

Human adaptation to climate change is, essentially, a matter of risk management, both in terms of society or community and individuals or households. Broadly, adaptation can be approached in three ways: **First**, by decreasing the probability of incidence of climate-related events – e.g. by constructing flood barriers along river banks and coastlines prone to flooding; or by providing irrigation facilities to cope with drought; and **second**, by mitigating the expected damage from climate-related disaster when they do occur – e.g. by putting buildings on stilts in flood plains and flood-prone coastal areas, or relocating populations away from flood-prone regions, or providing populations with meteorological facilities on storms, hurricanes, flooding, etc., or taking insurance policies against such disaster; and, **third**, by diversifying the economy away from sectors or activities very much vulnerable to climate change – e.g. agriculture, or investing in crop varieties that are resistance to drought conditions, etc. (Jones et al., 2008, Mills, op. cit., Jones and Keen, 2009).

Adaptation capacity referring to possession of the special type of the knowledge, resources and skills to cope with climate-related risks differs across countries and societies, and within the latter among individuals and households, determined by differential resource endowments in finance, infrastructure, technology, networks, etc. We illustrate with examples from Holland in Western Europe and Bangladesh in South Asia, both located in low-lying coastlines prone to damage from rising sea levels. Whereas Holland possesses adequate physical infrastructure, technology and finance to cope with such disasters, Bangladesh lacks such endowments. Whereas Holland illustrates the high adaptation capability of an industrialized society, Bangladesh illustrates the low adaptation capability of a developing society. Within the latter, the poorest strata of society – those with the lowest per capita income, subsisting on precarious agricultural and informal employments – are often not only the most exposed to threats from climate change disasters but are, also, the least able to cope with its challenges. Among other disabilities of the low-income groups is that they are most likely to depend for livelihood on a single crop or other income sources most vulnerable to climate change; most likely to lack the necessary networks and types of social capital to provide support in time of climate-related disasters such as flooding, hurricanes, droughts, etc. (see Adams, op. cit., especially chapters 8-11).

Climate-change related disasters have tended to escalate over time: roughly 12-fold during the half century between 1950 and 2005, when the incidence of recorded weather events grew from 21 to over 90 (Hoffman, 2007A; Mills, 2008). Estimates on overall losses put the costs at $48 billion in 1950-1959 and $151.7 billion during 1970-1979; it escalated to well over $700 billion during 1979-1999. During the 2000s more violent climate-related disasters have occurred – e.g. flooding in India, tsunami in East and Southwest Asia, hurricanes and floodings in southern United States and the Carribeans etc. – whose losses far outweigh those of earlier times (see Coumou and Ratimstorf, 2012; the Economists, September, 2017 pp. 17 - 20). Overall, Asia and the Pacific, the Amirican Gulf Coast and the Caribbian Islands seem to be the regions of the world most prone to climate-related disasters. (see Vuchani and Usmani, 2005; Thomas, Albert and Perez, 2013; Thomas, Albert and Hepburn, 2014). Table 14.8 provides some insight on the human costs of climate-change related disasters in Africa during 1993-2003; drought and famine, followed by flood, are the key extreme weather-related disasters in Africa.

Table 14.8 Numbers of People Affected by Extreme Weather-Related Disasters in Africa 1993-2003

Type	Killed	Affected
Flood	9,642	19,939,000
Drought/famine	4,453	110,956,000
Windstorms	1,335	5,687,000
Extreme temperatures	147	8,000
Total	**15,713**	**136,591,000**

Source: Conway (2009, Table 2, p. 14); citing sources in: EM – DAT data set, Centre for Research on the Epidemiology of Disaster (CRED), Université de Louvain, Belgium, (http://www.cred.be).

14.3.1 Role of Insurance

Recent literature recommends 'fiscal self-insurance' whereby governments budgets make adequate provisions for 'adaptation expenditure' or 'reserve fund', and social safety nets considered most important for developing countries prone to extreme environmental changes: droughts, hurricanes, flooding, earthquakes, volcanic eruptions, etc. (Hoffman, 2007A). Other innovations being suggested include, for instance: 'catastrophe insurance pools' for homeowners, 'micro-insurance' characterized by low premiums or coverage and is typically targeted at lower income groups who are unable to afford or access more traditional insurance; 'risk pooling' which seeks to aggregate risks regionally (or nationally) allowing individual risk holders to spread their risk geographically; 'insurance-linked securities' (also called 'cat bodies') offer an avenue to share risk more broadly with the capital markets (issued by a government or insurance firm and trigger payments on the occurrence of a specified disaster event) (See Arnold, 2008; The Munich Climate Insurance Initiative, 2009).

The question, however, is whether insurance is an appropriate adaptation strategy for climate-change disasters. With climate change, insurance tools, whatever their type, will be challenged to cover increasingly frequent and intense disasters. Much more importantly, insurance on its own could fail to reduce risk and to advance adaptation unless it is implemented along with disaster risk reduction measures (The Munich Climate Insurance Initiative, op. cit.). Key limitations of insurance could be identified as follows: it fails to prevent or reduce the likelihood of direct damage and fatalities from extreme weather events; and it is not always the most appropriate tool to manage risk – e.g. in terms of affordability by the poor. Available data show that, by the first decade of the 2000s, insurance covered only 3% of disaster losses in developing countries, compared to 40% in industrialized countries. Nevertheless, however, macro-level insurance schemes are known to have been implemented in the Carribean Island of Jamaica (the world's first multi-country catastrophe insurance pool, reinsured in the capital markets, to provide governments with immediate liquidity in the aftermath of hurricanes or earthquakes). The World Bank and other institutions are reported to be planning to extend similar pool benefits to climate-change disaster prone areas of Asia[16] and Southern Europe (see The Munich Climate Insurance Initiative, op. cit.).

14.4 Conclusion

It seems obvious that the costs of adapting to the effects of climate change are often too high for developing countries and, within the latter, often quite out of reach for low-income groups and individuals. Apart from the requirements of implementing new technologies in non-carbon energy (e.g. solar, wind, etc.) to reduce atmospheric CO_2 concentrations, there are, also, the costs of investments in energy-efficiency technologies in industry, buildings, transportation, etc.

The question then emerges: How do we reduce the costs of adapting to climate change? Basically, three factors are involved here. The first is the extent fossil fuels consumption can be minimized by adopting relatively cheaper energy-efficient technologies in buildings, transportation, industry, etc. The second is the pace at which the price of renewable energy technologies (e.g. solar, wind) will decline from their current high levels. [17]Some of these technologies are currently at the early stages of their life cycle, which suggests that as they mature and manufacturing volumes increase, their prices will fall.

The third factor is how fast CO_2 emissions are reduced. Economists, generally, tend to recommend a gradual approach, arguing that, as CO_2 hangs around in the atmosphere for around 200 years, a ton emitted now is not much worse than a ton emitted in 20 years' time; that reducing CO_2 emissions gradually is more cost-effective than doing so quickly, because machinery will be replaced with new, lower-emission models as they reach the end of their life cycle instead of being retired prematurely. The economists' slow-paced approach constrasts with the scientists' and engineers', who recommend a fast approach to CO_2 emission reductions. But economists seem to be more sensitive to the uncertainties about the extent of global warming (IPCC model predictions on the linear relationship between temperature rise of 1°C and doubling of CO_2 concentrations in Earth's atmosphere have been found to fall short of the predictions) that makes it unwise to implement costly mitigation strategies. This is especially relevant for developing countries, where attempts to reduce CO_2 emissions could easily run counter to the more immediate goal of fast-tracking economic development to bring about poverty reduction.

Finally, whereas global attempts to mitigate global warming through reducing GHG emissions have not been so successful due to the free-rider problem, adaptation strategies seem be succeeding relatively. In sub-Saharan Africa, for example, rural populations are taking various measures to adapt to extreme weather events – e.g. farmers in drought-prone areas are diversifying from growing wheat to sorghum (a drought-resistant crop); in cyclone, prone South Asia (e.g. Bangladesh) both government and communities are building thousands of cyclone shelters; in drought-prone Ethiopia rural farmers have

"… by tweaking their farming techniques. The villagers now plant potatoes two to three weeks later than they used to and harvest them a week earlier. The growing seasons for wheat and barley have also contracted by about a month. Yields are lower, but that is preferable to losing an entire crop to flooding or drought" (The Economist, 2015, 28th November, - Special Report Climate Change, p. 11).

African agronomists, as elsewhere in the developing world, are developing crops that can survive more extreme weather – e.g. "scuba rice", which can endure being submerged for up to two weeks; farmers in Bangladesh are being advised to switch from ordinary rice to salt-tolerant varieties, or to grow sunflower instead of rice. During the monsoon floods farmers raise freshwater fish in their flooded fields; as the latter recedes, the fish move to a pool at one end, freeing the remainder of the field for rice cultivation. Few of the rural people making the adjustments cited above are thinking explicitly about global warming; it is their individual comfort and security that are uppermost in their mind. As **The Economist** sums up these actions:

"… add up to the most profound and intelligent response to climate change so far" (ibid, p. 11).

End Notes

[1] Some such technological solutions aimed at removing GHGs from the atmosphere would involve limestone being tipped into the ocean to react with dissolved CO_2 to create bicarbonate ions, allowing the water (H_2O) to absorb more CO_2 from the air. Also, plants could be grown and then burned in power stations capable of capturing the carbon dioxide that the plants had removed from the air (through photosynthesis); the gas could then be captured and compressed and buried under the ocean; etc. For the various explanations given to geoingeneering, see, for instance, Biello (2010).

[2] See also the following references: Wright and Nebel, 2004, p. 525; Noble and Watson, 2006, pp. 229-33; Castro, 2014; Bosatti et al., 2014.

[3] See The Economist (2013, 5th January).

[4] (http://www.endler-energy.com/biofuels.ear)

[5] See The Economist (2009, 7th April).

[6] Accidents in deep coal mines caused by release of poisonous methane gas is regular phenomena in China, South Africa, United States, Russia, Ukraine (as in Donestkh in Eastern Ukraine in February 2015).

[7] The principle was developed by Forest Europe **Ministerial Conference on the Protection of Forests in Europe**, with signatories of 46 European countries, including the Holy See (Vetican). Sustainable forest management (FSM) has since been adopted by the Food and Agriculture Organization (FAO); it can be

described as the attainment of balance – i.e. balance between society's increasing consumption of forest products and benefits, and the preservation of forest health and diversity, which is critical to the survival of forests, and to the wellbeing of communities dependent on forest resources.

[8] On Nigeria, see, for instance, Morgan (1978) and Maconachie et al. (2009).

[9] Hydroelectric plant life cycle energy payback ratio (the ratio of total energy produced during normal lifespan divided by energy required to build, maintain and fuel) of a hydrofacility is high.

[10] See the following sources: Barros et al., 2011; Fearnside, 2004. (http://www.hydropower.org/climate initiatives.html).

[11] California, for example, has the capacity to produce over 1200 MW from wind energy.

[12] For more insight, see Energy Encyclopedia (no date); White (1962).

[13] PV systems contribute some 6% of Germany's national electricity consumption. A key energy policy objective in Germany is to increase the share of renewables in national electricity supply to 40-45% by 2025 and then to 55-60% by 2035.

[14] For useful insight, see Ürge-Vorsatz, Miladinova and Paizs (2006).

[15] Globally, the energy-intensive industries include: metal; metals/minerals/mining; pulp/paper; petro-chemicals; power and refineries.

[16] For insights into adaptation to climate change in Asia, see, for instance, Vachani and Usmani (2015).

[17] For instance, the cost of wind energy technology is reported to have declined from United States 8-10 cents to 3.5-4 cents per KWh since 1999 because of better-designed turbines and high production volumes (The Economist, 2006A, 9th September). Also, the cost of solar energy is reported to have plummetted (The Economist, 2015, June 13th, pp. 59-60).

CHAPTER 15

NATIONAL ECONOMIC AND REGULATORY POLICIES ON CLIMATE CHANGE

15.1 Introduction

Subsequent years since the 1970s have witnessed the evolution of economic and regulatory policies and mechanisms to cope with climate change, which can be broken into two broad types: (i) national policies adopted by individual countries to attempt to deal with the environmental problems peculiar to their particular contexts; and (ii) international or global policies adopted by the world community as a whole (through international agreements) to attempt to deal with environmental problems that transcend national boundaries such as threat to the ozone layer from CFCs. We deal with national policies in the present chapter, and returning to the international policies in chapter 16. It ought to be stated rightaway, however, that what we describe as national or international policies here are inter-twined in the sense that the environmental problems they are meant to solve are simultaneously global or national in their impact. Clunies-Ross et al. (2009, pp. 320-21) capture this fact where they stated that:

> "… an effective response to the environmental problems confronting developing countries must be twin-track-pursued simultaneously at two levels – global and national. No amount of enlightened, environmentally friendly policy … at the national level can enable a country to avoid depredations wrought by climate changes, a phenomenon which, by its nature, must be tackled by concerted, co-operative global action and cannot be solved piecemeal at national level. Equally, successful mitigation … of global warming will be rendered irrelevant in any developing country which fails to tackle local environmental problems …"

15.2 Imposing Taxes on Fossil Fuel Consumption to Correct the Negative Externality Problem Caused by GHG Emissions

By the end of the 1990s developments in climate change resurrected interest in environmental taxation; two policy instruments have dominated the policy literature: environmental taxation (taxation of fossil fuel consumption) and emission trading schemes (OECD, 2008; Fullerton et al., 2008; Jha, 2010). Apart from these two essentially economic or market-based approaches, there is the legislation or 'command-and-control' approach belonging to the wider field of legal rules and regulations guiding the activities of economic agents, which may involve, for example, introduction of controls by specifying minimum environmental standards on air quality, or imposing complete ban on use of particular inputs, etc.

Raising the prices of fossil fuels has been found to constitute one sure strategy to reduce GHG emissions; and the simplest and most cost-effective means to do this is to tax fossil fuels[1]. The theoretical rationale for this derives from Pigou's tax-subsidy solution to externality highlighted in chapter 1. When a tax is appropriately levied on fossil fuels the ensuing market price will cover the full costs of the fuel involved, including the costs of the damage to the environment, which would otherwise go unpaid by the polluting agents and, instead, be shifted to society or community at large, or to future generations. By imposing a tax on the polluting agents, the negative externality costs become thus internalized – that is, the costs of polluting the environment become fully incorporated into the cost functions of the private polluting agents.

15.2.1 Polluter-Pays Principle (PPP): Guiding Principle of Environmental Protection

In several countries policy makers have attempted to evolve guiding principles to identify pollution control policies – that is, an overarching policy criterion that supposedly sets guidelines for determining acceptance policies on environmental protection. In Japan, for example, environmental-protection policies were initially developed under the principle of 'harmonization', which required that pollution-control laws be 'harmonized' with the needs of economic growth. In China, the guiding principle is that new industrial construction be pursued within the principle of 'three at the same time', whereby each new construction plan is required to contain a special section on environmental protection showing how pollution control methods will be designed, installed, and operated (Jin and Liu, 1989). In Europe, pollution (environmental) taxes have been targeted on energy, transport, agriculture, and economy. As energy is a major source of both pollution and tax revenues in the OECD and European Union particularly, attention has been focused on restructuring energy pricing as a starting point in integrating environment and economy (Portier, 1996). In the literature, the concept of environmental taxes (also known as eco-taxes, green taxes, etc.) has several interpretations. One interpretation is that it refers to taxes with an environmental, rather than a fiscal or revenue objective, promoting protection and use of natural resource to promote sustainability. Another interpretation, perhaps the more conventional one, is that it refers to taxes to tackle the climate change challenge. (See: Kreiser et al., 2011; ILO, 2011; Milne and Andersen, 2012; EUROSTAT, 2013; OECD, 2013; Markandya, 2013).

Pollution taxes are thus intended to provide economic agents the incentive to shift from consuming products that generate large quantities of GHGs to existing 'clean goods' and 'clean technologies'. Pollution taxes are, generally, meant to raise the prices of products which create pollution as they are manufactured, or disposed of – e.g. lubricants; chemical (inorganic) fertilizers; pesticides (including insecticides, herbicides, fungicides, and other biocides); non-returnable containers; mercury and cadmium batteries; 'feedstock' chemicals; packaging materials; etc. By imposing a tax, the demand for such products will be reduced, which will induce the producers (firms) to take account of the external costs that their production activities impose on society.

In the OECD, pollution taxes, also known as eco-taxes or green taxes, are an affirmation of the 'polluter-pays principle' (PPP) adopted in 1972 and ratified by the European Community (now European Union) in 1975. The PPP has become accepted as a guide for environmental policymaking both by governments and agencies.

15.2.2 Reduction of Subsidies on Fossil Fuels

In several European countries, direct coal subsidies began to be reduced as from the 1980s to 'force change to different fuels'. By reducing domestic coal subsidies (and importing coal from South Africa, Australia or Central Europe e.g. Poland) West European countries had sought to reduce their volumes of GHG emissions, especially of methane and carbon dioxide. Methane emission would be lower because imported coal primarily comes from open-cast mines and not, as in West European mining regions, from deeper mines that generate large amounts of methane gas.

Yet coal prices are known to be the lowest in the European Union, which has encouraged coal-based energy generation. The amount of electricity generated from coal in Europe is rising at an annualized rate of as much as 50% in some European countries: in Britain, for example, in April 2012 coal replaced gas as the dominant fuel for electricity (The Economist, 5th January, 2013). In contrast to the United States, where coal-based electricity generation has plummeted replaced by shale-gas and natural gas, there is, as it were, golden age of coal in Europe (ibid. p. 161). Even so, coal-based electricity is still significant in United States energy supply. At its peak in the 1980s, coal provided upwards of 60% of electricity in the United States; even in 2010, when the shale-gas boom was well under way[2], coal still supplied more than 40%; by mid-2012, about 33% (ibid. p. 50).

On the other hand, in contrast, many developing countries subsidize consumption of energy; globally also petroleum product subsidies have increased in recent years. In 2003, global consumer subsidies for petroleum products totaled about $60 billion; rising to $520 billion by mid-2008 – more than 8-fold the 2003 level. Even as fuel prices rose sharply in the first decade of the 2000s, many governments chose not to fully pass those increases to domestic retail prices, which further increased subsidies. By 2010 petroleum product subsidies had exceeded $740 billion, if we include taxes both to contribute to government revenue requirements and to address domestic and global environmental damage (see IMF, 2010). Failure to reduce or remove fuel subsidies globally has had the effect of aiding excessive combustion of fossil fuels leading to over-supply of GHG emissions (see also Guilluame and Zytek, 2010). More recent studies find that fossil-fuel subsidies totaled $5 trillion per annum globally, including the failure to price in damages arising from pollution and climate change, which together constitute upwards of 60% of the total (see, for instance, Coady et al., 2015). But the social cost of fossil-fuel subsidies go beyond the market value of fossil fuels. There is need to factor in the externality effect – that is, damages on the environment by pollution and climate change.

The point stressed here is that to obtain the **real** costs of fossil-fuel subsidies we should include; besides, the costs of environmental damages inflicted by consumption of fossil fuels and not just focus on the market value of fossil fuels, which, typically, fails to capture the cost of externalities - e.g. deaths from air pollution, destruction of forests, climate change and destruction of ozone layer, etc. (Rohde and Muller, 2015 on China).

15.2.3 Tradeable Emissions Allowances

Emiseral European countries, direct coal subsidieade' referring to a legal limit on the quantity or level of a specific type of pollution an economy can emit each year – is a government- mandated, market-based method used to control environmental pollution. The term 'market-based method' in this context refers to the central objective of the strategy, namely, to encourage behavior that overcomes the free-rider syndrome that undermines most efforts to manage commons property (in this context, Earth's environment).

In this approach, a government agency sets a limit or cap on the level of a pollutant that may be emitted. The cap or limit is allocated and/or sold by the government agency in the form of emission permits or emission credits or emission standards or emission discharge permits issued to companies or producers, which represents a legal right or permit to discharge or emit a specified amount of a pollutant. A further aspect of this 'cap and trade' strategy is that it allows companies so permitted to trade their 'credits' to over-target companies. The total number of permits cannot exceed the cap, limiting total emissions to that level; those who need to increase their emission levels must purchase permits from those who require fever permits (Stavins, 2001). The term 'cap' describes existence of a limit on emission levels, which are lowered over time to reduce the amount of pollutants emitted into Earth's atmosphere. On the other hand, the term 'trade' describes the fact of creation of a market for carbon allowances, motivating or inducing companies towards innovation to meet, or achieve, their allocated limit. Given that the less companies emit, the less they pay (the less the need to purchase emission allowances or permits), this provides an economic incentive to engage in activities that generate less and less pollutants (EDF, 2014).

As to its theoretical roots, the emission trading scheme idea traces to Ronald Coase's (1960) classic, **The Problem of Social Costs**[3] which calls attention to an alternative to government tax-subsidy solution to the negative externality problem through a bargaining solution. It has been argued that, if private property (ownership) rights, and associated markets in which these property rights could be marketed (bought and sold like private goods) could be extended to incorporate all of the resources needed for, and affected by, production – and this would include all environmental resources (water, air, soils and the entire biosphere) – then this would provide resource owners an incentive to ensure that their resources attract appropriate compensation (or priced properly), and were never abused and used uncompensated in the style of many commons property. However, it was not until the 1990s, when the IPCC (The United Nations Intergovernmental Panel on Climate Change) through its reports which shed abundant light on the harm posed by rising levels of GHGs in Earth's atmosphere and global warming, that Coase's theory was transformed into a global policy instrument in the Kyoto Protocol, to which we return in chapter 16.

In the emissions allowances approach, the relevant national regulatory agency sets a global target for a reduction in a type of pollution, and proceeds to issue producers a license to emit pollutants up to specific levels or amounts. To illustrate, we highlight the experiences, respectively, of the United States and the European Union (EU), where empirical evidence has been systematically documented.

A. United States

As just noted, the United States has one of the best documented histories and, perhaps, the longest experience in the implementation of environmental management schemes dating back to the 1970s[4]. Under grassroots pressure from citizens, the United States Congress enacted the Clean Air Act (CAA) of 1970. Amended in 1977 and 1990, the CAA legislation, administered by the United States Environmental Protection Agency (EPA), represents the foundation of United States atmospheric pollution control effort. The EPA calls for: identifying the most widespread polluting chemicals; sets ambient standards or levels of environmental sanitation that must be met to protect environmental and human health; establishes control methods and time frames or deadlines to meet these standards.

The CAA identified for recognition the following chemicals as so-called **primary** pollutants: particulates, sulphur dioxide, carbon monoxide and nitrogen oxides. Primary pollutants are known to originate in fossil-fuel and waste combustion, which release particles consisting mainly of carbon emitted into Earth's atmosphere which are particulates we see as soot or smoke. In addition, various unburned fragments of fuel molecules remain in the atmosphere, which are known as VOCs (volatile organic compounds, present in Earth's atmosphere in the form of vapor, and are major factors in the formation of photochemical smog).

There is, also, so-called **secondary** pollutant ozone. Tropospheric (ground-level) ozone – a major compound in photochemical smog - is formed when nitrogen compounds react with VOCs. Secondary pollutants are most likely to be formed in valleys and low-lying basins (e.g. the Niger Benue Confluence around Lokoja in Nigeria, known to have higher-than-normal average temperatures, when winds are calm and warm, and sunny conditions obtain).

Lead was later included in the list of pollutants to constitute the criteria pollutants and are covered by the National Ambient Air Quality Standards (NAAQS) (EPA, 2000). The basic strategy of the 1970 CAA legislation was to regulate air pollution in the United States so that the criteria pollutants would not exceed the primary standard levels. Measured in parts per million (ppm), the primary standard levels describe the number of units of one substance present in a million units of another. The primary standard for each pollutant is based on the maximum level that can be tolerated (safety absorbed) by humans without noticeable ill effects, minus a 10% to 50% margin of safety. For carbon monoxide, for example, this was, as at 1997, 9 ppm for averaging time of 8 hours and 35 ppm for averaging time I hour (Wright and Nebel, op. cit., Table 22-2, p.556)[5].

It was assumed that human and environmental health could be significantly promoted by a reduction in the output of pollutants; if a region of the United States violated standards for any particular pollutant, the CAA legislation contains provisions for a local government agency to track down the origins and order reductions in emissions to the legally prescribed standards. Each state is required to develop State Implementation Plan (SIP) which must receive endorsement from the EPA.

Earlier application of the CAA legislative took the character of a 'command and control' approach (see below): regulations were handed to industry to achieve a set limit on each pollutant, to be effected or implemented by specific control equipment, etc., which proved difficult to implement, partly because most of the regulatory responsibilities fell on the states and municipal organs that lacked, quite often, the capability, or are unwilling, to enforce compliance.

By 1990, the CAA legislation was amended; one major change came in the form of a permit application process: polluters must apply for a permit that identifies the kinds of pollutants they release, the quantities of those pollutants, and the steps they employ to reduce pollution. Permit application involves payment of fees.

"Permit fees provide funds the states can use to support their air pollution control activities. The amendments also afford more flexibility than the earlier command-and-control approach, by allowing polluters to choose the most cost-effective way to accomplish the goals. In addition, the legislation uses a market system to allocate pollution among different utilities" (Wright and Nebel, op.cit, p. 556).

Coping with Automobile Emissions: In the United States, as in other major industrialized economies, vehicle exhausts (from cars, tracks, bases, etc.) release nearly 50% of the pollutants in the atmosphere; they emit the VOCs, carbon monoxide, and nitrogen oxides. Additional VOCs are known to originate in the evaporation of gasoline and oil vapors from fuel depots and engine systems. The CAA mandated installation of technologies to control fuel mixture and ignition timing, allowing more complete combustion of fuel and, hence, decreasing VOC emissions - e.g. the **catalytic converter:** as exhaust passes through this device, a chemical catalyst made of platinum-coated beads oxidizes most of the VOCs to carbon dioxides (CO_2) and water (H_2O) and most of the carbon monoxide (CO) into CO_2. Wright and Nebel (op. cit., pp.557-8) report that, despite the various efforts in the control of atmospheric pollution in the United States, there is evidence of failure to meet standards in many regions, manifested in "the aesthetically poor air quality in many cities". Nevertheless, the United States experience seems to have inspired other countries and regions of the world - e.g. the European Union (EU); - as well, the Kyoto Protocol, to which we return in chapter 16.

Tradable Permits for Ozone-Eroding Pollutants: As pointed out above, ozone is a secondary pollutant formed by other compounds. In August 1988, the EPA issued its first regulations implementing a tradable permit system to achieve the targeted reductions in ozone-destroying pollutants, which stipulated that all major United States, producers and users of the controlled substances, were allocated baseline production and consumption allowances using 1986 levels as the basis. Initially, each producer and consumer was allowed 100% of this baseline allowance; later, smaller allowances were granted after predefined deadlines.

The ozone permits allow for transfer of allowances within producer and consumer categories; as well, permits can be transferred across international frontiers to similar bodies in other signatory nations provided the deal has the approval of the EPA and results in the appropriate adjustments in the buyer or seller allowances in their respective countries. Further, production allowances can be increased by demonstrating the safe elimination or destruction of an equivalent amount of controlled substances by an approved technique. Finally, some inter pollutant trading is even allowed within categories of pollutants. We return to the international aspects of ozone depletion problem in chapter 16.

B. European Union (EU)

The European Union Emissions Trading System (EUETS) launched in 2005 to fight global warming was the first large GHG emission trading system in the world; at present, it remains the biggest (Ellerman et al., 2007)[6]. The EUETS covers more than 11,000 factories, power stations, and other installations with a net heat excess of 20 MW in 31 countries – all 28 EU member states plus Iceland, Norway and Liechtenstein (EUETS, 2010). The installation covered by the EUETS are collectively (as at the end of 2008) responsible for some 50% of the European Union's anthropogenic CO_2 emissions and 40% of its total GHG emissions (Wagner, 2004).

In the EUETS each country receives a fixed number of CO_2 emissions allowances for its companies in the so-called energy-intensive industries: electric power generation, oil refining, pulp and paper, steel, glass, and cement – these industries have been categorized as 'the dirtiest heavy industries'. All installations in these 'dirtiest heavy industries' with larger than approved thresholds, are included in the EUETS schedule. The EUETS work as follows: national governments decide how much carbon their 'dirtiest industries' may emit, they then allocate 'permits to pollute' to each company in the industry line. If a firm wants to exceed its limits, it must buy 'pollution permits' from 'cleaner firms' credits from developing countries that have set up special projects to lower GHG emissions - e.g. protection of the Amazon Rainforests in Brazil. Penalties for non-compliance were set at €40 per ton of CO_2 in the trading period ending in 2007, increasing to €100 in 2008-2012. The latter period coincided with the first commitment period of the Kyoto Protocol (to which we return in chapter 16). The current (third) trading period started in January 2013 and is expected to end in December 2020. The proposed caps for 2020 represent a 21% reduction of GHGs compared to 2005, when the EUETS was first implemented, a target that has been reached six years earlier as emission in the ETS declined to 1812 million tonnes in 2014[7].

Currently, the European Union disallows CO_2 credits under the EUETS to be obtained from natural sinks such as reducing CO_2 by planting trees or afforestation, though there is strong lobbying for its inclusion. It should be noted, however, that recognition that significant levels of additional CO_2 could be absorbed by the terrestrial biosphere – i.e. tress and soils – lies behind the Kyoto Protocol. Proponents have argued that this form of CO_2 sequestration is typically efficient or cost-effective in the sense not only that the given goal (of reducing CO_2 levels in Earth's atmosphere) at lower cost could be achieved, but also may likely increase the willingness (of negotiating agents or nations) to accept more stringent goals with closer deadlines. Besides, the strategy is likely to 'add economic values to sustainable practices' via limiting deforestation and/or preventing soil degradation and erosion, which in turn provides additional incentives for those practices (see Tietenberg and Lewis, 2010, p. 353, Debate, 16.1). The tree planting strategy for CO_2 sequestration, proponents argue, has the added advantage that the initial benefits will accrue to 'the poorest people in the poorest countries' (ibid.).

Opponents, including NGOs in the EU, argue, on the other hand, that our current knowledge and scientific understanding of the capacity of the terrestrial biosphere to absorb CO_2 is yet in its embryonic stage, which limits our capacity to predict precisely the amounts of credits that should be granted (see also Kenr and Mare, 1998).

15.3 Command-and-Control Approach

This approach, also known as the legislation approach, belongs to the wider field of legal rules and regulations guiding the activities of economic agents. Thus, this approach attempts to introduce direct controls, which may involve specifying minimum environmental standards on air and/or water quality, for example, or imposing complete law on use of inputs. For example, the effluents from a refinery or chemical plant may be permitted (by legislation) to a 'specified' level of a pollution. In some cases, legislation may require the installation of specific types of anti-pollution equipment. For instance, in the European Union, automobile firms are now required (as from the early 1990s) to fit exhaust systems (so-called **catalytic converters**) that reduce air pollution from automobiles and to develop fuel-efficient engines. Yet another example may be cited from the United States, where EPA has already proposed restrictions on carbon dioxide emissions which would in practice ban new coal-fired plants after 2013 unless fitted with carbon capture and storage (CCS).

To be effective, legislations setting minimum environmental standards apart from setting inspectorates to monitor and enforce compliance, must make sure that the monitoring agencies possess knowledge of what the optimal level of pollution ought to be on the product being legislated on. For the standard setting approach to be completely effective, the inspectorates must have knowledge of the marginal net private benefits curve and the external marginal cost curve to determine the optimal level of output and associated level of pollution. It is quite unlikely for such a situation to obtain in practice both for reasons of technology and information (data) constraints. Besides, when standards are set across the board for all firms, the process does not consider of the marginal cost of reducing pollution associated with individual firms.

15.4 Voluntary Approaches

It seems obvious that no single approach has been found to be sufficient to achieve the central objective of restraining global climate change and slowing the continued atmospheric concentration of GHGs. The conventional approaches highlighted above have centred on a combination of economic instruments; namely eco-taxes, incentives for switching to fuels with lower CO_2 content (e.g. biofuels) and change in particular taxes, trade and cap schemes, etc. These have been supplemented with voluntary approaches (VAs) particularly in the OECD Economies.

But governments in these countries are quite often reluctant to impose heavy fiscal or regulatory regimes on firms that, to survive must compete with other firms in international markets. Besides, such fiscal and regulatory measures tend to be 'politically unpopular'. Governments, therefore, began to innovate ways of working with industry as a sector or even with individual firms to achieve the mutual objectives of industrial and other public policies, embracing the whole spectrum of energy security, environmental protection and international commitments on trade and industrial competitiveness (Solsbery and Wiederkehr, 1995).

The first energy-related VAs evolved in the 1970s in the aftermath of the oil crisis, when the immediate concern was energy security rather than environment and was concerned with reducing the consumption of fossil fuels for heating, power and transport. Canada was the first member of the International Energy Agency (IEA) to evolve a VA approach. The Canada initiative on VAs included over 700 companies, representing about 70% of energy used by all industry and calls for promoting and monitoring of energy efficiency throughout the Canadian manufacturing and mining industries. The implementing institution was the Canadian Industry Programme for Energy Conservation (CIPEC), which survives today as part of government's programme on climate change.

By the 1990s under growing pressure to roll back atmospheric GHG emissions and stimulated by the commitments contained in the United Nation's Framework Convention on Climate Change (UNFCCC), energy-related VAs began to be revived among IEA member countries. Two types of approaches can be identified: first, informal activities where the parties entering into the VAs programme with the government set their own targets and often do their own monitoring and reporting; and, second, the formal approach, which is a form of contract between government and industry, and negotiated targets with commitments and time schedules on the part of all participating parties.

The main rationale for adopting VAs are to increase involvement by firms in rolling back GHG emissions, to increase motivation and responsibilities of industry and consumers alike in achieving environmental objectives and to use policy instruments that are better adapted to the economic and competitive context (Solsbery and Wiederkehr op. cit.). Evidence so far shows that properly designed VAs can achieve additional policy objectives, sometimes even exceeding those of minimum regulatory standards, and help integrate economic and environmental goals (ibid). Among their drawbacks may be cited the following: their effectiveness may depend on how they are structured or how closely they are monitored; being a purely voluntary approach, there is the high risk that their effectiveness will be undermined by the free rider syndrome – those not participating in the programme will want to take advantage of those participating in the programme.

15.5 Environmental Financing

How are revenues generated from eco-taxes used? Who finances environmental investments? In the OECD economies, eco-taxes are earmarked for specific environmental protection purposes – e.g. water and waste disposal management. For one thing, earmarking will help to bring political acceptability and support for otherwise politically unpopular taxes.

In Eastern Europe (as in most developing countries), the public sector plays the role of key provider – sometimes sole provider – of finances for environmental investments[8]. In the OECD economies, in contrast, the private sector and private households shoulder the largest part of the burden for spending on pollution control and environmental infrastructures (Gillespie, 1996). In the East European countries, the institutional framework for environmental financing has been strengthened in a number of countries by the establishment of funds, capitalized by environmental taxes and charges which are then reallocated to support important environmental investments in air and water pollution control and establishment of monitoring and enforcement mechanisms. Several other measures to strengthen environmental financing institutions have been put in place – e.g. 'green' equity schemes, to provide equity to projects and companies investing in environmental improvements – such as the Nordic Environment Finance Corporation (NEFCO), provide a model of such schemes in the Baltic region.

15.6 Conclusion

It has been shown that market-based policies (imposing taxes on fossil fuels, tradeable emission allowances, etc.), if effectively implemented, will frequently be less costly in meeting environmental goals than command-and-control alternatives. With market-based policies all polluters and resource users face the same price (penalty) and most choose their degree of control – e.g. a gasoline tax would encourage all car users (for instance, taxi drivers) to limit vehicle use 'to the point at which the value of benefits forgone is the same for each vehicle user'. On the other hand, by contrast, command-and-control approaches would restrict driving, for example, in certain parts of a city according to license plates, for example. This will encourage evasion and is costly because it forces all drivers "to give up the same proportion of trips, irrespective of the widely differing benefits they derive" (World Bank, 1992, p. 75).

With policies relying on market-based incentives, each resource user decides either to use fewer resources or to pay for using more resources. Command-and-control policies, on the other hand, leave those decisions to regulators (bureaucrats), who often lack adequate knowledge of the 'relative costs and benefits faced by users' (Ibid). Briefly, market-based approaches give the right long-term signals to agents regarding resource use; agents have an incentive to employ whichever technologies most cost-effectively reduce environmental damage.

However, market-based approaches will be effective only to the extent that polluters and resource users are sensitive to the market-based incentives/signals, which will depend on three factors (ibid.): ownership, competition, and differences among resource users. As experiences from different countries on pollution charges show, state-owned enterprises (SOEs) tend to be grossly incentives to economic incentives because they pay little attention to costs (but SOEs usually face different objectives compared to private firms which generally are profit driven). Absence of domestic and foreign competition often leads to a situation where there is insufficient pressure to minimize costs. Briefly, the effectiveness of using charges and tradeable permits would bring little benefits in countries with a large SOE sector, while bringing significant benefits in countries where competitive private industry drives the economy. Developing countries, generally, fall within the former category.

It is equally important to examine the distributional outcomes of using alternative approaches. One problem of using market-based policies is that some firms and individuals (households) may have difficulty investing in new technologies or pay for cleaner products. A relevant example would be, for example, poor urban households in developing countries who use kerosene as their principal cooking fuel; this category of households will have trouble switching to use of natural gas given the much higher cost of the infrastructure requirement – e.g. gas cookers, etc. Government subsidies on kerosene (or any fossil fuel, for that matter) conflict with the PPP. In such a situation, the subsidies should be well targeted, explicitly time-bound, and carefully monitored – which, however, is often difficult for most developing countries.

Finally, there is the fact that market-based policies – e.g. imposing taxes on fossil fuels/removing subsidies – raise revenues for governments. Such market-based policies may be recommended for governments seeking to replace more distorting sources of revenue common in developing countries – e.g. trade tariffs and corporate income taxes. Revenue generation and environmental protection then become complementary (see, for instance, Portier 1996 on OECD Countries).

End Notes

[1] See Jha, 2010 especially chapter 22; Field and Field, 2009, especially chapters 12-13. See also Kreiser et al., 2014.

[2] See Wang and Krupnick, 2013; Behr and Marshall, 2009; and Stevens, August 2012.

[3] Coase's 1960 article was preceded in 1959 by his 'The Federal Communications Commission' *Journal of Law & Economics*, 1959.

[4] The empirical facts and data rely on Wright and Nebel, 2004, chapter 22, especially pp. 554-65.

[5] The averaging time refers to the period over which concentrations are measured and averaged.

[6] See also Peeters and Deketaere (2006) and Peeters and Uylenburg (2015).

[7] http://www.environmentalistonline.com/article/2015-04-07/ets-emissions-decline-sharply.

[8] In Nigeria, the Federal Environmental Protection Agency (FEPA), a parastatal under the Federal Ministry of Environment, is the body charged with environmental protection matters, including funding (See Omofonmwan and Osa-Edoh, 2008).

CHAPTER 16

INTERNATIONAL INSTITUTIONS ON CLIMATE CHANGE

16.1 Introduction

The peculiar nature of climate change as a global negative externality, a 'global bad' that imposes costs on the international community has necessitated setting up international institutions to address the various issues relating to global warming and climate change. As was noted earlier, the global scope of many environmental problems was first highlighted by the United Nations Conference on the Human Environment (the Stockholm Conference of April, 1972), which led to the United Nations Environment Programme (UNEP) and the 'Earth Summits' of Rio de Janeiro in 1992 and Johannesburg in 2002.

The evolution of international institutions on climate change and (other environmental problems) has been motivated, as pointed out above, by the appreciation of the very nature of this environmental problem: it is an environmental 'global bad' inflicted by economic agents of one country or a group of countries but whose effects spill over into other countries. To tackle the problems posed by the climate change externality would require a multi-country approach in the form of international climate change agreements. In this chapter, we focus on highlighting some of the economic issues relating to creation of international climate change agreements and protocols, and the difficulties and incentives inherent in formulating and executing international climate change policy[1].

A key problem in the formulation and execution of international climate policy is that at the global level international enforcement mechanisms do not exist – even if they exist, they are not as effective as national ones. Thus, climate change policy at the global level consists essentially of international agreements among sovereign nations:

"... where each country pledges to follow certain specified courses of action as regards emissions reductions .... Enforcement then has to be carried out either through voluntary means like moral suasion, or else through retaliation by whatever pressure a country or a group of countries may be able to exert on recalcitrant countries. Sometimes environmental agreements are incorporated into international trade agreements, so that relaxation of restrictions on the trade of goods and services becomes linked to environmental regulations" (Field and Field, 2009, p. 449).

Such climate-related international trade agreements can be found in the 1987 Montreal Protocol for reducing ozone-destroying pollutants.

16.2 Current International Agreements on Atmospheric Pollution

As stated earlier, global awareness on the dangers posed by climate change began to evolve in the early 1970s starting with the United Nations Conference on the Human Environment in 1972. Table 16.1 carries a list of current multilateral agreements on air pollution. Field and Field (op. cit., Table 21.1, pp. 450-3) citing Barrett (2003) inform us that international agreements on the natural environment began evolving as from the early 1900s[2], proliferating, however, in the 1940s onwards, when "international treaties proliferated because of the rapidly expanding list of environmental problems involving multiple countries" (Field and Field, op. cit., p. 449).

Table 16.1 Multilateral Agreements on Atmospheric Pollution and Climate Change

Name of Agreement	Date of Adoption	Date of Entry into Force	Number of Signatories
Convention on Long-Range Transboundary Air Pollution	1979	1983	49
Protocol to the 1979 Convention on Long-Range Transboundary Air Pollution on Long-Term Financing of the Co-operative Programme for Monitoring and Evaluation of the Long-Range Transmission of Air Pollutants in Europe.	1984	1988	38
Protocol to the 1979 Convention on Long-Range Transboundary Air Pollution on the Reduction of Sulphur Emissions or Their Transboundary Fluxes by at Least 30 Percent	1985	1987	22

Protocol to the 1979 Convention on Long-Range Transboundary Air Pollution Concerning the Control of Emissions of Nitrogen Oxides or Their Transboundary Fluxes	1988	1991	29
Vienna Convention for the Protection of the Ozone Layer	1985	1988	176
Montreal Protocol on Substances that Deplete the Ozone Layer	1987	1989	175
Kyoto Protocol to the United Nations Framework Convention on Climate Change	1999	2005	163
Paris Conference to Limit Global Warming to less than 2°C Compared to Pre-Industrial Levels. Net Anthropogenic GHG Emissions to be Reached during the 2nd Half of the 21st Century.	2015	22nd April 2016	55 Representing 55% of Global Emissions

Source: Field and Field, 2009, Table 21.1, pp 450-3) except Kyoto Protocol data on number of signatories; Paris Conference, Sutter and Berlinger (2015).

Besides the multilateral treaties there are numerous others of a bilateral nature, addressing the environmental problems of just two countries. For instance, the United States and Canada have bilateral agreements, including those dealing with acid rain, management of the Great Lakes, etc.

16.3 Economic Interests Underlying Multilateral Agreements on Climate Policy[3]

International negotiations on climate policy (as in other global environmental problems) always appear on the surface to focus on politics; this is natural considering that what is going on are complex negotiations among sovereign nations often represented by their top diplomats (in some cases as during summits, for instance, by their heads of state and heads of government or prime ministers). However, beneath the political interactions among sovereign nations during international negotiations 'lie many bedrock economic factors that affect the perceived benefits and costs accruing to the different participants and the incentives they have for entering into environmental agreements' (Field and Field, op. cit., p. 454).

International agreements on climate policy are negotiated through the agency of multilateral institutions – e.g. the United Nations and its specialized bodies. In such agreements, countries that constitute our global community and contribute to climate change (through GHG emissions) negotiate how to share the cost of the damages caused by climate change. Typical examples here would be negotiations to eliminate production and trade in ozone-depleting CFCs, and reductions in the greenhouse effect stemming from CO_2 emissions. In these two environmental problems relating specifically to climate change what are negotiated are the damages suffered by individual countries of the global community related to the level of total emissions, present and probably past, of all the countries.

From a purely economic perspective, two issues usually come up for consideration: efficiency and equity. Specifically, there is the basic efficiency problem of how to balance overall benefits and costs – that is, arrange and compile the items and elements relating, respectively, to the costs and benefits of climate change so that elements of costs exactly equal the elements of benefits. However, in almost all climate agreements, given the truly global nature of climate change impacts, it is well near impossible to accurately estimate or compute the total global benefits. But as Field and Field (op. cit., p. 456) suggest, the impacts of truly global environment phenomena "are too massive, and there are extraordinarily difficult problems of trying to compare benefits across countries that are in very different economic circumstances". Consequently, the practical approach here is to, on the benefit side settle for an enumeration of the physical impacts of various climate-related changes and some ideas of how these impacts might be distributed among countries of the global community. This means that in these agreements most of the emphasis is placed on **abatement costs** and their distribution. Abatement costs in our present context refer specifically to the costs of reducing atmospheric GHG emissions, or of lowering ozone-depleting CFCs, considered on individual economy / country basis (which, of course, would differ among countries) or aggregated (considered on a global basis).

Two major questions relating to abatement costs are usually considered: first, what technologies (processes, means, etc.) to adopt by individual countries to meet the standards required by the agreements; and, second, how to distribute the total global costs among the various countries of the global community. If all countries adopted cost-effective abatement technologies, this can substantially reduce the global abatement costs to be distributed. This in practice is difficult.

The importance of cost distribution arises because, as seems clear, policy interventions to mitigate climate change represent a global public good – available to all countries of the global community at no cost. That is, the benefits accruing to say Nigeria, from a reduction in atmospheric CO_2 emissions by, say 15% will be the same for all other countries of the global community no matter where they are located, by who reduces the CO_2 emissions, and when the reductions are made. It is important to note, however, that the benefits will not be equal for all countries of the world, given that the global meteorological system or physical phenomena and processes taking place in Earth's atmosphere and its interactions with the ground surface differ across countries of the globe. This differential working of the meteorological system is bound to affect, also, the benefits accruing to each country from atmospheric CO_2 reduction. On the other hand, however, the effect of CO_2 reductions on individual countries are not sensitive to the source of the reduction or is invariant to who does the reductions: each country is affected even if, because of differences in how the global meteorological system works, the distribution of benefits will differ among countries.

Given the public goods characteristics of measures taken to mitigate the effects of climate change, each country has some incentive to get other countries to bear as much of the total global abatement costs as they can – the free-rider problem mentioned earlier. This has constituted the key constraint on getting international agreements on climate change to be effective: because the benefits of reducing CO_2 emissions take the form of an 'externality' meaning it is difficult to exclude anyone from enjoying the benefits, it is futile to ask nations to cut back CO_2 emissions with laws and regulations (see also Shiller, 2015). Indeed, free-riding tends to be a widespread problem in global public goods, as in any good the consumption of which produces externalities. Because of the 'free-riding impulse' individual countries (and their firms) will have difficulty recovering any costs incurred in climate-change related investments, which, in turn, undermines incentives to make the latter types of investments leading to undersupply of goods and services oriented on climate change mitigation. Because the global community cannot rely on the market mechanism or private agents to supply efficient quantities of this type of goods and services, there is need to rely on collective strategies involving all countries of the global community to supply them. As many countries of the global economy are induced to participate in such collective efforts the less the free-rider problem. Global climate policy emerges as the most effective strategy for coping with the threats and challenges posed for the international community by climate change.

16.4 The Distribution of Costs

To return to the problem of distribution of total abatement costs, the costs a country would face can be determined in three ways (Field and Field, op. cit.): (i) in the choices it makes on the modalities to reduce its CO_2 emissions – e.g. through the administrative command-and-control modality, or through greater use of market-based strategies, namely taxation of fossil fuels, emission trading, etc.; (ii) through the choice of the rules chosen in a particular climate change agreement as regards how overall emission reductions will be distributed among particular countries; and (iii) by payments or compensations made by some countries to others as part of the agreements to help offset costs in recipient countries – so-called **side payments**. For instance, as part of the Montreal Protocol dealing with global CFC elimination, the industrial countries, who are the producers and exporters of CFC-bearing goods, agreed to help the developing countries through technology transfer, whereby the developing countries are aided financially and technically in adopting and adapting technologies produced by the industrial countries for replacing CFC-bearing imports. We return to the Montreal Protocol later in this chapter.

16.4.1 Cost-Efffectiveness in Climate Policy Agreements

The way most international negotiations secure agreements on emission reductions from each participating country is to treat each country in the same way by applying the same emission reduction goals to each. However, in the treaty to reduce CFCs and the ozone-depleting pollutants this principle was never applied. Rather, there was differentiation among countries, whereby a simple distinction between developed and developing countries was made as distinct groups. Within each group, however, there is no differentiation among countries regarding the CFC-reducing targets.

The efficiency aspects of this approach have been discussed extensively (See ibid. especially chapter 21). The key problem is that it fails to exploit differences in marginal abatement costs among countries within the two distinct groups identified above. To accomplish this would require larger cutbacks from nations with relatively low marginal abatement costs and lower cutbacks from those with higher marginal abatement costs. But such non-uniform cutbacks appear to negate the principle of treating every country alike.

What happens in the case where each of two countries would benefit the same amount from reductions in emissions, but have different marginal abatement costs? In such a context, it will prove difficult to achieve cost-effectiveness if there is strong allegiance or adherence to applying the same cutbacks or emission reductions targets. In a global political economy with 200 or so odd countries, the principle of treating each country in the same way by applying the same emission reduction targets to each country does not seem feasible.

16.5 Global Policy Responses on Ozone Layer Depletion

As noted earlier in chapter 5, the history of the ozone issue illustrates, clearly, the emergence, persistence, and evolution of atmospheric pollution as both a national and global practical problem. The policy responses to the ozone problem have evolved in two phases: first, as an environmental and political issue, primarily in the United States (in the debate over the development of a commercial fleet of supersonic transports); and, second, as from the 1980s as an international environmental issue, when a global consensus began to be forged on the need to ban the production and use of CFCs.

The Montreal Protocol: The first international policy response came under the auspices of the United Nations in 1987, when the latter convened a conference in Montreal, Canada, to address the ozone depletion issue. The outcome of that conference became the Montreal Protocol, which aims to reduce the production and use of CFCs and halogen substances. As a result, the Montreal Protocol was developed and opened for signature in 1987. To date (2015) the protocol has been signed by 191 countries; its key components include: (a) phase-out of ODS (ozone destroying substances) according to prescribed timetables for developing and developed countries; (b) a ban on ODS trade with non-signatory parties and controls on ODS trade among parties; (c) creation of the multilateral fund – the financial mechanism of the Montreal Protocol that aids developing countries with Protocol compliance; and (d) a requirement for parties who produce and use ODS to provide a baseline and subsequent annual reports, and to conduct research, development, and information-sharing efforts on ODS substitutes.

The original Protocol has since undergone several amendments: the **London** Amendment (1990) required developed countries to eliminate CFCs, halons, and carbon tetrachloride by 2010; the **Copenhagen** Amendment required CFCs, halons, carbon tetrachloride, and methyl chloroform to be completely phased out in developed countries by 1996; the **Montreal** Amendment, produced a phase-out for HCFCs in developing countries, and targeted the complete phase-out of methyl bromide for developed countries by 2005 and developing countries by 2015; the **Beijing** Amendment (1999) increased Restrictions on HCFC production and trade, and scheduled complete phase-out of methyl bromide for developed countries by 2004; and the Montreal Adjustment on production and use of HCFCs included commitments to accelerate the freeze year and phase-out HCFCs in developed and developing countries (See GEP, 2013).

The Montreal Protocol as variously amended and adjusted has evolved to become one of the world's most successful multilateral environmental agreements, having set aggressive timelines for countries to phase out ODS. Due largely to the Montreal Protocol the global and annual production and use of ODS decreased by 95% between 1989 and 2005 (CCSP, 2008), leading, also, to the total levels of ODS and ODS substitutes emitted into Earth's atmosphere, including HFCs, decreasing during the same period.

There is evidence of a reversal of stratospheric ozone depletion though: due to larger atmospheric lifetimes, halon and HCFCs are yet to stabilize in the atmosphere. Consequently, atmospheric concentrations of these ODS continue to grow; in addition, CFC emissions have not decreased as significantly as other ODS, due, in part, to continued use by developing countries as well as emissions from stockpiles in developed countries (GEP, 2013).

16.6 Multilateral Institutions on Climate Change

This section highlights the various multilateral bodies and organizations set up at the global level to implement collective strategies on coping with the challenges posed by climate change, including their genesis, mandates and achievements with regard to climate change mitigation.

16.6.1 The United Nations Environment Programme (UNEP)

This institution plays a special coordinating function and has acted as the focal point for establishing legal frameworks for international environmental programmes. The UNEP grew from the April

1972 Stockholm Conference in which 26 **Principles** and 109 **Recommendations** for action on the environment were agreed on; it was established in December 1972 to act as a governing council for environmental programmes within the United Nations System (see Ivanova, 2007). Headquartered in Nairobi, Kenya (the first UN body outside the developed world), the UNEP seeks to act as a catalyst and think tank, the conscience of the UN System' (Clark and Timberlake, 1982, p. 49).

Critiques point out, however, that UNEP's small size, poverty of resources, relative weakness within the UN System and peripheral positions in Nairobi have constrained its effectiveness (Ivanova, op. cit.). Adams (2009, p. 64) explains that the UNEP's weakness or ineffectiveness originates in the fact that it is not an independent body like UNESCO or FAO:

"It is officially a unit of the UN Secretariat and gets administrative funds from that source, but money for projects comes from the Environment Fund. The contributions to that are voluntary, and have fallen short of needed targets (a reflection of the 'global public, goods' and 'free rider' problems) UNEP's influence on the UN agencies has been relatively small, and they have gone about their business as much as before" (bracketed words added).

UNEP's list of priorities defined at the Stockholm Conference is criticized as 'impossibly broad remit' and 'vague' (Adams, op. cit.). Its programmes have evolved to include several activities such as the Global Environment Monitoring System (GEMS), begun in 1972 (Gwynne, 1982), and the Regional Seas Programme launched in 1974. It coordinates intergovernmental action based on an agreed Action Plan – this is an approach for resolving a global environmental degradation problem through regional action, which by 1982 covered 10 regions and 120 coastal states (Bliss-Guest and Keckes, 1982)

UNEP had also organized the United Nations Conference on Desertification (UNCOD) in Nairobi in 1977, which was organized against the background of the Sahel droughts of 1972-1974 (see Karrar, 1984). Its anti-desertification programme has, so far, achieved "very little"; Swift (1996) notes that "by the 1980s and 1990s the whole subject had become beset by controversy…"[5] Adams (op. cit., p. 219) argues that 'Neo-Malthusian Blinkers' prevent environmental analysts 'make sense of the Sahel'. But neo-Malthusian arguments on desertification tend to ignore the role of economic organization and social relations, emphasizing only climatic factors, population pressure on resources – all factors rejected or, at best, de-emphasized in Marxist analyses (see Copans, 1983; Watts, 1983 A, B; Pepper, 1993). Neo-Malthusian arguments, typically, take their intellectual bearing from classical economics – in particular, the Malthus strand – that regarded or assumed natural resources (e.g. land) as fixed (by nature) and exhaustible in the long run, and not augmentable by technology (also assumed fixed). Specifically, the neo-Malthusian explanations of the Sahel drought have been premised on the argument that rapidly growing human population pressure exhausted the capacity of the African Sahel to regenerate and thus prevent desertification, and this problem is complemented by climate change and the intensification of drought. Marxist explanations reject this perspective, emphasizing, instead, the roles of economic organization and social relations. As pointed out earlier in chapter 11, the problem with both explanations is that they assume a homogenous African Sahel. The fact, however, is that different parts of the Sahel are subject to different demographic, economic and physical conditions that affect the desertification process. For instance, the conditions affecting desertification in the Lake Chad basin differ considerably from those affecting desertification in northern Mali or Nigeria's 'Far North', etc.

16.6.2 The Intergovernmental panel on Climate Change (IPCC)

The IPCC was established in 1988 (by the World Meteorological Organization (WMO) and (UNEP) with three working groups: on scientific evidence on climate change; environmental and socioeconomic impacts; and response strategies. IPCC's reports were released for the first time only in 1990.

IPCC's Science Assessment Working Group set out to fashion out a global consensus on the complex science of global warming and climate change; its reports have come to represent, as Houghton (1997, p. 159) put it, "… authoritative statements of the contemporary views of the international scientific community". Scientific evidence reports that atmospheric GHG concentrations are human-induced, and establishes that this is responsible for over 50% of the enhanced greenhouse effect, both historically and future (Jäger and O' Riordan, 1996).

The IPCC issued its First Assessment Report in 1990 establishing the consensus view of the actual role of fossil fuels combustion and atmospheric carbon dioxide concentrations. IPCC's position regarding the anthropogenic origin of carbon dioxide emissions 'cut directly at the heart of the interests of the industrialized northern countries', while also bearing significant implications for rapidly industrializing countries in the South such as India and China (Adams, 2009, p. 102).

IPCC's data and analysis of evidence on the anthropogenic origin of atmospheric carbon dioxide concentrations made a critical contribution to the negotiations leading to the adoption of the Kyoto Protocol (of the United Nations Framework Convention on Climate Change, UNFCC), to which we return. Meanwhile, the IPCC has continued to put out Periodic Assessment Reports: The Second was in 1995, the Third in 2001, the Fourth in 2007 and the 5th was issued in 2014. These Reports continue to put pressure on the international community by lending credibility and confirmation to the scientific consensus on the significance of increases in GHG concentrations in the atmosphere because of anthropogenic influences starting since the mid-1700s. Briefly, the IPCC consensus has come to dominate in climate science circles on how the global climate system works. The IPCC, indeed, currently embodies the mainstream of climate science. Its conclusion on climate change, regionally and globally, and the complexity of that process has become widely accepted in scientific circles (Parry et al., 2007).

IPCC's **Second Assessment Report** in 1995 concluded that the global mean temperature of the 20th century was at least as warm as any since 1400, and predicted 'an enhanced global mean hydrological cycle; meaning that there would occur more droughts and floods and storms (see Houghton et al., 1995). The **Third Assessment Report** in 2001 found a 100-year trend in temperature (1901-2000) was + 0.6°C, while the **Fourth Assessment Report** in 2007 noted that the period 1906-2005 had been hotter, at 0.74°C (IPCC, 2007); that eleven of the twelve years 1995-2006 were among the twelve warmest years since instrumental record started way back in 1850 (IPCC, 2007a); that impacts of anthropogenic climate change, globally and regionally, are highly complex (Parry et al., 2007); and that the implications for environment and society (particularly in the tropics) are huge.

The latest IPCC Report – the 5th Assessment Report, was completed in 2014; it includes, as usual, reports of three Working Groups (WGs). Working Group, I (WGI) concludes: that warming of the climate system is unequivocal, and since the 1950s many of the observed changes are unprecedented over decades to millennia; that human influence on the climate system is clear: likely that 95-100% probability that human influence was the dominant cause of global warming from 1951-2010.

The IPCC Report concludes that without new policies to mitigate climate change, global mean temperatures in 2100 of 3.7°C to 4.8°C, relative to pre-industrial levels could be reached. However, some key climate change predictions by IPCC's computer models have not materialized: for instance, that for each doubling of atmospheric carbon dioxide levels we get roughly 1°C of global warming. During the first decade of the 2000s, some 100 billion tonnes of carbon dioxide were pumped into Earth's atmosphere, an amount equal to a quarter of all human-induced carbon dioxide emissions since 1750. Yet the mean global temperature, though remaining almost 1°C above the level attained during 1900-1910, remained 'flat' during 2000-2010 (see The Economist, 30th March, 2013, p. 69). Thus, we observe what looks like a "mismatch" between rising GHG emissions and 'flat' trends in mean global temperature. This raises one of the 'biggest puzzles' in current climate science: there is a mismatch between the theoretical computer predictions of climate scientists and actual developments.

This 'mismatch' does not mean that global warming should be dismissed as a delusion but, rather, that Earth's climate is not as sensitive to higher GHG concentrations as hypothesized in IPCC's models, and that there exist individual climate influences and feedback reigning back global warming that current conventional climate science represented by IPCC are yet to explain. As **The Economist** has noted the explanation to this puzzle:

"… cannot rest on models alone. There must be other explanations – and, as it happens, there are: individual climate influences and feedback loops that amplify (and sometimes moderate) climate change" (**The Economist,** 30th March, 2013, p. 70; bracketed words in the original).

The Economist goes on to insist that:

"Despite all the work on sensitivity, no one really knows how the climate would react if temperature rose ..." (ibid., p. 71).

So, there are still 'clouds of uncertainty' as regards how the climate reacts to changes in carbon dioxide emissions.

16.6.3 The United Nations Framework Convention on Climate Change (UNFCCC)

Among the documents signed by Heads of State at the United Nations Conference on Environment and Development (UNCED) Earth Summit in Rio de Janeiro, Brazil in 1992 was the UNFCCC. Signed by over 150 states and the European Community (now European Union, EU), the UNFCCC formally came into force in March 1994. The Convention agreed, though on voluntary basis and without binding targets on countries, to aim at reducing GHG emissions to 1990 levels by the year 2000. Five years later, it became obvious that UNFCCC's voluntary approach was not eliciting any success. But all the developed countries except those of the European Union had increased their GHG emissions by 7-9% in the ensuing five years; the developing countries had increased their emissions by 25% (Wright and Nebel, op. cit., p. 41).

16.6.4 The Kyoto Protocol

The third Conference of Parties to the UNFCCC, prompted by a coalition of island nations whose existence is threatened by rising sea level caused by climate change, had met in Kyoto Japan, in December 1997 to fashion out a binding agreement on reducing GHG emissions, which came to be known as the Kyoto Protocol of the UNFCCC. The Kyoto Protocol was signed between 1998 and 1999; it set out binding obligations on developed countries to reduce six GHGs by 5.2% below 1990 levels by 2008-2012. Kyoto entered into force in February 2005 (after it had been ratified by the requisite number of countries). By 2006, 163 countries including the European Union (EU) had ratified Kyoto, the major abstaining ones being the United States and Australia.

The United States had complained that, in its own view, the costs of compliance were exorbitant, the exclusion of developing countries will render the undertaking ineffective, and the scientific uncertainties surrounding climate change remain too significant to warrant the actions taken. Table 16.2 contains the 'assigned amount obligation' to developed countries.

Table 16.2 Kyoto Protocol 'assigned amount obligations' for Reductions in GHGs for Developed Countries.

Country	Kyoto binding obligations (%) (1990 – 2010)	Observed change (1990 – 1998)	1998 GHG emissions (10^6 metric tons CO_2 equivalent)
European Union (EU)	- 8	n.a.	n.a
United Kingdom	- 12.5	- 8.9	695
Germany	- 21	- 16	986
France	0	- 1.1	489
Italy	- 6.5	+ 5.1	518
Iceland	+ 10	n.a.	n.a.
Australia	+ 8	+ 5.4	520
Canada	- 6	+ 17	670
Japan	- 6	+ 8.5	1, 226
United States	- 7	+ 22	5, 954
Russian Federation	0	- 58	1, 122
Ukraine	0	- 55	386

Source: Wright and Nebel (op. cit., Table 21-5, p. 527) EU and Iceland data from Adams (op. cit., pp. 103-164).

Under Kyoto, most of the developed countries agreed to reduce their GHGs emissions by an average of about 5% from 1990 levels between 2008 and 2012 when the treaty was due to expire. However, the negotiated emissions limits were differentiated according to countries and regions, ranging from a reduction of 8% to an increase not to exceed 10%. Developing countries were exempt from such firm commitments under Kyoto. Central elements of Kyoto included rules for compliance: land-use; land-use changes; and forestry provisions; and mechanisms which give countries some flexibility to achieve their GHG emissions reductions commitments.

The second mechanism is the so-called Joint Implementation (JI), which permits legal entities in one country that has an emissions commitment to earn emission credits towards that commitment by undertaking emissions reductions projects in another such country. Countries facing relatively high costs for emissions reductions can reduce their costs of compliance by earning such credits in countries where the costs are lower. Mindful of rising levels of atmospheric CO_2 and global warming, the Kyoto Protocol proposed that, if nations increased their forested areas, they should be given so-called emission credits to count for their CO_2 emission standards [their permissible and legally binding pollution maxima]. A further proposal, emission trading, would permit a nation with GHG emissions below its agreed target to trade its 'credits' to over-target nations. We highlighted the mechanism of the tradeable emissions allowances earlier in chapter 15 (see especially section 15.2.3).

The third mechanism is the Clean Development Mechanism (CDM), whose importance lies in bringing developing countries into the Kyoto protocol. Under CDM, as in JI, developed countries may accrue emissions credits towards their reduction commitment by sponsoring carbon emissions reduction projects in developing countries. The CDM not only gives the developed country an opportunity to meet its commitments at lower costs than otherwise, it also promotes sustainable development in the developing country at the same time it encourages the transfer of technology (Noble and Watson, 2006).

The IPCC had produced estimates of the costs to individual countries of complying with the Kyoto Protocol: these range from 0.2 to 2% of GDP in the absence of international carbon permits trading, and from 0.1 to 1.0% of GDP if such trading takes place. These costs could be reduced further by expanding the stocks of carbon sinks: afforestation, reforestation, and avoiding deforestation; and improved forest, cropland, and grassland management; implementing project-based emissions swapping between industrial and developing countries through the Clean Development Mechanism; and reducing emissions of other GHGs, including methane and halocarbons.

Assessments of progress towards the Kyoto emission targets have been mixed. Climate economists, generally, consider Kyoto to have been a noteworthy success: as of 2008, more than 95% of ozone-depleting substances have been phased out and the ozone layer is expected to return to its pre-1980 levels by the 2050s (Tietenberg and Lewis, op. cit., p. 354). Tietenberg and Lewis explain that:

"Part of the reason for the success of this approach was an early recognition of the importance of the need to solicit the active participation of developing countries. Part of the success in eliciting that participation was achieved by offering later phase-out deadlines for developing countries, but another important aspect involved providing some financial help for the phase-out" (p. 354).

(A) **Multilateral Fund** was established, designed to cover the incremental costs that developing countries incur because of taking actions to eliminate the production and use of ozone-destroying pollutants. The industrialized countries contribute to the multilateral fund which totaled some $2.4 billion by 2008 (see ibid.).

Other assessments are less positive: progress towards emission targets agreed at Kyoto has remained problematic; so, Kyoto has brought no decisive solution to the climate change threat (Najam et al., 2003; Shiller, 2015). It is widely agreed that climate change is, arguably, too complex a problem for the Kyoto Protocol emission control to solve, "treating tonnes of carbon dioxide like stockpiles of nuclear weapons to be reduced via mutually identifiable targets and timetables" (Prins and Rayner, 2007, p. 973). Even though world leaders agree that climate change is 'the most important issue we face as a global community', effective solution to this challenge is limited by serious constraints arising from the difficulty of bridging the protective self-interest of developed countries that have achieved industrialization yet are alarmed at the disastrous consequences of "drastic climate change", and those of developing countries yet seeking to industrialize and for whom 'crises of poverty', not climate change as such, are their immediate fears (see also Vira, 2002; Najam et al., 2003). Adams (op. cit., p. 102) reports that 'while the north argued the priority of environmental protection and that any measures agreed should be cost effective, the South pushed for development and industrialization, and the principle of historical responsibility.

16.6.5 Paris Climate Change Agreement of December 2015

The latest multilateral agreement on climate change, the Paris Agreement, saw 195 countries of the world adopt the first-ever universal, legally binding global climate deal. The Agreement sets out a global action plan to put the global community on tract to avoid dangerous climate change. The Agreement, due to enter into force in 2020 only if 55 countries that produce at least 55% of the global GHG emissions ratify, accept, approve or accede to the Agreement, is an agreement within the United Nations Framework Convention on Climate Change (UNFCCC). It aims to pursue three key objectives:

- limit global average temperature to well below 2°C above pre-industrial levels and adopt strategies to limit the temperature increase to 1.5°C above pre-industrial levels, which would significantly reduce the risks and impacts of climate change.
- enhance the ability of the global community to adapt to the adverse impacts of climate change and foster climate resilience and low GHG emissions development, in ways that do not undermine national and global food production capacities.
- make finance flows consistent with a pathway towards low GHG emissions and climate-resilient development.

Acclaimed to be the world's first comprehensive climate agreement, the Paris Agreement has the distinction that it carries on board as signatories the key countries of the world in GHG emissions: China (20.09%), United States (17.89%), Russia (7.53%), India (4.10%), Japan (3.79%), Brazil (2.48%), Canada (1.95%), South Korea (1.85%), Mexico (1.70%), United Kingdom (1.55%),

Indonesia (1.49%), South Africa (1.46%), Australia (1.46%), France (1.34%), Iran (1.30%), etc. The United States withdrew from the Paris Climate Agreement on 15th June, 2017, to which we return.

A. Naturally Determined Contributions (NDCs)

The contributions that each individual country should make in order to achieve the goal of the Paris Agreement are a decision determined by each country and called 'naturally determined contributions' (NDCs). The level of NDCs set by a country will set the targets for that country itself, as specified in Article 3 of the Paris Agreement. Countries are required to report their NDCs every 5 years and are to be recorded by the UNFCCC Secretariat. Further, every country's NDCs should follow the principle of "progression" – that is, each additional contribution should be more ambitious than the previous one. On the other hand, however, countries are free to cooperate and pool their NDCs.

B. Weaknesses of the Paris Agreement

Like all earlier multilateral climate agreements, the Paris Agreement contains serious loopholes that will undermine its effective implementation. One obvious problem is that "contributions" are set by individual countries and are not binding as a matter of international law, as they lack the specificity, normative character, or obligatory language necessary to create binding norms (see Brunnee, 2008). Another problem is that, as already suggested, the Agreement lacks mechanisms to force countries to set targets in their NDCs by a specific date and no enforcement if set targets are not met (Mark, 2015). The fact that the Agreement specifies no specific sanctions if a country fails to meet its commitments, other than to say that there will be only a "name and shame" system (see **Hindustan Times**, 14 December, 2015), creates room for the free rider syndrome – that is, it will encourage countries to free-ride on others' NDCs – which could lead to a total collapse of the Paris Agreement (see also Druzin, 2016).

For these and other reasons, criticisms began to surface no sooner than the Paris Agreement was announced. There is criticism about the fact that most of the Agreement consists of "promises" or aims and not "firm commitments". James Hansen, father of climate change awareness, felt frustrated and was quoted to have described the Paris Agreement "a fraud" (see Milman, 2015). Other criticisms centre on the obvious naïve assumption implicit in the Agreement, namely that the global high "polluters" – e.g. China, United States, Russia, India, Japan and Brazil, who together generate more than 55% of global GHG emissions – "will somehow drive down their carbon pollution voluntarily without any enforcement mechanism to measure and control CO_2 emissions at any level from factory to state and without any specific penalty gradation or fiscal pressure..." (see Firzli, 2016).

The first crack on the Paris Agreement came in June, 2017, when the United States withdrew from the Agreement. By this, the United States will join two other non-signatory nations, Syria and Nicaragua (however, in late 2017, Syria indicated interest in signing up to the Paris agreement). Donald Trump who was elected United States President earlier in November, 2015, is among many in the United States Republican Party who deny the anthropogenic source of global warming and climate change or that climate change is occurring at all. United States withdrawal has two potential implications. First, other countries' future pledges to cut or limit GHG emmissions will be less enthusiastic without the world's second largest polluter (after China) doing its own share. Second, the United States withdrawal could on the other hand galvanize other major global polluters – China, the European Union, Russia and India – to unite and fight further growth in GHG emissions, So far, fortunately, no other major country has indicated support for United States move to withdraw from the Paris agreement.

C. Green Climate Fund

Not part of the Paris Agreement though (and not legally binding), there is a plan to provide US$100 billion a year in aid to developing countries for implementing new procedures for minimizing climate change with additional amounts to be provided in subsequent years. Already, the United States has donated $300 billion to the Green Climate Fund.

16.7 The Role of the World Bank

The World Bank is involved in gloal efforts to mitigate and adapt to climate change mainly through two initiatives: the Global Environment Facility (GEF) and the Carbon Finance Portfolio (CFP). The GEF was established in 1991 to provide funding for projects to support diversity, climte change, international waters, land degradation, the ozone layer and persistent organic pollutants (see Box 16.1). Through the GEF, the World Bank distributes annually some $250 million for projects on energy efficiency, renewable energy and sustainable transportation.

The World Bank was among pioneers facilitating carbon trading under the CDM and JI flexibility mechanisms of Kyoto. The prototype carbon fund was launched in 1999 with a target of $180 million, and by 2006 the World Bank was managing nine funds with available funds to the value of about $2 billion.

Box 16.1 The Global Environment Facility: Priorities
for Greenhouse Warming Projects

The GEF has established principles and priorities to guide project design.

Principles

- More technologies are needed to offer options for reducing emissions at least cost.
- GEF funding should encourage promising but unproven technologies when the technology, economics, or market conditions are not yet 'right'.
- Successful technologies will be those that show potential for widespread use and could eventually attract investment from conventional sources.

Priorities for Support

I. **End-use efficiency**
- Reducing energy intensity of basic materials processing.
- Efficient motors and drivers
- Irrigation pump-sets
- Lighting and water heating
- Vehicle fuel use

II. **Reduction in the emission intensity of energy production**
- Renewable such as photovoltaics, solar-thermal, and wind power.
- Biomass gasifiers/gas turbines
- Sustainable biomass production to replace fossil fuels
- Advanced, efficient gas turbine cycles
- Micro-hydropower
- Fuel switching to natural gas

III. **Non – carbon – dioxide emissions reductions**
- Urban and rural waste treatment
- Reduction of flaring and venting natural gas
- Reduction of releases associated with coal mining

IV. **Generic areas**
- More efficient production, transmission, and distribution of energy
- Slowing deforestation
- Sequestering carbon dioxide (for example afforestation)

Source: World Bank (1992) Box 9.3, p. 176

16.8 Forest Carbon Emissions Reduction Mechanisms

The Post–Kyoto Protocol years have witnessed the emergence of the socalled carbon market to facilitate trading in GHG credits. The expectation that Kyoto would prevent further CO_2 concentrations in Earth's atmosphere beyond levels dangerous to human survival[6] – the ultimate objective of the 1992 United Nation's Framework Convention on Climate Change (UNFCCC) – had hardly been realized as the 1990s were coming to an end. This necessitated the setting up three institutions: (i) Clean Development Mechanism (CDM); (ii) Voluntary Carbon Market (VCM); and (iii) Reducing Emissions from Deforestation and Degradation plus promoting forest conservation, Sustainable forest management (Sfm), and enhancement of forest carbon stocks (REDD+). All these are targeted at forest carbon emissions which received no explicit attention in Kyoto.

As explained earlier, a carbon market refers to one created from the trading of GHG emissions allowances/credits. The sole aim of such a market is to encourage countries and production entities to limit their CO_2 emissions. A carbon credit/allowance is a generic term describing tradeable certificate or permit representing permission to emit one tonne of CO_2 or the mass of another GHG with a carbon dioxide equivalent (tCO_2e) to one tonne of CO_2. Carbon credits/allowance carbon markets – also known as carbon trading schemes – constitute an element of a natural and international effort to reign in the growth of atmospheric GHG concentrations. GHG emissions by economic entities are capped (they have quotas or upper limts) and then markets (exchange procedures) are used to allocate the emissions among the group of regulated sources (or production companies). The objective is to permit supply and demand forces to drive production in the direction of low CO_2 emissions or to use less carbon intensive processes than those used when there is no cost attached to emitting CO_2 and other GHGs into Earth's atmosphere. With GHG reducing production processes generate credits (benefits or profits), the carbon credid/trading approach can provide a framework to finance carbon reduction schemes between trading entities and around the world.

Under Kyoto, the quotas for GHGs for the industrial/developed Annex 1 countries are called 'Assigned Amount Obligations (see section 16.6.4 in this chapter) and are listed in Annex B, the quantity of the initial assigned obligations being denominated in individual units, called Assigned Amount Units (AAUs), each of which is represents permission/allowance to emit one metric tonne CO_2 equivalent. In turn, countries set quotas or 'caps' on the emissions of installations operated by local business and other units and manage these quotas through their national registries, which must be validated and monitored for compliance by the UNFCCC.

Each operator (business unit) has an allowance of credits where each unit is equivalent to a right to emit one metric tonne of CO_2 or other equivalent GHG. Business units who fail to use up their quotas can sell their unused quotas as carbon credits, while units that are about to exceed their quotas can purchase extra quotas as credits, privately or in an open trading system. By allowing quotas to be bought and sold, a business can seek out the most efficient means or technologies to minimize its emissions, either by installing 'cleaner' technologies or purchasing emissions from another excess-capacity business unit.

As from 2005 Kyoto was adapted for CO_2 trading within the European Union under its European Trading Scheme (EUETs). As from 2008, European Union participants are required to link with the other industrial/developed countries that ratified Annex 1 of Kyoto, and trade the six most significant anthropogenic GHGs: carbon dioxide CO_2; methane CH_4; nitrous oxide N_2O; Hydrofluorocarbons HFCs; Perfluorocarbons PFCs; Sulphur hexafluoride SF_6. We now proceed to describe and analyze the three-forest carbon emission market mechanisms identified above, highlighting their features, institutional framework and financing architecture.

16.8.1 Clean Development Mechanism, CDM

Defined in Article 12 of the Kyoto Protocol, CDM is intended to fulfill two purposes: first, assist parties not included in Annex 1 (largely developed countries) to achieve sustainable development and contribute to the goal of UNFCCC 1992, to prevent dangerous climate change; and, second, assist parties included in Annex 1 (largely developed countries) to achieve compliance with the Kyoto Protocol quotato cut GHG emissions. CDM meets the first objective by allowing Annex 1 countries to meet part of their Kyoto Protocol quota by purchasing Certified Emission Reduction (CER) units from CDM emission reduction projects in developing countries (Carbon Trust, 2009, p. 14).

CDM itself was expected to save up to 2 billion tonnes of CO2 emissions reduction by 2012. It allowed developed countries to purchase CERs and to invest in emission reductions in regions or countries considered to offer the cheapest or least-cost conditions. During 2001 – 2012 (September) CDM issued 1 billion CERs and by June 2013, 57% of CERs had been issued for projects for destroying either HFC-23 (38%) or N_2O (19%). By 2011, carbon capture and storage became included in CDM carbon offsetting scheme.

CDM projects involve a wild range of activities and technologies in various sectors: renewable energy[7]; waste handling and disposal; manufacturing; afforestation and reforestation (A/R) to enhance forest carbon sinks and reservoirs; landfill; transport; etc. Afforestation plant trees in areas that were never forests or have not been forested for over 50 years prior to CDM activities; reforestation generates forests through planting and seeding in areas that have been deforested.

Operational since 2006, CDM mechanism had registered more than 1,650 projects by 2012 and are anticipated to produce CERs amounting to more than 2.9 billion tonnes CO2 equivalent during 2008-2012 (the 1st commitment period of Kyoto)[8]. In 2008, the largest shares in location of CDM project went to China, India, and Brazil, in that order (Table 16.3); CDMs located in

Asia would total 79%. Table 16.4 carries data on CERs' country distribution and shows China and India again occupying the top positions.

Table 16.3 CDM Projects' location, November 2008.

Country	Project Number	Relative Contribution (%0
China	1500	36
India	1100	27
Brazil	300	7
Other Latin Countries	280	6
Other Asian Countries	210	5.5
Mexico	200	5
Malaysia	180	4.5
Indonesia	130	3.0
Africa	130	3.0
Philippines	130	3.0
Middle East	120	2.5
Europe and Central Asia	120	2.0

Source: Constructed from Corbera et al. (2009, figure 3) and may not conform to original data.

Table 16.4 Certified Emission Reductions (CERs)

Country	% of CERs originality in country
China	59.9
India	14.7
Rep. of Korea	9.1
Brazil	7.2
Mexico	1.6
Chile	1.0
Argentina	0.9
Others	5.9

The capacity of African countries attracting CDM projects has so far been constrained by a lack of human and technical resources (Arens et. al. 2011). By 2008 only 3% or so of CDM projects were in Africa (Table 16.3). It is unlikely that the situation has changed in any significant manner post-2008; if anything, it is quite likely to have deteriorated. The geographies of CDM projects seem to be an equity issue and should not detain us; of more relevance, perhaps, is capacity of CDM projects to reduce atmospheric GHG emissions – a key objective of the Kyoto Protocol. Studies show that CDM projects have been unevenly distributed both across regions and within countries, which limits CDM's capacity to contribute to global equitable development (Lohmann, 2006; Wara, 2007); nor have CDM projects created employments, given their concentration in large industrial projects with low employment creation capacity – e.g. HFC decomposition, fuel switching or methane mitigation, etc. It seems there are tradeoffs between capacity of CDM projects to effect low-cost emissions abatement and the realization of sustainable development benefits (Olsen, 2007).

16.8.2 Voluntary Carbon Market

The Voluntary Carbon Market[9] (VCM) functions outside the mandatory compliance market; it trades carbon emission credits for purposes other than meeting legally binding targets under the Kyoto Protocol obligations. Instead of being subjected to national approval from project participants and the registration and verification procedures from the UNFCCC, the calcculation and the certification of the emissions reduction are effected in accordance with many industry-created standards. VCMs enable business, governments, NGOs and individuals to offset their emissions by purchasing offsets (emission permits) that were created either through CDM or in the voluntary market.[10] VCMs allow for experimentation and innovation in that projects can be implemented with fewer transaction costs than CDMs or other compliance market projects. Unlike CDMs, there are no established rules and regulations for VCMs, which make them useful as a testing field for new procedures, methodologies and technologiesthat may later be introducd into regulatory schemes.

In VCMs, projects can be implemented with far fewer transaction costs than CDMs or other compliance projects. VCMs also serve as a niche for micro projects that are too small to warrant the administrative burden of CDMs.[11] On the negative side, the lack of quality control has led to the production of some low quality VERs, such as those generated from projects that appear likely to have happened anyway. VCMs differ from CDMs in two other fundamental ways. First, trading volums in VCMs tend to be smaller because demand is created only by voluntary wish to buy offsets in contrast to CDMs where demand is created by a regulatory instrument. Second, carbon offsets sold in VCMs tend to be' cheaper than those in CDMs. For instance, in 2006 the total volume of VCM offset projects amounted to 13 Mt CO_2, in contrast to 466 Mt CO_2 for CDM offset projects, which shows that the CDM market was 36 times larger than the VCMs market. Nevertheless, however, since 2006 the VCM market has expanded rapidly even if still remaining smaller than the CDM market. The growth of the VCM market does reflect the fact that:

"Companies and individuals are increasingly concerned about their environmental impact. Some will neutralize activities they cannot avoid by "offsetting" their own emissions. Individuals may seek to offset their travel emissions and companies claim they are 'carbon neutral' by buying large quantites of carbon offsets to 'neutralize' their own carbon footprint or that of their products. They see voluntary offsetting as part of their corporate responsibility and/or as part of their image strategy" [Ecosystem Marketplace (2016, May)].

16.8.3 Product Types

Table 16.5. VCM Project Category and Project Type.

Project Category	Project Type
Renewable Energy	Wind Run-of river hydro Biomass Biogas Solar Large hydro
Bio-sequestration	Redd+ Tree-planting Improved forest mnagement
Methane Capture	Landfill Methane Methane (Waste water and coal) Livestock
Industrial gases	Nitrous Oxide, N_2O F-gases, which includes: Hydrofluoro carbons, HFCs, Perfluoro carbons, PFCs, Sulfure hexa fluoride SF_6
Efficiency and fuel switching	Energy efficiency – industrial – focused Energy efficiency – community – focused Fuel switching Waste heat recovery

Source: Ecosystem Marketplace (2016, May); Kollmus et al. 2008.

Carbon reduction projects can be broadly categorized into five groups (Table 16.5): (i) renewable energy; (ii) bio-sequestration; (iii) methane capture; (iv) industrial gases; and (v) energy efficiency. There are differential capacities in the degree to which the different product types can reduce GHG emissions.

Renewable Energy: Renewable energy products include hydroelectricity, solar power, biomass power etc. As analyzed earlier (chapter 14), renewable energy projects are crucial for the long-term protection of Earth's climate because they help us to move away from current heavy reliance on fossil-fuel-based energy supplies; this makes, though in theory, demand for renewable energy products ideal for the carbon offset market. A key problem with renewable energy products is that many have high up-front capital costs – e.g. hydroelectricity – apart from legislative hurdles and opposition from environmental lobby groups. Renewable energy projects have had a significant position in the offsets sold in VCM projects (e.g. Hamilton et al., 2007).

Bio-sequestration: Examples of bio-sequestration are forestry mitigation projects which have been found in climate literature to make "very significant contribution to a low-cost global mitigation portfolio…" (IPCC, 2007, WG111). Emperical findings show that cumulative emissions from land-use changes, especially deforestation, have contributed some 25% of global GHG emissions. Projects aiming to reduce GHG emissions from land-use practices are collectively labelled afforestation, and reforestation, carbon storage by soil management techniques (e.g. no-till agriculture).

Methane capture: Methane (CH_4) has a GWP (global warming potential) 21 times greater than CO_2. Methane is produced from various sources: landfills, wastewater treatment, natural gas and petroleum systems, livestock production, rice paddies, coal mining, etc. Methane projects have accounted for just about 3% of VERs sold in the voluntary market (Hamilton 2007).

Industrial Gases: Some industrial gases have very high GWP, which makes the destruction of these gases a most effective way to reduce GHGs. The notable industrial gases include: nitrous oxide (N_2O), produced from chemical (inorganic) fertilizer production) is 296 times the GWD of CO_2; Hydrofluorocarbons (HFCs, used as non-ozone depleting refrigerants) has GWP 10005 times that of CO_2 and Sulphur Hexafluoride (SF_6, used in the electrical industry) has GWP 22,000 times that of CO_2. The Kyoto Protocol Conference in 1987 and Montreal Protocol in 2007 had agreed to phase out ozone-destroying CFCs. Developed countries had agreed to reduce CFC consumption by 75% by 2010 and by 90% in 2015 and finally phase out CFCs by 2020. On their part, developing countries agreed to phase out CFCs completely by 2030.

There is consensus that destruction of industrial gases is an effective way to reduce GHGs. Yet industrial gas offsets are controversial because, although they are the cheapest to conduct and generate large amounts of offsets (in the CDM market), 67% and 34% of all CERs transacted in 2015 and 2006, respectively, originated in HCF destruction projects (e.g. Capoor and Ambrosi, 2007), they fail to contribute to sustainable development.

Energy Efficiency: Energy efficienct products are less energy consuming than conventional technologies to perform the same or similar task – e.g. a new carfleet that replaces an old, fleet; homes fitted with more efficient bulbs; more efficient cooking stoves; etc. Energy efficient projects took up 5% of offsets in the voluntary markets in 2006 (Hamilton, et al. op. cit., 2007).

16.8.4 REDD+

REDD+ (reducing deforestation and degradation and the role of conservation and sustainable forest management) grew out of the post-Kyoto climate negotiations to capture a suit of activities beyond project level interventions. The term was first introduced as reducing emissions from deforestation (RED) at the 11th Conference of Parties (COP11) of the UNFCCC in Montreal in 2005. At COP13 in Bali in 2007, the concept of REDD was expanded to REDD+. At the UNFCCC Cancun Agreement, the REDD+ concept was defined to cover forest cover carbon emissions through five activities: (i) avoided deforestation; (ii) avoided forest degradation;[12] (iii) conservation; (iv) sustainable forest management (sfm); and (v) enhancement of forest carbon stocks. These five activities are not eligible types of projects under CDM or under any of the Kyoto Protocol's flexible mechanisms. It is obvious however, that such activities are necessary to reduce GHG emissions from land-use, land-use change, and forestry and to prevent GHG atmospheric concenrations from over-shooting the natural bound to levels dangerous to human survival – the ultimate objective of UNFCCC (see Section 16.6.3). Hence REDD+ has been proposed under UNFCCC as a new mechanism to be included in any future agreement which would provide a financial incentive to developing countries to conserve and enhance forest carbon sinks (see also RECOFT, 2011). In a way REDD+ is a mechanism to create financial value for the massive stock of carbon stored in forests, offering incentives for developing countries to reduce GHG emissions from forests and invest in low-carbon paths to sustainable development.

REDD+ has been defended because it possesses potential to unlock the climate mitigation potential of forests in developing countries, apart from generating other environmental spillovers additional to GHG reduction (e.g. Pfaff et. al., 2013). Forests, generally, have four major roles in climate change. First, they currently contribute 20 – 25% of global carbon emissions when cleared, over-used or degraded. Second, they react sensitively to changing climate – e.g. sustained drought conditions, as in the Brazilian Amazon (see Chapter3, section 3.5.1), lead to deforestation. Third, when managed sustainably, forests produce woodfuels as benign alternative to fossilfuels (woodfuels, however, are also a source of CO_2 emissions via charcoal production and firewood combustion). Fourth, they have the natural potential to absorb about 16% of global carbon emissions (through photosynthesis) into their biomass, soils and products and store them in principle in perpetuity. So, REDD+ if effectively implemented, has enormous potential to deliver on its proponents' argument, namely, that is a a low-cost mechanism to reduce atmospheric GHG concentration.

As noted above, 25 – 30% of annual GHG emissions, amounting to 1.6 billion tonnes, is caused by deforestation (e.g. Johnson, 2009). Trees have been proven to be constituted by 50% carbon; when they are felled or combusted, the CO_2 they store is unleashed on Earth's atmosphere. According to FAO, some 13 million hectares forests globally are lost every year, almost entirely in tropical South America, Sub-Saharan Africa, and Southeast Asia, where 80% of deforestation originates in new demand for farmland to grow food "to feed growing populations." However, as the UNFCCC negotiations on REDD+ progressed, it has been evident that REDD+ is "complicated, technically and politically, and more expensive to realize" (Cisneros, 2012; Pfaff et al., 2013; Gupta et al., 2016). Much of the initial debate focused on the global REDD+ architecture and how REDD+ can be built into a post-Kyoto climate agreement. Earlier discussion centred on the broad conceptual framing of REDD+; later, it shifted to how REDD+ can be implemented in individual developing countries so that REDD+ can deliver on its theorized capacity to provide a low-cost mechanism to reduce GHG emissions. The literature identifies five standards as national REDD+ claim of national reductions in carbon emissions: (i) a national REDD+ framework consisting effective strategies for reducing emissions; (ii) the necessary organizations and institutions to implement the national REDD+; (iii) a national reference emission level or reference level; (iv) a credible system to measure, monitor, repeat and verify the reductions in carbon emissions; and (v) a payment system to compensate those who have incurred opportunity costs in implementing REDD+.

We summarize below four key dimentions of REDD+, namely, the main features, institutional framework, financing architecture, and activity focus of REDD+, after which we provide insight into global and country-based implementation of REDD+.

MAIN FEATURES: REDD+ provides financial incentives to developing countries to conserve and manage their forests sustainably by offering financial rewards and incentives for decreased rates of deforestation and forest degradation, as well as conservation, sustainable forest management (SFM) and enhancement of carbon stocks. These activites are missing in CDM.

INSTITUTIONAL FRAMEWORK: This is yet to be fully worked out under the UNFCCC. National REDD+ readiness processes mostly follow UNFCCC, UN-REDD Programme, etc. but other instions intervene. Sub-national projects must follow VCM procedures while benefitting from official REDD+ finance.

FINANCIAL ARCHITECTURE: REDD+ finance is voluntary (credits do not contribute to countries' Kyoto emissions target). Financing comes from multilateral and bilateral sources, ODA and private funds. REDD+ is supported by World Bank, UN, NGO, etc.

ACTIVITIES: REDD+, SFM, conservation, enhancement of carbon stocks (see Section 16.8.3) are the key activities. Building local capacities for participating in future REDD+ mechanism currently occupies a central positon in many developing countries, especially in Sub-Saharan Africa.

16.8.4A Global Trends in REDD+

REDD+ projects are proliferating across tropical countries in the developing world; national REDD+ readiness activities are taking place in all regions, comprising over 50 countries, including 18 countries in Africa (as of 2012) stretching from Sierra Leone in West Africa[13] to Ethiopia in East Africa, and from Sudan in North Africa to Mozambique in Southern Africa (Cisneros and Fong, 2012).

However, to date the vast majority of REDD+ activities have been targeted towards readiness activities such as capacity building, training workshops, strengthening in-country institutional and technical capacities, and developing national REDD+ policies and strategies (Anelsen,2013). Such efforts are ultimately focused on preparing a country for verified emissions reductions on a payment for performance basis (Norman and Nakhooda, 2015).

Studies (up to 2014) find that aggregate pledges of both public and private financing for REDD+ amounted to U$ 9.8 billion for the period 2006-2014, of which about 90% originated in the the public sector, with a preponderance of funding concentrated among a relatively small number of donor countries and recipient countries. As of 2014, there were more than 20 REDD+ donors, among which are Norway, United States, Germany, Japan and United Kingdom, who combined, provided about 77% of identified funding (Norman and Nakhooda, op. cit.) Funding for REDD+ activities from bilateral and multilateral sources have not been distributed evenly among developing regions: about 44.7% has gone to South America and Caribbean; Africa has received only about 18%, and Asia and Pacific 17.1%; finally, less than 1% has gone to Europe and Central Asia.

For Africa, the Congo Basin rainforests are a prime location for REDD+ implementation. Currently, national REDD+ policy processes are on-going and many REDD+ pilot initiatives are being demonstrated (Fobissie et. al., 2014; Megevand, 2013; Cisneros and Fong, 2012). Cameroon and Democratic Republic of Congo harbour more than 60% of Congo Basin REDD+ activities. The Congo Basin rainforests have been spared high deforestation rates; because of this, vast swaths of prime rainforests still stand in this region often described as the 'Green Heart of Africa'.

16.9 Conclusions

The realization that climate change caused by GHG emissions is a global public bad has led to growing interest among countries to address that problem through international agreements. International agreements on climate change are, however, much more problematic than domestic policies, because enforcement is undermined by the free rider problem. Because in atmospheric pollution (GHG emissions) one country's pollution causes damage in another, including itself, the basic problem becomes how to get individual countries to abandon attempts to free ride on the control efforts of others. The incentive for individual countries to forgo free riding on others' efforts is provided by these agreements containing, apart from perceived benefits and costs, also side payments, monetary subsidies, technology transfers, etc.

End Notes

[1]   See, for example, Barret, 2003, 2007; Downie, 2013.

[2]   For instance, as far back as 1902 there was the 'European Treaty on the Conservation of Birds Useful to Agriculture' signed by 10 countries.

[3]   This Section relies heavily on insights in Fields and Fields (2009) especially chapter 21.

[4]   For the extensive literature on reasons why UNEP's anti-desertification campaign failed to achieve significant progress (see Adams, 2009, especially Chapter 8).

[5]   The debates and controversies surrounding this strategy were highlighted in chapter 15 (section 15.2.3).

[6] CO_2 atmospheric concentrations beyond 600-1000ppm would impair human health, which is what the 2015 Paris Climate Conference sought to prevent. Post-industrial revolution centuries have witnessed CO_2 concentrations rise from 2+ ppm to 400ppm and rising further – at a rate of 2+ppm a year. The fact, however, is that "… we do not know the threshold at which CO_2 levels begin to measurably impact human cognition" (Romm, 2015, October 26th)

[7]   E.g. a rural electrification project using solar panels – a renewable energy technology (see 14.2.3D)

[8]   http://cdm.unfccc.int/Statistics/Issuance/CERs/IssuedbyHostPartyPyeChart.html

[9]   This section relies on insight in Kellmus et. al. (2008) and Ecosystem Marketplace (2016, May)

[10]   When CDM credits are used for voluntary offsetting, they see retired, thus they do not go towards assisting or meeting any legally – binding Kyoto reduction targets

[11]   Carbon emission offset projects must reduce emissions minimum 5000 metric tonnes of CO_2/year in order to justify the CDM transaction costs (Kellmus et. al. 2008)

[12]   Forest degradation differs from deforestation; it refers to the destruction or reduction in the quantity of specific aspects of forests, a complete loss of the forest. Prolonged degradation can wipe a forest, or result in a decrease in tree cover, changes in their structure or a reduction in the number of species that can be found there. Forest degradation can be caused by forest fires, climate change (prolonged droughts and dry conditions reduce tree cover and dry out water bodies running through them); pest and diseases, etc. Degraded forests can often be restored

[13]   All but one (Mauritaania) West African country is involved in REDD+

CHAPTER 17

SUMMARY AND CONCLUSIONS

17.1 Introduction

This study set out to explore three broad issues connected with global warming and climate change: the causes; the symptoms in Earth's physical, ecological and socioeconomic systems; and the coping strategies evolved over the decades to deal with the climate change challenge. This final chapter summarizes the findings of the study and the policy conclusions that could be drawn from the findings.

17.2 Human Activities: Key Source of Global Warning and Climate Change

Global warming and climate change constitutes one of the major global problems of our time – indeed, the major environmental challenge of our time. Although a long-standing phenomenon, the current concern with climate change arises from two distinct facts: it is caused by human activities; and it is occurring at a pace hitherto not experienced in any part of the world. Scientific evidence shows that Earth's average surface temperatures have warmed up as much as by 6°C(42.8°F) over the past ten decades or so, 60% of this occurring in the 1970s upwards – that is, since the first decades of the 1900s – and is projected to rise further if no effective measures were taken to reduce significantly greenhouse gas atmospheric concentrations. Previous changes in Earth's average surface temperatures were caused by volcanic eruptions, changes in ocean currents, variations in the angle of Earth's rotation in its distance from the Sun; in contrast, current rise in Earth's temperature originates in human activities - specifically, GHG emissions from fossil fuel combustion to drive industrial, agricultural and domestic activities, deforestation and other changes in the use or management of land by humans, which may lead to change in land cover, which may, in turn, affect sources and sinks of GHGs, or other elements of the climate system.

Atmospheric concentrations of GHGs began to rise following the European Industrial Revolution unraveling by the mid-1700s and 1800s. But the Industrial Revolution was essentially an energy revolution: each succeeding phase has seen significant increases in fossil-fuel produced GHGs. The Industrial Revolution was driven by coal-based energy; in the postwar-II decades (the 1940s through the 1970s) petroleum (crude oil) displaced coal as the major energy source in industrial production and transportation; by the 1960s through the 1970s, the Industrial Revolution difused into the developing world, most notably East Asia, (Singapore, Hong Kong, Malaysia, South Korea, Thailand etc), China, and India in South Asia etc; and, also, by some countries of Latin America, most notably Brazil and Mexico.

The empirical literature shows that each year sees some 6.6 billion tons of fossil fuel carbon combustion, adding some 24 billion tons of carbon dioxide emissions into Earth's atmosphere. Carbon dioxide is the most abundant GHG: its current concentration equals some 370,000 parts per billion (ppb). During the 1970s to the first decades of the 2000s, GHG emissions measured in CO_2-equivalent increased at an annual average rate of 1.6%, with carbon dioxide emissions from fossil fuels growing at 1.9% per annum, which indicates that combustion of fossil fuels supplies the bulk of GHG emissions.

The geographical sources of anthropogenic GHG emissions correlate with the regional levels of industrial development. Expectedly, overall, the OECD countries account for some 80% of global carbon dioxide emissions over the long-term horizon. In terms of cumulative energy-related carbon dioxide emissions per capita, the United States, United Kingdom, Germany, Canada and Russia, in that order, top the ranks of the top-10 global GHG emitters. When it comes to the accelerating pace of carbon dioxide emissions witnessed since the 1980s, China emerges as the key geographical origin. The reason is that China is experiencing, currently, the highest pace of industrial development with coal as the key energy source – about 80% - of China's industrialization drive.

17.3 Symptoms of Climate Change

Rapidly rising carbon dioxide concentrations in Earth's atmosphere are driving the properties of Earth's physical, ecological, and socioeconomic systems towards conditions not observed for millions of years, with an associated risk of fundamental and irreversible transformations. Ozone layer depletion, disruption of the hydrologic cycle, melting of polar ice sheets and mountain snow caps, rising sea levels, droughts and desertification, declining agricultural yields and threat of famine in some parts of the developing world, etc- these are some of the most visible symptoms of climate change in Earth's natural and socioeconomic systems.

Ozone layer depletion is linked to atmospheric concentrations of chlorine and bromine through large emissions of anthropogenic nitrogen oxides produced from aircrafts and, more importantly, chlorofluorocarbons (CFCs). Five categories of environmental and health changes are linked to ozone depletion: human health; plants; marine ecosystems; biogeochemical cycles; and materials.

The hydrologic cycle has been found to be very much sensitive to global warming. Climate change has had the effect of speeding up the rate at which water evaporates and falls again as rain or snow; this has the effect of making humid regions (e.g. tropical countries) yet wetter and humid, and arid regions (e.g. deserts) even drier. Indeed, much of the effect of climate change tends to show its symptoms and effects on the intensity of precipitation (rain and snow) and temperatures.

Rising sea levels is caused both by thermal expansion of sea water and by partial melting of the vast sheets of ice in the polar regions. Scientific research confirms that already the mean global sea level has risen by between 10 and 25 centimeters. The Intergovernmental Panel on Climate Change (IPCC) forecasts an additional rise of between 8 and 88 centimeters by 2100. Rising sea levels threaten the very existence of small island states as well as the existence of a variety of biologically rich and economically important ecosystems such as coral reefs, mangrove forests, and other wetlands. Besides, rising sea levels pose serious environmental problems for low-lying alluvial plains and cities, which can only avoid being submerged by building costly protective infrastructures.

The symptoms of climate change in socioeconomic systems have been found to be most significant and visible in agriculture. But agriculture is the aspect of human activity most sensitive to changes in the key elements of climate such as temperature and precipitation. The extremes of heat and humidity in the tropical regions contribute to deteriorating soil quality and the rapid deterioration and, hence, depreciation of many natural assets. Such extreme tropical geographic conditions contribute, as well, to the low productivity of certain crops, the weakened regenerative growth of forests, and poor health of both animals and human beings, leading to lower levels of productivity and efficiency.

17.4 What to do? Mitigation and Adaptation Strategies to Cope with Climate

However, not every change in global warming and climate conditions will be considered bad: countries in the cold regions, such as Russia, Canada, Scandinavian, Greenland, etc. could benefit immensely from warming global temperatures. Specifically, warming global temperatures are predicted to lead to GDP growth of the range of 11% in the former Soviet Union and 0.3% in North America; in contrast, United States GDP would decline by some 0.5%. As for the developing world, Africa and India, for instance, will be made yet hotter, which will damage agricultural productivity. Overall, global warming will lead to a tailing off of agricultural productivity across the globe in the range of 3% with a rise of 2.5°C in global temperatures. Damage will be, generally, higher for countries located closer to the equator, where temperatures tend to be close to crop tolerance levels – and these countries and regions are mostly located in Sub-Saharan Africa. Finally, even though technological change will likely offset the loses in agriculture arising from climate change, the fact of the widening technology deficits in the developing world, especially Sub-Saharan Africa, will likely worsen the food crisis in the latter.

17.5 How to Cope with Climate Change

Coping with climate change has involved adopting two types of strategies: **mitigation** and **adaptation**. Mitigation strategies aim to moderate or reduce global temperatures by employing measures to reduce atmospheric GHG emissions; otherwise, they seek to enhance Earth's capacity to assimilate GHGs through carbon sequestration in the terrestrial biosphere – that region of Earth's surface, the seas and oceans, and air and land that is inhabited by living matter (humans, plants, microbes). Steps taken in mitigation include: innovation in fossil fuel technologies; developing biofuels as alternative to fossil fuels; developing new technologies in non-carbon energy; improving energy efficiency; and land-use changes.

The cost of mitigating the effects of climate change depends principally on three factors. The first relates to the extent energy demand can be effectively reduced by adopting relatively cheap energy-efficient technologies. Currently, global dependence on non-renewable fossil energy sources ranges up to 80.4%. The International Energy Agency (IEA) estimates that there are abundant cheap energy-efficient measures – e.g. new buildings, for instance, can be made 70% more efficient than average existing ones, reckoning that by the next four to five decades energy-efficient technologies can reduce emissions back to 2000 levels at moderate cost. The second factor relates to how fast renewable energy prices can be made to decline, which depends on reducing the costs of supplying wind power or solar energy, for example. The gap between some of them and the fossil-fuel-based energy should shrink, as technologies mature and manufacturing volumes rise – e.g. the cost of wind power is reported to have declined from 8-10 cents to 3.5-4 cents per KWh since 1990 because of better-designed turbines and higher volumes. The third factor is how fast emissions are rolled back: economists, in contrast to scientists and engineers, tend to recommend a gradual approach, pointing out that, as carbon dioxide hangs around in the atmosphere for up to two centuries (200 years), a tonne emitted now is no much worse than a tonne produced in 20 years' time; that cutting emissions gradually is a great deal cheaper than doing it quickly, because machinery can be replaced with new, lower-emission varieties at the end of its life cycle instead of being scrapped prematurely.

Adaptation, essentially, is a matter of managing the risks posed by climate change – both in terms of society or community and individuals or households. Adaptation strategies involve, therefore, for instance, construction of flood barriers along coastlines and river banks prone to flooding or providing irrigation to cope with drought conditions, taking out insurance policies on climate change related disasters, etc. Generally, developing countries possess far less adaptation capacity than developed countries – both in terms of financial resources and technological capability to deal with losses arising from extreme weather events e.g. flooding, tsunamis, etc.

The ultimate mitigation strategy lies in reducing GHG atmospheric emissions to be effected through reducing fossil fuel combustion through a combination of market-based policies (e.g.

imposing taxes on fossil fuel consumption) and administrative controls and regulation. On the other hand, adaptation capacity differs significantly across societies and individuals determined by differences in resource endowments, finance, infrastructure, networks and technology.

17.6 Policies and Institutions on Climate Change

These policies and institutions can be categorized into two: national or domestic and international. National policies refer to policies adopted by individual governments to attempt to address climate change problems to their countries – such as pollution taxes imposed on fossil fuel consumption in the European Union. In Europe as a whole pollution taxes have been targeted on energy, transport, agriculture, and economy. As energy is a major source of both pollution and tax revenue in the OECD economies particularly, attention has tended to be focused on restructuring of energy pricing as a starting point in integrating environment and economy. Air pollution is a major environmental problem in the OECD; strategies here include pollution (emission) taxes, direct controls or legislation, etc. Pollution taxes are aimed at reducing damage to the environment by cutting emissions of GHGs such as methane gasses or carbon dioxide. The rationale for a pollution tax, therefore, is to compel polluting producers to include in their prices the full social costs of production. In the OECD, pollution taxes or eco-taxes are an affirmation of the 'polluter-pays principle' adopted way back in 1974 and ratified by the European Community [now European Union (EU)] in 1975.

International policies transcend national boundaries – e.g. ozone layer depletion caused by chlorofluorocarbons (CFCs). The latter is a global or international problem precisely because all atmospheric concentrations of CFCs, regardless of their geographical origin, affect the ozone layer, which, in turn affects climate. International climate policies are formulated and implemented collectively by national governments who accede to multilateral treaties which usually form the basis of implementing global policies such as the 1997 Kyoto Protocol on climate change in which many nations agreed to impose strict taxes on carbon emissions. However, international efforts to respond to the climate change challenge have produced limited success; such efforts have, until now, foundered on a fundamental free rider problem: briefly, individuals and nations that bear the immediate costs of measures to protect the Earth's atmosphere will experience only a small fraction of the benefits, whereas the latter are shared by all individuals and nations on planet Earth, which encourages individuals and countries to free-ride on others' efforts. Given that climate change is a negative externality, it is, for the most part, futile to appeal to individuals to volunteer to fix it – by taking actions like taking public transport to get to work instead of driving own car to reign in emissions or, in the case of governments, to enforce laws and regulations.

17.7 Factors Undermining International Effort to Reach Agreement on Climate Change

The difficulty of responding to the climate change challenge via international or multilateral agreements arises from the fact, namely, that the costs and benefits of measures to mitigate the GHG effect tend to be shared rather unevenly by countries of the world community. Consequently, negotiations on international climate change agreements tend to be difficult and long-drawn; specifically, among the factors that have affected such negotiations may be identified from the following (World Bank, 1992, p. 158):

- Climate change dynamics differ across countries, defined by geophysical or ecological differences.

- Because climate change dynamics differ across countries, the nature and extent of damage differ across countries and regions: some may find their climate improving (e.g. warmer temperatures and more precipitation, which improve agriculture) and, therefore, gain from climate change, while others may observe opposite effects.

- Even when the pattern of climate change seems similar – as, for instance, for countries in the same equatorial region or temperate region, - it may affect individual countries differently because of differences in ecology, economic activity, or the values placed on natural habitats and other ecosystem or natural resources.

- GHG emissions into Earth's atmosphere differ among countries both in terms of volume and mix. The industrialized economies have been emitting far larger volumes of GHGs for far longer period and have thus contributed a disproportionate share of accumulated GHGs in the atmosphere – some 80% of carbon dioxide from fossil-fuel combustion. On the other hand, GHG emissions from the non-industrialized, low-income countries, starting from a lower base, are growing at a higher rate and are expected to become more important in the future.

- Strategies to **mitigate** GHG emissions are one response to the climate change challenge – they seek to prevent global warming and climate change. Another response seeks to **adapt**, by investing in assets that will mitigate or reduce the losses arising from the impacts of climate change on socioeconomic systems – that is, economic and social activities. The relative costs and benefits of the mitigation and adaptation strategies are bound to differ across countries.

- Some countries are heavily dependent on exports of fossil fuels or forest products (e.g. timber exports from tropical rainforests) and are bound to be adversely affected from policies that would reduce global trade in these products. They might respond by taking measures that undermine international efforts to reach agreements on strategies or global warming and climate change.

17.8 Impact of Globalization

Current world economy is undergoing profound changes reflected most importantly in globalization, whose key features may be summarized in the following five features:

- The rise of the multinational corporations (MNCs) owing allegiance to customers and suppliers dispersed in different parts of the globe rather than to countries or governments as such.
- The development of truly global, intricately interlinked financial markets – investment banks, stock markets, etc.
- The emergence of so-called newly industrialized countries (NICs) located largely in East and Southeast Asia and Latin America, which evolved from the ranks of previously developing countries by exploiting opportunities in global trade, technology transfer, etc. complemented by heavy investments in human capital.
- The evolution of 'huge new regional trading blocs' – e.g. ASEAN, the EU, etc.
- The massive structural transformation in the former Soviet bloc and its reintegration into the global trading and financial systems.

On the one hand, globalization has had profound environmental implications, including climate change, driven by increasing levels of trade and technology transfer processes between and among countries of the global community. On the other hand, this increased global integration between countries has made it yet more difficult for individual countries to legitimately put restrictions on their trade by restricting either imports or exports to mitigate the effects of climate change or maintain environmental quality. Also, globalization has made it difficult for the global community acting as a single collective body – e.g. through the United Nations and its various agencies – to effectively mitigate climate change by regulating international trade flows.

A dilemma facing the global community currently is how to reconcile the need of protecting the global environment from climate change through regulations of global trade flows with that of promoting free trade – a goal that has been pursued since the 1940s with the formation of the General Agreement on Tariffs and Trade (GATT) in 1944, which metamorphosed into the World Trade Organization (WTO) in 1994[1]. WTO rules allow governments to regulate international trade through restrictions on products that have direct health implications, so long this is done in a nondiscriminatory manner. This is interpreted to mean that, for example, setting tight emission standards for automobiles, the use of which increases CO_2 emissions, should apply both to domestic firms and imports. In some cases, global climate agreements have incorporated trade elements – e.g. the Montreal Protocol to reduce and later eliminate trade in emissions below 1990 levels. The actual compliance target is determined as a weighted average of six GHGs: carbon dioxide, methane, nitrous oxide, HFCs, PFGs, and sulphur hexafluoride. Reilly et al. (2002) explain that defining the target in terms of this mitigation index rather than only CO_2 reduced compliance costs by some 22%.

17.9 Over-exploitation and Degradation of Earth's Atmosphere

To return to the key argument of this study, there has occurred over the past two centuries – socalled period of "modern economic growth" *a la* Simion Kuznets – over-exploitation and degradation of Earth's atmosphere as a waste 'sink'. This has resulted in current global warming and climate change facing the global community. The economic literature explains that this over-exploitation and degradation of Earth's atmosphere arises from the fact that the later represents a common pool resource *par excellence*, so that it is impossible to exclude any individual or firm or government from exploiting the services of Earth's atmosphere as a waste 'sink'. As a common-pool resource, Earth's atmosphere raises problems similar to 'public goods'whose 'carrying capacity' ultimately gets undermined and destoyed through over-exploitation and degradation – the tragedy of the commons thesis propounded by ecologist Garret Jones Hardin in a famous 1968 paper in *Science* (vol. 162, no 3859, pp. 1243-1248).

The atmosphere's 'carrying capacity' in the present context refers to the maximum amount of GHGs or gaseous pollutants Earth's atmosphere as a natural waste 'sink' can effectively assimilate without its chemical structure changing to a significantly different state. We have shown that the maximum amount of GHGs Earth's atmosphere can process as a 'sink' has been exceeded; as a result, large stocks of unassimilated GHGs are now left in Earth's atmosphere leading to a fundamental change in Earth's chemical structure – the source of current global warming and climate change problem.

Current atmospheric CO_2 concentrations are significantly higher than anything experienced since the beginning of 'modern economic growth'. In the mid-1700s, around the beginning of the English Industrial Revolution, Earth's atmosphere had 280ppm of CO_2 by the beginning of the 2000s (21st Century), the concentration had exceeded 400ppm. Various IPCC *Assessment Reports* have consistently reported that in order to keep Earth's average surface temperatures from heating up more than 2°C, which would prevent the most disastrous climate outcome, CO_2 concentrations in Earth's atmosphere most not exceed 450ppm. This 2°C target permit the world to emit about 3,200 gigatonnes (Gt) of CO_2 in total. The tally so far is 2,000Gt; and, if annual emissions remain at current levels, the next 30-40 years will witness the balance of 1,200Gt completely exhausted!

At that point in time planet Earth will get over-heated to levels that pose serious danger to human health.

The ideal long-term goal would be to return to 350ppm; this, however, will require negative growth in CO_2 concentrations, apart from limiting further increase in atmospheric CO_2 concentrations. The culprit in the pollution and degradation of Earth's atmosphere is combustion of fossil fuels to drive industrial production and various economic activities. Since the beginning of the 2000s, global increase in coal-based energy has expanded rapidly, thanks to rapid industrial growth in China and India (see Chapter 4). China emits more GHGs than any country in the world presently, because, inter alia, it has a large population: 1.4 population, compared with 250 million for the United States and 550 million for the European Union. However, much of China's pollution, as we have shown, originates in producing goods consumed in other countries.

China was responsible for upwards of 75% of the net coal-based power-generating capacity added world-wide during the period 2000-2014. Apart from China's coal-based energy plants producing GHGs, there is, also, pollution generated in domestic coal-based heating and in textile plants. The situation has turned Chinese cities, especially those located around China's coastal regions, where industrial development has progressed farthest, into "19th Century Manchester" (The Economist, 2015, 28th November).

Other major anthropogenic sources of GHG emissions originate in land-change. The latter has received considerable attention in recent climate change literature, the bulk of this focusing on deforestation in the Brazilian Amazonia region of South America, the Congo basin in Central Africa, and the monsoon rainforests of Southeast Asia-socalled 'hotspots' of tropical rainforest deforestation. Tropical Asia or monsoon Asia presents the highest rates of deforestation and forest degradation among the three 'hot spots' cited above, driven by both high rural population pressure and actually planned conversion programs – e.g. large settlement schemes, involving forest exploitation to extract timber, land conversion for purposes of plantation agriculture, etc. Other dimensions of land-use change, apart from deforestation, involve livestock production (most dominant in South America) and fire burning (of which the peat fires of Indonesia and Malaysia are best known for their CO_2 emissions estimated to amount to 203 megatonnes (Mt) per year – equivalent to emissions from 70 coal plants (Harris and Sargent, 2016). Besides, there is the fire burning episodes in grasslands, of which the African savannas are most notable.

17.10 The Paris Climate Agreement and Bonn Summit

Global strategies to limit Earth surface temperatures to 1.5°C above pre-industrial levels and move towards low GHG emission path or evolve a low GHG emission deveiopment path have been spelled out in the Paris Climate Agreement of December 2015 and re-emphasized in the Bonn Summit of the November 2017. Earlier agreements to mitigate global warming and climate change via imposition of 'caps' on countries'GHG emissions, which was described in the 1997 Kyoto Protocol as holding promise to save planet Earth, seems to have been abandoned after it expired in 2012. But the Kyoto Protocol had achieved little, crippled and beset by disputes right from inception.

In the 2015 Paris Agrement, 195 countries of the world set out to pursue these climate objectives: (i) limit global average temperature increases to 1.5°C above pre-industrial levels; (ii) boost the global community's ability to adopt to the adverse effects of climate change in ways that do not undermine national and global development potentials; and (iii) provide financial flows consistent with a pathway that aligns with low GHG emissions and climate-resilient development. In the Paris Agreement, countries agreed, instead, to reduce, or at least restrain, their own CO_2 emissions on a voluntary basis – socalled "intended nationally determined contributions" (NDCs). The level of NDC set by individual countries will set their emission's targets; and countries are required to report their NDCs every 5 years to the UNFCCC Secretariat and reset their NDCs on the basis of the principle of 'progression' – i.e. each additional contribution should be more ambitious than the previous one.

Perhaps it is too early to conclude that the Paris Agreement will suffer a similar fate as the Kyoto Protocol. But the Paris Agreement, it is pointed out by critics, contains serious loopholes that will undermine its effective implementation. For instance, the NDCs are simply 'promises' lacking no enforcement mechanisms to implement and no sanctions should a country fail to meet its NDC. *The Hindustan Times* of India insists that the Paris Agreement creates room for the free rider syndrome that encourages countries to "free ride on others'" NDCs, which could lead to total collapse of the Agreement (Druzin, 2016).

Meanwhile, economies around the world are pushing forward with strategies to decarbonize their energy systems by moving towards renewable energy sources at a speed hitherto unimagined. At the November 2017 Climate Change Summit in Bonn, Germany, the international community reaffirmed its commitment to the pledges made in the Paris Climate Agreement in December 2015. The Bonn Summit reemphasized the global commitment to limit global warming to a maximum temperature rise of 2°C above pre-industrial levels by 2040-2050. This will require global emissions to decline by more than 50% by 2040-2050, and thereafter continuing to decline towards net zero.

The Bonn Summit was presented with new research from 15 major countries; its sole aim was to give confidence to the countries of the world community that near-zero atmospheric CO_2 emissions could be achieved without undermining economic growth. These 15 countries, in alphabetical order, include: Australia, Brazil, Canada, China, France, Germany, India, Indonesia, Japan, Mexico, Russia, South Africa, South Korea, the United Kingdom (UK) and United States together produce 70% of global GHG emissions (Canadell, et al., 2017). Since these 15 countries have evolved different pathways to move towards the low-carbon energy system by 2050 while sustaining economic growth, their message to the global community would seem to be: every country is free to evolve their own distinct path to achieve the low-carbon development objective and there is no single model for achieving that type of energy transition.

17.11 Global Energy Transition: Shifting from Fossil Fuels to Rewnewable Energy

Shifting from fossil fuels to renewables seems to be the strategy to move the world towards a low-carbon development path that could mitigate the adverse effects of global warming and climate change. Such a path of global economic development, if achieved, would be described as an energy transition. Generally, an energy transition refers to a significant change in the state of an energy system (referring to all components related to the production, conversion, delivery and consumption of energy; an energy system is designed, primarily, to supply energy services to end-users or consumers).

A global energy trasition will involve fundamental structural shifts in the energy systems of all countries of the world. In the present context, this will be reflected in increasing share of renewables (wind, solar, hydro, ocean waves, etc.) in the energy mix and promotion of energy efficiency combined with phasing out fossil fuels. It will involve fundamental changes in terms of structure, scale, prices of energy products, energy policies (referring to the manner in which government decides to address the issues of energy development, including production, distribution and consumption) whose attributes may include, also, legislation, international agreements and treaties, incentives to attract investment into the industry, guidelines on energy conservation, taxation, etc.

Why do energy transitions occur? What induces a shift from one energy sytem to another? The explanation will differ across countries and overtime. Generally, however, energy trasitions seek to achieve one or the other of the following objectives: (i) overcome supply bottlenecks, as for instance, reducing import dependence (eg. United States) or seeking to expand supplies to meet rapidly growing domestic demand (e.g., China); (ii) achieve competitiveness by employing least-cost strategies for supply expansion (e.g., France as from the early 1970s in the wake of the OPEC fuel price hikes); (iii) public pressure to phase out nuclear energy (e.g., Germany in the wake of the 2011 Fukashina nuclear accident in Japan); and (iv) mitigate climate change or protection of the environment (this is the current global objective).

History teaches us that energy trasitions occur for several reasons (Riihl et al., 2012; Podobnik, 1999): exhaustion or depletion of existing energy resource leading to a crisis, as when Britain had to shift from fuelwood to fossil fuels (initially coal) after exhausting its forest trees through deforestation in the 1500s through the 1700s – the later Middle Ages - when Europe was in the throes of the primary capital accumulation that launched the Industrial Revolution by the mid-1700s (Nef, 1977; Fouquet and Peearson, 1998).

17.12 Transition to Clean Energy: Can It Lead to Climate Change?

Given that burning fossil fuels (coal, petroleum, natural gas) has been established by scientific research to be responsible for the greater percentage of global atmospheric GHG emissions, transition to clean energy has been touted to hold the key to addressing the climate change challenge – the most serious environmental problem currently facing the international community. Apart from the climate objective, transition to clean fuel would bring other benefits: energy diversification and security; innovation in new technologies; green jobs; sustainable economic development; improvement in health and welfare through cleaner environment; etc. But what really is meant by clean energy? What potentials are there for clean energy to mitigate climate change? The term clean energy is used in the climate literature to describe all energy resources that generate low-to-zero atmospheric GHG emissions. But this is a rather malleable and elastic definition that creates room for disputes and controversies as to what energy resources actually qualify to be admitted into the clean energy category. Clean energy is sometimes used to describe, specifically, the 'new' renewable energy resources that have zero GHG emission potential. Other definitions include, also, biomass, natural gas, nuclear power, and even 'clean coal' or 'gasified coal'; these energy sources have far lower contribution to atmospheric CO_2 emissions, and take from or degrade Earth's environment to a far less degree than fossil fuels.

In the Paris Climate Change Agreement of 2015, socalled nationally declared contributions (NDCs), as explained earlier, set out the actions and targets nations plan to implement to achieve the objectives of the Paris Agreement, focused on limiting global average temperature increases to well below 1.5°C above pre-industrial levels. Of the 194 Parties to the UNFCCC that submitted NDCs, 145 referred to renewables as a means to mitigate climate change, while 109 cited specific renewable energy targets.

It is expected that countries' upgraded NDCs would feature in the next round of NDCs in 2020. Rapid deployment of renewables, coupled with energy efficiency, could contribute around 90% of the expected decline in GHG emissions in the energy sector needed by 2050, the year the global community is expected to make transition from fossil fuels to renewables. Controversies and disputes still surround 'how clean' some of the renewable fuels classified as clean energy really are? We are referring, specifically to nuclear energy, biomass, and 'clean coal'. We proceed below to highlight elements of these controversies.

17.12.1 Nuclear Power

Nuclear energy is derived from naturally occurring uranium (see Section 14.2.3 of this study). The International Atomic Energy Agency declares that:

"Nuclear power is among the energy sources and technologies…that could help meet the climate-energy challenge. GHG emissions from nuclear power plants (NPPs) are negligible, and nuclear power, together with hydropower and wind-based electricity, is among the lowest GHG emitters when emissions over the entire life cycle are considered, standing at less than 15grams CO_2-equivalent (GCO$_2$-eq) per KW.h (kilowot-hour)." (IAEA, 2016, p.1).

IAEA (op. cit.p.4) points out that climate mitigation is one the salient reasons for considering nuclear energy in future national energy portfolios. However, when, by how much and under what arrangements nuclear energy will contribute to climate mitigation will depend on local conditions, national priorities and international arrangements. The most important factors influencing future CO_2 levels of nuclear energy involve the nuclear life cycle, which includes the following: the quantity and the ore grade of the fresh uranium needed; the efficiency of the enrichment technology; the fuel enrichment requirements; and the carbon intensity of the electricity used in the different process steps in the life cycle (e.g. in the enrichment cycle) (OECD, 2013).

The nuclear capacity required to meet the stringent climate objectives of the Paris Climate Agreement is estimated to range around 950GW by the year 2030. This is more than double the worldwide capacity of the 441 nuclear power plants (NDPs), which was 383GW(c) at the end of 2015. An important outcome of the Paris Agreement is that innovation is absolutely critical for an effective, long-term global response to climate change. It is argued that innovation, together with investment and R&D in cleaner and sustainable technologies and strategies, rather than continued subsidies for polluting activities, is necessary to reach the goal of low-carbon development. It is estimated that during 2015-2030, more than US$400 billion/year would need to be invested in low-carbon power supplies, including US$81 billion/year in nuclear power.

Globally, the top-10 countries in nuclear-based electricity are: France (75%); Luthuania (73%); Belgium (58%); Bulgaria (47%); Slovokia (47%); Sweden (47%); Ukraine (44%); South Korea (43%); Hungary (38%), and Armenia (36%). France's high dependence on nuclear-based electricity has its genesis in the energy crisis of the early 1970s that destabilized the energy balance of several European countries driving them to seek alternatives outside petroleum-based energy. The climate benefits of nuclear-based energy vis-à-vis fossil fuels are key factors in France's and other European countries' – e.g. Belgium – high dependence on this energy source. There is, besides, the well known slow pace of developing alternatives in traditional renewables.

Nuclear energy has, however, gone out of favour in much of the world, much as a result of the potential risk of deadly nuclear accidents (e.g., Christodouleas et al., 2011). Globally, the share of nuclear-based electricity in total supply has declined to about 11% from a peak of 18% in 1996, though some countries – e.g., China, Russia, India, and several Middle East countries including the biggest oil producers, Saudi Arabia, Kuwait, Qatar, United Arab Emirates (UAR), Iran, etc. – are expanding their nuclear-based electricity capacities (Perry, 2010). By 2025 at least 15 new reactors are expected to come on stream in the Middle East (ibid.). World-wide, there are some 450 nuclear plants; China leads with 24 plants under construction, followed by Russia, South Korea, and India. Other countries seeking to expand their capacities include South Africa, Argentina, Brazil, Indonesia, Vietnam and Morrocco. On the other hand, the United States has the 'largest fleet' of nuclear power plants in the world: 104 reactors producing some 20% of the country's electricity generation.

Why the upsurg of interest in nuclear-based energy inspite of the potential for deadly accidents? Why is nuclear-based electricity preferred to other renewables? Several reasons are given for different countries to explain their need to expand nuclear-based electricity. For the United States, for instance, revival of interest in nuclear energy is said to be driven not only by the need for more generating capacity (diversify electricity supply base), but also by favourable "cost comparisons with other fuels, concern about climate change, and improved licensing procedure" (Perry, op. cit.). Other reasons are that while "nuclear plants produce electricity about 90 percent of the time, wind turbines generate, on average, only 30 percent of the time and require back-up electricity from fossil fuel turbines on days when the weather isn't cooperating. Solar electricity is inefficient, providing electricity only 20 percent of the time" (ibid.).

17.12.2 Biomass Energy

Biomass is an alternative energy source that can be based on a number of primary feedstocks (various crops, residues, waste streams and algae). Biomass can provide multiple services such as heat, power, liquid fuels for transport and act as a feedstock for non-energy uses such as chemicals (see Daioglou, 2016; Koch, et al., 2007). Briefly, biomass energy originates in biological or organic matter, namely wood, crops and animal waste. Globally, biomass provides up to 10% of the total primary energy supply in the world. In the developing world, generally, biomass (e.g. wood sourced from communal forests) is the major fuel source for houscholds' cooking and heating purposes aften meeting up to 90%. Extraction of fuelwood from forests is a major cause of deforestation and, hence, major contribution to climate change. In the EU, biomass energy constitutes the largest renewable fuel, accounting for 50% of Europe's total renewable supply, although this share differs across countries: e.g. in Poland, it ranges up to 80% while in Germany, it is just 38%.

Biomass can generate both positive and negative outcomes and its deployment needs to balance a range of environmental, social and economic objectives that could be conflicting (Gustavsson, et al., 2007). Our concern is with the environmental outcomes in particular, and the extent biomass can mitigate climate change. Scientific research finds that biomass has vast potentials from the environmental standpoint. Producing and using biomass limits the use of fossil fuels (Gustavsson, et al., 2007). Biomass use for energy is also climate-friendly because the CO_2 released during biomass combustion is found to be equivalent only to that absorbed by the plants and crops during photosynthesis – i.e., during their growth. So using the plants and crops as biomass simply recycles the CO_2 to the atmosphere, with zero net addition in the concentrations of CO_2 in Earth's atmosphere, plants and soils. Real world conditions differ, however, from this ideal situation in three important ways (Field, Campbell, Lobell, 2007; The Economist, 6th April).

First, the production of biomass energy almost always entails the use of fosil fuels for the farming, transportation and manufacturing phases of the process. Other GHG emissions from agriculture, particularly nitrous oxide, can greatly increase the next climate forcing from biomass energy production. Given that the 100-year global warming potential (GWP) of nitrous oxide is 296 times that of carbon dioxide, small effects on nitrous oxide emissions can have significant effects on overall GHG forcing. Second, the next effect of biomass energy production on climate forcing needs to take into account the changes in the carbon content of the site – e.g. deforestation, which, typically, releases a large fraction of the GHG emissions to the atmosphere.

Third, biomass effect on climate forcing involves the balances between absorption and reflection of solar energy at the surface of the Earth: darker vegetation produces local warming and lighter vegetation produces local cooling. In the tropics, forests produce evapotranspiration and cloud cover, which produce cooling effect, which is an addition to the cooling effect of that caused by the trees.

17.12.3 Biomass Combustion through Fire Burning

As pointed out earlier (see Section 3.6), fire burning produces carbon dioxide, methane, etc. through combustion of biomass. Van der Werf et al. (2010) report that during 1997-2001, over 40% of carbon dioxide emissions came through forest fires in grasslands and savannas. It is found that fire burning in grasslands has the most significant effect on global warming and climate change. African savanna fires may produce a little over of global emissions from biomass combustion, almost all originating in human activities. African savannas are known to be quite vunerable to wild fires, whose emissions are transported over vast areas, including the mid-Atlantic, South Pacific and Indian Oceans (e.g. Levine, 1991).

Both biomass combustion and wind-driven dust also produce large quantities of aerosols; indeed, aerosols (both fossil fuel and industrial processes generated) exert complex influences on climate: both cooling and warming effects. In cooling effect, aerosols reflect away solar radiation; and in warming effect, they trap heat and thus add to the greenhouse effect.

17.12.4 Clean Coal

Also known as 'gasified coal', clean coal has been presented as a low-carbon fuel, whose pollution and other environmental effects (normally associated with combustion of coal widely accepted as the 'dirtiest' fuel) have been permanently captured and sequestered. In its modern usage, clean coal describes coal whose energy efficiency has been greatly boosted by gasification processes to mitigate its CO_2 emissions. Critics dismiss the notion of clean coal as a myth (e.g. Bigger, 2009; Pearce, 2008, 2009; Nijhais, 2014).

Coal combustion is the largest source of anthropogenic GHG emission into the atmosphere. Electricity production using coal produces approximately twice the GHG per kilowat compared to generation based on natural gas. Coal mining, in particular, produces methane, a potent GHG, naturally occurring product of decay of organic matter as coal deposits are formed over geological time. A portion of the methane is absorbed by the coal and later released from the coal seam during the mining process. On the other hand, methane accounts for roughly 11% of the anthropogenic GHG emissions, and has a GWP 21 times greater than that of carbon dioxide over a 100-year time line. The release of methane gas during coal mining is a potential source of deadly coal accidents if 'methane draining' prevention methods are not applied.

Scientists have analysed the effect of coal phase-out on atmospheric carbon dioxide levels, using their baseline mitigation scenerios of global coal emissions by 2050. If current coal-based carbon dioxide emissions continued atmospheric carbon dioxide peaks at 563ppm in the year 2100; if coal is phased out, (under 4 scenerios) atmospheric carbon dioxide peaks at 422-446ppm between 2047 and 2060, declining thereafter (Charecha and Hansen, 2008).

17.13 Renewables Slowing Down Growth in CO_2 Emissions?

There are signs that global CO_2 emissions are slowing down. Flat trends were observed three years in a row (2014-2016) in global CO_2 emissions from combustion of fossil fuels and industries: global CO_2 levels amounted to 36.3 billion tonnes in 2015, the same in 2014, and grew by only 0.2% in 2016 to reach 36.4 billion tonnes (Canadell et al. op. cit). These trends are a departure from CO_2 emission growth rates of 2.3% in previous decades (ibid.).

The decline in CO_2 emissions during 2014-2016 origiated primarily in China: after relatively slow growth in earlier decades, China's CO_2 growth rose rapidly in the 2000s up until 2014 and then began to flatten out, a change explained as originating largely in economic factors such as the end of the construction boom, weaker global demand for steel, etc.These efforts by China to reduce its air pollution reflected in the growth of solar and wind energy. The USA and EU also have contributed to the slowdown, largely driven by growth in energy efficiency, movement away from coal-based electricity and replacement with natural gas, and renewable energy. What distinguishes the flattening of CO_2 emissions growth during 2014-2016 is that global economic growth continued (at more than 3% per annum). This contrasts with previous experiences that were driven by stagnant or shrinking economies – e.g. the global financial crisis of 2008.

End Notes

[1]   The WTO was announced in the Marrakesh Declaration of April 15, 1994, which marked the successful conclusion of the long-drawn-out Uruguay Round of multilateral negotiations on elimination of barriers to international trade. By July 2008 the WTO had 153 member countries – very close to the total membership of the United Nations (at 192 in 2008).

REFERENCES

Abate, R.S. and Warner, E.A.K., (eds.) 2013 *Climate Change and Indigenous Peoples – The Search for Legal Remedies;* Edward Elgar.

Abbasi, T., Premalatha, M. and Abbasi, S.A. 2011 "The Return to Renewables: Will it Help in Global Warming Control?" *Renewable and Sustainable Energy Reviews,* Vol. 15, No. 1, pp. 891-894. doi: 10.1016/j.rser.2010.09.048.

Achard, F., Eva, H.D., Stibig, H.J., Mayoux, P., Gallega, J., Richards, T., and Malingreau, J–P. 2002 "Determination of Deforestation Rates of the World's Humid Tropical Forests" *Science,* 297, 999 – 1002.

Adams, W.M. 1992 *Wasting the Rain: Rivers, People and Planning in Africa;* London: Earthscan.

Adams, W.M. 2009 *Green Development: Environment and Sustainability in a Developing World* 3rd edition; London & New York: Routledge Taylor & Francis Group.

ADB 2009 *The Economics of Climate Change in Southeast Asia: A Regional View*; Manilla: Asia Development Bank.

Adhikari, U., Nejadhashemi, A.P., Woznicki, S.A. 2015 "Climate Change and Eastern Africa: A Review of Impact on Major Crops". *Food and Energy Security,* 4(2), 110-132 (July).

Adler, J., Arthurton, R., Ash, N. et al. 2006 *Marine and Coastal Ecosystems and Human Well-Being;* Nairobi: United Nations Environmental Programme.

AfricaFiles (http://www.africafiles.org).

Agardy, T., Adler, J., Dayton, P. et al. 2005 "Coastal Systems" In: Rashid Hassan, Robert Schoks and Neville Ash, (eds.), *Ecosystems and Human Well-being: Current Status and Trends*, pp. 513-19 Washington D.C.: Island Press.

Agence France Presse (2015, 17th September) "Southeast Asia's Haze: What's Behind the Annual Outbreak"? *Agence France Presse,* 17th September.

Agyei, Y., 2009 "Deforestation in Sub-Sahara Africa" *African Technology Forum,* 8(1).

Ainsworth, E.A. and Long, S.P. 2005 "What have we learned from 15 years of free-air CO_2 enrichment (FACE)? A meta-analysis of the responses of photosynthesis, canopy properties and plant production to rising CO_2" *New Phytology,* Vol. 165, pp.351-372. doi: 10.1111/j.1469-8137.2004.01224x.

Akinbami, J. 2003 "An Integrated Strategy for Sustainable Forestry-energy-environment Interaction in Nigeria" *Journal of Environmental Management,* Vol. 69, No. 2, pp. 115-28.

Alenar, A., Nepstad, D. and Moutinho, P. 2005 "Carbon Emissions Associated with Forest Fires in Brazil" In P. Moutinho and S. Schwantzman, (eds.,) *Tropical Deforestation and Climate Change,* Washington D.C.: Environmental Defense / IPAM Brazil.

Ali, A. 1996 *Vulnerability of Bangladesh to Climate Change and Sea Level Rise through Tropical Cyclones and Storm Surge;* Springer Link.

Aligica, P.D. 2009 "Julian Simon and the "Limits to Growth" Neo-Malthusianism" *The Electronic Journal of Sustainable Development,* Vol. 1, No. 3.

Allen, J. (2001, 6th September) "Ultraviolet Radiation: How It Affects Life on Earth" *NASA Earth Observatory,* September 6. (Accessed 19th April 2016).

Allen, J.C. and Barnes, D.F. 1985 "The causes of deforestation in developing countries" *Annals of the Association of American Geographer,* Vol. 75, pp. 163-84.

Allen, W. 1958 "Solar Radiation" *Quarterly Journal of the Royal Meteorological Society,* Vol. 84, Issue 362 (October), pp. 307-318.

Allison, I. 2010 *The Science of Climate Change: Questions and Answers;* Canberra: Australian Academy of Science.

Allwood, J.M., Bosetti, V., Dudash, N.K., Gimo-Echeverri, L, von Stedow. 2014 "Annex 1: Glossory, acronyms and chemical symbols". In: *IPCC Climate Change 2014: Mitigation of climate change, contribution of Working Groups III to the Fifth Assessment Report of the Intergovernmental Panel on Climate Change,* Cambridge University Press.

Aluko, M.A.O. 2004 "Sustainable development, environmental degradation and the entrenchment of poverty in the Niger Delta of Nigeria" *Journal of Human Ecology,* Vol. 15, pp. 63-8.

American Climate Choice 2011 *American Climate Choice;* Washinigton D.C.: The National Academy Press.

American Geophysical Union, (1999, 12th July)"Sahara's Abrupt Desertification Started By Change: In Earth's Orbit, Accelerated By Atmospheric and Vegetation Feedbacks" *Science Daily,* Retrieved September 8, 2013 from http://www.sciencedaily.com/releases/ 1999/ 990712080500.htm.

Ames, P. 2009 "Climate Change in Palau: one of the world's smallest and newest nations" *Global Post,* December 16. http://www.globalpost.com/notebbok/global-green/091216/climate-change-palau-one-the-worlds-smallest-and-newest-nation Retrieved 8 August 2013.

Amsalu, A. and Adem, A. 2009 *Assessment of climate change-induced hazards, impacts and responses in the Southern lowlands of Ethiopia*; Addis Ababa: Forum for Social Studies.

Anand, P.B. 2010 *Scarcity, Entitlements and the Economics of Water in Developing Countries;* Edward Elgar.

Anderson, D. 1987 *The Economics of Afforestation: A Case Study in Africa*; Baltimore: The Johns Hopkins University Press.

Andrady, A.L., Hamid, H.S. and Torika, A. 2003 "Effects of Climate Change and UV-B Materials" *Photochem Photobiol. Sci.,* Vol. 2, No. 1, pp. 68-72.

Andrady, A.L., Hamid, S.H., Hu, X. and Torikai, A. 1998 "Effects of Increased Solar Ultraviolet Radiation on Materials" *Journal of Photochem Photobiol* B., Vol. 46, No. 1-3, pp. 8-103.

Andrae, G. and Beckman, B: 1985 *The Wheat Trap: Bread and Underdevelopment in Nigeria;* London: Zed Books.

Angelson, A. 2008 "Moving Ahead with REDD: Issues, Options and Implications" CIFOR:Indonesia (http://www.cifor.org/publications/pdffiles/Books/BAngelson0801.pdf

Angelson, A. and Kaimovitz, D. 1999 "Rethinking the Cause of Deforestation: Lesson from Economic Models" *The World Bank Research Observer,* Vol. 14, No. 1, pp 73-98.

Angelson, A. and Rudel, T.K. 2013 "Designing and Implementing Effective REDD+ Policies: A Forest Transition Approach" *Review of Environmental Economics and Policy,* Vol. 7, No. 1.

Angelson, A., Brockhaus, M., Sunderlin, W.D., and Verchot, L.V. 2012 *Analyzing REDD+ Challenges and Choices;* Boger (Indonesia): CIFOR Available @ http:www.cifor.org/publications/pdf_files/Books/BAngelsen/201.pdf

Angelson, A., Strack, C., Paskett, L., Brown, J. and Luttrell, C. 2008 *What is the Right Scale for REDD? National, Subnational and Nested Approaches;* CIFOR: Indonesia.

Anthoff, D.I., Nicholls, R.G., and Tol, R.S.J. 2010 "The economic impact of substantial sea-level rise" *Mitigation and Adaptation Strategies for Global Change,* Vol.15, pp. 321-335.

Anthony, K.R.N., Kline, D.I., Diaz-Pulido, G., Dove, S. and Hoegh-Guldberg, O. 2008 "Ocean Acidification Causes Bleaching and Productivity Loss in Coral Reef Builders" *Proceedings of the National Academy of Sciences,* Vol. 105, No. 45, pp. 17442-446.

Appeldoorn, Van G.J. 1981 *Perspective on Drought and Famine in Nigeria;* London: Allen & Unwin.

Aredo, D. 2010 "The Iddir: An informal insurance arrangement in Ethiopia" *Savings and Development,* 1 (xxxiv), pp. 53-72.

Aren't, D.J., Wise, A. and Gelman, R. 2010 "The Status and Prospects of Renewable Energy for Combating Global Warming" *Energy Economics,* Vol. 33, No. 4, pp. 584-593. doi: 10.1016/eneco.2010.11.003.

Arnold, J.E.M. and Jongma, J. 2016 "Fuel wood and Charcoal in Developing Countries: An Economic Survey" FAO (www.fao.org/docrep/12015e/12015e01.htm).

Arnold, M. 2008 "The Role of Risk Transfer and Insurance in Disaster Risk Reduction and Climate Change Adaptation" *Commission on Climate Change and Development. (htt://www.ccdcommission.org),* January.

Arnolds, O. 2000 "Desertification: An appeal for a broader perspective" *In: Rangeland Desertification,* (eds.), Arnolds, O. and Archer, S. Klniver, Academic Publishers.

Aronsson, T. and Lofgreen, K. (eds.) 2010 *Handbook of Environmental Accounting:* Edward Elgar.

Arrhenius, S. 1896 "On the Influence of Carbonic Acid in the Air upon the Temperature of the Ground". *Philosophical Magazine and Journal of Science, (Fifth Series),* Vol. 41, pp. 237-76, April.

Arrhenius, S. 1908 *Worlds in the Making;* New York: Harper & Brothers.

Arrow, K.J. 2000 "Keynote Address: Knowledge as a factor of production". In: Boris Pleskovic and Joseph E. Stiglitz, (eds.) *Annual World Bank Conference on Development Economics 1999,* Washington D.C.: The World Bank.

ASEAN, 2011 "Peatlands in Southeast Asia: Profile" *ASEAN Secretariat and Global Environment Centre.*

Asiyanbi, P.A., Arhin, A.A., Isyaku, U. 2017 "REDD+ in West Africa: Politics of Design and Implementation in Ghana and Nigeria" *Forests,* March. (doi:10.3390/f8030078)

Associated Press, (2002, 21st July) "1970-85 Famine Blamed on Pollution" *Associated Press,* 21 July.

Associated Press, (2011, 6th July) "Dust Storm Swallows Phoenix" *Associated Press,* July 6.

Astaiza, R. (2012, 12th October) "Islands that will vanish when Sea Levels Rise" *Business Insider.* (http://www.businessinsider.com/isla) Retrieved August 6, 2013.

Astyanbi, P.A., Arhin, A.A., and Isyaku, U. 2017 "REDD+ in West Afrrica: Politics of Design and Implimentation in Ghana and Nigeria" *Forests,* (March) (doi: 10:10.3390/f8030078)

Atkinson, G., Dietz, S. and Neumayer, E. (eds,) 2008 *Handbook of Sustainable Development;* Edward Edgar.

Atkinson, G., Dietz, S. and Neumayer, E. (eds.) 2007 *Handbook of Sustainable Development;* Edward Elgar.

Aubréville, A. 1949 *Climates, forêts et désertification de Afrique tropicale* (Climates, forests and desertification of Tropical Africa), Société d' Edition Geographiques, Maritimes et Coloniales, Paris.

Australian Broadcasting Corporation, (2009, 23rd September) "Brisbane on alert as dust storms sweep east" *Australian Broadcasting Corporation.*

Baker, K.M. 1995 "Drought, agriculture and environment: a case study from the Gambia, West Africa" *African Affairs,* Vol. 94, pp. 67-86.

Baker, T., 1995 *Equity and Social Considerations in Climate Change 1995: Economic and Social Dimensions of Climate Change* (Contribution of Working Group III to the 2nd Assessment Report of IPCC); Cambridge University Press.

Bannock, G., Baxter, R.E. and Davis, E. 1998 *The Economist Books Dictionary of Economics;* John Wiley & Sons Inc.

Barbier, E. B. 1998 "Valueing environmental functions: tropical wetlands" pp. 344-69 In: E.B. Barbier *The Economics of Environment and Development Related Essays* Cheltenham: Edward Elgar.

Barrett, S. 2003 *Environment and Statecraft: The Strategy of Environmental Treaty-Making;* Oxford: Oxford University Press.

Barrett, S. 2007 *Why Cooperate? The Incentive to Supply Global Public Good;* Oxford: University Press.

Barros, et al. 2011 "Carbon Emission from Hydroelectric Reservoirs Linked to Reservoir Age and Latitude" *Nature Geoscience,* Vol. 4, pp. 593-96.

Barry, J.P., Baxter, C.H., Sagarin, R.D. and Gilnon, S.E. 1995 "Climate- Related, Long-Term Faunal Changes in a California Rocky Intertidal Community" *Science,* 267, no. 5198, pp.672-675.

Batterbury, S. 2001 "The Sahel region: assessing progress twenty-five years after the great drought" Republished paper from 1998-R GS-IBG Conference: *Global Environmental Change,* Vol. 11, No. 1, pp. 1-95.

Baykoff, M. and Baykoff, J. 2004 "Balance as Bias: Global Warming and US Prestige" Press 1 *Global Environmental Change,* Part A 14, 2, 125-36.

BBC News (2008, 18th June) "Australian rivers 'Face Disaster'" *BBC News,* London.

BBC News (2008, 28th May) 'Nature loss to hurt global poor' *BBC News,* London.

BBC News (2008, 29th May) "Nature Loss to Hurt Global Poor". *BBC News,* London.

BBC News (2015, 16th September) "What Causes South-East Asia's Haze?" *BBC News,* London.

Behr, P. and Marshall, C. (2009, 5th August) "Is shale gas the climate bill's new bargaining chip?" *New York Times.*

Behrenfeld, M.J. et al. 2001 "Biopherii Primary Production during the ENSO Transition", *Science,* 291, 2594-2597.

Berg, H. 2011 *Transition of Energy Regime: An Evolutionary Economic Interpretation,* Dissertation, Borgische Universitat Wupertal, Germany.

Berg, M. and Hudson, P. 1992 "Rehabilitating the Industrial Revolution" *The Economic History Review,* Vol. 45, No. 1, pp. 24-50.

Bergstrom, J.C. and Randall, A. 2010 *Resource Economics: An Economic Approach to Natural Resource and Environmental Policy;* 3rd edition, Edward Elgar.

Bernstein, L., Pachauri, R.K. and Reinsinger, A. 2008 *Climate Change 2007: Synthesis Report;* IPCC.

Bernus, E. 1975 "Human Geography in the Sahelian Zone" In *The Sahel: Geographical Approaches to Land Use, MAB Technical Report,* UNESCO Press.

Bertani, R. and Thain, I. 2002 "Geothermal Power Generating Plant CO_2 Emission Survey" *IGA News* (International Geothermal Association), Vol. 49, pp. 1-3.

Bewket, W. and Conway, D. 2007 "A note on the temporal and spatial variability of rainfall in the drought-prone Anihara Region of Ethiopia" *International Journal of Climatology,* Vol. 27, pp. 1467-1477.

Bewket, W. and Sterk, W. 2005 "Dynamics in land cover and its effect on stream flow in the chemoga watershed, Blue Nile Basin, Ethiopia" *Hydrological Processes,* Vol. 19, pp. 445-58.

Bhargava, V. (ed.) 2006 *Global Issues for Global Citizens* Washington D C.: The World Bank.

Biazin, B. and Sterk, G. 2013 "Drought vulnerability drives land-use and land cover changes in the Rift Valley dry lands of Ethiopia" *Agriculture, Ecosystems and Environment,* Vol. 164, pp. 100-113.

Biello, D. (2010, 6th April) "What is Geoingeneering and why is it considered a Climate Change Solution?" *Scientific American.*

Bigger, J. (2008, 2nd March) "'Clean Coal'? Don't Try to Shovel That" *The Washington Post.*

Bindoff, N.L. et al, 2007 "Observations: Oceanic climate change and sea level." In: *Climate Change 2007: The Physical Science Basis. Contribution of Working Group 1 to the Fourth Assessment Report of the Intergovernmental Panel on Climate Change* Solomon, S. et al (eds.), Cambridge (UK) and New York: Cambridge University Press 2007.

Binswanger, H.P. 1991 "Brazilian policies that encourage deforestation in the Amazon" *World Development,* Vol. 19, pp. 821-29.

Birkett, M.-T.S, 2000 "Fishing and Farming at Lake Chad: Responses to Lake-level Fluctuations" *Geographic Journal,* Vol. 166, No. 2, pp. 156-172.

Black, J., 2002 *Oxford Dictionary of Economics*; 2nd edition Oxford and New York: Oxford University Press.

Black, R. (2006, 12th October) "New Dawn for Liberia's "Blood Forests" *BBC News,* London.

Black, R. (2008, 8th October) "Fisheries waste costs billions" *BBC News,* London

Blackwell, J.M., Roger, N.G., and Richard, W. 1991 *Environment and Development in Africa; Selected Case Studies;* EDI Development Policy Case Series, Analytical Case Studies No. 6, Washington D.C.: The World Bank.

Blaikie, P. 1985 *The Political Economy of Soil Erosion in Developing Countries;* London: Longman.

Blaikie, P. and Brookfield, H. 1987 *Land Degradation and Society*; London: Methuen.

Blakemore, Bill (2009, 9th December) "Micronesia: A Third Kind of Nation, Written Off?" *ABC News.*

Bliss–Guest, P.A. and Keckes, S. 1982 "The Regional Sea Programme of UNEP" *Environmental Conservation,* Vol. 9, pp. 43-9.

Bloeman, S. 2011 "Lake Chad's receding water level heightens risks of malnutrition and disease" http://www.unicef.org/infobycountry/chad_57642.html.

Bodeen, C. (2010, 11th April) "China's sandstorms blast Beijing with dust, sand" *Associated Press.*

Boden, T.A., Marland, G. and Andres, R.J. 2017 Natural CO_2 Emissions from Fossil-fuel Burning, Cement Manufactoring, and Gas Flaring: 1751-2014. Carbon Dioxide Information Analysis Center, Oak Ridge National Laboratory, US Department of Energy. doi: 10.3334/ CDIA/0000_V2017

Boden, T.A., Marland, G., and Andres, R.J. 2017 *National CO₂ Emissions from Fossil-Fuel Burning, Cement Manufacturing and Gas Flaring 1751-2014;* Carbon Dioxide Information Analyzing Centre, Oak Ridge, USA.

Bohm, P. 1997 *The Economics of Environmental Protection; Theory and Demand Revelation (New Horizons in Environmental Economics);* Edward Elgar.

Bohm, R.,A., Ge, C., Russel, R., Wang, J. and Yang, J. 1998 "Environmental Taxes: China's Bold New Initiative" *Environment,* Vol. 40, no 1 (September).

Bolster, W.J. 2012 *The Mortal Sea: Fishing the Atlantic in the Age of Sail* Belkap Press.

Bonnie, R. and Schwartzman, S. 2003 "Tropical Reforestation and Deforestation and the Kyoto Protocol" *Conservation Biology,* Vol. 17, pp. 4-5.

Booth, A. 2012 "Woodfuel Causes Deforestation in Congo Basin yet is Potential Renewable Energy Source" *CIFOR Forest News: Center for Internationational Forest Research (CIFOR).* Accessed 21 May, 2016.

Bosetti, V. and Lubowski, R. (eds.,) 2010 *Deforestation and Climate Change;* Edward Elgar.

Bosetti, V., Carraro, C., Massetti, E. and Tavoni, M. (eds.) 2014 *Climate Change Mitigation, Technical Innovation and Adaptation: A New Perspective on Climate Change Policy*; Edward Elgar.

Botkin, D.B. 1990 *Discordant Harmonies: A new ecology for the twenty-first century;* New York: Oxford University Press.

Boubacar, I. 2010 "The Effect of Drought on Crop Yield and Yield Variability in Sahel" Selected paper for presentation at the Southern Agiculture Economics Association Annual Meeting, Orlando: Florida, February 6-9.

Boubacar, I. 2012 "The Effects of Drought on Crop Yields and Yield Variability: An Economic Assessment" *International Journal of Economics and Finance,* Vol. 4, No. 12.

Bowen, A., Romani, M., and Stern, N. 2010 "Challenge of the Century" *Finance & Development*, March.

Boykoff, M. and Boykoff, J. 2004 "Balance as Bias: Global Warming and the US Prestige Press" *Global Environmental Change,* Part A Vol. 14, No. 2, pp. 125-136.

Bradley, R.S., Briffa, K.R., Cole, J., Hughes, M.K. and Osborne, T.J. 2003 "The Climate of the Last Millennium" In: K.D. Alverson, R.S. Bradley and T.F. Pederson *Paleoclimate, Global Change and the Future*, pp. 105-141 Springer.

Brahic, C. 2006, 6ᵗʰ May) "Wet or Dry? Sahel's uncertain future" *SciDevNet.* Retrieved 26 August 2013.

Bren, L. 2003 "The genetic engineering: the future of food" *FDA Consumer Magazine*, November – December (http://www.fdd.gov/educ/features/2003/603_food.html).

Bringezu, S., Schutz, H., Steger, S., and Bandisch, B. 2004 "International comparison of resource use and its relation to economic growth" *Ecological Economics,* Vol. 51, 1-2.

Brink, A.B. and Hugh, D.E. 2009 "Monitoring 25 years of land cover change dynamics in Africa: a sample based on remote sensing approach" *Applied Geography,* Vol. 29, no. 501-512 doi: 10.1016/j.apgeog.2008.10.004.

Broecker, W., 1975 "Climate Change: Are we on the Brink of a Pronounced Global Warming", *Science,* 189, 460-63.

Broecker, W.S., 2006 "Breeding Easy: et tu, O_2" Columbia University.

Brooks, N. 2003 "Vulnerability, risk and adaptation: A conceptual framework" Tyndall Centre for Climate Change *Research Working Paper 38*, November http:/www.tyndall.ac.uk/sites/default/files/wp38.pdf. Retrieved 4 Sept. 2013.

Brooks, N. 2004 "Drought in the African Sahel: Long term perspectives and future prospects" *Saharan Studies Program and Tyndall Centre for Climate Change Research Working Paper 61*, October.

Brooks, R. (2013, 13th August) "A New Study shows Sea-Level Rise Made Flooding from Harrican Sandy Worse. Surprise!" *BBC News.* http.//www.bbc.co.uk/news/world_europe_227525444_sandy_flooding.php. Retrieved 13th August 2013.

Brough, W.T. and Kimenyi, M.S. 2004 "Desertification of the Sahel – Exploring the Role of Property Rights" *PERC Report, Vol. 22. No.2* (Summer) http://perc.org/articles/desertification_sahel.

Brown, T.C., Bergstron, J.C. and Loomis, J.B. (2007) "Defining, Valuing and Providing Ecosystem Foods and Services", *Natural Resource Journal,* Vol. 77, No.2 pp. 329-76.

Brundtland, H. 1987 *Our Common Future;* Oxford University Press for the World Commission on Environmental and Development (WCED).

Brunnee, J. 2008 "International Legislation" *Max Planck Encyclopedia of Public International Law*, Oxford University Press.

Bryden, H.L., Longworth, H.R. and Cunningham, S.A. 2005 "Slowing of the Atlantic Meridional Overturning Circulation at 250N" *Nature,* Vol. 438, pp. 655-7, 1 December.

Buchheim, J. 1998-2013 *Coral Reef Bleaching.* (http://www.marinebiology.org/coral bleaching.htm) Retrieved 14th August 2013.

Budyko, M.I. 1969 "The Effect of Solar Radiation Variations on the Climate of the Earth", *Tellus,* 21, 611-19.

Budyko, M.I. 1971 *Climate Life;* Leningrad.

Budyko, M.I. 1972 "The Future Climate", *EOS, Transactions of the American Geographical Union,* 53, 868-74.

Budyko, M.I. 1977 *Climate Changes: Translation of Izmeniia Klimata (Leningrad: Gidrometeoizdat, 1974);* Washington D.C.: American Geophysical Union.

Budyko, M.I. and Kerol, I.L. 1975 "Man's Impact on the Global Climate" In: *Proceedings of the WMO/IAMAP Symposium on Long-Term Climate Fluctuations, Norwich,* August 1975 (WMO Dec. 421), ed. WMO, pp. 465-71, Geneva: World Meteorological Organization.

Buijs, B. 2011 "Why China Matters" Chapter 15 *Energy, Sustainability and the Environment:Technology, Incentives, Behavior;* Elsevier, Inc.

Buis, A., Ramsayer, K. and Rasmursen, C. 2015 "A Breathing Planet, Off Balance" *NASA* (13 November).

Butler, R. 2012 "A World Imperiled: Forces Behind Forest Loss" *rainforests.mongabay.com* Accessed 17 May 2015.

Byron, N. and Arnold, M. 1999 "What Future for the People of the Tropical Forests?" *World Development,* Vol. 27, pp. 789-805.

Cahoon, Jr., D.R., Stocks, B.J., Levine, J.S., Cafer III, W.R. and O'Neill, K.P. 1992 "Seasonal Distribution of African Savanna Fires" *Nature,* Vol. 359, pp. 812-815 doi: 10.1038/35 9812aO.

Callendar, G.S. 1938 "The Artificial Production of Carbon Dioxide and Its Influence on Climate" *Quarterly Journal of the Royal Meteorological Society,* Vol. 64, pp. 223-40.

Callendar, G.S. 1939 "The Composition of the Atmosphere through the Ages" *Meteorological Magazine,* Vol. 74, pp. 33-39.

Callendar, G.S. 1940 "Variations in the Amount of Carbon Dioxide in Different Air Currents" *Quarterly Journal of the Royal Meteorological Society,* Vol. 66, pp. 395-400.

Callendar, G.S. 1941 "Infrared Absorption by Carbon Dioxide, with Special Reference to Atmospheric Radiation" *Quarterly Journal of the Royal Meteorological Society,* Vol. 67, pp. 263-75.

Callendar, G.S. 1949 "Can Carbon Dioxide Influence Climate" *Weather,* Vol. 41, pp. 310-14.

Callendar, G.S. 1958 "On the Amount of Carbon Dioxide in the Atmosphere" *Tellus,* Vol. 10, pp. 243-48.

Callendar, G.S. 1961 "Temperature Fluctuations and Trends over the Earth" *Quarterly Journal of the Royal Meteorological Society,* Vol. 87, pp. 1-12.

Canadell, J.C. and 9 Others 2007 "Contributions to accelerating atmospheric CO_2 growth from economic activity, carbon intensity, and efficiency of natural sinks" *Proceedings of the National Academy of Sciences,* USA.

Canadell, P., Le Quere, C., Peters, G., Andrew, R.I., Jackson, R., Havard, V. (2017,13[th] November) "Fossil fuel emissions hit record high after unexpected growth: Global Carbon Budget 2017", *The Conversation.*

Cane, M. et al. 1997 "Twentieth-century sea surface temperature trends" *Science,* 275: 957-960.

Canfield, C. 1982 *Tropical Moist Forests: The Resources, The Forests;* London: Earthscan/HED.

Capoor, K. and Ambrosi, P. 2007 *State and Trends of the Carbon Market 2007;* World Bank Institute.

Carbon Trust, 2009 "Global Carbon Mechanisms: Emerging lessons and implications", *Carbon Trust,* March. Retrieved May 28, 2017.

CARE ALP 2013 *Climate change vulnerability and adaptive capacity in Garissa country; Kenya* CARE Adaptation Learning Programme (http://www.careclimatechange.org/ files/CVCA Kenya Report.pdf).

Carina, E. and Keskitalo, H. (eds.) 2012 *Climate Change and Flood Risk Management: Adaptation and Extreme Events at the Local Level;* Edward Elgar

Castro, P. 2014 *Climate Change Mitigation in Developing Conutries: A Critical Assessment of the Clean Developing Mechanism;* Edward Elgar.

Cavendish, W. 1999 "Poverty, Inequality and Environmental Resources: Quantitative Analysis of Rural Households" *Working Paper Series WPS / 99-99,* Centre for the Study of African Economies (CSAE), University of Oxford.

CCSP 2008 United States Climate Change Science Programme. Montzka, S.A. et al. (eds.) *Trends in Emissions of Ozone-Depleting Substances, Ozone Layer Recovery and Implications for Ultraviolet Radiation Exposure* Asheville; NC: Department of Commerce, NOAA's National Climate Data Center.

Central Europe Floods 2013 "2013 European Floods" http://en.wikipedia.org/ wiki/2013_European_floods.

Cerda, E. and Lanbandeira, X. (eds.) 2010 *Climate Change Policies;* Edward Elgar.

Change-Seng, D. 2004 *Sechelles climate change scenarios for vulnerability and adaptation assessmen;* prepared for the seqchelles 2nd Natural communication (SNC) under the UNFCCC and with the Guidance of the Natural Climate Change Committee, October.

Chapin III, F.S. and Eleven Others 2000 "Consequences of changing biodiversity" *Nature,* Vol. 405, 234-242 (11 May) doi: 10. 1038 / 35012241.

Chapin, F.S., Muston, P.A., Mooney, H.A., (2002) *Principles of Terrestrial Ecosystem Ecology;* New York: Springer.

Charecha, P.A. and Hansen, J.E. 2008 "Implications of 'peak oil' for atmospheric $CO2$ and climate", *Global Biogeochem. Cycles,* 22. doi: 10.29/2007GB003142

Charney, J .G. 1975 "Dynamics of deserts and drought in the Sahel" *Quarterly Journal of the Royal Meteorological Society,* Vol. 101 (428), pp. 193-202.

Chen, R.J.C. 2011 "Effects of Climate Change in North America: An Overview" *Journal of Sustainable Development,* Vol. 4, No. 3 doi: http://dx.doi.org/10.5539/jsd.v4n3p32).

Chidumayo, E.N. and Gambo, D.J. (eds) 2010 *The dry forests and woodlands of Africa: managing for products and services;* London: Earthscan.

Chidumayo, E.N. and Gambo, D.J. 2013 'The Environmental Impacts of Charcoal Production in Tropical Ecosystems of the World: A synthesis". *Energy for Sustainable Development,* Vol. 17, No. 2, pp. 86-94.

Chomitz, K.M. and Kumari, K. 1998 "Domestic Benefits of Tropical Forests: A Critical Review" *The World Bank Research Observer,* Vol. 13, No. 1, pp. 13-35.

Christensea, J.H. and Christensea, O.B. 2003 "Climate modelling: several summertime flooding in Europe" *Natural,* 421,805-806.

Christian-Albrechts-Unviersitaet Zu Kiel, (2008, 7th October) "The Green Sahara, A Desert in Bloom" *Science Daily.* Retrieved September 8 2013, from http://www.sciencedaily.com.

Christodouleas, J.P., Forrest, R.D., Ainsley, C.G., Tochner, Z., Hahn, S.M., Glatstein, E. 2011 "Short-Term and Long-Term Health Risks of Nuclear-Power-Plant Accidents" *The New England Journal of Medicine,* Vol. 364, pp. 2334-2341. doi: 1056/NEJMra1103676.

Christy, J.R., Norries, W.B. and McNider, R.T. 2009 "Surface temperature variation in East Africa and possible causes" *Journal of Climate,* Vol. 22, pp. 3342-56.

Chueca., J., Asuncion, J., Lopez- Morino, J.I. 2007 "Recent evolution (1981-2005) of the Maladeta glaciers, Pyrenees, Spain: extent and volume losses and their relation with climatic and topographic factors" *Journal of Glaciology,* Vol. 53, No. 183, pp. 547-57, Retrieved 9th August 2013.

Church, J.A. and White, N.J. 2006 "A 20th century acceleration in global Sea Level Rise" *Geophysical Research Letters,* 33: 4 pp.

Church, J.A. et al., 2001 "Changes in Sea Level". In J.T. Houghton et al. (eds) *Climate Change 2001: The Scientific Basis,* pp539-694 New York: Cambridge University Press.

Church, J.A., White, N.J., Coleman, R., Lambeck, K. and Mitrovica, J.X. 2004 "Estimates of the regional distribution of sea level rise over the 1950-2000 period" *Journal of Climate,* 17, 2609-2625.

CIFOR, 2007 Centre for International Forestry Research (CIFOR) "Beef Exports Fuel Loss of Amazonian Forest" *Centre for International Forestry Research,* (2007-11-27).

Cisneros, J, and Fong, A. 2012 *Forest Carbon Projects in Africa: A Mapping Study;* Background Report for the Political Ecologies of Forest Carbon in Africa Rsearch Project, 28 November, STEPS Centre.

Cisneros, J.A.F. 2012 *Forest Carbon Projects in Africa: A Mapping Study;* Background Report for the Political Ecologies of Forest Carbon in Africa Research Project, 28 November, STEPS Center.

Clark, D. (2011, 21st April) "Which Nations are most responsible for Climate Change?" *theguardian. com* (Accessed 1st June 2016).

Clark, R. and Timberlake, L. 1982 *Stockholm Plus Ten: Promises? The Decade since the 1972 UN Environment Conference;* London: Earthscan.

Cleaver, K. 1994 "Deforestation in the Western and Central African forests: The agricultural and demographic causes, and some solutions" pp. 65-78 In: K. Cleaver (ed.) *Conservation of West and Central African Rainforests,* World Bank Environmental Paper No. 1, Washington D.C.

Cleaver, K. and Schreiber, G. 1993 "The population, agriculture and environment nexus in sub-Saharan Africa." *Africa Technical Department Working Paper.* World Bank, Washington D.C.

Cline, W.R. 2007 *Global Warming and Agriculture: Impact Estimates by Country;* Washington: Centre for Global Development and Peterson Institute for International Economics.

Cline, W.R. 2008 "Global Warming and Agriculture", pp.23-27 *Finance & Development,* March.

Cloud, P. 1983 "The Biosphere" *Scientific American,* Vol. 249 (September) pp. 176-189.

Clunies-Ross, A., Forsyth, D. and Huq, M. 2009 *Development Economics;* McGraw-Hill Higher Education.

Coady, D. Parry, I., Sears, L. and Shang, B. 2015 "How Large Are Global Energy Subsidies" *IMF Woking Paper 15/105,* Washington D.C.: International Monetary Fund.

Coase, R. 1960 "The Problem of Social Cost" *The Journal of Law and Economics,* Vol. 3, pp 1-44.

Coe, M.T. and Foley, J.A. 2001 "Human and Natural Impacts on the Water Resources of the Lake Chad Basin" *Journal of Geophysical Reserarch,* Vol. 106, pp 3349-56.

Cohen, D. 2007 "Earth's natural wealth: an audit" *New Scientist,* May; and Reed Business Information Ltd. Also at: www.science.org.an/nova/newscientist/027n5_005.htm .

Coldwell, M.M., Bjorn, L.O., Bornman, J.F., Flint, S.D., Kulandaiuelu, G., Teramura, A.H. and Terini, M. 1998 "Effects of increased solar ultraviolet radiation on terrestrial ecosystems" *Journal of Photochemistry and Photobiology,* Vol. 46, pp. 40-52.

Coldwell, M.M., Borman, J.F., Ballare, C.C., Flink, S.D. and Kulandaivelu, G. 2007 "Torrestrial Ecosystems, Increased Solar Ultraviolent Radiation, and Interaction with Other Climate Change Factors" *Photochem Photobid Sci.,* Vol. 6, No. 3, pp. 252-66.

Colins, M. and G. Evans 1986 "The influence of fluvial sediment supply on coastal erosion in West and Central Africa" *Shoreline Management,* Vol. 2, pp. 5-12.

Collins, M. and 11 Others 2010 "The Impact of Global Warming on the Tropical Pacific Ocean and EL Niňo" *Nature Geoscience,* 3, 391-397.

Connah, G. 1981 *Three Thousand Years in Africa: Man and His Environent In the Lake Chad Region of Nigeria;* London: Cambridge University Press.

Conway, D. and Shipper, E.C.F. 2011 "Adaptation to climate change in Africa: Challenges and opportunities identified from Ethiopia" *Global Environmental Change,* Vol. 21, pp. 227-37.

Conway, E. 2008 "What's in a Name? Global Warming vs Climate Change" *NASA,* 5th December.

Conway, G. 2009 *The Science of Climate Change in Africa: Impacts and Adaptation;* Imperial College, London, Grantham Institute for Climate Change Discussion Paper No. 1 (October).

Conway, G., Krol, M., Alcamo, J., and Hume, M. 1996 "Future water availability in Egypt: The interaction of global, regional and basin-scale driving forces in the Nile Basin" *Ambio,*25, pp.336-342..

Cook, J. 2011 "Infographic on where global warming is going" *Skeptical Science.com,* January 20.

Copans, J. 1983 "The Sahelian Drought: Social Sciences and The Political Economy of Underdevelopment" pp. 83-97 In: K. Hewitt, (ed.) *Interpretations of Calamity: from the Viewpoint of Human Ecology,* Allen and Unwin.

Corbera, E., Estrada, M., and Brown, K. 2009 "How do regulated and voluntary carbon-offset compare?" *Journal of Integrative Environnental Sciences,* Vol. 6, Issue 1 pp. 25-50.

Cordel, D., Draugert, J.-O., and White, S. 2009 "The story of phosphorus: Global food security and food for thought", *Global Environmental Change,* Vol. 19, No. 2 (doi:10. 1016/j. gloenvcha2008.10.009).

Corden, W.M. and Neary, J.P. 1982 "Booming sector and industrialization in a small open economy" *Economic Journal,* Vol. 92, pp. 25-48 doi: 10.2307/2232670.

Corte, 2014 "Climate Change: The Externality that came in from the Cold" *TriplePundit*, April 24th.

Costanza, R., d' Arge, R., de Groot, R., Farber, S., Grasso, M., Hanon, B., Limburg, K., Naem, S., O'Neill, R.V., Parneco, J., Raskin, G., Sutton, P. and Van den Belt, M. 1997 "The value of the world's ecosystem services and natural capital" *Nature,* Vol. 387, pp. 253-60. doi: 10.1038/387253a0

Cotula, L., Vermuelen, S., Leonard, R. and Keeley, J. 2009 *Land grab or development opportunity? Agricultural investment and international land deals in Africa;* London & Rome. IIED/FAO/FAD (http://www.ifad.org/pub/land_grab.pdf.)

Coumou, D. and Rahmstorf, S. 2012 "A Decade of Weather Extremes" *Natural Climate Change,* Vol. 2, No. 7, pp. 491-497.

Cox, P.M., Betts, R.A., Jones, C.D., Spall, S.A. and Totterdell, I.J. 2000 "Acceleration of global warming due to carbon-cycle feddbacks in a coupled climate world" *Nature,* 408, 184-187.

Creatzig, F., Rarindranata, N.H., Bendes, G., Suh, S., Masere, O. 2015 "Biodiversity and climate change mitigation: An assessment", *GCB Bioenergy,* 7(5), 916-944.

Cromwell, C. and Winpenny, J.T. 1991 *Has Economic Reform Harmed the Environment? A Review of Structural Adjustment in Malawi;* London: ODI.

Culas, R.J. 2007 "Deforestation and the Environmental Kuznets Curve: An Institutional Perspective" *Ecological Economics,* Vol. 61, Nos 2-3, pp. 429-37.

D'Almeida, C., Vörösmarty, C.J., Hurt, G.C., Marengo, J.A., Dingman, S.L. and Keim, B.D. 2007 "The effects of deforestation on the hydrological cycle in Amazonia: a review on scale and resolution" *International Journal of Climatology,* 27, 633-47.

Dai, A. 2011 "Drought Under Global Warming: A Review" *Wiley Interdisciplinary Reviews: Climate Change,* Vol.2, pp. 45-65 doi:10.1002/weo.81.

Dai, A., Lamb, P.J., Trenberth, K.E., Hulme, M., Jones, P.D., and Xie, P. 2004 "The Recent Sahel Drought Is Real" *International Journal of Climtology,* Vol. 24, Issue 11, pp.1323-1331.

Daily, G.C. 1997 *Nature's Services: Societal Dependence on Natural System;* Washington: Island Press.

Danielson, F. et al. 2008 "Biofuel Plantations on Forested Lands: Double Jeopardy for Biodiversity and Climate" *Conservation Biology,* Vol. 23, pp. 348-58.

Dasgupta, P., Meiler, K.G. 1991 "The Environment and Emerging Development Issues" In: Stanley Fischer, Denis de Tray and Shekhar Shah, (eds.) *Proceedings of the World Bank Annual Conference on Development Economics 1990,* Washington DC.: World Bank.

Davenport, C. (2015, 12th December) "Nations Approve Landmark Climate Accord in Paris" *New York Times.* Retrieved 21 October 2016.

Davis, S.J. and Caldeira, K. 2010 "Consumption-based Accounting of CO_2 Emissions" *Proceedings of the National Academy of Science,* (USA) Vol. 107, No. 12, March 23 (doi: 10.1073/pnas.0906974107.

De Waah, A. 1989 *Famine that Kills: Darfur, Sudan, 1984 – 1985;* Oxford: Clarendon.

Degefu, M.A. and Bewket, W. 2014 "Trends and spatial patterns of drought incidence in the Omo-Ghibe river basin, Ethiopia" *Geografiska Annaler: Series A, Physical Geography.*

Demirbas, A. 2009 "Political, Economic and Environmental Impacts of Biofuels: A Review" *Applied Energy,* 86, S108-S117.

Diarrassouba, M. and Boubacar, I. 2009 "Deforestation in Sub-Saharan Africa" Paper for presentation at the Southern Agricultural Economics Association Annual Meeting, Atlanta Georgia, USA.

Diaz, D., Hamilton, K. and Johnson, E. 2011 "State of the Voluntary Carbon Markets 2011: From Canopy to Currency", Washington D.C.: Forest Trends. Available @ http://www.forest-trends.org/documents/files/doc_2963.pdf

Diaz, R. Virginia Institute of Marine Research htt://www.youtube.com/wath: V = Ojempo M 115 C.

Dike, E. 1986 The Agricultural Foundations of the Nigerian Economy, Unpublished Manuscript, Department of Economics, Ahmadu Bello University, Zaria, (Nigeria).

Dike, E. 1990 "Problems of Large-Scale Irrigation Schemes in Nigeria" *Science, Technology & Development,* Vol. 8, No. 3 (December) pp.245-52.

Dike, E. 2007 "Environmental Problems in Economic Development: A Review of Key Issues" Chapter 3: In: E.E. Udoye et al. (eds.) *Environment and Conflicts in Africa: Issues and Problems,* Enugu: Prefag Investment Limited.

Dike, E. and Dike, N.I. 2012 "Economics and Environmental Resources: Review" *International Business Research,* Vol. 5, No. 12, pp. 161-174.

Dinar, A. and Mendelsohn, R. (eds.) 2013 *Handbook on Climate Change and Agriculture;* Edward Elgar.

Ding, Y., Hayes, M.J., and Widhalm, M. 2010 "Measuring Economic Impacts of Drought: A. Review and Discussion" *Papers in Natural Resources,* Paper 196 University of Nebraska- Lincoln.

Ding, Y., Hayes, M.J., Widholm, M. 2011 "Measuring economic impacts of drought: A review and discussion" *Disaster Prevention and Management,* Vol. 20, No. 4.

Dixon, J.A. 1997 "Comment in "Enviroment, Poverty, and Economic Growth" by Karl-Göran Mäler." In: Boris Pleskovic and Joseph E. Stiglitz, (eds.), pp. 277-81, *Annual World Bank Conference on Development Economics 1997,* The World Bank, Washington D.C.

Dlamini, C., Larwanou, M. and Chirwa, P.W. 2015 "A brief review of the capacities of public forest administrations in climate change work in the moist forest countries of sub-Saharan Africa" *International Forest Review,* Vol. 17 (S3).

Dobson, T. 1992 *Loss of Biodiversity: An International Environmental Policy Perspective;* Hein Online. Retrieved 14th August 2012.

DOE / EIA 2006 United States Department of Energy. Country Analysis Briefs: *China Energy Information Administration,* August.

Dore, M.H.I. 2005 "Climate change and changes in global precipitation patterns: what do we know?" *Environment International,* Vol. 31, No. 8 (October) pp. 1167-1181.

Dow Jones *Financial New*s (2016, 25th January). Retrieved 21 October 2016.

Dowing, T.E., Susanna, B.H. and Pearson, H.A. (eds.) 1992 *Development or Deforestation? The Conversion of Tropical Forest to Pasture in Latin America;* Boulder, Calo: Westview Press.

Downie, C. 2013, *The Politics of Climate Change Negotiations: Strategies and Variables in Prolonged International Negotiations;* Edward Elgar.

Dowsett, H. et al, 1994 "Joint Investigations of the Middle Pliocene Climate 1: PRISM Palcoenvironmental Reconstructions" *Global and Planetary Change,* 9: 169-195.

Doyle, A. (2015, 1st June) "Climate Change Boosts Rain in Africa's Sahel Region: Study", *Reeuters.*

Dracup, J.A., Lee, K.S., Paulson, Jr., E.G. 1980 "On the definition of drought" *Water Resources Research,* Vol. 16, Issue 2, pp. 297-302 (April).

Dregne, H.E. 1984 "Combating desertification: evaluation of progress" *Environmental Conservation,* Vol. 11, pp, 115-121.

Dregne, H.E. and Tucker, C.J. 1988 "Desert Encroachment" *Desertification Control Bulletin,* 16, pp. 16-19.

Druzin, B. 2016 "A Plan to Strengthen the Paris Agreement" *Fordham Law Review,* March 3.

Dukiya, J.J. and Galhot, V., 2013 "Remote Sensing and GIS Based Assesssment of Flood Vulnerability in Lokoja (Nigeria)" *Journal of Enviromental Science and Sustainabilty,* Vol. 1, No. 3, pp. 74-80.

East, A.J. 2008 "Vegetable Industry Carbon Footprint Scoping Study" *Discussion Paper I* Horticulture Australia Ltd.

Eden Foundation, 1994 "Desertification- a Threat to the Sahel" *Eden Foundation,* August. Retrievd 26 August 2013.

EDF 2014 "How Cap and Trade Works" *Environment Defense Fund 2014.* http/www.edf.org/climate/how-cap-and-trade-works.

EEA 2014 "National adaptation policy processes across European countries – 2014", EEA Report No. 4/2014, Copenhagen Denmark: *European Environment Agency.*

Egeru, A. 2012 "Role of indigenous knowledge in climate change adaptation: a case study of the Teso sub-region, Eastern Uganda" *Indian Journal of Traditional Knowledge,* Vol. 11, No. 2, pp. 217-24.

Eilperin, J. (2006, 29th January) "Debate on climate change shifts to issue of irreparable change" *The Washington Post*, Sunday. (http://en.wikipedia.org/Kiribati#cite_ref_10). Retrieved 7 August 2013.

Ekins, P. and Jacobs, M. 1995 "Environmental Sustainability and the Growth of GDP Conditions for Compatibility" pp. 9-46. In: V. Bhaskar and A. Glyn, (eds.), *The North, The South and The Environment: Ecological Constraints and the Global Economy,* United Nations University Press & Earthscan, London.

El- Sayed, S.Z., Van Dijken, G.L., Gonzalez, G. 1996 "Effects of ultraviolet radiation on marine ecosystems" *International Journal of Environment Studies,* 51(3).

Ellerman, A., Denny, B. and Barhara, K. 2007 "The European Union Emissions Trading Scheme: Origins, Allocation, and Early Result" *Review of Environmental Economics and Policy,* Vol. 1, No. 1 pp.66-87. doi:10.1093/reep/rem003.

Elliot, J.A. 2005 *An Introduction to Sustainable Development;* 3rd Edition, London: Routledge.

Energy Encyclopedia (no date) "History Wind Energy" *Energy Encyclopedia,* Vol. 6.

Enfield, D.B. and Cid-Serrano, L. 2009 "Secular and multidecadal warming in the North Atlantic and their relationships with major hurricane activity" *International Journal of Climatology,* 30.

Environmental Investigation Agency and Telapak, 2004 *Profiting from Plunder: How Malaysia Smuggles Endangered Wood, eia – global.org*

EORC 2005 "Huge glaciers retreat on a large scale in Patagonia, South America" *Earth Observation Research Center,* Japan (http.//www.eorc.jaxa.jp/en/imgdata/ topics/2008/ tp080903.html) Retrieved 10th August 2013.

EPA 2000 United States Environmental Protection Agency (EPA) Office of Air and Radiation Office of Air Quality Planning and Standards 2000.

EPA, 2010 *Protecting the Ozone Layer Protection Eyesight: A Report on Cataract Incidence in the United States Using the Atmoshperic and Health Effects Framework Model;* Washington D.C.: US Environmental Protection Agency.

Eskeland, G.S. and Samuel J. 1992 "Policy Instruments for Pollution Control in Developing Countries" *The World Bank Research Observer,* Vol. 7, No. 2 (July) pp. 145-169.

EUETS 2010 *European Union Emissions Trading System* European Comission 15 November.

European Floods 2013 "Germany Evacuated after river Elbe breaks its banks again" http:// en.wikipedia.org/wiki/2013_European_Floods.

EUROSTAT 2013 *Environmental Taxes: Detailed Analysis;* EUROSTAT.

Evans, T.E. (http://www.fao.org). *The effects of changes in the world hydrological cycle on availability of water resources;* FAO, Natural Resources Management and Environment Department. http://www.fao.org Accessed 4 Feb. 2015.

Evenson, R.E. and Gollins, D. 2003 "Assessing the Impact of the Green Revolution, 1960-2000" *Science,* Vol. 300, pp. 758-62.

Faber, D. 2008 *Capitalizing on Environmental Injustice: The Polluter-Industrial Complex in the Age of Globalization;* Rowman & Littlefield.

Falconer, J. 1990 *The Major Significance of "Minor" Forest Products: The Local Use and Valuable of Forests in the West African Humid Forest Zone;* Rome: FAO.

Falconer, J. and Arnold, J.E.M. 1989 *Household Food Security and Forestry: An Analysis of Socio-Economic* Issues; Rome: FAO.

FAO 1996 *World Food Summit, Corporate Document Repository*; Rome.

FAO Newsroom 2005 "Cattle Ranching in Encroaching on Forests in Latin America" Rome: Food and Agriculture Organization.

FAO, (2006, 4th September) "Deforestation Causes of Global Warming" *FAO Newsroom*, Rome: Food and Agricultural Organization.

FAO, 2005 *Global Forest Resources*; Rome: Food and Agriculture Organization.

FAO, 2008 FAOSTAT database. Available at: faostat.fao.org.

FAO, 2009 *State of the World's Forest 2009;* Rome: FAO.

FAO, 2011 *The state of food insecurity in the world: How does international price volatility affect domestic economies and food security?* Rome: Food & Agricultural Organization.

FAO, 2014 *Agriculture, Forestry and Other Land Use Emissions by Sources and Removal by Sink;* FAO: Climate, Energy and Tenure Division.

Fargoine, J.E., Plevin, R.J., and Hill, J.D. 2010 "The ecological impact of Biofuels" *Annual Review of Ecology, Evolution and Systematics,* Vol. 41, pp. 351-77.

Farley, K.A. 2007 "Grasslands to tree plantations: Forest transition in the Audes of Ecuador" *Annals of the Association of American Geographers,* Vol. 97, pp. 755-71.

Fearnside, P.M. (1997) *Transmigration in Indonesia: Lessons from Its Environmental and Social Impacts;* New York: Springer – Verlag.

Fearnside, P.M. (2000) "Global Warming and Tropical Land-Use Change: Greenhouse Gas Emissions from Biomass Burning, Decomposition and Soils in Forest Conversion, Shifting Cultivation and Secondary Vegetation" *Climate Change,* 46, pp. 115-158.

Fearnside, P.M. 2004 "Greenhouse Gas Emissions from Hydroelectric Dams: Controversies provide a Springboard for Rethinking a Supposedly 'Clean' Energy Source – An Editorial Comment" *Climate Change,* Vol. 66, Issue 1/2.

Fearnside, P.M. 2005 "Deforestation in Brazilian Amazonia: History, Rates, and Consequences" *Conservation Biology,* Vol. 19, pp. 680-88.

Fearnside, P.M. and Laurence, W.F. 2004 "Tropical Deforestation and Green-House Gas Emission" *Ecological Applications*, Vol. 14, Issue 4 (August), pp. 982-86.

Few, R., Satyal, P., McGahey, D., Leavy, J., Budds, J., Assen, M., Canfield, L., Loubser, D., Adnew, M. and Bewket, W. 2015 *Vulnerability and Adaptation to Climate Change in Semi-Arid Areas in East Africa* ASSR; Working Paper, ASSAR PMU South Africa.

Field, B.C. and Field, M.K. 2009 *Environmental Economics: An Introduction;* McGraw Hill International Edition.

Field, C.B., Campbell, J.E., Lobel, D.B. 2008 "Biomass Energy: The Scale of the Potential Resource" *Trend in Ecology and Evolution,* 23(2).

Field, F. (2006, 8th October) "How can you Save the Rainforest?" *Times*, London.

Finance & Development 2008 "Global Energy: Increasingly Unsustainable" *Finance & Development,* March, 16-17.

Financial Times (2008, 2n June) "The end of abundance" *Financial Times* Series, Part I, p. 13, London.

Financial Times 2008 "Seeds of Change" *Financial Times* Series, Part 2, pp. 13, London.

Firzli, M. Nicholas J. (2016, 25th January) "Investment Governance: The Real Fight against Emissions is Being Waged by Markets" *Dow Jones Financial News.*

Fischer, G., Shah, M. and Van Velthuizen, H. 2002a *Climate Change and Agricultural Vulnerability,* Special Report to the UN World Summit on Sustainable Development Johannesburg 2002 Luxenburg, Austria: IISA.

Fischer, G., Shah, M., Tabiello, F.N. and Van Velthuizen, H. 2002b *Climate Change and Agricultural Vulnerability Report to the UN World Summit on Sustainable Development;* Johannesburg / Luxemburg.

Fischer, G., Shah, M., Tubiello, F.N. and Van Velthuizen, H. 2005 "Socio-economic and climate change impacts on agriculture: an integrated assessment, 1990-2080" *The Royal Society: Philosophic Transactions B,* Vol. 360, Issue: 1463.

Fischer, G., Van Velthuizen, H. Shah, M., Nachtergaele, F.O. 2002c *Global agro-ecological assessment for agriculture in the 21st Century: Methodology and results;* IIASA RR-02-02 Laxenburg, Austria: IISA.

Fischlin et al. 2007 "Ecosystems, their Properties, Goods and Services" In Intergovernmental Panel on Climate Change (IPCC), *Climate Change 2007, Synthesis Report 2007,* Chap. 4.

Fisher, B. 2010 "African exception to drivers of deforestation" *Nat. Geosci.,* Vol. 3, pp. 375-76 doi: 10.1038/nge0873.

Fisher, T.M. 2009. "Modeling the Global Water Cycle" http://www3.geosc.psu.edu/_dmb53/Davies Stella/water/ global%2010. Accessed 30 August 2013.

Fleming, J.R. 1999 "Joseph Fourier, the "Greenhouse Effect", and the Quest for a Universal Theory of Terrestrial Temperatures" *Endeavour,* 23, 2, 72-75 doi:10.1016/s0160-9327(99)01210-7.

Flint, E.P. and Richards, J.F. 1991 "Historical Analysis of Changes in Land Use and Carbon Stock of Vegetation in South and Southeast Asia" *Canadian Journal of Forest Research,* Vol. 21, pp. 91-110.

Floyd, M. 2007 "Long-lived deep-sea fishes imperilled by techology overfishing" *AAAS* (American Association for the Advancement of Science).

Fobissis, K., Alemagi, D. and Minang, P.A. 2014 "REDD+ Policy Approaches in the Congo Basin: A Comparative Analysis of Cameroon and Democratic Republic of Congo (DRC), *Forests 2014*, 5,2400-2424 (doi:10.3390/f5102400)

Foley, J.A., Coe, M.T. Scheffer, M. and Wang, G. 2003 "Regime Shifts in the Sahara and Sahel: Interactions between Ecological and Climatic Systems in Northern African". *Ecosystems,* Vol. 6, Issue 6, pp. 524-532. dol: 10. 1007/5/0021 − 002 − 0227 − 0.

Folwer, H. and Tietenberg T. (2006) *The International Yearbook of Environmental Resource Economics 2005/2006: A Survey of Current Issues;* Edward Elgar.

Forero, J. and Eilperin, J. (2011, 18th December) "Brazil's forest policy could undermine its climate goals" *The Washington Post.*

Forest Carbon Partnership Facility (FCPF) 2010 Incorporating Environmental and Social Considerations into the Process of Getting Ready for REDD+ Draft March 7.

Formula One, 2009 "Bahrain day two-sandstorm curtails running at Sakhir" *Formula One,* February 11.

Fouquet, R., Pearson, P.J.G. 1998 "A thousand years of energy regime: use in the United Kingdom" *Energy Journal,* 19(4).

Fowler, A.M. and Hennessy, K.J. 1995 "Potential impacts of global warming on the frequency and magnitude of heavy precipitation" *Natural Hazards,* Vol. 11, No 3 (May) pp. 283-303.

Francou, B., Ramirez, E., Caceres, B., and Mendozo, J. 2000 "Glacier Evolution in the Tropical, Andes during the last decades of the 20th century: Bolivia, and Antizana, Ecuador" *Ambio,* Vol. 29, No. 7 (November) (www.unisci.um/stories/20011/0117013.htm).

Freeman, P., Keen, M., and Mani, M., 2003 "Dealing with Increased Risk of Disasters: Challenges and Options" *IMF Working Paper No. 03/197,* Washington, D.C.: International Monetary Fund.

Fridleifsson, I.B., Bertani, R., Huenges, E., Lund, J.W., Ragnarsson, A. and Rybach, L. 2008 *The Possible Role and Contribution of Geothermal Energy to the Mitigation of Climate Change;* (O. Hohmeyer and T. Trittin (eds.) pp. 59-80 Luebeck, Germany.

Friedlingstein, P., Houghton, R.A., Marland, G., Hacker, J., Boden, T.A., Conway, T.J., Canadell, J.G., Raupach, M.R., Ciasis, P., Le Quere, C., 2010 "Update on CO_2 Emissions" *Nature Geoscience. doi: 1038/ngeo.1022.*

Fthenakis, V. and Kim, H.C. 2009 "Land Use and Electricity Generation: A Life-Cycle Analysis" *Renewable and Sustainable Energy Review,* Vol. 13, No. 6, pp. 1465-1474. doi:10.1016/j.rser.2008.09.017. Retrieved 24 April 2016.

Fullerton, D., and Metcalf, G.E. 1998 "Environmental Taxes and the Double-dividend Hypothesis: Did you Really Expect Something for Nothing?" *Chicago-Kent Law Review,* Vol. 73, No. 1, pp. 221-56.

Fullerton, D., Leicester, A. and Smith, S. 2008 "Environmental Taxes" *NBER Working Paper 1497.*

Fullerton, D., Leicester, A., and Smith, S. 2008 *Green Development: Environmental and Sustainability in a Developing World;* 3rd Edition, London & New York: Routledge Taylor & Francis Group.

Gallup, J.G., Saiha, J.D., and Mellinger, A.D. 1999 "Geography and Economic Development" *Annual World Bank Conference on Development Economics 1998,* Washington D.C: World Bank.

Gao, H., Bohn, T.J. Podest, E., McDonald, K.C. and Lettenmaier (2011) "On the Causes of the Shrinking of Lake Chad" *Environmental Research Letters,* Vol. 6, 034021 (7pp).

Gardner, A.S. and 16 Others 2013 "A reconciled estimate of glacier contribution to sea level rise: 2003 to 2009" *Science,* 340, 852-857.

Gash, J.H.C., Nobre, C.A., Roberts, J.M. and Victoria, R.I. (eds) 1996 *Amazonian Deforestation and Climate;* Chichester: Wiley.

Gebre Senbet, F. and Kefale, A. 2012 "Traditional coping mechanisms for climate change of pastoralists in South Omo, Ethiopia" *Indian Journal of Traditional Knowledge,* Vol. 11, pp. 573-79.

Geerts, B. (no date) "Global warming and the hydrological cycle" (http:/www.watrencyclopedia.com/Ge-Hy/Global-warming-the–hydrologic) Retrieved 18 August 2013.

GEF 2009 Global Environment Facility, *GEF Impact Evaluation of the Phase-Out of Ozone-Depleting Substances in Countries with Economies on Transition, Vol. 1: Theory of Change;* Washington, D.C.: GEF. http:/www.thegef.org/gef/node/2033.

GEF 2013 Global Environment Facility, *Investing In the Phase-Out of Ozone-Depleting Substances – The GEF Experience* http://www.thegef.org

Geist, H. 2005 *The Causes and Progression of Desertification;* Ashgate Publishing.

Geist, H.J. and Lambdin, E.F. 2002 "Proximate causes and underlying driving forces of tropical deforestation" *BioScience,* Vol. 52, pp. 143-50.

Geist, H.J. and Lambin, E.F. 2004 "Dynamic causal patterns of desertification" *Bioscience,* 54 (19) pp. 817-829.

Gemeda, D.O. and Siina, A.D. 2015 "The impacts of climate change on African continent and the way forward" *Journal of Ecology and the Natural Environment,* Vol. 7, No. 10, pp. 256-262.

Gerber, P.J., Steinfeld, H., Henderson, B., Motter, A., Opio, C., Dijkman, J., Falcucci, A. and Tempio, G. 2013 *Tackling Climate Change through Livestock – A Global Assessment of Emissions and Mitigation Opportunities;* Rome: Food and Agriculture Organization.

Ghatak, S. and Tuener, R.K. 1978 "Pesticide use in less Developed Countries: Economic and Environmental Considerations" *Food Policy,* Vol. 3, pp. 136-46.

Giannimi, A., Saravanan, R. and Chang, P. 2003 "Oceanic forcing of Sahel rainfall on international to interdecadal timescales", *Science,* 302 (5647), 1027-1030.

Gidden, A. 2009 *The Politics of Climate Change;* Polity Press.

Gilis, J. (2014, 31st March) "Panel's Warming on Climate Risk; Worst is Yet to Come" *The New York Tmes.*

Gill, M., Smith, P., Willkinson, J. 2010 "Mitigating Climate Change: The Role of Domestic Livestock" *Animal,* 4, pp. 323-333.

Gillespie, B. 1996 "Pollution in Eastern Europe" *The OECD Observer,* No. 198 (Feb/March) pp. 29-32.

Girard, P. (no date) Charcoal Production and Use in Africa: What Future? FAO Corporate Document Repository (www.fao.org/docrep/005/y4450e/y4450e10.htm).

Glaeser, B. (ed.) 1984 *Ecodevelopment: Concept, Project, Strategies;* Oxford: Pergamon.

Glickman, J. and Teter, D. 1991 "Debt, Structural Adjustment, and Deforestation: Examining the Links a Policy Exercise for the Sierra Chile" Consultant's Report, Sierra Chile, Washington, D.C.

Global Biodiversity, 2010, *Global Biodiversity Outlook Report 3;* Montreal (May).

Global Wind Report 2014: *Annual Market Update;* Istanbul.

Globaltimber.org.uk "Exports by, and imports from, Africa" (http://www.globaltimber.org.uk/Africa.htm).

Goa, H., Bohn, T.J., Podest, E., McDonald, K.C. and Lettenmaire, 2011 "On the causes of the shrinking of Lake Chad" *Environmental Reseach Letters,* Vol. 6.

Goldman, M. 2006 *Imperial Nature: The World Bank and Struggles for Social Justice in the Age of Globalization;* Yale University Press.

Gonzales, P. 2001 "Desertification and a shift of forest species in the West African Sahel" *Climate Research,* Vol. 17, 217-228.

Gordon, R.B., Bertram, M. and Graedel, T.E. 2006 "Metal Stocks and Sustainability" *Proceedings of the National Academy of Sciences,* Vol. 103, No. 5, pp. 1200-4.

Gore, A. 2006 *An Inconvenient Truth: The Planetary Emergency of Global Warming and What we can do About it;* London: Bloombury Publishing.

Gore, A. 2009 "Our Choice: A Plan to Solve the Climate Crise" Chap. 9, *Forests,* pp. 170-95, Bloombury.

Goria, A., Sgobbi, A., and Homeyer, (eds.) 2010 *Governance for the Environment: A Comparative Analysis of Environmental Policy Integration;* Edward Elgar.

Gouldner, L.H. and Kennedy, D. 1997 "Valuing ecosystem services: philosophical bases and empirical methods" pp. 23-47, In: G.C Daily (ed) *Nature's services; societal dependence on natural ecosystems,* Washington: Island Press.

Goulet, D. 1971 *The Cruel Choice: A New Concept on the Theory of Development;* New York: Atheneum.

Grafton, R. Quentin, (ed.) 2008 *Economics of Water Resources;* Edward Elgar.

Gratzfeld, J. (ed) 2003 *Extractive Industries in Arid And Semi-Arid Zones: Environmental Planing and Management;* IUCN, Gland, Switzerland & Cambridge, UK.

Grear, A. and Kotzé, L.J. (eds.) 2015 *Research Handbook on Human Rights and the Environment;* Edward Elgar.

Gregory, J.M. and Huybucht, P. 2006 "Ice-sheet contributions to future sea-level change" *Phih. Trans. Roy. Soc. A*; 364 (1844), 1709-1732.

Gregory, P.J., Ingram, J.S.I. and Brklacich, M. 2005 "Climate change and food security" *Philosophical Transactions of the Royal Society B;* Vol. 360, pp. 2139-48.

Griffin, K. 1979 *The Political Economy of Agrarian Change: An Essay on the Green Revolution;* Macmillan.

Grise, K.M., Polvani, L.M., Tselioudis, G., Wu, Y., Zelinka, M.D. 2013 "The Ozone hole indirect effect: cloud-radiative anomalies accompanying the paleward shift of the eddy-driven jet in the Southern Hemisphere" *Geophysical Research Letters,* 40, 41: 3688-3692.

Grove, A.T. 1973 "A Note on the Remarkably Low Rainfall of the Sudan Zone in 1913" *Savanna,* Vol. 2, pp. 133-8.

Grove, A.T. 1977 "Desertification" *Progress in Physical Geography,* Vol. 1, pp. 296-310.

Guan, D., Peters, G.P., Weher, C.L. and Hubercek, K. 2009 "Journey to the World Top Emitter: An Analysis of China's Recent CO_2 Emissions Surge" *Geophysical Research Letters,* 36: L 04709.

Guezuraga, B., Zauner, R. and Pölz, W. 2012 "Life Cycle Assessment of two different 2 MW Class Wind Turbines" *Renewal Energy,* Vol. 37, pp. 37-44. doi.10.1016 /j.renene.2011.05.008. Retrieved 24. April.

Guillaume, D. and Zytek, R. 2010 "Reducing the Staggering Costs of Cheap Energy" *Finance & Development,* June, pp. 39-41.

Gupta, A., Pistorius, T., and Vijge, M.J. 2016 "Managing Fragmentationin Global Environmental Governance: The REDD+ Partnership as Bridge Organization" *International Environmental Agreements,* Vol. 16, Issue 3, pp. 355-374.

Gustavsson, L., Holmberg, J., Dornburg, V., Sathre, R., Eggers, T., Mahapatra, k., Marland, G. 2007 "Using Biomass for Climate Change Mitigation and Oil Use Reduction" *Energy Policy,* 35(11), 5671-5691.

GWEC 2015 "GWEC Global Wind Statistics 2014" *Global Wind Energy Council Update*, 10 February.

Gwynne, M.D. 1982 "The Global Environment Monitoring System (GEMs) of UNEP" *Environmental Conservation*, Vol. 9, pp. 35-42.

Haberl, H., et al. 2007 "Quantifying and Mapping the Human Appropriation of Net Primary Production in Earth's Terrestrial Ecosystems", *Proc. Natl. Acad. Sci.*, USA, 104 12942-12947

Hafele, W. and Sassin, N. 1979 "The Global Energy System" *Annual Review of Energy*, Vol.2 pp. 1-30. https://doi.org/10.1146/annurev.eg.02.110177.000245

Hails, C., Loh, J., and Goldfinger, S. (eds.) 2006 *Living Planet Report 2006* WWF International, Zoological Society of London, and Global Footprint Network, Gland, Switzerland.

Hall, R. and Jones, C. 1999 "Why do some Countries Produce so much more Output per Worker than Others?" *Quarterly Journal of Economics*, Vol. 114, pp. 83-116.

Hamilton, K., Bayon, R., Turner, G., and Higgin, D. 2007 "State of the Voluntary Carbon Market 2007: Picking up Steam". *Ecosystem Marketplace and Carbon Finance*. Available @ http://ecosystemmarketplace.com/documents/cms/s/2...

Hansen, K. 2007 "Sahara Dust Has Chilling Effect on North Atlantic" *Goddart Space Flight Centre*, December 14.

Hanski, I. 2005 Landscape Fragmentation, Biodiversity Loss and Societal Response National Center for Biotechnology Information (NIH) www.ncbi.hlm.nih.gov. Retrieved 8/14/2012.

Hardin, G. 1968 "The Tragedy of the Commons" *Science*, Vol. 162 (3859) pp.1243-1968 (doi: 10.1126/science.162.3859.1243).

Hardjono, J. 1989 "The Indonesian Transmigration Program in Historical Perspective" *International Migration*, Vol. 26, pp. 427-39.

Hardwick, P., Khan, B. and Langmead, J. 1994 *An Introduction to Modern Economics;* 4th ed., Longman Group, UK.

Harris, N. and Sargent, S. (2016, 21st April) "Destruction of Tropical Forestland is an Overlooked Source of Emissions" *World Resource Institute*.

Hartford, E. 2012 "Lake Chad Desertification: A Symptom of Global Climate Change" http://www.earthreform.org.

Hartman, D.L., et al. 2013 "Observations: Atmosphere and Surface:" In: *Climate Change 2013: The Physical Science Basis. Contribution of Working Group I to the Fifth Assessment Report of IPCC,* Cambridge University Press.

Hayami, Y. 2001 "Ecology, History, and Development: Perspective from Rural Southeast Asia" *The World Bank Research Observer*, Vol. 16, no. 2, pp. 169-198.

Haywood, J.M., Jones, A., Bellovin, N. and Stephenson, D. 2013 "Asymmetric forcing from stratospheric aerosols impacts Sahelian rainfall" *Nature Climate Change* (2013) doi: 10.1038/nclimate 1857.

Hecht, S.B., Kandel, S., Gemes, I., Cueller, N., Rosa, H., 2006 "Globalization, Forest Resurgence, and Environmental Politics in E1 Salvador" *World Development,* Vol. 34, No. 2.

Heil, A. and Goldammer, J.G. 2001 "Smoke-haze Pollution: A Review of the 1997 Episode in Southeast Asia" *Regional Environmental Change,* Vol. 2, No. 1, pp. 24-37.

Heimann, M., 2010 "How Stable is the Methane Cycle?" *Science,* 327, 1211-1212.

Held, I.M. and Soden, B.J. 2006 "Robust Responses of the Hydrological Cycle to Global Warming" *Journal of Climate,* Vol. 19, 5686-5699.

Held, I.M., Delworth, T.C., Lu, J., Findel, K.L., and Knutson, T.R. "Simulation of Sahel Drought in the 20th and 21st Centuries" *Proceedings of the National Academy of Science* (PNAS), Vol. 102, No. 50, 17891-17896.

Hert, T.W., Ramankutty, N. and Baldos, U.L.C. 2014 "Agricultural Revolution in Africa and Increase Global Carbon Emissions" *Proceedings of the National Academy of Science,* September, 8.

Hertwich, E.G. and Peters, G.P. 2009 "Carbon Footprint of Nations: A Global Trade-Linked Analysis" *Environment, Science and Technology,* Vol. 43, pp. 6414-6420.

Hiernaux, P. 1996 "The Crisis of Sahelian Pastoralain: Ecological or Economic?" *Pastoral Development Network,* January.

Hill, J., Nelson, E., Tilman, D., Polasky, S., and Tiffany, D., (2006) "Environmental, Economic and Energetic Costs and Benefits of Biodiesel and Ethanol Biofuels" *Proc. Natc Acad Sci., USA,* 103 (30) 11206-11210.

Hindustan Times (2015, 14 December) "Paris Climate Deal: What the Agreement means for India and the World" *Hindustan Times,* 14 December. Retrieved 21 October 2016.

Hirsch, T. (2005, 5th October) "Animals hit by global warming" *BBC News.* (see also: Climate Change and Ecosystmes: http:/www.en.m.wikipedia.org).

Hobsbawn, E. 1982 *The Age of Revolution: Europe 1789-1848;* Weidenfield & Nicholson.

Hoegh-Guldberg, O. (2011, January 21) "Coral reef ecosystems and anthropogenic climate change" *Regional Environmental Change,* Vol.11, No. 1, Supplement pp. 215-27.

Hoegh-Guldberg, O. 1999 "Climate change, coral bleaching and the future of the world's coral reefs", *Marine and Freshwater Research,* Vol. 50, No. 8, pp. 839-866.

Hoegh-Guldberg, O. 2011 "Climate Change Impacts on Ocean Systems" *Climate Shifts,* January 21.

Hoegh-Guldberg, O. and 15 Others 2007 "Coral Reefs under Rapid Climate Change and Ocean Acidification" *Science,* Vol. 318, No. 587, pp. 1737-1742.

Hoffman, D. 2007A "Time to Master Disaster" *Finance & Development,* March pp. 42-5.

Hoffman. J. 2007 "The Maldives and Rising Sea Levels" *ICE Case Studies,* 206, May.

Holland, A. and Roxbee Cox, J. 1992 "The Valuing of Environmental Goods: A Modest Proposal' pp. 12-24 In: A. Coker and C. Richards, (eds.) *Valuing the Environment: Economic Approaches to Environmental Valuation,* London: Belhaven.

Hollis, G.E., Adams, W.M., and Aminu-Kano, (eds.) 1994 *The Hadejia-Nguru Wetlands: environment, economy and sustainable use of a Sahelian floodplain wetland;* IUCN Wetlands Programme, Gland, Switzerland.

Holmberg, J., Thomson, K., and Timberlake, L. 1993 *Failing the Future: Beyond the Earth Summit;* Earthscan/International Institute for Environment and Development, London.

Hooke, R.L. 1989 "Englacial and subglacial hydrology: a qualitative review" *Arctic and Alpine Research,* Vol. 21, No. 3, pp. 221-33.

Houghton, J. 1997 *Global Warming: The Complete Briefing;* 2nd Edition, Cambridge University Press.

Houghton, J.T. et al. 2001 "Climate Change 2001: The Scientific Basis" Intergovernmental Panel on Climate Change (IPCC).

Houghton, J.T., Meira Filho, L.G., Callanden, B.A., Harris, N.N., Kattenberg, A., and Maskell, K., (eds.), 1995. *Climate Change 1995: The Science of Climate Change (Contribution of Working Group I to Second Assessment Report of the Intergovernmental Panel on Climate Change);* Cambridge, UK: Cambridge Press University.

Houghton, R.A. 2005 "Tropical deforestation as a source of greenhouse gas emissions" In: P. Moutinho and S. Schwartzman, (eds.), *Tropical Deforestation and Climate Change,* Washington D.C.: Environmental Defense / IPAM Brazil.

Houghton, R.A. and Hackler, J.L. 2001 "Carbon Flux to the Atmosphere from Land-Use Changes: 1850 to 1990" Environmental Sciences Division Office of Biological and Environmental Research (doi: 10.3334/CDIAC/ue.nd p 050) US Department of Energy.

Houghton, R.J.A., Skole, D.L., Noble, C.A., Hackler, J.L., Lawrence, K.T., and Chomentowski, W.H., 2000. "Annual Fluxes of Carbon from Deforestation and Re-growth in the Brazilian Amazon" *Nature,* 403, pp. 301-304.

Huang, J., and Van den Dool, H.M. 1993 "Monthly Precipitation-Temperature Relations and Temperature Prediction over the United State" *Journal of Climate,* Vol. 6, pp. 1111-1132.

Hulme, M. 1995 *Climate Change and Southern Africa: An Exploration of Some Potential Impacts and Implications in the SADC Region;* Norwich, Climate Research Unit and World Wide Fund for Nature.

Hulme, M., Kelly, M., 1993 "Climate change, desertification and dessication, and the case of the African Sahel" *CSERGE Working Paper GEC G3-17,* The Centre for Social and Economic Research on the Global Environment, University of East Anglia and University College London.

Huq, S., Karim, Z., Asaduzzaman, Mahtab, F. (1994) *Vulnerability and Adaptation to Climate Change for Bangledesh;* Springler- Science-Business, Media, B.V.

Hyde, W.F., Amacher, G.S. and Magrath, W. 1996 "Deforestation and Forest Land Use: Theory, Evidence and Policy Implications". *The World Bank Research Observer,* Vol. 11, No. 2, pp. 223-48.

Hyden, G. 1968 "The Tragedy of the Commons" *Science,* Vol. 162, No.1, pp. 243-48.

Häder, D.-P., Kamaar, H.D., Smith, R.D. and Worrest R.C. 2007 "Effects of solar UV radiation on Aquatic ecosystems and interactions with climate change" *Photochemical & Photobiological Sciences,* Vol. 6, pp. 267-285.

I.A.E.A, 2016 *Climate Change and Nuclear Power 2016;* Vienna: International Atomic Energy Agency.

Ibe, A.E. and Nwufo, M.I. 2005 "Domestication of Medicinal Plants in Southeastern Nigeria" *Africa Development,* Vol. 30, No. 3, pp. 66-77.

Ibrahim, J. 1989 "Lake Chad as an Instrument of International Cooperation" In: Asiwaju, A.I. and Adeniyi, P.O. (eds.), *Borderlands in Africa: A Multidisciplinary and Comparative Focus on Nigeria and West Africa,* Lagos: University of Lagos Press.

Ickowitz, A. 2006 "Shifting cultivation and deforestation in tropical Africa: Critical reflections" *Development and Change,* Vol. 37, pp. 599-626.

IEA, 2007 *World Energy Outlook* (Edition – China and India Insights); Paris: International Energy Agency.

IEA, 2009 International Energy Agency, *World Energy Outlook 2009;* Paris: IEA.

IEA 2014 "Technology Roadmap: Solar Photovoltaic Energy" *International Energy Agency* (htt://www.iea.org).

IEA 2016 International Energy Agency (IEA) *Snapshot of Global Photovoltaic Markets;* Vienna: 22 April.

IEA/OECD, 1995 International Energy Agency/Organization for Economic Cooperation and Development, *Voluntary Approaches for Mitigating Energy-Related CO$_2$ Emission;* Paris: IEA/OECD Publications.

Ikegbunam, F.I. 2007 "Biodiversity Loss and Crisis in the Environment: Issues and Options to Man". In: E.E Udoye et al., (eds.), Chap.5. *Enviromental and Conflict in Africa: Issues and Problems,* Enugu: Frefbag Investment Ltd.

Ikporukpo, C.O. 1983 "Environmental deterioration and public policy in Nigeria" *Applied Geography,* Vol. 3, pp. 303-16.

ILO, 2011 *Green Policies in the EU: A Review;* Geneva: ILO.

IMF, 2010 "Petroleum Product Subsidies: Costly, Inequitable, and Rising" www.imf.org/external/pubs/ft/spn/1005/pdf.

Indonesia-UK Study 1999 Indonesia-UK Tropical Forestry Management Programme 1999 *Illegal Logging in Indonesia*. ITFMP Report No. EC/99/03.

Inikori, J.E. 2002 *Africans and the Industrial Revolution in England*; Cambridge University Press.

IPCC 2000 Intergovernmental Panel on Climate Change *Report on Land Use, Land Use Change and Forestry*; Cambridge University Press.

IPCC 2001 Intergovernmental Panel on Climate Change, *Graph of 20 glaciers in retreat worldwide: Climate Change 2001 (Working Group1: The Scientific Basis).* Retrieved 9th August 2013.

IPCC 2001a *Intergovernmental Panel on Climate Change, 2001: Synthesis Report*, edited by Robert T. Watson, Cambridge University Press.

IPCC 2007 AR4 Intergovernmental Panel on Climate Change, *Climate Change 2007: The Physical Science Basis: Contribution of Working Group 1 to the 4th Assessment Report;* Cambridge University Press.

IPCC 2007A Intergovernmental panel on climate change 2007: *Assessing Key Vulnerabilities and Risks from Climate Change* Sect. 19. 23 *Ecosystems and Biodiversity;* Cambridge University Press.

IPCC 2007a The Fourth Assessment Report of the Intergovernmental Panel on Climate Change (IPCC). *Climate Change 2007. The Physical Science Basis* (Solomon, S., D. Qin, M. Manning, Z. Chen, M. Marquis, K.B. Averyt, M. Tigner and H.L. Miller, eds.) Contribution of Working Group I, Cambridge University Press.

IPCC 2007b *Synthesis of the Fourth Assessment Report of the Intergovernmental Panel on Climate Change*; Geneva: Intergovernmental Panel on Climate Change (www.ipcc.chl.).

IPCC 2012 *Managing the Risks of Extreme Events and Disasters to Advance Climate Change Adaptation. A Special Report of Working Groups I and II of the Intergovernmental Panel on Climate Change* (Field, C.B., Barros, V., Stocker, T.F. and 9 Others (eds); Cambridge UK and New York: Cambridge Unviersity Press (http://www.ipcc-wg2.gov/SREX/images/uploads/SRES-All_Final.pfd). Retreved 17 August 2013.

IPCC 2013 *Climate Change 2013: The Physical Science Basis. Working Group 1 Contribution to the Fifth Assessment Report of the Intergovernmental Panel on Climate Change*, Stocker;, T.F., Qin, D., Plattner, G. – K, et al (eds.) Cambridge University Press.

IPCC 2014 Climate Change 2014: *Synthesis Report of the Contribution of Working Group I, II, III to the 5th Assessment Repor;*, Cambridge University Press.

IPCC 2014 *Summary for policymakers. In: Climate Change 2014: Impacts, adaptation, and vulnerability. Part A: Global and sectoral aspects. Contribution of WG II to the Fifth Assessment;* Report of the IPCC, Cambridge University Press.

IPCC AR5 2014 *Climate Change 2014: Mitigation Climate Change. Contribution of Working Group III to the Fifth Assessment Report of the Intergovernmental Panel on Climate Change* (Edenhofer, O. et al.); Cambridge and New York: Cambridge University Press.

IPCC AR5 2014 Intergovernmental Panel on Climate Change (IPCC): The Fifth *Assessment Report: Impacts, Adaptation and Vulnerability.* http://www.ipcc.ch/report/ ar5/wg2.

IRENA, 2017 International Renewable Energy Agency, *Global Renewable Energy Capacity 2000-2015;* Masdar City, Abu Dhabi.

Ite, U. E. 2004 "Multinationals and corporate social responsibility in developing countries: a case study of Nigeria" *Corporate Social Responsibility and Environmental Management,* Vol. 11, pp. 1-11.

IUCN, 1980 *The World Conservation Strategy;* World Wild-Life Fund, Geneva.

Ivanova, M. 2007 "Moving Forward by Looking Back: Learning from UNEP's History" pp. 262-47. In: L. Swart and E. Perry, (eds), *Global Environmental Governance: Perspectives on the Current Debate,* Center for UN Reform New York (see http://www.centerforunreform.org/node/251).

Jablonski, L.M., Wang, X. and Curtis, P.S. *2002* "Plant production under element CO_2 conditions: a mete-analysis of reports on 79 crops and wild species" *New Phytology,* Vol. 156, pp. 9-26 doi:10.1046/1469-1837 2002-00494.x

Jacob, M.C., 2007 "Industrial Revolution" In: *World Bank Encyclopedia* (Delux Edition). http://www.justfacts.com/globalwarming. Retrieved 21st August 2012.

Jäger, J. and O' Riodan, T. 1996 "The History of Climate Change Science and Politics" pp. 1-31. In: T.O. O' Riordan and J. Jäger (eds.) *Politics of Climate Change: A European Perspective,* London.

Jarvis, L.S. 1986 *Livestock Development in Latin America;* Washington, D.C.: World Bank.

Jha, R. 2010A "Environmental taxation and emission trading schemes" chapter 22. In: Righbendra Jha, *Modern Public Economics,* Second Edition, London – New York: Routledge Taylor & Francis Group.

Jha, R. 2010B *Modern Public Economics;* Second Edition, London & New York: Routledge Taylor.

Jin, Rui Lin, and Liu, W. 1989 "Environmental Policy and Legislation in China", In: *Proceedings of the Sino-America Conference on Environmental Law,* Natural Resource Law Center, University of Colarado School of Law, Boulder.

Johnson, B. 2010 "Wally's World" *Foreign Policy;* 3rd August.

Johnson, D.E., Phetteplace, H.W. and Seidl, A.F. 2002 "Methane, Nitrous Oxide and Carbon Dioxide Emissions from Ruminant Livestock Production Systems". In: J. Takahashi and B.A. Young (eds.) pp. 77-85 *GHGs and Animal Agriculture, Proceedings of the 1st International Conference,* Obihiro, Japan, November.

Johnson, I. 2009 *Deforestation and Greenhouse Gas Emissions* (http://www.cfr.org/naturalsources.ma) Retrieved 21st August 2012.

Johnson, T. (2009, 21st December) "Deforestation and Green-house Emissions" *Council on Foreign Relations.*

Jones, B. and Keen, M. 2009 "Climate Policy in Hard Times" *Finance & Development,* December, pp. 7-9.

Jones, B., Keen, M. and Strand, J. 2008 "Paying for Climate Change" *Finance and Development*, March, pp. 28-31.

Jones, P.G. and Thornton, P.K. 2003 "The potential impacts of climate change on maize production in Africa and Latin America in 2055" *Global Environmental Change*, Vol. 13, pp. 51-59.

Joosten, H. 2009 "The Global Peatland CO_2 Picture: Peatland Status and the Drainage Related Emissions in All Countries of the World" *Wetlands International*.

Journal of Geophysical Research 15th January 2013.

Kanalley, C. (2011, 6th July) "Beijing Sandstorm 2010: PHOTOS of Major China Storm" *Huffington Post. Associated Press.*

Kandzewicz, Z. 2008 "Climate change impacts on the hydrologic cycle" *Ecohydrology & Hydrobiology*, Vol.8, No 2 doi: 10.2478 / v 10104-009-0015-y

Karim, M. F. and Mimura, N. (not dated) *Sea Level Rise in the Bay of Bengal: its Impact and Adaptations in Bangladesh;* Center for Water Environment Studies, Ibaraki University Hitachi, Japan http:/wcrp.ips.jussieu.fr/workshops/SeaLevel/ Posters/2_12_Fazlulkarin. pdf. Retrieved 7 August 2013.

Karl, T.R. and Knight, R.W. 1998 "Secular trends of precipitation amount, frequency, and intensity in the United States" *Bulletin of America Meteorological Society*, Vol. 79, pp. 231-41.

Karl, T.R., 2003 "Modern Global Climate Change" *Science*, 302 (5651) 1719-23.

Karrar, G. 1984 "The UN Plan of Action to Combat Desertification and the Concomittant UNEP Campaign" *Environmental Conservation*, Vol. 11, pp. 99-102.

Kasky, T. 2010 *Encyclopedia of Earth and Space Science.* (http://en.wikipedia.org/wiki/ Retreat of glarciers since 1850) Retrieved 10th August 2013.

Kemp, A.C. and Bengamin, P. 2013 "Contribution of relative sea-rise to historical hurricane flooding in York City" *Journal of Quaternary Science*, 1st published online: 8 August 2013 doi: 10. 1002/jqs.2653.

KENYA MENR 2002 "First Kenya communication to the conference of the parties of the UNFCCC" *National Environment Secretariat, Ministry of Environment and Natural Resources*, Nairobi. (http://unfccc.int/resources/docs/natc/kennc1.pdf).

Kerr, S. and Mare, D. 1998 *Transaction Costs and Tradable Permits. The United States Lead Phasedown*, Mimeos, Motu Research Trust, NZ htt:/www.meta.org.nz/pdf/transaction_costs.pdf.

Kete, N. 1992 "The U.S. Acid Rain Control Allowance Trading System". In: T. Jones and J. Corfee-Morlot, (eds). (pp. 69-93) *Climate Change: Designing A Tradeable Permit System.* Paris: OECD.

Kgope, B.S., Bond, W.J. and Midgleg, G.F. 2010 "Growth responses of African savanna trees implicate atmospheric CO_2 as a driver of past and current changes in savanna tree cover" *Austral Ecology*, Vol. 35, pp. 451-63.

Khan, T.M.A. and Quadir, D.A. 2002 "Relative Sea Level Changes in Maldives and Vulnerability of land due to abnormal coastal inundation" *Marine Geodesy,* 25, 133-143.

Kharin, N.G. 1994 *Climate change and desertification in Central Asia* Ashgabat, Turkmenistan: Desert Research Institute.

Kiehl, J.T. and Kerin, E.T. 1997 "Earth's Annual Global Mean Energy Budget" *Bulletin of the America Meteorological Society,* 78, 2, 197-208.

Kiehl, J.T. and Trenberth, J.T. 1997 "Earth's Annual Global Mean Annual Energy Budget" *Bulletin of the America Meteorological Society,* 78, (2): 197-208.

Kimbal, B.A., Kobayashi, K., Bindi, M. 2002 "Responses of agriculture crops to free-air CO_2 enrichment" *Advances in Agronomy,* Vol.77, pp. 293-368.

Kirby, K.R., Lawrence, W.F., Albernaz, A.K., Schroth, G., Fearnside, P.M., Bergen, S., Venticinque, E.M., de Costa, C. 2006 "The Future of Deforestation in the Brazilian Amazon" *Features of Bioregions,* Vol. 38, pp. 432-53.

Kleidon, A. and Heimann, M. 1999 "Deep-rooted Vegetation, Amazonian Deforestation and Climate: Results from a Modelling Study" *Global Ecology and Biography,* Vol. 8, pp. 397-405 doi: 10.1046/j. 1365-2699.1999.00150.x.

Klein, A.G. and Kincaic, J.L. 2008 "On the disappearance of the Puncak Mandala ice cap, Dapua" *Journal of Glaciology,* 54, 195-198.

Koch, H.-J. et al. 2007 *Climate Change Mitigation by Biomass – Executive Summary of the Special Report of the SRU Adversary Council on the Environmen;,* Berlin: German Advisory Council on the Environment, Jury.

Koop, G. and Tole, L. 1999 "Is there an environmental Kuznets curve for deforestation?" *Journal of Development Economics,* Vol. 58, doi: 10. 1016/S0304 – 3878 (98) 00110 – 2.

Kosten, S. et al. 2010 "Climate-dependent CO_2 Emissions from Lakes" *Glob. Biogeochem. Cycles,* Vol. 24. GB 2007.

Krales, A.H. (2011, 18th October) "As Danger Laps at Its Shores, Tuvalu Pleads for Action" *The New York Times..*

Kreiser, L., Duff, D., Milne, J.E., and Ashiabon, H. (eds.) 2014 *Market Based Instruments: National Experiences in Environmental Sustainability;* Edward Elgar.

Kreiser, L., Sirison, J., Ashiabor, H. 2011 *Environmental Taxation and Climate Change: Achieving Environmental Sustainability through Fiscal Policy;* Edward Elgar Publishing.

Kummar, D.M. 1992 *Deforestation in the Postwar Philippines;* University of Chicago Press.

Kummar, D.M. and Turner II, B.L. 1994 "The Human Causes of Deforestation in Southeast Asia" *Bioscience,* Vol. 44, No. 5, pp. 323-28.

Kunzig, R. 1995 "Twilight of the Cod" *Discovery,* 52.

Kurlansky, M. 2002 *Salt: A World History;* London: Pengium.

Kurz, W.A. Dymond C.C., Stinson, G. et al. 2008 "Mountian pine beetle and forest carbon feedback to climate change" *Nature,* 452 (7190), pp. 987-90.

Kuznets, S. 1966 *Modern Economic Growth: Rate, Structure, and Spread;* New Haven, CT: Yale University Press.

Lamb, P.J. 1979 "Some Perspectives on Climate and Climate Dynamics" *Progress in Physical Geography,* Vol. 3, pp. 215-35.

Lambin, E.F., Turner, B.L.., Geist, H.J., Agbola, S.B. et al. 2001 "The causes of land-use and land-cover change: moving beyond the myth" *Global Environmental Change,* Vol. 11, No. 4, pp. 261-269.

Lamprey, H. 1988 "Report on the desert encroachment reconnaissance in northern Sudan, October 21 – November 10, 1875" *Desertification Control Bulletin,* Vol. 17, 1-7 (reprinted).

Latif, M. and Keenlyside, N.S. 2009 "EL Niňo / Southern Oscillation response to global warming" *Proceedings of the National Academy of Sciences of the United States of America (PNAS),* Vol. 106, No. 49, December 8, 20578-20583. (http://www.pnas.org/content/106/49/20578. fall#f1) Retrieved 22 September 2013.

Laurence, W.F. 1999 "Reflection on the Tropical Deforestation Crisis" *Biological Conservation,* Vol. 91, Issues 2-3, pp. 109-117.

Le Houerou, H.N. 1977 "Biological Recovery vs Desertization" *Economic Geography,* Vol. 53, pp. 413-20.

Le Houerou, H.N. 1996 "Climate change drought and desertification" *Journal of Arid Environments,* Vol. 34, pp. 133-85.

Le Trent, H. Somerville. R., Cubasoh, U., Ding, Y., Mauritzen, C., Hoksill, A., Patterson, T., and Prather, M. 2008. "Historical Overview of Climate Change Science" In: Solomon, S., Quin, D., Manning, M., Chen, Z., Marquis, M., Averyt, K.B., Tighor, M., and Miller, H.C., (eds.) *Climate Change 2007: The Physical Science Basis,* Cambridge University Press.

Lele, S.M. 1991 "Sustainable Development: A Critical Review" *World Development,* Vol. 19, pp. 607-21.

Lemke, P.J. et al. 2007 "Observations: changes in Snow, Ice and Frozen Ground" In: S. Solomon et al. (eds) *Climate Change 2007: The Physical Science Basis. Contribution of Working Group I to the Fourth Assessment Report of the IPCC,* Cambridge University Press.

Levine, J.S. (ed) 1991 *Global Biomass Burning: Atmospheric, Climate and Biospheric Implication;* Cambridge, MS: MIT Press.

Levitus, S., et al. 2000 "Warming of the World Ocean" *Science,* Vol. 287, March 24.

Li, G., Harrison, S.P., Bartlein, P.J., Izumi, K., and Colin Prentice, I. 2013 "Precipitation scaling with temperature in warm and cold climates: An Analysis of C M I P 5 simulations" *Geophysical Research Letters,* Vol. 40, doi: 10, 1002/grl. 50730.

Limbery, B. 2009 "Technology, Not Talks will Save the Planet" *Finance & Development*, December, pp. 13-14.

Lindsey, R. 2007 "Tropical Deforestation" *NASA Earth Observatory*, March 30.

Lindsey, R. 2010 "Spring Sandstorm Scours China" *Earth Observatory National Aeronautics and Space Administration,* March 20.

Lipton, M. and Longhurst, R. 1989 *New Seeds and Poor People*; Baltimore: The Johns Hopkins University Press

Lloyd, W.F. (1833) *Two Lectures on the Checks to Population,* Oxford University Press. (see *Population and Development Review,* Vol. 6, No. 3, Sep. 1980, pp. 473-96).

Lohmann, L. 2006 *Carbon Trading: A Critical Conversation on Climate Change, Privatization and Power;* Uppsala: Dag Hammarrskjold Foundation.

Lomborg, B. 2009 "Technology, Not Talks Will Save the Planet" *Finance & Development,* December pp. 13-14.

Lopez, R. 1998 "The tragedy of the commons in Cote d' Ivoire Agriculture: Empirical Evidence and Implications for Evaluating Trade Policies" *The World Bank Economic Review,* Vol. 12, No.1, pp. 105-31.

Lopez-Acevedo, Gladys, 2003 "Mexico: In-firm training for the knowledge economy" *Policy Research Working Paper Series, 2947,* The World Bank.

Lotstayn, Z.D. and Lohmann, U. 2002 "Tropical Rainfall Trends and the Indirect Arosal Effect" *Journal of Climate* (American Meteorological Society). http://eu.wikipedia.org/wiki/sahel_drought.

Low, N. and Glesson, B. 1998 *Justice, society and nature: An exploration of political ecology;* London: Rouledge.

Lu Hu (ed) 2006 "Pollution, overfishing destroy East China Sea Fishery" *Xinhua* on Gov. on 26th August.

Lucas, R., McMichael, T., Smith, W. and Armstrong, B. 2006 "Solar Ultraviolet Radiation: Global Burden of Disease from Solar Ultraviolet Radiation" In: Pŕuss-Ustun, A. et al. (eds.) *Environmental Burden of Disease Series,* No. 13 World Health Organization, Geneva. (see also WHO Website: http:..www.who.int/UV/health/solaruvradfull_180706.pdf?ua=1).

MA 2005 *Millennium Ecosystem Assessment: Ecosystems and Human Wellbeing: Synthesis;* Washington: Island Press.

Mabbut, J.A. and Floret C. (eds.) 1980 *Case Studies on Desertification;* Paris: United Nations Educational, Scientific and Cultural Organization (UNESCO).

Mabbutt, J.A. 1984 "A New Global Assessment of the Status and Trends of Desertification" *Environmental Conservation,* Vol. 11, pp. 103-113.

Mabogunje, A.L. 1995 "The Environmental Challenges in Sub-Saharan Africa" *African Technology Forum,* Vol. 8, No. 1; also *Environment* Vol. 37, No. 4.

MacAndrews, C. 1978 "Transmigration in Indonesia: Prospects and Problems" *Asian Survey,* Vol. 18, No. 5, pp. 458-72.

Machi, Y., Roberts, J.T., Betts, R.A., Killeen, T.J., Li, W. and Noble, C.A. 2009 "Climate Change, Deforestation, and the Fate of the Amazon" *Science,* Vol. 319 (5860) pp. 169-172.

Maconachie, R., Tanko, A. and Zakariya, M. 2009 "Descending the Energy Ladder? Oil Price Shocks and Domestic Fuel Choices in Kano, Nigeria" *Land Use Policy,* Vol. 26, No. 4, pp. 1090-1099 doi: 10.1016/j.landnsepal.2009.01.008. Accessed 29 May 2016.

Maes, F., Cliquet A., Due Plessis, W., McLeoa-Kilmurray (eds) 2013 *Biodiversity and Climate Change: Linkages at International and Local Levels;* Edward Elgar.

Mahowald, N.M. and Kiehl, L.M. 2003 "Mineral Aerosol and Cloud Interactions" *Geophysical Research Letters,* Vol. 30, No. 9, 1475.

Malaisse, F. and Binzangi, K. 1985 "Wood as a source of fuel in Upper Shaba (Zaire)" Commonwealth *Forest Review,* Vol. 64, pp. 227-39.

Maler, K. 1998 "Environmental Poverty and Economic Growth" In: Boris Pleskovic and J.E. Sitglitz, (eds.), pp. 251-70 *Annual World Bank Conference on Development Economics 1997,* Washington DC: World Bank.

Marcoax, A. 2000 *Population and Deforestation*; Rome: FAO.

Marglis, S. 2004 "Causes of Deforestation of the Brazilian Amazon" *World Bank Working Paper* No. 22, Washington, D.C.: The World Bank.

Marine, J – N., 2009. "Peri-Urban Forests and Wood Energy: What are the Perspectives for Central Africa?" In: C. de Wasseige et al. (eds.) *The Forests of the Congo Basin – State of the Forest 2008,* Luxemburg: European Union Publication Office.

Mark, K. (2015, 14th November) "COP21: What does the Paris Climate Agreement mean for me?" *BBC News.*

Markandya, A. 2013 "Environmental Taxation: What have we learnt in the Last 38 Years?" In: Laura Castellucci, Anil Markandya, *Environmental Taxes and Fiscal Reform,* Basingstoke. Palgrave Macmillan.

Master, C. 1990 *The Redesigned Forest*; Toronto: Stoddart.

Mather, A. 1992 "The forest transition" *Area,* Vol. 24, pp. 367-79.

Maurya, P.R. 1987 "Impact of Irrigation Water Logging and Salinity in Kano River Irrigation Project, Northern Nigeria" *Samaru Journal of Agricultural Education,* Vol. 1, No.1., pp. 46-55.

Mayhell, H. (2001, 26th April) "Shrinking African Lake Offers Lesson for Finite Resources" *National Geogrhaphic.*

Mayhew, S. 2009 *Oxford Dictionary of Geography;* 4th edition, Oxford University Press.

Mayoux, P. et al. 2013 "State and evolution of the African rainforests between 1990 and 2010" *Philosophical Transactions of the Royal Society B,* Vol. 368, 201 20300.

Mbow, C., Skole, D., Dieng, M., Justice, C., Kwesha, D., Mane, L., El Gamri, M., von Vordzogbe, V. and Virji, H. 2012 *Challenges and Prospects for REDD+ in Africa: Review of REDD+ Implimentation in Africa;* START: Copenhagen, Denmark.

McCormick, J. 1986 "The Origins of the World Conservation Strategy" *Environmental Review,* Vol. 10, No. 2, pp.177-87.

McCormick, J. 1997 *Acid Earth;* London: Earthscan.

McCormick, J. 1997 *The Global Environmental Movement: Reclaiming Paradise;* London: Belhauen.

McGranaham, G., Back, D. and Anderson, B. 2007 "The rising tide: assessing the risks of climate change and human settlement in low elevation coastal zones" *Environment & Urbanization,* Vol.19, No 1, pp.17-37.

McLean, I. and McMillan A. (eds) 2003 *Oxford Concise Dictionary of Politic;* Oxford University Press.

McMillan, M., Shepherd, A., Sundal, A., Briggs, K., Mair, A., Ridout, A., Hogg, A. and Wingham, D. 2014 "Increased Ice Losses from Antarctica Detected by Cryostat-2" *Geophys. Res. Le H* 41, 3899-3905.

McPhaden, M. J. et al 1998 "The Tropical Ocean Global Atmosphere Obscuring System: A Decade of Progress" *Journal of Geophysical Research,* 103: 14169-14240.

Mechl, G.A. et al. 2007 "Global Climate Projections" In: S. Solomon, et al (eds.) *Climate Change 2007: The Physical Science Basis. Contribution of Working Group I to the Fourth Assessment Report of IPCC,* Cambridge (UK) and New York: Cambridge University Press.

Megerand, C. 2013 *Deforestation Trends in the Congo Basin: Reconciling Economic Growth and Forest Protection;* Washington D.C.: The World Bank.

Mendelsohn, R. and Ariel Dinar 2009 *Climate Change and Agriculture;* Edward Elgar Publishing.

Mendelsohn, R. and Schlesinger, M.E. 1999 "Climate Response Functions" *Ambio,* Vol. 28 (June) pp. 362-66.

Mendelsohn, R.A., Dinar, et al. 2006 "The Distributional Impacts of Climate Change on Rich and Poor Countries" *Environmental and Development Economics,* Vol. 11, pp. 159-178.

Menzel, A and 30 Co-authors, 2006 "European Phenological Response to Climate Change Matches the Warming Pattern" *Global Change Biology,* Vol. 12, No. 10, pp. 1969-76.

Mertens, B. and Lambin, E.F. 2000 "Land-cover change trajectories in Southern Cameroon" *Annals of the Association of American Geographers,* Vol. 90, pp. 467-94.

Metcalf, G.E. 2009 "Designing a Carbon Tax to Reduce U.S. Greenhouse Gas Emissions" *Review of Environmental Economics & Policy,* Vol. 3, No.1, pp. 63-83.

Meyer, W.B. and Turner II, B.L. 1992 "Human Population Growth and Global Land-Use/ Cover Change" *Annual Review of Ecological Systems,* Vol. 23, pp. 39-61.

Michael, P. (2007, 2nd August) "Rising Seas Threat to Torres Strait Islands" *The Courier – Mail* (Nuos Queenland), (http://en.wikipedia.org/wiki/Torres_Strait_Islands.

Middleton, N.J. and Goudie, A.S. 2000 "Sahara dust: sources and trajectories" *Transactions of the British Institute of Geographers,* NS 26 165-181.

Midgley, T. and Henne, A.L. 1930 "Organic Fluorides as Refrigerants 1" *Industrial & Engineering Chemistry,* Vol. 22, No. 5, doi: 10.1021/ie 502459031.

Mijindadi, N.B. and Adegbehin, J. O. 1991 "Drought, Desertification and Food Production in Nigeria" *Savanna,* Vol. 12, No. 2 (December), pp. 25-40.

Miklin, P., and Aladin, N.V. 2008 "Reclaiming the Aral Sea" *Scientific American.* Retrieved 4 Feb 2015.

Millennium Ecosystem Assessment 2005 *Ecosystem and human well-being: Synthesis;* Washington, D.C.: Island Press.

Milliman, J.D., Broadus, J.M., and Gable, F. 1989 "Environmental and Economic Implications of Rising Sea Level and Subsiding Deltas: The Nile and Bengal Examples" *Ambio,* Vol. 18, No. 6, pp. 340-345.

Mills, P. 2008 "The Greening of Markets" *Finance & Development,* Vol. 45, No. 1 (March) pp. 32-41.

Milman, O. (2015, 12th December) "James Hansen, Father of Climate Change Awareness, Calls Paris Talks 'a Fraud'" *The Guardian,* London. Retrieved 21 October 2016.

Milne, J. E. and Aderson, M.S. 2012 *Handbook of Research on Environmental Taxation;* Edward Elgar Publishing.

Mishia, A.K., and Singh, V.P. 2011 "Drought modeling – A review" *Journal of Hydrology,* Vol. 403, p. 157. doi:10.1016/j.jhydrol.2011.03.049.

Mobjörk, M., and van Baalen, S. 2016 *Climate change and violent conflict in East Africa-implications for policy,* Stockholm International Peace Research Institute (SIPRI) Policy Brief, April.

Mölg, T. 2005 "Worldwide glacier retreat" *Real Climate: Climate Science from Climate Scientists,* 18th March.

Mongillo, J.F., Zierdt-Warshaw, L. 2000 (ed.) *Encyclopedia of environmental science;* University of Rochester Press.

Mooney, C. (2015, 15th October) "How Indonesia's Gigantic Fires are Making Global Warming Worse" *The Washington Post.*

Mooney, H.A. and Ehrlich, P.R. 1997 "Ecosystem Services: a Fragmentary History" pp. 11-19, In: G.C. Daily, (eds.) *Natures Service: Societal Dependence on Natural Systems,* Washington: Island Press.

Moorhead, R. 1988 "Access to resources in the Niger Inland Delta, Mali" pp. 27-39, In: J. Seeky and W.M. Adams (eds.) *Enviromental Issues in African Development Planning,* Cambridge African Monorgraphs No. 9, African Studies Centre, Cambridege (UK).

Moran, E.F. 1993 "Deforestation and Land Use in the Brazilian Amazon" *Human Ecology,* Vol. 21, No. 1.

Morgan, W.B. 1978 "Development and the Fuelwood Situation in Nigeria" *Geo Journal,* Vol. 2, Issue 5, pp. 437-442.

Morrisette, P.M. (1989) "The Evolution of Policy Responses to Stratospheric Ozone Depletion" *Natural Resources Journal,* 29, 793-820. Retrieved 28 August 2013.

Mortimore, M. 1989 *Adaptinig to Drought: Farmers, Famines and Desertification in West Africa;* Cambridge Univeristy Press.

Mortimore, M. 1998 *Roots in the African Dust: Sustaining the Sub-Saharan Drylands*; Cambridge University Press.

Mortimore, M. and Adams, W.M. 1999 *Working the Sahel: environment and society in northern Nigeria;* London: Routledge.

Mote, P.W. and Kaser, G. 2007 "The shrinking glaciers of Kilimanjaro: Can Global Warning be blamed?" *American Scientists,* 95, 4: 318-325.

Mouafo, D., Fotsing, E.R., Sighomnou, D., and Sigha, L. 2002 "Dam, environment and regional development: case study of the Logone floodplain in Northern Cameroon" *Water Resource Development,* Vol.18, pp. 209-19.

Moutinho, P. and Schwartzman, S. (eds.) 2005 *Tropical Deforestation and Climate Change;* Washington D.C.: Environmental Defense / IPAM Brazil.

Mulvaney, D. 2014 "Solar Energy Isn't Always as Green as You Think. Do Cheaper Photovoltaics come with a Higher Environmental Tag?" *IEEE Spectrum,* 26 August.

Munasinghe, M. 1993 "Environment Economics and Sustainable Development" *World Bank Environmental Paper* 3, World Bank, Washington.

Munasinghe, M. 1993a "Environmental economics and biodiversity management" *Ambio,* Vol. 22, pp. 126-35.

Munasinghe, M. 2008 "Rising Temperatures, Rising Risk" *Finance and Development,* March, pp. 37-41.

Muoghalu, L.N. 2007 "Environment and Conflict in Africa: Issues and Problems (Focus on the Niger Delta Region of Nigeria)" In: E.E. Udoye, M.E. Onuorah, M.E. Meze, E.O. Ibezim, S.C. Okafor Udah, T.O. Onyefulu, V.N. Okonkwo (eds.) *Environment and Conflicts in Africa: Issues and Problems,* Enugu: Prefabag Investment.

Murray, J.W. 1992 "The Oceans" *International Geophysics,* Vol. 50, pp. 175-211 doi: 10.1016/50074-6142 (08) 62692 – 3.

Myers, N. 1980 *Conversion of Tropical Moist Forests;* Washington: National Academy of Sciences.

Myers, N. and Tucker, R. 1987 "Deforestation in Central America: Spanish Legacy and North American Consumers" *Environmental Review* ER, 11, No. 1, pp. 55-71.

Myint, H. 1965 *The Economics of Developing Countries;* New York: Praeger.

Myint, H. 1971 *Economic Theory and Underdeveloped Countries;* New York: Oxford University Press.

Najam, A. Huq, S. and Sokona, Y. 2003 "Climate Negotiations beyond Kyoto Development Countries, Concerns and Interests" *Climate Policy,* Vol. 3, pp. 221-31.

Naoto, J. 2006 "International trade and terrestrial open-access renewable resources in a small-open economy" *Canadian Journal of Economics,* Vol. 39, No. 3, pp. 790-808.

Narayanan, D.L., Saladi, R.N. and Fox, J.L. 2010 "Review: Ultraviolet radiation and skin cancer" *FAAD2 International Journal of Dermatology,* Vol. 49, Issue 9, pp. 978-986, Septmber.

NASA (2004, 9th June) "NASA Data shows deforestation affects climate in the Amazon" *NASA News.*

NASA (2011, 5th July) "Dust Storm in Phoenix" *NASA Earth Observatory.*

National Academy of Sciences, 1979 "Carbon Dioxide and Climate" *National Academy of Sciences.*

National Non-Feed Crops Centre "GHG Benefits from Use of Vegetable Oils for Electricity, Heat, Transport and Industrial Purposes, NNFCC 10-016" http://en.wikipedia.org/wiki/biomass_fuels.

National Research Council 1994 *Solar Influence Can Global Change;* Washington D.C.: National Academy Press.

Ndzibah, E. 2010 "Diffusion of Solar Technology in Developing Countries: Focus Group Study in Ghana" *Management of Environmental Quality: An International Journal,* Vol. 21, No. 6. doi: 10.1108/14777 831011077637.

Nef, J.U. 1977 "Early Energy Crisis and its Consequences" *Scientific America,* 237(5).

Negin, J., Rome, R., Karnti, S. and Kanzo, J.C. 2009 "Integrating a broader notion of food security and gender improvement into African Green Revolution" *Food Security,* Vol. 1, pp. 351-360.

Nelson, G.C. 2009 *Climate change: Impact on agriculture and costs of adaptation;* International Food Policy Research Institute, Washington, D.C.

Neptad, D., McGrath, d., Stickler, C., Alencer, A., Swette, B. et. al. (2014) "Slowing Amazon deforestation through puplic policy and intervention in beef and soy supply chains" *Science,* Vol. 344, No. 6188, pp. 1118-1123.

Neptad, D., Soares-Ficho, B.S., Merry, F., Lima, A., Mortinho, P., Carter, O. 2009 "The end of deforestation in the Brazillian Amazon" *Science,* Vol. 326, No. 5958, pp. 1350- 1351.

Neumayer, E. 2010 *Weak versus Strong Sustainability: Exploring the Limits of Two Opposing Paradigms;* 3rd edition, Edward Elgar.

New Scientist (2003, 23rd July) "Biodiversity Wipeout Facing Southeast Asia" *New Scientist.*

New York Times (2012, 24th July) "Rare Burst of Melting Seen in Greenlands Ice Sheet" *New York Times.*

News Archives, AAAS 2005 "New Study in Science Find Glaciers in Retreat on Antarctic Peninsular" *American Association for the Advancement of Science,* April 21. (http://www.aaas.org/news/releases/2005/0421glaciers.shtml) Retrieved 10th August 2013.

Newson, C. 2012 "Renewable Energy Potential in Nigeria" *International Institute for Environment and Development* (IIED), London.

Niasse, M. 2005 "Climate-induced Water Conflicts Risks in West Africa: Recognizing and Coping with Increasing Climate Impacts on Shared Watercourses" Paper to *International Workshop on Human Security and Climate Change*, Asker, 21-23 June.

Nicholls, R.J., Wong, P.P., Burket, V. et al. 2006 "Coastal system and low-lying areas" In: *IPCC WGII Fourth Assessment Report – Draft for Government and Expert Review.*

Nicholson, S. 2005 "On the question of the "recovery" of the rains in the West African Sahel" *Journal of Arid Environments,* Vol. 63, No. 3, pp. 615-41.

Nicholson, S.E. 1978 "Climate variation in the Sahel and other African regions during the past five centuries" *Journal of Arid Environment,* Vol. 1, pp. 3-24.

Nicholson, S.E. 1996 "Environmental change within the historical period" pp.60-88 In: W.M. Adams, A.S. Goudie and A.R. Orme (eds.) *The Physical Geography of Africa,* Oxford: Oxford University Press.

Nicholson, S.E. 2001 "Climatic and environmental change in Africa during the last two centuries" *Climate Research,* Vol. 17, No 2, pp. 123-144.

Nicholson, S.E. 2013 "The West African Sahel: A Review of Recent Studies on the Rainfall Regime and its Interannual Variability" *ISRN Meteorology.* (http:/dx.doi.org /10.1155/2013/453521. Vol 2013 (2013) article ID 453521.

Nicholson, S.E., Tucker, C.J. and Ba, M.B. 1998 "Desertification, Drought and Surface Vegetation: An Example from the West African Sahel" *Bulletin of the American Meteorological Society.*

Nijhuis, M. (2014, April) "Can Coal Ever be Clean?" *National Geographic*, April.

Niklitschek, M. 1990 *Economic Growth in Sub-Saharan Africa: The Implications for Environmental Degradation,* PhD Dissertation, University of Maryland, College Park.

Ninani, K.N. 2014 *Valuing Ecosystem Services: Methodological Issues and Case Studies;* Edward Elgar.

NMA 2007 *Climate change natural adaptation program of action (NAPA) of Ethiopia;* National Meteorological Agency, Addis Ababa.

NOAA 2013 National Oceanic and Atmospheric Administration: "Stratospheric Ozone: monitory and Reseacrh in NOAA" http:/wwwozonelayer.noaa.gov/science/basics.htm. Accessed 27August 2013.

Noble, I. and Watson, R.T. 2006 "Confronting Climate Change" pp. 219-44. In: Vinay Bhargava, ed. *Global Issues for Global Citizens: An Introduction to Key Development Challenges,* Washington D.C.: The World Bank.

Noble, I. et al 2005 "Climate Change" In: *Ecosystems and Human Well-Being: Policy Responses,* Washington, D.C.: Island Press.

Nordhaus, W. and Boyer, J., 2000 *Warming the World: Economic Models of Global Warming;* MIT Press.

Nordhaus, W.D. 1994 "Expert Opinion on Climate Change" *American Scientist,* Vol. 82, pp.45-51.

Norman, M. and Nakhooda, S. 2015 "The State of REDD+ Finance" *Centre for Global, Working Paper,* 378, May.

Norris, F.T. 1997 "Where Did the Villages Go? Steamboats, Deforestation and the Archaeological Loss in the Mississippi Valley" In: *Common Fields: An Environmental History of St. Louis,* Andrew Hurley, (ed.) St. Louis, MO: Missouri Historical Society Press.

North America Climate Change Impacts 2016 "North America: Climate Change Impacts" *Climate Change: in Context,* Encyclopedia.com 3 Dec (http://www.encyclopedia.com)

North India Floods, 2013 "2013 North India Floods" http//en.wikipedia.org/wiki/2013_North_India_Floods.

NOVA 2006 "Dimming the Sun" *NOVA,* Public Broadcasting Service 18th April Retrieved 26 August 2013.

Nunes, A.L.D., Kumar, P. and Dedeurwaerdere, T. (eds.) 2014 *Handbook on the Economics of Ecosystem Services and Biodiversity*; Edward Elgar.

O'Riordan, T. and Jager, J. 1996 "The History of Climate Change Science and Policies" pp. 11-31 in T. O' Riordan and J. Jager, (eds.) *Politics of Climate Change in European Perspective,* London: Routledge.

Obasi, G.O.P 2005 "The impacts of ENSO in Africa" In: Pak Sum Low (ed) *Climate Change and Africa<* pp. 218-30, Cambridge University Press.

Odihi, J. (2003) "Applied Geography – Deforestation in Afforestation Priority Zone in Savanna-Sahelian Nigeria" *Applied Geography,* Vol. 23, Issue 4 (October) pp. 227-59.

Odjugo, P.A. 2010 "General Overview of Climate Change Impacts in Nigeria" *Journal of Human Ecology,* Vol. 29, No. 1, pp. 47-55.

OECD, 2008 *Environmentally Related Taxes and Tradable Permits Systems in Practice;* Paris: Organization for Economic Cooperation and Development.

OECD, 2012 *The Role of Nuclear in a Low-Carbon Energy Future*; OECD Nuclear Energy Agency, Paris.

OECD, 2013 *Taxing Energy Use: A Graphical Analysis;* Paris: OECD.

Oladipo, E. O. 1988 "Drought in Africa; A Synthesis of Current Scientific Knowledge" *Savanna,* Vol. 9, No. 2, pp. 64-82.

Olesen, J.E., Bindi, M. 2002 "Consequences of Climate Change for European Agricultural Productivity, Land Use and Policy" *European Journal of Agronomy,* Vol.6, pp. 239-262.

Olsen, K.H. 2007 "The Clean Develpoment Mechanism's Contribution to Sustainable Development: A Review of the Literature" *Climate Change,* Vol. 84, pp. 59-73.

Olsen, K.H. and Fenhann, J. 2008 Sustainable Development Benefits of Clean Development Mechanism Projects: A New Methodology for Sustainability Assessment Based Text

Analysis of the Project Design Documents Subjected for Validation, *Energy Policy* 36, 2819-2830.

Omofonmwan, S.I. and Osa-Edoh, G.I. 2008 "The Challenges of Enviromental Problems in Nigeria" *Journal of Human Ecology*, Vol. 23, No.1, pp.53-57.

Omondi, P.A. et al 2014 "Change in temperature and precipitation extremes over the greater Horn of Africa region from 1961 to 2010" *International Journal of Climatology*, Vol. 34, pp. 1262-77.

Onuoha F.C. 2008 "Saving Africa's shrinking lakes through inter-basin water transfer: reflections on the Lake Chad replenishment project" *Nigeria Journal of International Affairs*, Vol. 34, pp 65-84.

Oollimi, J. 2015 *Shiftihg Cltivation, Gender and REDD+ in Cameroon and Democratic Republic Congo. USAID – Supported Forest Carbon, Markets and Communities (FCMC) Program:* Washington D.C.

Oosterhais, F. H. and Brink, P. ten (eds.) 2014 *Paying the Polluter: Environmentally Harmful subsides and their Reform*; Edward Elgar.

Oreskes, N. and Conway, G. (no date) *Merchants of Doubt: How a Handful of Scientists Obscured the Truth on Issues from Tobacco Smoke to Global Warming;* (First Edition), Bloomberg Press.

Osadchaya, I. 1983 *Keynesianism Today: A Critic of Economic Theory and Economic Policy;* Moscow: Progress Publishers.

Osman, J. (2011) *100 Ideas that Changed the World;* Random House.

Osueke, C.O. and Ezugwu, C.A.K. 2011 "Study of Nigeria Energy Resources and Its Consumption" *International Journal of Scientific & Engineering Research*, Vol. 2, Issue 12 (December).

Osueke, C.O., Uzendu, P. and Ogbonna, I.D. 2013 "Study and Evaluation of Solar Energy Variation in Nigeria" *International Journal of Emerging Technology and Advanced Engineering*, Vol. 3, Issue 6 (June).

Oxford Dictionary of Biology, 2000 *Oxford Dictionary of Biology*, 4th edition, Oxford University Press.

Oxford Dictionary of Physics 2009 *Oxford Dictionary of Physics*, 6th edition Oxford University Press.

Oxford Dictionary of Science, 2005 *A Dictionary of Science*, 5th edition, Cambridge University Press.

Oyiga, B., Mekibib, H. and Christine, W. 2011 *Implications of climate change on crop yield and food accessibility in Sub-Saharan Africa;* Bonn University, Germany.

Paltsev, S., Morris, J., Cai, Y., Karplu, V. and Jacoby, H. 2012 "The role of China in Mitigating Climate Change" *Energy Economics*, Vol. 34, S444-S450 doi.10.1016/j.eneco.2012.o4.007.

Palumbi, S.R. 2001 "Humans as the wold's greatest evolutionary force" *Science*, 293 (5536), 1786-90.

Panayotou, T. 1993 *Green Markets: The Economics of Sustainable Development;* San Francisco, C.A.: ICS Press.

Pantuliano, S. and Pavanello, S. 2009 *Taking drought into account: Addressing chronic vulnerability among pastoralists in the Horn of Africa;* London: Overseas Development Institute (ODI).

Pappas, S. 2013 "Melting glaciers are causing almost a third of sea-level rise" *Science,* May 16.

Parikka, M. 2004 "Global biomass fuel resources" *Biomass and Bioenergy,* Vol. 27, Issue 6, December, pp. 613-620.

Parmiesan, C. 2006 "Ecological and Evolutionary Responses to Recent Climate Change" *Annual Review of Ecology, Evolution and Systematics,* 37: 637-69.

Parry, M., Canziani. O., Palutikof J., Van der Linden, P. and Hansen, C. (eds.) 2007 *Climate Change 2007: Impacts, Adaptation And Vulnerability, Contribution of Working Group II To The Fourth Assessment Report of the Intergovernmental Panel on Climate Change;* Cambridge University Press/Published for IPCC.

Parry, M.L. 2001 "Millions at risk defining critical climate change threats and targets" *Global Environment Change,* Vol.11, pp.181-183.

Pear, D. and Atkinson, G. 1993 "Capital Territory and the Measurement of Sustainable Development: An Indicator of 'Weak Sustainability'" *Ecological Economics,* 8(103-8) (htt://dx.doc.org/10.1016/0921-8009/83) 90039-9.

Pearce, D. 2009 *Environmental Valuation in Developed Countries: Case Studies;* Edward Elgar.

Pearce, D. and Brown, K. 1994 "Saving the world's tropical forests" pp. 2-26 In: K. Brown and D. Pearce (eds) *The Causes of Tropical Deforestation. The Economic and Statistical Analysis of Factors giving rise to the loss of the Tropical Forests,* London: University College, London Press.

Pearce, D. and Puroshothaman, S. 1993 "Protecting Biological Diversity: The Economic Value of Pharmacentical Plants" In: Timothy Swanson, ed., *Biodiversity and Botany: the Values of Medicinal Plants,* http:/www.cserge.ac.uk; accessed 3 August 20014.

Pearce, D.W. and Turner, K. 1990 *Economics of National Resoruces and the Environment;* Baltimore: Johns Hopkins University Press.

Pearce, D.W., Barbier, E., and Markandya, A. 1989 *Sustainable Development: Economics and Environment in the Third World;* London: Edward Elgar.

Pearce, F. (2008, 30th October) "Time to Bury the 'Clean Coal' Myth" *The Guardian* (UK).

Pearce, F. (2009, 28th February) "Green wash: Why 'Clean Coal' is the Ultimate Climate Change Oximoron" *The Guardian* (UK).

Pearse, A. 1974 "Green Revolution" *Journal of Peasant Studies,* Vol. 1, No. 3 (April) pp.386-7.

Pechony, O. and Shindell, D.T. 2010 "Driving Forces of Global Wildfires over the Past Millennium and the Forthcoming Century" *Proceedings of the National Academy of Sciences,* Vol. 107, No. 45, pp. 19167-170.

Peeters, M. and K. Deketaere 2006 *EU Climate Change Policy: The Challenge of New Regulatory Initiatives;* Edward Elgar.

Peeters, M. and Uylenburg, R. (eds.) 2015 *EU Enviromental Legislation: Legal Perspectives on Regulatory Strategie;* Edward Elgar.

Pelto, M.S. and Hedlund, C. 2001 "Terminus behavior and response time of north Cascade glaciers, Washington, USA" *Journal of Glacciology,* 47 (158): 497-506.

Pelto, P.M. (no date) North Cascade Glacier Climate Project - Recent Global Retreat Overview. http://www.nichols.edu/Departments/glaciers_retreat.htm.

Pepper, D. 1993 *Eco-Socialism: From Deep Ecology to Social Justice;* London: Routledge.

Perkins, D.H., Radelet, S., Snodgrass, D., Gillis, M. and Roemer, M. 2001 *Economics of Developent;* 5th edition, W.W. Norton & Company.

Perry, M.J. (2010, 11th November) "Nuclear Power Needed Now" *Detwit News.*

Peters, G.P. 2008 "From Production-based to Consumption-based National Emission Inventories" *Ecological Economics,* Vol. 65, pp. 13-23.

Peters, G.P. and Hertwich, E.G. 2008 "CO_2 Embodied in International Trade with Implications for Global Climate Policy" *Environment, Science and Technology,* Vol. 28: 1401-1407.

Peters, M. and Fudge, S. 2010 *Low Carbon Communities: Imaginative Approaches to Combating Climate Change Locally;* Edward Elgar.

Pezzy, J. 1989 "Economic Analysis of Sustainable Growth and Sustainable Development" *Environment Working Paper 15,* World Bank, Washington D.C.

Pfaff, A., Amaecher, G.S., and Sills, E.O. 2013 "Realistic REDD+: Improving the Forest Impacts of Domestic Policies in Different Settings" *Review of Environmental Economicsand Policy,* Vol.7, No. 1, pp. 114-135. Doi:https://doi.org/10.1093/reep/res023

Philander, S.G.H. 1990 *EL Niño, La Niña, and the Southern Oscillation;* London: Academic.

Piazza-Georgi, B. 2002 "The role of human and social capital in growth: extending our understanding" *Cambridge Journal of Economics,* Vol. 26, pp. 461-477 http://dx.doi.org/10.1093/cje/26. 4.461.

Pidwirny, M. 2012 "Glacier" In: *The Encyclopeia of Earth.* Retrieved from http://www.eoearth.org/view/article/152981.

Pigou, A.C. 1932 *The Economics of Welfare;* London: Macmillan.

Podobnik, R., Pearson, P.J.G., 1998 "Toward a Sustainable Energy Regime: A Long-wave Interpretation of Global Energy Shifts" 62(3), doi: 10.1016/S0040-1625(99)00042-6

Polet, G. and Thompson, J.R. 1996 "Maintaining the floods: hydrological and institutional aspects of managing the Komaduga - Yobe River Basin and its floodplain wetlands" pp. 73-91. In: M.C. Acreman, and G.E. Hollis (eds.) *Water Management and Wetlands in Sub-Saharan Africa,* IUCN, Gland: Switzerland.

Porrini, D. 2005 Environmental Policy". In: M. Peter Van der Hoek, ed., *Handbook of Public Administration and Policy in the European Union;* Chapter Twenty, pp. 501-13, Taylor & Francis Group.

Portier, M. 1996 "Integrating Environment and Economy" *The OECD Observer,* No. 198, (February/March) pp. 6-10.

Post, A. and Chapelle, E. 2009 *Glacier Ice;* Seattle, WA: University of Washington Press.

Powell, D. 2012 "Himalaya Rush: Scientists scurry to figure out the status of glaciers on the tall roof of the world" *Science News,* Vol. 182, No.4, August 25.

Prather, M. and Ehhalt, D. 2001 "Atmospheric Chemistry and Greenhouse Gases" pp. 239-87. In J T. Houghton and 8 others (eds.) *Climate Change 2001: The Scientific Basis, Contribution of Working Group I to the 3rd Assessment Report of the IPCC,* Cambridge UK and New York: Cambridge University Press.

Prentice, I.C. www.grida.no/CLIMATE/IPCC_TAR/wg1/pdf/TAR_03PDF *The Carbon Cycle and Atmospheric Carbon Dioxide,* IPCC.

Price, T.J. 2005 "James Blyth – Britain's First Modern Wind Power Engineer" *Wind Engineering,* Vol. 29, No. 3, pp. 191-200.

Prins, G. and Rayner, S. 2007 "Time to Ditch Kyoto" *Nature,* 449, pp. 973-5.

Prugh, T., et al. 1995 *Natural Capital and Human Economic Survival;* Sunderland: MA: Sinauer Assouaales, Inc.

Qian, Y., Flanner, M.G., Leang, L.R. and Wang, W. 2010 "Sensitivity Studies on the Impacts of Tibetan Plateau Snowpact Pollution on the Asian Hydrological Cycle and Moonsoon Climate" *Atmospheric Chemistry & Physics,* Vol. 11, pp. 1929-1948.

Radford, T. (2002, 9th November) "World may be warming up even faster" *The Guardian* (UK).

Radford, T. 2015 "Peat Bog Fires are Burning Issues in Climate Calculations" *Climate News Network,* January 9.

Radić, V. and Hock, R. 2010 "Regional and global volumes of glaciers derived from statistical upscaling of galcier inventory data" *Journal of Geophysical Research,* Vol. 115.

Rahmstorf, S. 1996 "On the freshwater forcing and transport of the Atlantic thermehaline circulation" *Climate Dynamics,* Vol. 12, pp. 799-811.

Rahmstorf, S. 2003 "The concept of the thermohaline circulation" *Nature,* 421 (6924): 699.

Rahmstorf, S. 2007 "Sea-Level Rise: A Semi-Empirical Approach to Projecting Future" *Science,* 315: 368-370.

Ramage, C. 1971 "Monsoon meteorology" *International Geophysics Series,* Vol. 15.

Ranpach, M.R. et al. 2009 "Global and Regional Drivers of Accelerating CO_2 Emissions" *Pro. Natl. Acad. Sc.,* USA, 104,10288-10293

Raupach, M.R. et al. 2007 "Global and Regional Drivers of Accelerating CO_2 Emissions" *Proceedings National Academy of Sciences,* (USA) Vol. 104, no. 24.

RECOFTC 2011 What is REDD+? Bangkok: RECOFTC- The Centre for People and Forests. Availale @ http://www.recoftc.org/sits/What-is-REDD-

Redcliff, M.R. 2005 *Sustainability: Critical Concepts in the Social Sciences* (Routledge Major Works – Four Volumes); London: Taylor & Francis Group.

Redcliff, M.R. and Benton, T. (eds.) 1994 *Social Theory and the Global Environment;* London: Routledge.

Redcliff, M.R. and Grasso, M. (eds) 2013 *Handbook on Climate Change and Human Security;* Edward Elgar.

Rediff India Abroad (2007, 24th July) "Ganges, Indus may not survive: climatologist" *Rediff India Abroad.*

Redo, D.J., Gran, H.R., Aide, T.M. and Claak, M.L. 2012 "Assymetric Forest Transition Driven by the Interaction of Socioeconomic Development and Environmental Heterogeneity in Central America" In: *Proceedings National Academy of Sciences,* (United States), June 5, Vol. 109, No. 23.

Reed, D. (ed.) 1992 *Structural Adjustment and the Environment;* Boulder, Colorado: Westview

Reguly, E. (2015, 14th December) "Paris Climate accord marks shift toward low-carbon economy" *Globe and Mail,* Toronto. Retrieved 21 October 2016.

Reilly, J., Mayer. M., and Harnisch, J. 2002 "Multiple Gas Control under the Kyoto Agreement" In: J.A. Van Ham, P.M. Baede, L.A. Mayer, and R. Ybema, (eds.) *Seconda International Symposium on Nen - CO_2 Greenhouse Gases,* Dordrecht, Netherlands: Kluwer Academic Publishers.

Reilly, J., Tubiello, F.N., McCarl, B., Mellilo, J. 2001 "Climate change and agriculture in the United States" In: *Climate change impacts on the United States: Foundation,* USGCRP Mellilo, J., Janetos, G. and Karl, T. 2001 pp. 379-403 (eds.) Cambridge University Press.

Reuveny, R. 2007 "Climae change-induced migration" *Political Geography,* Vol.26, Issue 6 (August) pp. 656-672.

Reynolds, L. 2013 "Agriculture and Livestock Remain Major Sources of Greenhouse Gas Emissions" *Worldwatch Instutite,* May 8 (see section 5.7 and 5.8).

Rhines, P.B. and Hakkinea, S. 2003 "Is the Oceanic Heat Transport in the North Atlantic Irrelevant to the Climate in Europe" *ASOF Newsletter,* Issue No.1 September.

Richards, P. 1985 *Indigenous Agricultural Revolution: Ecology and Food Production in West Africa;* London: Longman.

Rico, R. 1995 "The U.S Allowance Trading System for Sulfur Dioxide; An Update" *Environmental and Resources Economics,* Vol. 5, No. 2, pp. 115-29.

Riddle, R. 1981 *Ecodevelopment;* Aldershot, UK: Glower.

Rigg, J. 1991 "Land Settlement in Southeast Asia: The Indonesian Transmigration Program" In: *Southeast Asia: A Region in Transition,* pp. 80-108 London: Unwin.

Robinson, J. 2004 "Squaring the Circle? Some thoughts on the Idea of Sustainable Development" *Ecological Economics,* Vol. 48, pp. 369-84.

Robinson, N. (ed.) 1993 *Agenda 21: Earth's Action Plan, IUCN Environmental Policy and Law Paper 27;* New York: Ocean Publications.

Rocmmich, D. and McGowan, J. 1995 "Climatic Warming and Decline of Zooplankton in the California Current" *Science,* 267, No. 5202, pp. 1324-1326.

Rohde, R.A. and Muller, R.A. 2015 "Air Pollution in China: Mapping of Concentrations and Sources" *PLoS ONE,* Vol. 10, No. 8.

Romm, J. (2015, 26th October) "Exclusive: Elevated CO2 Levels Directly Affect Human Cognition, New Harvard Study Shows" *Thinkprogress.*

Ronchail, et al. 2002 "Internannual Rainfall Variability in the Amazon Basic Sea-Surface Temperatures in the Equatorial Pacific and the Tropical Atlantic Oceans" *International Journal of Climatology,* Vol. 22, pp.1663-1686.

Root, T.L., Price, T.T., Hall, K.R., Schneider, S.H., Rosenzweig, C. and Pounds, A. 2002. "Finger prints of global warming on animals and plants" *Nature,* Vol. 421, No. 6918, pp. 57-9.

Rose, A. 2009 *The Economics of Climate Change Policy: International, Natural and Regional Mitigation Strategies,* Edward Elgar.

Rosenzweig C., Tubiello F.N., Goldberg R.A., Mills E., Bloomfield J. 2002 "Increased crop damage in the U.S From excess precipitation under climate change" *Global Environmental Change,* Vol. 12, pp. 197-202. doi: 10.1016/50959-3780 (02) 00008-0.

Rosenzweig, C. and Iglesia, A. 2006 "Political Impacts of Climate Change on World Food Supply: Data" (http://www.sedac.ciesin.columbia.ed).

Rosenzweig, C. and Parry, M.L. 1994 "Potential impact of climate change on world food supply" *Nature,* 367, 133-138.

Rostagno, M. C. 1994 Comments on climate change drought and desertification in Patagonia Pnerto-Madryn: CONICET/CENPAT.5.

Rowell, A. 1996 *Green Blackcash: global subversion of the environment movement;* London: Routledge.

Rowell, C.P. 2003 "The Impact of Mediterranean SSTs on the Sahelian Rainfall Season" *Journal of Climate,* Vol.16, pp. 849-862.

Rozhnov, K. (2012, 15th August) "Oil Futures – Crude Prices Stable: DOE Data, Brent Rolllover Eyed" *The Wall Street Journal.*

Rudel, T.K. 2005 *Tropical Forests, Regional Paths of Destruction and Regional Regeneration in the Late 20th Century,* Columbia University Press.

Rudel, T.K. 2013 "The national determinants of deforestation in Sub-Saharan Africa" *Philosophical Transactions of the Royal Society B,* Vol. 368, Issue 1625.

Rudel, T.K. and Roper, J. 1997 "The paths of rainforest destruction: Cross-national patterns of tropical deforestation" *World Development,* 25, 53-65.

Rudel, T.K., Coomes, O.T., Moran, E., Achard, F., et al. 2005 "Forest transitions: towards a global understanding of land use change" *Global Environmental Change.*

Rudel, T.K., Schneider, L. and Uriate, M. 2010 "Forest transitions: An introduction" *Land Use Policy*, Vol. 27, No. 2.

Ruhl, C., Appleby, P., Fennema, F., Naumov, A., Schuffer, M. 2012 "Economic Development and the Demand for Energy: A Historical Prospective on the Next 20 Years" *Energy Policy*, 50.

Russel, R. 2007 "The Greenhouse Effect and Green Gases" *University Corporation for Atmospheric Research Windows to the Universe*, 16th May.

Rybach, L. 2007 "Geothermal Sustainability" *Geo-Heat Centre Quarterly Bulletin*, Oregon Institute of Technology, Vol. 28, pp. 2-7.

Saatchi, S., Asefi-Najafabady, S., Malhi, Y., Aragao, L.E.O., Anderson, L.O., Myneni, R.B., and Nemani, R. 2013 "Persistent effects of a severe drought on Amazonian forest camopy" *Proceedings of the Natural Academy of Sciences of the United States of America (PNAS)*, Vol. 110, N0. 2 (January 8).

Sach, I. 1979 "Ecodevelopment: A Definition" *Ambio*, Vol. 8, No. 2/3, p.113.

Saghir, J. and O'Sullivan, K. 2006 "Toward a Sustainable Energy Future." In: Vinay Bhargava, (ed.,) *Global Issues for Global Citizens: An Introducton to Key Development Challenges*, The World Bank, Washington D.C.

Sahel, 2013 "Sahel, Africa" *Global Warming Science*. www.appinsys.com/Global/Warming.

Salkida, A. (2012, 30th April) Africa's Vanishing Lake Chad: Action Needed to Counter an "Ecological Catastrophe" http://www.an.og/en/africarenewal/vol26No/lake-chadhtml Accessed 11 March 2015.

Sambrook, R.A., Pigozzi, B.W. and Thomas, R.N. 1999 "Population Pressure, Deforestation, and Land Degradation: A Case Study from the Dominican Republic" *The Professional Geography*, Vol. 51, Issue 1, pp. 25-40. (Online 15 March, 2010).

Samuelson, P. 1976 "Economics of forestry in an evolving society" *Economic Inquiry*, Vol. 14, No. 4, pp. 466-92.

Samuelson. P.A. 1954"The Pure Theory of Public Expenditure" *Review of Economics and Statistics*, Vol. 36, No. 4, pp. 387-389.

Samueslon, Paul A. and William D. Nordhaus 2005 *Economics*; 18th edition, Tata- McGraw-Hill Publishing Company Limited.

Sandoval, I.S., Bechberger, M. and Tergens, H. (eds.) *A Guide to Renewable Energy Policy in the EU: Actors, Processors and Policy Change*; Edward Elgar.

Sayer, J.A., Harcourt, C.S., and Collins, N.M. (eds.) *The Conservation Atlas of Tropical Forests: Africa*; New York: Simon & Schuster.

Scales H. (2007, 29th March) "Shark Declines Threaten Shellfish Stocks, Study Says" *National Geographic News*. Retrieved 17 Feb. 2015.

Schanche, D. 2007 "Scarce Resources, Ethnic Strife Fuel Darfur Conflict" (http://www.npr.org) Retrieved 4th September 2013.

Schimel, D.S. and 28 other 2001 "Recent Patterns and Mechanisms of Carbon Exchange by Terrestrial Ecosystems" *Nature,* 414, pp. 169-172.

Schlesinger, W.H. and Bernhadt, E.S. 2013 "The Global Water Cycle" In: *Biogeochemistry,* chap 10, pp. 399 – 417 doi: 10. 1016/B978 – 0 – 12 – 385874 – 0 – 00010.8.

Schmidt, G. 2005 "Water Vapour: The Feedback or Forcing?" *Realclimate,* 6th April.

Schmidt, G.A. Ruedy, R.A., Miller, R.C. and Lacis, A.A. 2010 "Attribution of the present-day total greenhouse effect" *Journal of Geophysical Research,* 115 D20106, doi: 10.1029/2010JD014287, 2010.

Schmitz, C. et. al., 2015 "Agricultural trade and tropical deforestation: Interaction and related policy option" *Regional Environmental Change,* Vol. 15, No. 8, pp. 1757- 1772.

Schneck, R. and Moshbrugger, V. 2011 "Simulated Climate Effects of Southeast Asian Deforestation: Regional Processes and Teleconnection Mechanisms" *Journal of Geophysical Research,* Vol. 116, D 11116.

Schneider Von Deimling, T, Ganopolski, A., Hed, H., Rabmstorf, S. 2006 "How cold was the last Glacial Maximum?" *Geophysical Research Letters,* 33: 5pp.

Schubert, S.D., Snarez, M.J., Pegion, P.J., Koster, R.D., and Bacmeister, J.T "On the causes of the 1930s Dust Bowl" *Science,* Vol. 303, No. 5665, pp. 1855-1859 doi: 10. 1126/ Science.1095048.

Science News, (2008, 18th March) "Glaciers Are Melting Faster Than Expected, UN Reports" *Science News.*

Scoones, I. 1991 "Wetlands in drylands: key resources for agricultural and pastoral production in Africa" *Ambio,* 20, 366-71.

Scott, J. and Marshall, G., (eds.) 2005 *Oxford Dictionary of Sociology,* Oxford University Press.

Seager, R. 2006 "The Source of Europe's Mild Climate" *American Scientist,* Vol. 94, No. 4. (http:/ www./americanscientist.org/issues/feature/2006/4/the–source-of-europe). Retrieved 14 August 2013.

Secretary of the Convention on Biological Diversity 2006 *Global Biodiversity Outlook 2,* Montreal.

Sejian, V. and Naqvi, S.M.K. (no date) *Livestock and Climate Change: Mitigation Strategies to Reduce Methane Production* (http://www.intechopen.com).

Sejian, V., Lal, R., Lakritz, J. and Ezeji, T. 2011 "Measurement and Prediction of Enteric Methane Emission" *International Journal of Biometeorology,* Vol. 55, pp. 1-16.

Sen, A. 1981 *Poverty and Famine: an essay on entitlements and deprivation;* Oxford: Oxford University Press.

Serdeczny, O., Adams, S., Baarsch, F., Coumou, D., Robinson, A., Hare, W., Schaefer, M., Perrette, M., and Reinhardt, J. 2015 "Climate change impacts in Sub-Saharan Africa: from physical changes to their social repercussions" *Regional Environmental Change, January 2016,* Vol. 15, No. 8 (doi: 10.1007/S10113-015-0910-2).

Seychelles News Agency (2014, 19th October) "An uncertain future for Seychelles? A study shows sea levels are at their highest in the past 6000 years" *Seychelles News Agency.*

Shah, A. 2014 "Climate Change affects biodiversity" *Global Issues,* 19 (January) (see also <http://www.globalissues.org/article/172/climate-change-affects-biodiversity).

Shanahan, T., Overpeck J.T. et al. 2009 "Atlantic Forcing of Persistent Drought in West Africa" *Science,* 324 (5925), pp. 377-380.

Sharp, M., Burgess, D.O., Cogley, J.G., Ecclestone M., Labine, C., and Wolken, G.J., 2011 "Extranet melt on Canada's Arctic ice caps in the 21st century" *Geophyiscal Research Letters,* 38.

Shepherd A. and Wingtam, D. 2007 "Recent sea-level contributions of the Antarctic and Greenland ice sheets" *Science,* 315 (5818): 1529-32.

Shepherd, J.M., "Carbon, Climate Change, and Controversy" <u>http://animalfrontiers.fass.org/conte.</u> <u>Retrieved 30th August 2012</u>.

Shiller, R.J. (2015, 30th March) "Fighting climate change with idealism" p. 15 *International New York Times.*

Shindell, D.T. 2005 "An Emissions-Based View of Climate Forcing by Methane and Tropospheric Ozone" *Geophysical Research Letters,* 32, 4.

Sills, B. (2011, 29th August) "Solar May Produce Most of World's Power by 2060;" *Bloomberg.*

Sills, E.O., Atmadja, S.S., de Sassi, C., and Sunderlin, W.D. 2014 *REDD+ on the Ground: A Case Study of Sub-national Initiatives across the Globe,* CIFOR

Simonsen, A. H. 1995 "Where oil kills: the Ogoni story" *Indigenous Affair*s, Vol. 4, pp. 52-7.

Sivakhuman, M.V.K. and Ndiang' ni, N., (eds.) 2007 *Climate and Land Degradation;* Springer.

Skinner, J.R. 1992 "Conservation of the Inland Niger Delta in Mali: the interdependence of ecological and socioeconomic research" pp. 41-7 In: E: Maltby. P.J. Dugan and J.C. Lefeuve (eds.) *Conservation and Development: the Sustainable Use of Wetland Resources,* IUCN, Gland, Switzerland.

Smil, V. 1994 *Energy and Civilization: A History*; MIT Press.

Smil, V. 1994 *Energy in World History;* Boulder, Co.: Westview.

Smil, V. 2011 *Energy Transition: History Requirements, Prospects;* Praeger.

Smith, D. 2000 "Death Stalks Millions in Drought-Stricken Areas" *National Geographic News,* December 27 http://www.news.nationalgeographic.com. Accessed 11 March 2015.

Smith, Joel B., Richard J.T., Klein, and Saleemul Huq, 2003 *Climate Change, Adaptive Capacity and Development;* London: Imperial College Press.

Smith, S.V. and Baddemeier, R.W. 1992 "Global change and coral ecosystems" *Annual Review of Ecological Systems,* Vol.23, 89-118.

Smyth, S.J., Phillips, P.W.B., and Castle, D. (eds.) 2014 *Handbook of Biotechnology and Development;* Edward Elgar.

Soderbaum, B. 1996 "Revaluing Wetlands" *The OECD Observer,* 198 (February/March) pp. 47-50.

Solberg, L. and Wiederkehr, P. 1995 "Voluntary Approaches for Energy-Related CO_2 Abatement" *The OECD Observer,* No. 196 (October / November).

Solomon, S., Qin, D., Manning, M., Chen, Z., Marquis, M., Averyt, K.B., Tiguer, M. and Miller, H., (eds.) 2007 *Climate Change 2007: The Physical Science Basis: Contribution of Working Group 1 to the 4th Assessment Report of the Intergovernmental Panel on Climate Change,* Cambridge University Press.

Solsberg, L. and Wiederkehr 1995 "Voluntary Approaches for Energy-related CO_2 Abatement" *The OECD Observer,* No. 196, October /November, pp. 41-45.

South America Climate Change 2016 "South America: Climate Change Impacts" *Climate Change in Context* (http://www.encyclopedia.com.).

Spash, C.L. 1999 "The Development of Environment Thinking in Economics" *Environmental Values,* Vol. 8, pp. 413-35.

St. Fleur, N. (2015, 11th November) "Atmospheric Greenhouse Gas Levels Hit Record, Report Says" *The New York Times.*

Stavius, R.N. 2001 "Experience with Market-Based Environmental Policy Instruments" *Discussion Paper 01-58,* Washington D.C.: Resources for the Future.

Stebbing, E.P. 1935 "The Encroaching Sahara; The Threat to the West African Colonies" *Geographical Journal,* Vol.85, pp. 506-24.

Stebbing, E.P. 1938 "The advance of the desert" *Geographical Journal,* Vol. 91, pp. 356-59.

Steinfeld, H., Gerben, P., Wassenar, T., Castel, V., Rosales, M., de Hann, C., 2006 "Livestock's Long Shadow: Environmental Issues and Options" *FAO Livestock, Environment and Development (LEAD) Initiative,* Rome: FAO.

Steininger, K.W. and M. Logoy 2006 *Economics of Global Environmental Change: International Cooperation for Sustainability;* Edward Elgar.

Stern, D.I. 2004 "The rise and fall of the Environmental Kuznets Curve" *World Development,* Vol. 29, pp. 1419-39.

Stern, N, et al. 2007 *The Economics of Climate Change: The Stern Review;* Cambridge: UK Cambridge University Press.

Stern, N. 2006a *Stern Review on the Economics of Climate Change* (Pre-Publication Edition); Executive Summary, London: HM Treasury.

Stern, N. 2006b *"Introduction". The Economics of Climate Change The Stern Review,* Cambridge University Press.

Stern, N. 2008 *The Economics of Climate Change;* Richard T. Ely Lecture, AEA Meetings, New Orleans, January 4.

Stern, N. 2009a *The Global Deal: Climate Change and the Creation of a New–Era of Progress and Prosperity;* Public Affairs.

Stern, N. 2009b *Blueprint for a Safe Plane;* The Bradley Head.

Stern, P., Young, O. and Druckman, D. (eds.) 1992 *Global Environmental Change: Understanding the Human Dimensions;* Washington, D.C.: National Academy Press.

Stevens, P. August (2012) *The Shale Gas Revolution: Developments and Changes;* Chathan House.

Steward, T. A., Pickett, V., Parker, T., and Feidler, P. 1992 "The new paradigm in ecology: implications for conservation biology above the species level Biology" pp. 65-88 In: P.L. Feidler and S.K. Jain, (eds.) *Conservation Biology; the theory and practice of nature conservation, preservation and management,* London: Chapman and Hall.

Stewart, R. 2000 "Economic Incentives for Environmental Protection: Opportunities and Obstacles" In: R. Revesz, P. Sands and R. Stewart (eds). *Environmental Law, the Economy and Sustainable Development,* Cambridge University Press.

Stier, S.C. and Siebert, S.F. 2002 "The Kyoto Protocol: An Opportunity for Biodiversity Restoration Forestry" *Conservation Biology,* Vol. 16, pp. 575-6.

Stiglitz, J.E., Jaramillo-Vallejo, J., and Park Y.C., 1993 "The role of the state in financial markets" *Proceedings of the World Bamk Annual Conference on Development Economic*s, 1993, p. 19-61, Washington, D.C.

Stringer, L.C. et al 2009 "Adaptations to climate change, drought and desertification: local insights to enhance policy in Southern Africa" *Environment Science and Policy.* doi: 10.1016/J. envsci.2009.04.002 Retrieved 20 August 2013.

Stutz, F.P. and Warf, B. 2007 *The World Economy: Resources, Location, Trade, and Development;* 5th edition, Pearson / Prentice-Hall.

Suliman, M. 2008 "The War in Darfur: The Resource Dimension" *Respect, Sudanese Journal of Human Rights…* 8th Issue August http://en.sudan-foral/.org Retrieved 4 September 2013.

Sultan, B., Baron, C., Dingkahn, M., Sarr, B. & Janicot, S. 2005 "Agricultural impacts of large-scale variability of the West African Monsoon" *Agriculture & Forest Meteorology,* 128 (1/2), 19-110.

Sutter, J.D. and Berlinger, J. (2015, 12th December) "Final Draft of Climate Deal formally accepted in Paris" *CNN Cable News Network,* Turner Broadcasting System, Inc Accessed 24 April 2016.

Suzuki, D. (2013, 14th August) "Is Alberta Flooding a Sign of Climate Change?" *Huff Post, Alberta, Canada.*

Swift, J. 1996 "Desertification Narratives: Winners and Losers", pp. 73-90. In: M. Zeach and R. Mearns, (eds.) *The Lie of the Land: Challenging Received Wisdom on the African Environment,* London: James Currey / Heinemann.

Swiss Glacier Monitoring Network 2011 *Glacier Length Variations of the Year 2011* (http://glaciology. ethz.ch/messnetz/glacienlist.html) Retrieved 9th August, 2013.

Tacconi, L., Mahanty, S., and Suich, H., (eds.) 2010 *Payments for Environmental Services, Forest Conservation and Climate Change;* Edward Elgar.

Tamirisa, N. 2008 "Climate Change and the Economy" *Finance & Development,* Vol.45, No.1 (March) pp. 18-22.

Tansley, A.G. 1935 "The use and abuse of vegetational terms" *Ecology,* Vol. 14, No. 3, pp. 284 -307.

Tegel, S. 2012 "Antisana's Glaciers: Victims of Climate Change" *Globalpost* (http://en.wikipedia.org/wiki/Retreat_of_glaciers_since_1850) Retrieved 10th August 2013.

Terborgh, J. 1999 *Requiem for Nature;* Washington: Island Press.

The Economist (2005, 23rd April) "Environmental Economics: Are you being Served?" *The Economist*, London.

The Economist (2006, 18th November) "Soot, Smoke and Mirrors" p.28, *The Economist*, London.

The Economist (2006, 18th November) "Special Report: Investing in Clean Energy" pp.68-70, *The Economist,* London.

The Economist (2006, 19th December) "Waiving or Drowning" p. 97, *The Economist,* London.

The Economist (2006, 9th September) "Selling Hot Air" pp. 16-19, *The Economist,* London.

The Economist (2006, 9th September) "The Heat is On: A Survey of Climate" *The Economist,* London.

The Economist (2007, 2nd June) "Cleaning Up: A Special Report on Business and Climate Change" *The Economist,* London.

The Economist (2008, 20th September) "Water for Farming: Running Dry" *The Economist,* London.

The Economist (2009, 11th April) "The Environment: Biofuels" p. 73, *The Economist,* London.

The Economist (2009, 11th April) "Water: sine aqua non" pp. 54-56, *The Economist,* London.

The Economist (2009, 24th September) "A catastrophe is Looming" *The Economist,* London.

The Economist (2009, 7th April) "The Environment: Biofuels" *The Economist,* London.

The Economist (2012, 16th June) 'The Global Environment: Boundary Conditions" pp. 87-88, *The Economist,* London.

The Economist (2012, 16th June) "Special Report The Arctic: The Melting North" *The Economist,* London.

The Economist (2012, 23th June) "China; Climate Change: Warmed Up Numbers" *The Economist* London.

The Economist (2012, 5th January) "Europe's Dirty Secret: The Unwelcome Renaissance" pp. 51-52, *The Economist,* London.

The Economist (2013 10th August) "Briefling China and the Environment: The East is Grey" pp. 17-20, *The Economist,* London.

The Economist (2013, 11th May) "The Climate of Tibet; Pole-Land" pp. 76-77, *The Economist,* London.

The Economist (2013, 19th January) "Global Warming: The New Black" *The Economist,* London.

The Economist (2013, 1st June) "Arctic Ecology Sacred Geese" p. 75, *The Economist,* London.

The Economist (2013, 30th March) "Climate Science: A Sensitive Matter" pp. 69-71, *The Economist*, London.

The Economist (2013, 5th January) "Briefing Coal in the Rich World: The Mixed Fortunes of a Fuel" *The Economist*, London.

The Economist (2013, 6th April) "Wood: the Fuel of the Future" *The Economist*, London.

The Economist (2013, 8th June) "Energy: Blown Away" p. 43, *The Economist*, London.

The Economist (2015, 13th June) "Banishing the Clouds", pp 59-60, *The Economist*, London.

The Economist (2015, 28th November) "Adaptation: If You Can't Stand the Heat – How Farmers in Poor Countries are Responding to Climate Change" pp.10-12, *The Economist* (Special Report Climate Change), London.

The Economist (2015, 28th November) "China: Seeing Daylight" *The Economist*, London.

The Economist (2015, 28th November) "Clear Thinking Needed" *The Economist*, London.

The Economist (2015, 28th November) "Nuclear Power in the Middle East: Wasting Energy" p. 35, *The Economist*, London.

The Economist (2015, 28th November) "The Way Forward: Second-best Solutions" p. 15, *The Economist*, London.

The Economist (2015, 4th July) "Why the Dutch Oppose Windmills: Dutch Quixote" pp.22-23, *The Economist*, London.

The Economist (2017, 15th July) "100% Renewable Energy: At What Cost?" pp. 61-62, *The Economist*, London.

The Economist (2017, 2nd September) "Briefing Flooding: Submerged", pp. 17-20, *The Economist*, London.

The Economist (2017, 2nd September) "How to Cope with Floods", p.9, *The Economist*, London.

The Economist, (2009, 11th April) "Water Rights: Awash in Waste" pp.17-18, *The Economist*, London.

The Guardian (UK) (2006, 17th July) "Drought Threatens Amazon Basin" *The Guardian (UK)*.

The Independent (2006, 23rd July) "Dying Forest: One Year to Save the Amazon" *The Independent (UK)*.

The Munich Climate Insurance Initiative, 2009 "Adaptation to Climate Change: Linking Disaster Risk Reduction and Insurance" Paper submitted to the UNFCĆC for the 6th Session of the Ad Hoc Working Group on Long-Term Cooperative Action under the Convention (AWG-LCA 6).

The New York Times (1997, 3rd May) "Sandstorm kills 12 in Northern Egypt" *The New York Times*.

The New York Times (2016, 2nd July) "A Remote Pacific Nation, Threatened by Rising Seas" *The New York Times*.

The Royal Society, 2010 *Climate Change: A Summary of the Science*; London: The Royal Society – Science Policy Centre.

The Sidney Morning Herald, (2009, 23rd September) "Sydney turns red: dust storm blankets city" *The Sidney Morning Herald.*

Thirgood, J.V. 1986 "The Barbary Forests and Forest Land: Environmental Destruction and Vicissitudes of History" *Journal of World Forest Resource Management,* Vol. 2, pp.137-84.

Thomas, C.D. 2010 "Climate, climate change and range boundaries" *Diversity and Distribution,* Vol. 16, pp. 488-495.

Thomas, D.S.G. and Middleton, T. 1994 *Desertification: Exploding the Myth;* Wiley.

Thomas, V., Albert, J.R.G. and Perez, R.T. 2013 "Climate-Related Disasters in Asia and the Pacific" *Asian Development Bank Economics Working Paper Series,* 358 (July) (http://www.adb.org/publications/climate-related-disasters-asia-and-pacific).

Thomas, V., Albert, J.R.G., Hepburn, C., 2014 "Contributors to the Frequency of Intense Climate Disasters in Asia-Pacific Countries" *Climate Change,* Vol. 126, Issue 3 (October), pp. 381-398. (doi: 10.1007/s10584 – 014 – 1232 – y).

Thornton, P., Boone, R., Galvin, K., BurnSilver, S., Waithaka, M., Kuyiah., Karanja, S., Gonzales – Estrada, E. and Herrero, M. 2007. "Coping strategies in livestock-dependent households in East and Southern Africa: A synthesis of four case studies" *Human Ecology,* Vol. 35, No. 4, pp. 461-76.

Thuiller, W. 2007 "Biodiversity: Climate change the ecologist" *Nature,* 448, 550-552 (2nd August) doi: 10.1038/44855a.

Tietenberg, T. 1988 *Environmental and Natural Resource Economics;* 4th ed., Gleaview, Illinois: Scott. Foreman.

Tietenberg, T. 1995 "Design Lessons from Existing Air Pollution Control Systems: The United States" In: S. Hanna an Munasinghe, (eds.), pp. 15-32 *Property Rights in Social and Ecological Contexts Cases Studies and Design Applications,* Washington DC: The World Bank.

Tietenberg, T. and Lewis, L. 2010 *Environmental Economics & Policy;* sixth edition, Pearson Puplications.

Tietenberg.T. 2000 *Environmental and National Resource Economics;* 5th edition, New York: Addison-Wesley.

Titus, J.G. 1989 *The Potential Effects of Global Climate Change on the United States;* United States Environmental Protection Agency, December.

Tobey, J. 1996 "Economics Incentives for Biodiversity" *The OECD Observer,* No. 198 (Feb/March) pp. 25-8.

Todaro, M.P. and Smith, S.C. 2009 *Economic Development;* 10th edition, Addison-Wesley.

Tolba, M.K. 1986 "Desertification In Africa" *Land Use Policy,* Vol.3, pp. 260-268.

Touffut, J.P., ed. 2009 *Changing Climate, Changing Economy;* Edward Elgar.

Trade and Environment Database 1999 "Peruvain Anchovy Case: Anchovy Depletion and Trade" *Trade and Environment Datbase,* Accessed 18 February 2015.

Trenberth, K.E., Stepaniak, D.P., and Caron, J.M. 2000 "The global monsoon as seen through the divergent atmospheric circulation" *Journal of Climate,* Vol.13, 3969-3993.

Trujillo, A.P. and Thurman, H.V. 2008 *Essentials of Oceanography;* 9th edition, New Jersey: Pearson Education, Inc.

Tucker, C.J. Townsend, J.E.G. and Goff, T.E. 1985 "African land cover classification using satellite data" *Science,* Vol. 277, pp 187-198.

Tucker, C.J., Dregne, H.E. and Newcombe, W.W. 1991 "Expansion and Contraction of the Sahara Desert from 1980 to 1990" *Science,* 253, pp. 299-301.

Tucker, C.J., Holben, B.N. and Goff, T.E. 1984 "Intensive forest clearing in Rondônia, Brazil, as detected by satellite remote sensing" *Remote Sensing and the Environment,* Vol. 15, pp. 255-61.

Tucker, C.J., Justice, C.O. and Prince, S.D. 1986 "Monitoring the grasslands of the Sahel, 1984-1985" *International Journal of Remote Sensing,* Vol. 7, pp. 1571-83.

Tucker, C.J., Townsend, J.E.G. and Goff, T.E. 1985 "African land cover classification using satellite data" *Science,* Vol. 277, pp. 369-75.

Turcotte, D.L. and Schubert, G. 2002 *Geodynamics,* 2nd Edition, Cambridge University Press.

Turner, B. 1977 *The Fadama lands of Central Northern Nigeria: Their classification, spatial variation, present and potential use.* Unpublished Ph.D Thesis, University of London.

Turner, M.D. 2003 "Methodological Reflections on the Use of Remote Sensing and Geographic Information Science in Human Ecological Research" *Human Ecology,* Vol. 31, No. 255 doi: 10. 1023/A. 1023 984813957.

Tyndall, J. 1861 "On the Absorption and Radiation of Heat by Gases and Vapours ..." *Philosophical Magazine Ser.* 4, 22: 169-94, 273-85.

Tyndall, J. 1863 "On Radiation of Radiant Heat to Aqueous Vapor" *Philosophical Magazine,* Ser. 4, 26: 30-54.

U.S. Senate Committee 23rd June 1988 United States Senate Committee on Energy and National Resources, Greenhouse Effect and Global Climate Change, Part 2. 100th Congress 1st Session, 23rd June, p.44.

UN Global Biodiversity Outlook 2010, *Global Biodiversity Outlook 3, May 2010;* New York: United Nations Secretariat of the Convention on Biological Diversity.

UN, Water 2007 United Nations Department of Economics and Social Affairs (ECOSOC) 2008, *Trends in Sustainable Development; Agriculture, Rural Development, Land, Desertification and Drought;* New York: United Nations.

UNCCD 1994 *United Nations Convention to Combat Desertification (UN Earth Summit) Convention on Desertification. UN Conference on Environment and Development (UNCED);* Rio de Janeiro, Brazil June 3-14, 1992 DP1/SD/1576 New York: United Nations.

UNCCD 1995 *Down to Earth: A Simplified Guide to the Convention to Combat Desertification, why it is Necessary and what is important and different about it;* Bonn Germany: Secretariat for the UNCCD (htt://www.unccd.int/knowledge. menu.php).

UNCCD 2012 "United Nations Convention on Combating Desertification (UNCCD): About the Convention". http://www.unccd.int/en/about-the-convention/pages/ about-the-convention. aspx.

UNECA/OECD 2014 *The 2014 Mutual Review of Development Effectiveness in Africa: Promise and Performance* (Topic 19 – Climate Finance).

UNECE 2012 United Nations Economic Commison for Europe (UNECE) *Wood Confirmed as the Primary Source of Renewable Energy in Europe,* Februrary.

UNEP (on line) "Impacts on Africa's Lakes: Case Studies of Africa's Changing Lakes" http:// na.unep.net/AfricaLakes/AtlasDownload/PDFs/Africa–Chapters3–0–Screen.pdf. (Accessed 7 March 2015).

UNEP 1995 *Global Biodiversity Assessment,* Cambridge University Press.

UNEP 2002 United Nations Environment Programme, *Africa Environment Outlook: Past, Present and Future Perspectives* http./www.unep.org/dewa/Africa/publications/AEO-1/056.htm. Retrieved 20 September 2013.

UNEP 2007 *United Nations Environmental Program (UNEP): Global Environmental Outlook – GE04 Environement for Development* Nairobi: UNEP.

UNEP 2008 United Nations Environmental Programme, *Africa: Atlas of Our Changing Environment* Chapter 1, p. 18 (http://www.unep.org/dewa/africa/AfricaAtlas/PDF/ en/chapter1.pdf).

UNEP, 1992 United Nations Environmental Programme, *World Atlas of Desertification;* New York: United Nation.

UNEP/WMO 2011 *Integrated Assessment of Black Carbon and Tropospheric Ozone: Summary for Decision Matters;* United Nations Environmental Programme/ World Meteorological Organization.

UNEP-Interpol, 2012 United Nations Environmental Programme-Interpol, "Illegal Logging Decimates Forests" *Africa: AllAfrica.com*

UNESCO 2007 United Nations Educational, Social and Cultural Organization, "Lake Chad Basin" *Water Portal Weekly Update* No. 178 (March).

UNFCC 2007 *Investment and Financial Flows to Address Climate Change,* United Nations Framework Convention on Climate Change.

UNFCCC 2007 United Nations Framework Convention on Climate Change, *Climate Change: Impacts, Vulnerabilities and Adaptation in Developing Countries,* UNFCC Secretariat: Bonn, Germany.

UNFCCC 2011 United Nations Framework Convention on Climate Change (UNFCCC) *Compilation and Synthesis of the Fifth National Communications Executive Summary*, Geneva: United Nations.

UNFCCC 2015 *Paris Agreement, FCCC/CP/2015/L.9/Rev.1* UNFCCC Secretariat.

United Nations 2014 United Nations, *World Urbanization Prospects*, Department of Economic & Social Affairs, Population Division.

United States EPA, (2017, 14th February) Greenhouse Gas Emissions: Understanding Global Warming Potentials. Washington D.C.: United States Environmental Publication Agency.

United States National Research Council 2010 United States National Research Council of the National Academies; America's Climate Choices: Panel on Advancing the Science of Climate Change, Board on Atmospheric Sciences and Climate, Division on Earth and Life Studies. *Sea Level Rise and the Coastal Environment*, Washington D.C.: The National Academies Press.

University of Wyoming (2004, 13th January) "2004/01/040113080810. htm Ocean Floor Reveals Clues to Global Warming" *Science Daily*. .(http://en.wikipedia.org/wiki/Effects_of_global_warming_on_oceans).

Ürge-Vorsatz, D., Miladinova, G. and Paizs, L. 2006 "Energy in Transition: From the Iron Curtain to the European Union" *Energy Policy*, Vol. 34, No. 15, pp. 2279-2297. doi:10.1016/j.enpol.2005.03.007.

US Environmental Protection Agency, 1987 "*Regulatory Impact Analysis: Protection of Stratospheric Ozone; Vol. II, Appendix E*, Washington, DC: pp.E3-E4.

USEIA 2016 U.S. Energy Information Administration, 2016 "Carbon Dioxide Emissions Coefficients" *U.S. Energy Information Administration (EIA) Environment*, Feb. 2.

USEPA 2002 United States Environmental Protection Agency (USEPA), Office of Atmospheric Greenhouse Gases and Global Warming Potential Values. Excerpts from the Inventory of US Greenhouse Emissions and Sinks: 1990-2000.

Vachani, S. and Usmani, J. (eds.) 2014 *Adaptain to Climate in Asia*; Edward Elgar.

Van der Werf, C.R., Randerson, J., Ciglio, L., Lollatz, C., Mu, M., Kasibhtia, P., Morton, D., Defries, R., Jin, Y., Van Leeuwen, T., 2010 *Global Fire Emissions and the Contribution of Deforestation, Savana, Forest, Agricultural and Pent Fire (1997-2009)*, Atmospheric Chemistry – Physics Discussion.

Van Der Werf, G.R., Merton, D.C., Defries, R.S., Olivier, J.G.J., Kasibhatla, P.S., Jackson, R.B., Collatz, G.J. and Randerson, J.T. 2009 "CO_2 emissions from forest loss" *Nature Geoscience*, Vol. 2, No. 11, pp. 737-38.

Vecchi, G.A. and Soden, B.J. 2007 "Global Warming and the Weakening of the Tropical Circulation" *Journal of Climate*, Vol. 20: 4316 - 4340.

Vecchi, G.A. and Wittenberg, A.T. 2010 "EL Niño and our future climate: where do we stand?" *Climate Change,* Vol. 1, Issue 2, pp. 260-270 (March – April).

Vecchi, G.A., A. Clemet, and B.J. Soden 2008 "Examining the Tropical Pacific's Response to Global Warming" *EOS,* 89: 81, 83.

Vellinga, M. and Wood, R.A. 2002 "Global Climate Impact of a Collapse of the Atlantic Thermohaline Circulation" *Climate Change,* Vol. 54, No. 3, pp. 251-67.

Verón S.R., Paruelo, J.M. and Oesterheld, M. 2006 "Assessing desertification" *Journal of Arid Environments,* Vol. 66, pp. 751-63.

Verstraete, M.M. 1986 "Defining Desertification: A Review" *Climate Change,* Vol. 9, pp. 5-18.

Vira, B. 2002 "Trading with the Enemy? Examining North-South Perspectives in the Climate Change Debate" pp. 164-80 In: D.W. Bromley and J. Paavola, (eds.), *Economics, Ethics and Environmental Policy: Contested Choices,* Oxford: Blackwell.

Vitousek, P.M. et al. 1986 "Human appropriation of the products of photosynthesis", *Bioscience,* 36, 368-373.

Volkov, M.I., (ed.) 1985 *A Dictionary of Political Economy,* Moscow Progress Publishers.

Waelbroeck, C. et al 2002 "Sea-level and deep water temperature changes derived from benthic foraminifera isotopic records" *Quarternary Science Review,* 21: 295-305.

Wagner, G. and Weitzman, M.L. 2015 *The Economic Consequences of a Hotter Planet;* Princeton University Press.

Wagner, M. 2004 *Firms, the Framework Convention on Climate Change and the EU Emissions Trading System. Corporate Energy Management Strategies to Address Climate Change and GHG Emissions in the European Union;* Lünebarg: Centre for Sustainability Management.

Wang, M.J.E. 2009 "A Sea Ice Free Summer Arctic within 30 Years?" *Geophys. Res. Lett.,* Vol.36, No.7.

Wang, Z and Krupnick, A. 2013 "A Retrospect Review of Shale Gas Development in the United States" *Resources for the Futures,* April.

Wara, M. 2007 "Is the Global, Carbon Market Working?" *Nature,* Vol. 445, No. 8, pp. 595-596.

Warren, A. 1993 "Desertification as Global Environmental Issue" *Geo Journal,* Vol.31, pp. 11-14.

Warren, A. 1996 "Desertification" pp.342-55. In: W.M. Adams, A.S. Goudie and A. Orme, (eds.), *The Physical Geography of Africa,* Oxford: Oxford University Press.

Warren, A. and Khogali, M. 1992 *Assessment of Desertification and Dronght in the Sudano-Sahelian Region 1985-1991;* New York: United Nations Sudano-Sahelian Office (UNSO), UNDP.

Watson, R.T., Noble, I.R., Bolin, B., Ravindranath, N.H., Verardo, D.J. 2000 *Special Report of the Intergovernmental Panel on Climate Change 2000;* Cambridge University Press.

Watts, A. 2013 "Ozone may be warming factor due to wind shifts" http.//wattsupwith that.com/tag/ozone-depletion Retrieved 28 August 2013.

Watts, M.J. 1983A *Silent Violence: Food, Famine and Peasantry in Northern Nigeria;* Berkeley, CA: University of California Press.

Watts, M.J. 1983B "On the poverty of theory: natural hazards research in context" pp. 231-62. In K. Itewitt, (ed.), *Interpretations of Calamity from the Viewpoint of Human Ecology,* London: Allen & Unwin.

WCED 1987 "World Commission on Environment and Development" *Our Common Future,* Oxford University Press.

Weart, S. 2014 "The Discovery of Global Warming – A History" *American Institute of Physics.*

Weart, S.R. 2008 *The Discovery of Global Warming;* 2nd ed., Harvard University Press.

Webb, A.P. and Kensh, P.S. 2010 "The dynamic response of reef islands to sea-level rise: Evidence from multi-deca Ral analysis of island change in the Central Pacific" *Global Planetary Change.*

Weber, K.T. and Horst, S. 2011 "Desertification and livestock grazing: The roles of sedentarization, mobility and rest" *Pastoralism: Research, Policy and Practice,* Vol.1: 19 doi: 10. 1186 /2041 – 7136 – 1 – 19.

Webster, P.J., Holland, G.J., Curry, J.A., and Chang, H.R., 2005 "Changes in Tropical Cyclone Numbers, Duration, and Intensity in a Warming Environment" *Science,* Vol.309 (September), pp. 1844-46.

Weishaar, S.E. 2014 *Emissions Trading Design: A Critical Overview;* Edward Elgar.

Werth, D. and Avissar, R. 2005 "The Local and Global Effects of Southeast Asian Deforestation". *Geophysical Research Letters,* Vol. 32, L 20702.

Wertz-Kanounnikoff, S. and Alvarado, L.X.R. 2007 "Bringing 'REDO' into a new deal for the Global Climate" *Analyses,* N. 2 Institute for Sustainable Development and International Relations.

White, L. Jr. 1962 *Medical Technology and Social Change,* Oxford University Press.

WHO 2003 *WHO Climate Change and Human Health-Risk and Responses 2003;* Geneva: World Health Organization (WHO).

Wiedmann, T. and Minx, J. 2008 "A Definition of 'Carbon Footprint'". In: *Ecological Economics Research Trends,* C.C. Pertsova: Chapter 1, pp. 1-11 Nova Science Publishers, Inc.

Wijen, F., K. Zoelman and J. Pieters, 2006 *A Handbook of Globalization and Environmental Policy: National Government Interventions In a Global Arena;* Edward Elgar.

Wikipedia, 2013 "Current sea level rise" http://en.wikipedia.org/wiki/current_sea_level_ rise Retrieved 7 August 2013.

Wilanski, E. (ed.) 2006 *The Environment in Asia Pacific Harbours;* Dordrecht: Springer.

Wilhite, D.A. and Glantz, M.H. 1985 "Understanding the drought phenomenon; the role of definitions" *Water Interntional,* Vol. 10, Issue 3, pp. 111-120 doi: 10.1080/02508068508686328.

William, M. 2006 *Deforesting the Earth: from Prehistory to Global Crisis;* The University of Chicago Press.

Williams, J.C. 2006 "The History of Energy" *The Franklin's Institute's Resources for Science Learning,* April 25 (http://www.fi.edu/learn/case-files/energy.html.

Williams, M. 1990 "Forests" pp. 179-201: In: B.L. Turner II, W.C. Clark, R.W. Kates, J.T. Richards, J.T. Mathews, and W.B. Meyers (eds.) *The Earth as Transformed by Human Action,* New York: Cambridge University Press.

Williams, M. 1994 "Forests and Tree Cover" pp. 97-124. In: W.B Meyer and B.C. Turner II., (eds.), *Changes in Land Use and Land Cover: A Global Perspective,* Cambridge: Cambridge University Press.

Williams, M.A.J. 2001 "Interactions of desertification and climate: present understanding and future research imperatives" *ARIDLAND,* No. 49 (May- June).

Willianms et al. 2007 "Industry, Settlement and Society" *In: Intergovernmental Panel on Climate Change* 2007, Chap. 7.

Willis, A.J. 1997 "The ecosystem: an evolving concept viewed historically" *Functional Ecology,* Vol. 11, No. 2, pp 208-71.

Willis, K. 2004 *Thories and Practices of Development;* London: Routledge.

Willis, K.G. and Garrod, G. (eds.) 2012 *Valuing Environment and Natural Resources,* Edward Elgar.

Wilson, E.O. 1992 *The Diversity of Life;* Harmondsworth: Penguin.

WMO, 1975 *Drought in Agriculture* (prepared by C.E. Hounam and 4 others), Technical Note No. 138, WMO No. 392 Geneva: World Meteorological Organization.

Woodworth, P.L. 2005 "Have there been large recent sea level changes in the Maldive Island"? *Global and Planetry Change,* Vol. 49, pp. 1-18.

World Bank, 1992 *World Development Report 1992: Development and the Environment;* Oxford University Press.

World Bank, 1997 *Expanding the Measure of Wealth: Indicators of Environmentally Sustainable Development;* Environmentally Sustainable Development Studies and Monograph Series 17, Washing D.C.: World Bank.

World Bank, 2002 *Process framework for the Mitigation of Social Impacts of the Lake Chad Basin Commission (LCBC) Project,* World Bank.

World Bank, 2003 *World Development Report 2003: Sustainable Development in a Dynamic World;* Oxford University Press.

World Bank, 2004 *Forest Law Enforcement. The Pernvian Environmental Law Society (2003). Case Study on the Development and Implementation of Guidelines for the Control of Illegal Logging with a View to Sustainable Forest Management in Peru;* Washington D.C.: World Bank.

World Bank, 2006 *Ethiopia: Managing water resources to maximize sustainable growth;* World Bank: Washington, D.C.

World Bank, 2010 *World Development Report 2010: Development and Climate Change;* Wastington D.C.: World Bank.

World Resources Institute 2000/2001 *People and Ecosystems: The Fraying Web of Life;* Washington D.C.: World Resource Institute.

World Resources Institute 2011 *Climate Analysis Indicators Tool (CAIT): Indicators GHG Emissions: Cumulative Emissions;* Washington, D.C.

World Resources Institute, 2005 *Millennium Ecosystems Assessment 2005. Ecosystems and Human Well-Being: Desertification Synthesis;* Zafar Adeel et al. (eds.) Washington D.C. Retrieved 10th September 2013.

World Wind Energy Association, 2014 *Half-Year Report,* pp. 1-8 The World Wind Energy Association.

Wright, L., Kemp, S. and Williams, I. 2011 "Carbon Footprinting: Towards a Universally Accepted Definition" *Carbon Management,* Vol. 2, No. 1, pp. 61-72.

Wright, R.T. and Nebel, B.J. 2004 *Environmental Science: Toward a Sustainable Future;* 8th edition, Delhi: Prentice-Hall (India) Private Ltd.

Wrigley, E.A. 2010 *Energy and the English Industrial Revolution,* Cambridge University Press.

Wrigley, T., 2011 "Opening Pandora's Box: A New Look at the Industrial Revolution" http://www. org/article/industrial-revolution. Retrieved 26th August, 2012.

Wunder, S. 1992 "Dutch disease theory and the case of Colombia" *Institute of Economics* PhD Thesis, Copenhagen University, Denmark.

Wunder, S. 2003a *When the Dutch Disease met the French Connection: Oil, Macroeconomics and Forests in Gabon*; Center for International Forestry Bogor, Indonesia.

Wunder, S. 2003b *Oil wealth and the fate of the forest: A comparative study of eight tropical countries;* London: Routledge.

Wunsch, C. 2002 "What is the Themohaline Circulation"? *Science,* 298 (5596).

WWF 2006 "Climate change a treat to Amazon rainforest, warns WWF" *World Wide Fund for Nature,* March 22.

WWF 2007 (November) "Russia's Boreal Forests" *WWF,* November.

Yale Global Online 2007 *The Double Edge of Globalization;* Yale University Press.

Yoshino, M. 1992 "Wind and rain in the desert region of Xin–Jiang, Northwest China" *Grkunde,* Vol. 46, pp 203-216.

Yoshioka, M., Mahowald, N.M., Conley, A.J., Collins, W.D. Fillmove, D.W., Zender, C.S., Colemen, D.B. 2007 "The impact of desert dust radiation forcing on sahel precipitation: relative importance of dust compared to sea surface temperature variations, vegetation, and green house gas warming" *Journal Climate,* Vol. 20, pp. 1445-1467.

Yousef and Ghilly, no date "Alert el Sahel countries: drought is appreciating" http://www. virtualacademia.can/pdf/di209_220.pdf.

Yu, J - Y. and Kim, S.T. 2013 "Identifying the types of major EL niño events since 1870" *International Journal of Climatology,* Vol. 33, Issue 8 (30 June), pp. 2105-2112.

Yuan, R. and Zhao, T. 2016 "Changes in CO_2 Emissions from China's Energy-Intensive Industries: A Subsystem Input-Output Decomposition Analysis" *Journal of Cleaver Production,* Vol. 117, pp. 98-109.

Yulianti, N. and Hayasaka, H. 2013 "Recent Active Fires under El Niño Conditions in Kalimantan, Indonesia" *American Journal of Plant Science,* Vol. 4, pp. 685-696. Accessed 26th May, 2016.

Yung, Y.L. et al 1996 "Dust: A Diagnostic of the Hydrologic Cycle during the Last Glacial Maximum" *Science,* Vol. 271, pp. 862-63.

Zehner, O. 2011 "Unintended Concequences" In: Paul Robbins, Dustin Mulvancy and J. Geoffrey Golsom (eds.), Green Technology, London: Sage, pp. 427-432.

Zemp, M., Roe, I., Kääb, A., Hoelzle, M., Paul, F., and Haeberli, W. 2008 United Natoins Environment Programme – Global Glacier Changes: Facts and Figures (Report) (http://www.grid.unep.ch/glaciers/pdfs/samary.pdf) Retrieved August 8, 2013.

Zhang, R. and Delworth, T.L. 2006 "Impact of Atlantic Multidecadal Oscillations on India/ Sahel Rainfall and Atlantic Hurricanes" *Geophysical Research Letters,* 33: L17712.

Zielinski, S. 2012 "Are We Headed for another Dust Bowl"? *Science & Nature,* November 16.

Zimmer, C. 2013 "Black Carbon and Warming: It's Worse than We Thought" *Environment, 360,* 17th January (Accessed 7th April, 2016).

Zukeruen, W. 2010 "Shape-shifting Islands Defy Sea-Level Rise" *New Scientist,* No. 2763.

Zwedie, A. 2012 "Impacts of climate change on food security: A literature review in Sub-Saharan Africa" *Journal of Earth Science & Climate Change,* 5: 225 (doi: 10.4172/2157. 1000225).